The American Foreign Policy Library

Edwin O. Reischauer, Editor

Robert V. Daniels

RUSSIA

The Roots of Confrontation

Harvard University Press

Cambridge, Massachusetts, and London, England   1985

27203

This book is printed on acid-free paper, and its binding materials
have been chosen for strength and durability.

Library of Congress Cataloging in Publication Data

Daniels, Robert Vincent.
    Russia, the roots of confrontation.

    (The American foreign policy library)
    Bibliography: p.
    Includes index.
    1. Soviet Union—History. I. Title. II. Series.
DK40.D28   1985   947   84-19152
ISBN 0-674-77965-7

Foreword by Edwin O. Reischauer

It is a truism that history repeats itself, and those who are least aware of this fact are the most likely to suffer its consequences. A student of East Asian history like me cannot but be struck by the parallels between the course of international relations in the modern Occident and the story of political rivalries in ancient China. The states of the central Chinese heartland fought one another fiercely, engaging in "checkerboard diplomacy," as it was later to be known in the West. Those in the center, like the nations of western and central Europe, lacked the space to grow, but those on the periphery expanded into superpowers. Eventually the states began to destroy and consume one another, until only two great peripheral states remained. When one of these absorbed the other in 221 B.C., the Chinese Empire was born in the general shape it still maintains today. The winner in this dog-eat-dog contest was the state that was most bureaucratized, closely controlled, ruthless, and even totalitarian to the degree allowed by the technology of the day.

The history of ancient China presents a chilling parallel to our own age, in which the Soviet Union and the United States clearly play the role of the peripheral powers that expanded. Together they come close to equaling the land area and population of all the rest of the Western states combined. In military power they are incomparably stronger. Expand the focus to include the whole world, and, while the proportions of land and people change radically, the preponderance of military strength is little affected. In military power the world is clearly bipolar, and either of the two superpowers could easily annihilate not just the rest of the lesser powers but also its rival, and no doubt itself too in the process.

A historically minded alarmist has ample reason to proclaim that the end of civilization is near. But a more sophisticated look at history also tells us that history repeats itself only in a selective way.

Much of the past can never be repeated. An agricultural society cannot revert to the ways of a hunting economy; the classic empires could not be restored to their days of pristine innocence; the modern nation-state cannot revive the patterns of feudalism; the spread of nationalism has made nineteenth-century imperialism seem like remote antiquity; nuclear weapons make the repetition of the first two world wars impossible. We need to differentiate between what in the experience of humanity is repetitive, being either part of man's unchanging nature or deeply ingrained in the social patterns of some particular grouping of mankind, and what is likely to change as knowledge and technology grow. A Soviet-American Armageddon is by no means inevitable, but, given the present state of affairs in the world, nothing is more important than that Americans and Russians should understand each other better. Because of the nature of the Soviet Union, this involves largely the Soviet leadership on one side, but for the United States, as a democratic nation, it concerns the whole people.

Mutual understanding between Russians and Americans is not easy to achieve. As Professor Daniels points out in this book, no part of the Western world is more alien to Americans than is Russia. Russia stems culturally from the Byzantine area of southeastern Europe, while the United States is an offshoot of the British Isles in the extreme northwest. Russia grew up on the defenseless North European Plain, swept by invading hordes and conquerors; the United States, across the Atlantic Ocean, where it found no dangerous rivals. No two countries within the bounds of Western civilization could have had more dissimilar histories or developed more divergent attitudes toward the outside world and the problems of their own societies.

The situation is complicated by the strong emotional reactions evoked among Americans by their country's Russian rival on the eastern periphery of the European heartland. At times, small bands of zealots have looked on the Soviet Union as the promised land of the future. Much more prevalent have been feelings of deep distrust, fear, hatred, and even revulsion. Certainly all outsiders have found Russia an enigma.

It is no easy task to present to Americans a clear, evenhanded view of Russia. Many have attempted it, but few with much success. It does not help that Russia has chosen to cloak itself under the name "Soviet Union," or more fully "USSR," in which even the *R* does not stand for "Russia," as one might assume, but for the generic term "Republic." Whatever its name, however, the nation is clearly the modern continuation of the historic Russian state, in which Russians make up the majority and the entirely dominant element of the population. It appears to be a land in which the tendency of history to repeat itself is strong, particularly in intellectual attitudes, emotional reactions, and political organization. As Professor Daniels makes clear, the present Soviet Union cannot be understood except as the outcome of a long historical process. The broad historical perspective in which he describes it makes the picture he paints and the judgments he passes credible and illuminating.

Professor Daniels has traced the experiences of the Russian people and state from our earliest knowledge of them up through the great Revolution of 1917 and from it to the present. Bit by bit the pieces seem to fall into place. While he is scrupulously fair in describing the various differing interpretations that have been made about Russia and its past, he is forthright and clear in stating his own judgments. The result is a book of exceptional balance, insight, and clarity. The Foreign Policy Library has long lacked an up-to-date book on Russia. It is proud now to present Professor Daniels' book, which admirably fills the bill.

Preface

Of all the nations whose import for the United States has been set forth in the American Foreign Policy Library, Russia may well be the most difficult to bring within the compass of one reasonably objective volume. The problems are obvious enough. Russia is a vast and complex country whose long history has followed paths far removed from the American experience. The Russian Revolution and the rule of Communism have made Russia the focus of unending controversy among outsiders, while within the country both its present and its past must pass through the astigmatic lenses of official ideological legitimation. Most unsettling of all, Russia and the United States have confronted each other for four decades as the world's two nuclear-armed superpowers, joined in a contest of power and will that could decide the fate of the globe. Much hangs on the correct understanding of Russia, yet no author can be sure that he has the ultimate answer.

In exploring the perspectives and the legacies conferred on present-day Russia by the different epochs of its past, I have organized this book into large chunks of chronology. My intention is to define the salient contributions of each distinctive period and to discuss separately, for the sake of convenience, Russia's internal and external evolution. Throughout, my aim is to reflect upon the ways in which Russia's many-layered past shapes the present and sets the terms for the future.

Although this work is not intended as a policy paper on the issues of the day, it naturally bears on the perspectives and assumptions that underlie American efforts to deal with the Soviet Union. To the extent that it may contribute some clarity and calm to thought processes that are often overtaxed by the alarms of each passing moment, I will consider the effort amply rewarded.

All works on Russia must address the technical peculiarities of rendering Russian names and converting dates. I have followed a modified Library of Congress system of transliteration, reserving for the best-known personages the English form of their given names. Dates are given according to the Western (Gregorian) calendar, with reference where necessary to the Russian dating (thirteen days behind in the twentieth century, until the calendar reform of February 1918). Where place names and other terms have been changed, I have used the form appropriate to the period under discussion.

I am indebted to the John Simon Guggenheim Foundation for fellowship support and to the University of Vermont for sabbatical leave time, both of which contributed vitally to the completion of this work. The International Research and Exchange Board and the USSR Academy of Sciences made it possible for me to pursue research and discussions in the Soviet Union on the theme of the book. Aida Donald provided constant encouragement and editorial guidance in the course of this project. In addition, I wish to extend my thanks to Maria Ascher for her thorough editorial polishing; to Carolyn Perry, Susan Lacy, and Linda Gustavson for their expert assistance in preparing the manuscript; and to Alice Daniels for her careful reading and critique of the text. Needless to say, all idiosyncrasies and imperfections in the work remain my own responsibility.

R.V.D.

Contents

Illustrations

Illustrations on pages 75, 95, and 119 are reproduced courtesy of the Library of
Congress; those on pages 151 and 191, courtesy of Wide World. All other
photos are by the author.

Maps

Russia: The Roots of Confrontation

1

The Moscow River at Arkhangelskoe

The Past in the Present

For citizens of the United States, the specter of Soviet Russia may well be the most stressful intrusion upon their political consciousness since the American Civil War. Never since the War of Independence has the re-action to a single foreign country figured so deeply in

America's formulation of its own alternatives and its own destiny. This is so, paradoxically, even though there has been little or no conflict of power and interest between the United States and Russia until the relatively recent past.

Russia has always been an abstraction for Americans. Before the Revolution it was a dim and backward wasteland; afterward, an embodiment of cosmic destructiveness. Only for a few Americans did Russia become a distant utopia; for many, it was a terrifying revelation of evil; for most, it was an inchoate menace to their national existence. Rarely have any of these responses rested either on direct experience or on sufficient knowledge about where Russia came from before the Revolution or where it has gone since. For Americans, Russia is a creature of newspaper headlines.

My guiding premise in this book is the belief that history matters in the understanding of Russia today. For any other country, this proposition would be a patent truism. It must be underscored in this case only because the belief is so often expressed or implied that in Soviet affairs history does *not* matter, that the Communist revolution swept away everything that went before and determined everything that came after. In truth, the Revolution did not efface Russia's historical legacy or put an end to new formative influences. Both the most remote and the most recent of the country's experiences must be considered when trying to comprehend the Russian enigma.

This is not to suggest that history will supply clear and undisputed answers; Russia will remain one of the most controversial topics in human affairs. In viewing Russia, enemies and friends alike have often sought substantiation of their own philosophical commitments more than real enlightenment. Objectivity is not enhanced by the Soviet government's practice of manipulating the historical record for the sake of ideological appearances. At the same time, foreign judgments of the Soviet Union have often been determined more by particular political biases and the swinging pendulum of politics than by independent assessment of Soviet reality.

▪ The Old in the New

Even if we grant that Russia, like any other country, is the product of its past, understanding the Russian experience remains a difficult task for Westerners, and particularly for Americans, because it has been so remote and so different from their own. Russia's grim saga of invasion, despotism, servitude, and obscurantism, of inner impoverishment and outward violence, of holy visions and devilish obsessions, has no parallel in Americans' historical consciousness. By the same token, the pragmatism, legalism, commercialism, and individualism that have governed American public values since colonial times, the free competition in the marketplace of goods and ideas, are all foreign to the Russian tradition. In the origins and vicissitudes of the nation, its experience with political authority, its opportunities to establish its identity, its mode of survival, Russia has negotiated a path to the present which Americans have no basis of their own to comprehend.

Americans tend to think by classification rather than by degrees of difference, and to respond to the Russian mystery by presuming either unreal parallels or Manichaean contrasts. It is common in the United States to take the official Marxist philosophy at its face value and explain all Soviet behavior since the Revolution as a single-minded plan to impose World Communism. At the opposite end of the spectrum, Americans have sometimes imagined that the Soviet Union has found a formula for curing all the evils that they see in their own system. Both extremes assume that Russia is easy to understand because the Revolution wiped out the past, and that the Marxist program has ordained everything the Communists have done since then. Such a view is naturally encouraged by the Soviet regime, as well as by some of its noted opponents: "Russia is to the Soviet Union," wrote Alexander Solzhenitsyn, "as a man is to the disease afflicting him." However, any attempt, whether positive or negative, to represent the Soviet Union in terms of its revolutionary ideology alone is unhistorical, unrealistic, and dangerous as a basis for policy judgments by the United States government.

Americans would like to be able to perceive Russian reality clearly and unambiguously, and this helps explain why they are attracted to the ideological explanation of Soviet behavior. It is more difficult to comprehend how the history of a country makes a revolutionary upheaval possible and how revolution generates confrontation with the rest of the world. Americans—unlike Europeans, who have long known the Russian presence in tsarist guise—find it hard to understand how in the aftermath of a revolution, old and new are woven into a remade social fabric in which the stuff of revolutionary change is tailored to fit the design of a new status quo patterned in many ways like the old one.

The revolutionary experience which the United States seems to share with Russia fosters not understanding but confusion and antagonism. The Russian Revolution was not like the American either in cause or course, values or effect: the two events were as different as any that could be called by the common term "revolution." Russia's revolution was a convulsion of modernization intersecting with radical millenarianism; America's was a restrained assertion of the rights of self-rule already flourishing in the mother country. America's revolution has been deeply absorbed into the traditions of a stable society; Russia's wounds are near the surface, and the pains of revolution are still felt. Russia can in no way be construed as a new nation emerging from its revolution, as the United States was. However much the Revolution altered its political physiognomy, Russia remains a very old country, long accustomed to its role in the international community, but all the while faced with the superiority of the West and plagued with doubts about its own character and identity. America is the reverse: cockily self-assured about its national identity and virtues (from 1776 at least until the mid-twentieth century), but forever unclear about the role it should assume in the world, until the Soviet challenge and the collapse of alternatives forced it to become a world policeman.

The depth of Russia's national sense of insecurity, psychic and cultural as well as military and strategic, is lost on Americans, who proceed from their own country's confidence and wonder how a nation as large as Russia, half girdling the globe, could leave its citizens with any legitimate basis for an inferiority complex. Here again it is history's legacy that makes the difference. Russia originated and developed under the cloud of foreign military and cultural superiority. The country was continually being invaded by the armies and beliefs of other nations; not until the eighteenth century was the situation reversed in the military sphere, and not until the twentieth in the realm of ideas. Overwhelmed by the realization that foreigners do everything better, Russia has remained a closed society, in which the government claims total responsibility and demands total justification. In these respects the Revolution only made matters worse, sharpening contrasts with the West, heightening the need to dissimulate for the sake of ideological legitimacy, and enhancing the power of the state over all facets of life.

▪ The Geographical Base

Russia's unique geography would by itself assure the nation a place of international preeminence no matter what kind of regime was in power. Considering its size, strategic setting, and endowment of natural resources, Russia—or, in present-day terms, the Soviet Union—is potentially the most powerful country in the world. It is in area by far the largest political entity on the surface of the globe, its 8.6 million square miles dwarfing the runner-up, Canada (3.8 million square miles), as well as the continental United States (3 million square miles). Occupying virtually the entire northern half of the Eurasian land mass, the territory of the Soviet Union curves west to east around the Arctic Ocean through no less than eleven time zones, and its population is exceeded only by China and India.

Russia's vast area is situated in what the English geopolitician Halford Mackinder called the "heartland" of the Eurasian "world island," affording it the advantage of central location over its neighbors around the continental rim, and also an almost limitless defensibility thanks to the space available to draw invaders in and exhaust them. At the same time, this key position has been a liability in exposing Russia to enemy invasion on one border or another throughout its history. By contrast, the United States is unrivaled by any other major power on the North American continent—or anywhere in the Western hemisphere, for that matter—and has been secure for most of its history behind two broad oceans.

Russia has been repeatedly threatened and blocked over the centuries by major adversaries all around its periphery. To the west, lacking any natural frontier, it has been exposed to invasion—by Germans, Poles, Swedes, French, Germans again—across the plain of northern Europe. To the east, it was repeatedly invaded by nomadic hordes coming in waves across the open steppes. In the Far East, Russia has been confronted by Japan and now by China. Along its southern border Russia faced the Turkish and Persian empires, more recently buttressed by European and American power. The stresses of this vast and continuing continental exposure have, according to many historians, compelled Russia to accept centralized and despotic government as the price of survival.

An age-old strategic problem for the Russians is access to the sea. Russia is fundamentally a continental, not a maritime power. For all its vastness, it enjoys no free and direct contact with the open ocean except on remote and inaccessible coasts. The Baltic is controlled by the Danish narrows and their North Sea approaches; the Black Sea is doubly bottled in by the Turkish Straits and by the Gibraltar and Suez exits from the Mediterranean; the Caspian is landlocked. Only in the European Far North and the Pacific Far East does Soviet territory extend to the high seas, and these two regions are separated by the frozen Arctic, traversable only by ice-breakers. Moreover, the Pacific shore and the White Sea are icebound in winter. Russia has always been trying to secure ice-free ports; only the Black Sea, Murmansk on the Kola Peninsula (warmed by the Gulf Stream), and the base at Kaliningrad on the Baltic (taken from Germany after World War II) qualify as such. (Odessa, on the Black Sea, is the country's main commercial port.) In sum, Russia's maritime activity involves five separate coasts, none within easy reach of the others, none offering both free access to the oceans and proximity to the principal settled parts of the country. Consequently, sea power has—almost to the present day—played a lesser role in Russia's strategic calculations than for any other major power in modern times. To be sure, internal communication, particularly in European Russia, has always been facilitated by rivers and by the lack of serious mountain barriers, but Siberia is still traversed by only one rail line, running along the Mongolian and Chinese frontiers. An alternative connection, the "Baikal-Amur Mainline," is now under construction at great cost further north in the permafrost region.

Despite its size, the Soviet Union does not enjoy an easy superiority over other nations in terms of national power and economic success. It has immense mineral resources, but distance makes many deposits inaccessible. More serious are the obstacles imposed by latitude and climate on the exploitation of resources, and above all on agriculture. Since nearly all of the Soviet Union lies north of the forty-fifth parallel (except in Central Asia), the proper geographical and climatic comparison in North American terms is not with the United States but with a greatly magnified Canada plus Alaska and the Mountain States.

The Soviets do not enjoy anything approaching the vast agricultural potential of the United States. Generally speaking, successful agriculture in the Soviet Union is restricted by two conditions—cold

in the north and lack of rainfall in the south. To the north is the
taiga, a band of coniferous forest five hundred miles wide or more,
and beyond it lies the tundra on the Arctic coast. Almost everywhere
in these zones, which resemble the Canadian North and Alaska, the
ground is permanently frozen beneath the surface. This permafrost
impedes mining and construction, as well as agriculture. South of
the central, mixed forest zone there is a progression of vegetation
zones resembling the east-west sequence in the United States: first,
the fertile steppes—the celebrated "black-earth" region, akin to Illi-
nois and Iowa; then the dry steppes, similar to the Great Plains,
running from the Black Sea, around the Caspian, and across Central
Asia; finally, the Central Asian desert and mountain rim, closely resembling the American Southwest.

As one progresses eastward from European Russia into Siberia,
the increasingly continental climate causes northern cold and
southern drought to converge, so that agriculturally based settlement is mainly confined to a long wedge-shaped central zone of the
country (basically the mixed forest zone and the fertile steppe). This
band is broad in the west (along the Baltic coast and the border from
the Leningrad area down to the Black Sea littoral) but narrows toward the east, especially beyond the Urals, into a thin strip of populated territory extending to the Pacific along the Trans-Siberian
Railway and the Mongolian and Chinese frontiers. Apart from the
fertile wedge, agriculture and dense populations are confined to
coastal and river valley areas of Transcaucasia and Central Asia,
where irrigation is available and conditions are almost subtropical.
The country's total arable acreage is not much greater than that of
the United States, and most of it, due to conditions of soil and climate, is less productive. Given these circumstances, it is no mean
feat that the Soviet Union leads the world in wheat production and
produces over a third of the total world harvest of oats and barley.
(The American lead in total grain output comes from corn, with
which the Soviets experimented unsuccessfully under Khrushchev.)

The USSR ranks among the top three world producers for practically every strategic mineral, with untold reserves locked away in
the frozen Siberian wastes. However, the major industrial centers
have often arisen far from the sources of raw materials and energy,
and this strains a transportation system that has never been ade-
quately developed. More convenient is the industrial district of the
Donets Basin (the "Donbas") in the eastern Ukraine, whose iron

and steel base makes it almost as important as the Ruhr or the Pittsburgh-Youngstown area. Another famous center for ferrous and nonferrous metallurgy is the Urals, an area richly endowed with minerals but distant from much of its fuel supply. Overall, energy supplies are abundant: the USSR is the world's largest producer of petroleum, coal, and hydroelectric power. The fact that it is also the world's second largest source of gold is an important element in balancing its foreign exchange accounts. Altogether the Soviet Union comes closer, potentially, than any other country to the elusive goal of complete self-sufficiency.

■ The Ethnic Mosaic

Just as important as geography, as a foundation of history, is nationality—the existence of peoples with their languages, cultures, and continuous sense of identity attached to certain territories. This did not cease to be true for Russia just because the Communists imposed a new order. The Russian Revolution was not, as some have imagined, incited by a foreign conspiracy; it was inflicted by Russians on one another, and they did not stop being Russians on that account.

One of the most basic continuities from prerevolutionary Russia to the Soviet era is the unique complexity of the country's nationality makeup. As a result of its extraordinary territorial expansion between the sixteenth and nineteenth centuries, the Russian state does not coincide with the Russian nation. It is a multinational empire, politically dominated by the Russian half of its population, but encompassing a host of other nationalities who still maintain their linguistic and cultural identity in their own ancestral regions. For an American parallel, one would have to look beyond the melting-pot mix of European immigrants and consider the fate of the Native Americans, the seizure of the Spanish-speaking Southwest, and the annexation of Puerto Rico. In the same way—by conquest—the Soviet minorities were brought under the rule of the Russian emperors.

Reflecting the difference between cultural and political identity, the Russian language has two words for "Russian"—*russkii,* which refers to the language and the individuals of the Russian nation, and *rossiiskii* (from *Rossiya,* meaning Russia), which refers to the governmental and territorial entity with all its subject minorities. In postrevolutionary parlance, the term *sovetskii* has replaced *rossiiskii* to reflect the new official name of the empire: Union of Soviet Socialist Republics. In this book I generally use the terms "Russia" and "Soviet Union" interchangeably, except of course in prerevolutionary contexts, where "Russia" alone must serve. This is not to deemphasize the multinational character of the Russian-Soviet state, but only to facilitate reference to its historical continuity.

Beginning in the 1920s Russia's ethnic complexity was given administrative form in the Union of Soviet Socialist Republics, with its fifteen union republics corresponding to the major nationalities. By far the largest, comprising over half the country's population and roughly three quarters of its land area (including Siberia) is the RSFSR—the Russian Soviet Federated Socialist Republic—where "Great Russians," or speakers of the standard Russian language, predominate. The Russian Republic includes substantial pockets of lesser nationalities whose ethnic identity is reflected in lower administrative units—depending on how large their population is, either "autonomous republics" (corresponding to Russian-speaking provinces), "autonomous regions," or "autonomous areas," the latter encompassing large northern regions thinly populated by Siberian aborigines.

A Soviet citizen's nationality is not based on residence or citizenship in a union republic or other nationality unit, as those familiar with the American federal system might suppose. Nationality in the Soviet Union is now an inherited legal classification of individuals, based on the traditional identification of minorities by their language. It is reinforced by differences of religion, custom, and historical experience. Thus, it is something like the recent legal designation of Hispanics, Native Americans, and other minorities in the United States. However, the Soviet concept of nationality is not, strictly speaking, racial. Between Russians and the European national minorities there are no uniform racial distinctions at all, nor are they very clear among many of the Asiatic nationalities, though a general European-Asian physical contrast is quite apparent. Russia has had a long tradition of assimilating foreign ethnic and racial elements, from the west as well as the east, by intermarriage or religious conversion, so that the distant ancestry of most Russians is very much a mixture. However, the initial Soviet effort at promoting equal rights for nationalities by legal categorization has had the reverse effect: it has abetted covert racism by locking individuals by heredity into labeled groups where in practice they can be treated as second-class citizens. This is particularly so in the case of the Jews.

The great majority of the Soviet population consists of European nationalities who share the Christian religious tradition in one form or another (with the exception of the Jews) and for the most part speak languages descended from the same Indo-European source. Paramount among the European nationalities are the Slavs.

"Slavic" is sometimes thought of by the Slavs themselves as a term of racial community. This is a nineteenth-century myth, with no basis in any identifiable and exclusive set of hereditary physical characteristics, though most Slavs in the Soviet Union do tend toward fair coloring and broad faces. "Slavs" are simply speakers of Slavic languages, constituting one of the major groups of the vast Indo-European language family. The modern Slavic languages took form in relatively recent times, in the early centuries of the Christian era, as speakers of the ancestral language, Common Slavic, migrated in different directions to the areas in which they eventually settled. Though they are linguistically classified further into the East Slavic, West Slavic, and South Slavic subgroups, the relationship among all of the Slavic languages in terms of vocabulary, phonetics, and (except for Bulgarian) grammar remains very close.

The Slavic languages of the Soviet Union are the East Slavic: Russian, which is by far the most widely spoken, Ukrainian (or "Ruthenian"), and Belorussian ("White Russian"). The latter two, though they have their own literary standards, are so close to Russian as to constitute mutually intelligible dialects, and prerevolutionary Russian nationalists were reluctant to recognize them as separate languages in their own right. All three East Slavic languages use the Cyrillic alphabet, invented by Saints Cyril and Methodius in the ninth century in order to translate the scriptures into Slavic. The major West Slavic languages are Polish, Czech, and Slovak; South Slavic includes Slovenian, Serbo-Croatian, Macedonian, and Bulgarian. All, by coincidence, are spoken in countries brought under Communist rule during and after World War II.

Sensitivity about national identity is most acute among Ukrainians, especially those from the Western Ukraine who never lived under Russian rule until the Soviet annexation of the Lvov region in 1939. Since the Ukrainians, almost a third as numerous as the Russians, are such a large and economically crucial minority, their sentiments are the crux of the Soviet nationality problem.

The Soviet Slavs, accounting for three fourths of the population of the country, share a nearly identical cultural tradition and are in most respects indistinguishable in their way of life. They have traditionally belonged to the Russian national branch of the Greek Orthodox Church. However, there are a fair number of religious sectarians among them, both Old Believers, who broke away from the official church in the seventeenth century, and converts to various evangelical Protestant denominations—Baptists, Seventh-Day Adventists, Jehovah's Witnesses—in more recent times. In addition, many Ukrainians, especially in the west, were communicants of the Uniate Church, or Catholic Church of the Eastern Rite, which is Orthodox in liturgy and rules but recognizes the authority of the papacy. The Soviet regime has striven vigorously to suppress this particular denomination.

The non-Slavic nationalities of the European portion of the Soviet Union are small in number but important economically, culturally, and historically. The three Baltic peoples, annexed by the Russian Empire in the eighteenth century, are strongly oriented toward the West by culture, religion, and previous political ties. Estonia and Latvia, once ruled by the German Teutonic Knights and then by Sweden, are Lutheran; Lithuania, as a result of its old association with Poland, is the one Roman Catholic region in the Soviet Union (making it a source of constant friction and dissent). Lithuania and Latvia speak closely related Indo-European languages of the Baltic family (originally related to the Slavic). Estonian is quite different—a non-Indo-European member of the Finno-Ugric language family and a very close cousin of the Finnish spoken in Finland. All three languages of the Baltic states use the Latin alphabet with diacritical marks. The Baltic republics retain a very strong sense of cultural identity (thanks in part to their experience of independence between the World Wars), despite their small population and the considerable number of Russian immigrants, drawn by the employment opportunities offered by their advanced economies. Average educational levels, worker skills, and living standards in the Baltic states remain significantly above those in the Russian Republic, and couples in mixed marriages more often than not opt for the Baltic nationality for their children. Much less distinctive is the Moldavian Republic, a rural area on the southwestern border roughly coinciding with the old province of Bessarabia, which was taken by Russia from the Turks in 1812 and largely populated by

Greek Orthodox speakers of Rumanian. The Soviets maintain that the "Moldavians" are a separate nationality and have instituted the use of the Cyrillic alphabet, though the Rumanians deny the legitimacy of this truncation of their nation.

Ethnically most distinctive and varied of all the regions of the Soviet Union is the area between the Black and Caspian seas, including the region of the North Caucasus (on the northern slopes of the Caucasus mountains) and Transcaucasia (which extends south from the Caucasus range to the Turkish and Iranian frontiers). All this territory was acquired by the Russian Empire early in the nineteenth century. Transcaucasia comprises the three union republics of Georgia, Armenia, and Azerbaijan, all distinctive historically and culturally. The Georgians, to the west, are Orthodox Christian; their most famous son, Joseph Stalin, born Dzhugashvili, was at one time a candidate for the priesthood. Their language, however, is unrelated to any major group. Armenia, on the southern border, speaks an Indo-European language (though one that is independent of any other subfamily); it follows an independent Christian church theologically akin to Protestantism. Georgia has a national history going back to the Middle Ages, and Armenia to the second millenium B.C. But since both have suffered harsh treatment at the hands of the Turks and the Persians, national sentiment in these regions has not been particularly anti-Russian. Both of these republics are unusually homogeneous, and Moscow has allowed the local cultures and religions to flourish with relatively little interference. The third Transcaucasian republic, Azerbaijan, which includes the metropolis of Baku and the great oil field on the Caspian Sea, is quite a different matter: its people are Turkish-speaking Shiite Moslems (apart from a large influx of Russians, Armenians, and other nationalities), and it thus belongs culturally with Central Asia. The North Caucasus, administratively part of the Russian Republic, is an incredible patchwork of diverse ethnic groups, mostly Moslem, who speak languages related variously to the Georgian (Caucasian), Turkic, Iranian, and Mongolian. Most famous in history are the Circassians (in Russian, *Adygei*), Caucasian-speaking Moslem mountaineers from the western end of the Caucasus Mountains who fought Russian rule throughout the first half of the nineteenth century.

Elsewhere in European Russia there are perhaps 10 million members of national minorities scattered in rural areas between the Volga and the Urals and in the Far North. These peoples are speakers of Finnish dialects, descendants of the aboriginal inhabitants of the North Russian forests, long ago absorbed into the Orthodox Church; or Turkic speakers (mainly Tatars), who remain Moslem despite the fact that they were conquered by the Russians in the sixteenth century.

The Asiatic portion of the Soviet Union presents yet another complex of nationalities. Siberia proper, explored and claimed by Russia in the seventeenth century, has a majority of Russian and Ukrainian settlers (some 20 million), but they are concentrated in the narrow agricultural and industrial zone along the Trans-Siberian Railway. The rest of the region, to the north, is thinly populated by a variety of formerly nomadic aboriginal peoples, most of whom adhere to animistic religious traditions and speak languages in the Altaic family; the Yakuts in the northeast speak a Turkic language; the Buryats around Lake Baikal, a variety of Mongolian; the Evenki (Tungus), a tongue related to the Manchu spoken by China's last imperial rulers. Some of the smaller nationality groups are no larger than American Indian tribes, and their "autonomous areas" invite comparison with American Indian reservations. The difference is that the Soviet units are part of the regular governmental and economic structure and are not restricted to members of the named ethnic group: imagine New Mexico as the "Chicano Autonomous State" even with its Anglo majority, or preemption of county government in northeastern Arizona by the Navaho and Hopi Indian reservations.

Central Asia, the general term for the southern bulge of the Soviet Union between the Caspian Sea and the border of China's Sinkiang Province, is altogether different from the rest of the country in its ethnic makeup. This was a region of long-established Moslem civilization, urban and agricultural in the irrigated valleys along the Iranian and Afghan frontiers, nomadic in the steppe and desert region further north. Mostly Turkic-speaking and Arabic-writing, the people of Central Asia had little national consciousness beyond their Orthodox Sunni Islam and their loyalty to local khans, until the Russians conquered the area in the course of the nineteenth century. The Soviets have been harsh on Islam, regarding it as superstitious, antimodern, and anti-Communist, though they have nominally tolerated its observance. Considerable local guerrilla activity by the so-called Basmachi rebels had to be suppressed before Soviet rule was consolidated in the 1920s. Soviet policy has been to subdivide the ethnic consciousness of the substantial bloc of now nearly 25 million Moslem Turks by cultivating old historical and dialectal differences and enshrining these in four different union republics—the Uzbek, Kazakh, Turkmen, and Kirghiz (plus one autonomous republic)—even though the languages are more or less mutually intelligible and their speakers are intermingled across all the boundaries. In the case of the Tadzhik Republic, the distinction is much more meaningful, for here the principal language is a dialect of Persian and hence a member of the Indo-European family. All of the nationalities of Central Asia had their alphabets changed from Arabic to Latin in the 1920s and then to Cyrillic in the 1930s, but, significantly, with different phonetic equivalencies and different diacritical marks, making it artificially difficult for a speaker of one language to read the others.

Of all the Soviet nationality groups, the Jews present the most problematic and tension-ridden situation. As in other times and places, they have been the object of popular hostility and official persecution; their status as a nationality has been complicated by religious differences and racial myths, and the legal rights of Soviet Jews have in recent years become a matter of international controversy. As with other Soviet nationalities, Jewish nationality is based on heredity—that is, the identity ascribed to parents or grandparents. This, in the case of the Jews, has been a combination of language and religion: the Jewish faith, together with the Yiddish language traditionally spoken by the majority of Jews in Russia (a language derived from medieval German with Hebrew borrowings and written in the Hebrew alphabet).

The Jews originally came under Russian rule in the same manner as most of the other Soviet minorities—that is, by conquest. In this instance it was through the partitions of Poland in the late eighteenth century, when the eastern provinces, settled by large numbers of Jewish refugees from central Europe during the previous two centuries, were annexed by Catherine the Great. Thanks to the opportunities made available by reform, modernization, and revolution in the nineteenth and twentieth centuries, Jews were able to move out of the old Pale of Settlement (the region to which the tsars had originally confined them) and enter the mainstream of Russian life through linguistic assimilation and secularization. Assimilated Jews became prominent in the arts and sciences and in the revolutionary movement (including early leaders of the

Communist Party, notably Leon Trotsky). Following the Second World War, when at least a third of the Jewish population of the Soviet Union fell victim to Hitler's Holocaust, Stalin adopted a thinly veiled anti-Jewish line himself. Since that time Soviet Jews have been under heavy pressure to abandon both their religion and their language, but continue nonetheless to be identified legally as Jews and subjected to employment discrimination and educational quotas. Thus, the Soviet regime has adopted in practice a racial definition of the Jews, devoid of rights but burdened with disabilities.

▪ Ethnodemographics

According to the census of 1979 the USSR had a population of approximately 262 million, recorded by nationality (as by race in the United States), as well as by the usual particulars of age, sex, residence, and so on. Of the total, Russians accounted for 137 million, or just over 52 percent, residing mostly in the RSFSR but constituting a significant minority in every other union republic except Armenia (which retains an extraordinary degree of ethnic homogeneity). The Ukrainians were the second-largest group (42 million), concentrated in the Ukraine but spilling over eastward into the North Caucasus and Central Asia. Then came the Uzbeks of Central Asia (12 million) and the Belorussians (9.5 million), mostly in their respective republics. The Kazakhs followed with 6.5 million, but they are a minority in their own republic, which is heavily populated by Russians and Ukrainians in the north—the "Virgin Lands" area. The other nationalities of union republic status ranged from the Azerbaijanis (5.5 million) and the Armenians (4 million) down to the Turkmen and Kirghiz (about 2 million each), the Latvians (1.5 million), and the Estonians (a little over a million). Of the minorities recognized through autonomous republics and other administrative areas, the largest are the Tatars, numbering over 6 million, about half in the Tatar Autonomous Soviet Socialist Republic (ASSR) on the middle Volga and the rest scattered through Central Asia, where they have been a traditional trader class in recent centuries. About half a million Tatars from the Crimean Peninsula were deported to Central Asia during World War II for alleged collaboration with the Germans; recent agitation for their return has been in vain. The same punishment befell the Chechens and Ingush of the North Caucasus—who, however, had their ASSR status restored in 1957.

While as many as fifty-three different nationalities have their designated home territories in the Soviet administrative structure, ranging in size down to groups as small as the Koryak and Dolgani (Siberian tribes of less than 10,000 each), certain significant nationalities of European derivation have no place in the administrative scheme at all. There are, according to the 1979 census, nearly 2 million ethnic Germans, descendants of eighteenth-century settlers; a concentration of them on the lower Volga was at one time recognized as an ASSR, but they were deported during World War II, like the Crimean Tatars. There are also more than a million Poles, some resident in the lands annexed by the Soviet Union during World War II, others descendants of Poles who had spread through the empire when Poland proper was a subject province. Finally, the census reported nearly 2 million citizens of Jewish nationality. Between the world wars the Soviet government tried to compete with Zionism by creating a "Jewish Autonomous Province" around the town of Birobidzhan on the Chinese border. However, the experiment never told hold and was virtually suspended after Stalin's anti-Jewish purges; Birobidzhan remains a rural backwater with a small population more Russian than Jewish.

The rate of growth of the Soviet population and its composition in terms of age and sex reflect both the transition from an agrarian to an industrial society and the devastating experiences to which the country has been subjected in this century. As in other industrialized countries, Western and Communist alike, the Soviet birthrate has been steadily declining, to its present 18 per thousand per year, almost as low as the American. Among the Russians and other European nationalities it is even lower, scarcely above the rate required for zero population growth, whereas in Central Asia, reflecting its lesser degree of modernization, the birthrate remains fairly high. The result is that non-Russians as a whole are gaining in their share of the total population, and it seems certain that by the next census in 1989 the Russians will themselves be a minority.

War, purges, and labor camps have taken a terrible human toll in the Soviet Union. The dissident physicist Iosif Dyadkin has calculated "unnatural deaths" from 1927 to 1958 at 23–32 million, not counting war losses. Deaths directly caused by the Second World War, military and civilian combined, totaled, according to Khrushchev, more than 20 million. Furthermore, there was a severe birth deficit during the war years when the men were at the front, and in the postwar years when millions of women could not find husbands. As a result, the net recorded population increase between the two Soviet censuses of 1939 and 1959 was only about 23 percent (from 170 million to 209 million, including the population gained by annexation after World War II). By contrast, the war caused hardly a wrinkle in the American demographic pattern: the U.S. population grew approximately 36 percent in the same span of time. Wartime casualties left the Soviet sex ratio highly skewed, with substantial constriction in the population pyramid among men born between 1900 and 1925. As recently as 1959, men constituted only 45 percent of the population, a deficit that made the recruitment of women into the work force all the more imperative.

The Soviet population is now expected to level off at a figure not much above the American, except for the factor of Central Asian growth noted above. Efforts to encourage families larger than the current norm of one or at most two children per family have run up against the economic realities of the housing shortage and the material aspirations of a population that has had a taste of consumer amenities. Industry and the army find themselves compelled to make better use of non-Russian manpower resources. Population is not an unlimited resource for the Soviet leadership in its quest for greater national power.

■ The Geology of Historical Experience

The bedrock of geography and ethnicity underlying a country's past naturally continues to shape everything that happens in its present. Overlying this foundation is the legacy of human history—the accretion of circumstances, beliefs, habits, and institutions from the depths of the past that mold the present even as the present is adding new experiences to the total accumulation. This relationship of old and new is complicated in Russia by the distinctiveness of different eras of its history—imperial, revolutionary, postrevolutionary— whose contributions to the country's present character are like layers of geological deposits. To be sure, the great discontinuity of the Revolution makes it difficult to recognize older influences, as well as more recent changes. Yet the key to understanding Russia historically is to see how the Revolution, in transmuting elements of the past, reaffirmed them and amalgamated them with the promise of the future.

In Russian political life the unacknowledged parallels between tsarism and Stalinism are obvious to the objective observer. Centralization, autocracy, an official belief, police methods unrestrained by law, suspicion and repression of initiatives independent of the state—all these have been the rule for old and new regimes alike. Russia's history generated the possibility, if not the necessity, of revolution, while the Russian political culture invited recourse to old despotic tactics by the revolutionaries. Time and again during the development of the Soviet system from Lenin to Stalin, autocratic Russian experience set the line where doctrine failed to guide.

Perhaps even more of a burden than the autocratic tradition was prerevolutionary Russia's legacy of economic backwardness and cultural underdevelopment in comparison with the West. Neither in tsarist nor in Soviet times have Russia's natural and human resources been sufficiently developed to satisfy the appetites of individuals and the government at the same time. This deficiency has compelled the Russian state to pursue Western goals of modernization with the most un-Western forms of coercion and exploitation. But as the objective was approached, in both tsarist and Soviet times, new stresses arose between a changed society and the state that had changed it, and in the first instance the upshot was revolution. Soviet Russia now faces a problem of peculiar complexity: how to overcome the legacy of the Russian-style political methods that were used to overcome the legacy of economic backwardness.

Some of Russia's tradition contributed to Soviet Communism in a direct and acknowledged, though reactive, way. This was the current of political and philosophical thought generated among nineteenth-century Russian intellectuals under the combined impact of Western inspiration and governmental repression. With a dogmatic intensity rivaling that of the Orthodox faith, the intelligentsia embraced the latest in Western radical belief—scientism, socialism, and atheism—while the boldest among them took up the cause of revolutionary conspiracy. This philosophical atmosphere readily accepted Marxism, which moreover recognized the ultimate revolutionary potential in Russia's economic Westernization and the rise of the working class. However, Marxism did not square so easily with the Russian idea of conspiratorial politics, and it was as a result of Lenin's effort to synthesize the two that the Marxist movement split in 1903 into the Menshevik and Bolshevik factions.

The historical impact of Marxism and its refinement as Marxism-Leninism is one of the most complex and subjective questions in the entire effort to interpret Soviet Russia. One thing is clear: ideology has never operated in a vacuum. Marxism took root where the ground was receptive, and flourished selectively according to the experience and ambitions of its devotees; and it was subject to constant (though after a point unacknowledged) updating, selection, and revision. The most enduring function of Marxist ideology for Soviet Russia has been to provide a single, official, obligatory code of public belief, superseding and exceeding the mission of the Orthodox Church under the Old Regime. The strongest surviving elements in Soviet Marxism—its scientism, socialism, and atheism—are precisely those that distinguished the pre-Marxist intelligentsia; other elements—equalitarianism, antistatism, and internationalism—yielded sooner or later to the continuity of Russian statism.

Revolution, the millennium both for Russian radical tradition and for Marxism, had a force of its own beyond the ken of any of its makers. Releasing a restive nation from the habits of submission, the Revolution allowed the whole fabric of a functioning society to be torn apart. Then it strove to rebuild a viable structure of authority without the services of the country's most competent elements, who had been its victims. Although no law of revolution dictated which party and what philosophy would eventually prevail, the outbreak of revolution made virtually inevitable the surge of extremism that brought the Communists to power. The shock of revolution continued to energize the pendulum swings between the new and the old, between experiment and expediency, until Soviet society eventually reached a stable postrevolutionary form.

The events of the Russian Revolution between 1917 and 1921 left a lasting imprint on the Soviet system of rule, uniting the goals of the future and the methods of the past. Out of the civil war that followed the Revolution came a ruling organization of desperate fanatics, militarized and dogmatized, inured to despotism and terror. Their long-term survival was unique in the annals of revolution, reflecting their combination of ruthlessness and adroitness, and it gave to the postrevolutionary system a revolutionary cast that only heightened the demands and cruelties of a regime constantly at war with its own people.

The problems of a modernizing society—how to foster development, how to administer effectively—compelled or hastened the
abandonment of the more utopian facets of the revolutionary impulse. Workers' control of the factories, equality of rewards, liberation from coercive traditions, and blending of manual and mental
labor all fell by the wayside sooner or later. The Communist regime
accommodated itself to the imperatives of industrialization by
jumping ahead of capitalism, sociologically speaking, to a managerial society in which the entire nation was organized as one giant
corporation. Alfred Meyer has termed it "USSR Incorporated"—a
system complete with company towns, company stores, company
unions, company police, company public-relations men, and company manipulation of the stockholders.

Did all this necessarily lead to Stalinism? Stalin's role as a personality was fortuitous and unpredictable, but the possibility of power
falling into the hands of such a man arises in the wake of any revolution, when a torn and disillusioned society offers to the most determined ego the opportunity to create a stable new synthesis in
whatever way he will. Stalin drew from all levels of the Russian heritage—Russian autocracy, Marxist class struggle, Leninist organization—to fashion his political machinery. He directed his terroristic
measures at real problems in Russia's development, and devised
from the country's experience his own despotic answer to those
problems.

Stalin's revolution of the early thirties was the decisive step, fil-
tering and mixing all of the historical ingredients that formed the
extraordinarily stable character of the modern Soviet system. From
the Revolution and the civil war, Stalinism retained and perfected
the Communist Party dictatorship, the militarized style of rule, and
the nominal ideology of Marxism-Leninism, including its antireligious component. From the pragmatic period of the 1920s, Stalinism retained the restored money economy and the social hierarchy
of unequal power and rewards. It suppressed the revolutionary spirit
of social justice and cultural experimentation, and it overrode the
compromise policy of "market socialism" in favor of a vastly
strengthened "War Communism" model of economics. Beyond this,
Stalinism contributed the totalitarianism that is reflected in the
party's control of every form of organized social life, in the immense
power of the police state, and in the authoritarian-traditionalist system of public values that is billed as Marxism but (terminology and

the religious issue aside) is difficult to distinguish from movements of the extreme right.

What appeared in this mix that warrants speaking of a synthesis of revolutionary and prerevolutionary Russia? Little that was direct or acknowledged; much that was indirect and subtle. Culturally speaking, the Revolution did the most damage to the attitudes and practices that had been most recently imported from the West. Stalinism then revived, with a new vocabulary, some of the oldest, crudest, and harshest habits and premises from the Russian cultural heritage. Until the limited reform efforts of the mid-nineteenth century, the imperial government was a centralized bureaucratic despotism, backward and inefficient; the Stalinist government was also a centralized bureaucratic despotism, though vastly more effective both in its reach and in its grasp. Imperial Russia was nationalistic, chauvinistic, and imperialistic; Stalin shed all inhibitions in dealing with the outside world. Imperial Russian society was a hierarchy based originally on service to the state; Stalinist society took the same form and the same purpose. Imperial Russia maintained a state religion and discouraged the import of ideas from abroad (except in technology); Stalinist Russia found another, more rigorous basis in Marxism to achieve the same ends. In terms of the revolutionary process, by extirpating the spirit of revolutionary innovation and liquidating the vast majority of the makers of the Revolution, Stalinism became the functional equivalent of a royal Restoration.

Did anything really remain of the Revolution, apart from the ideological pretensions of the regime? The answer is simultaneously much and little—little of unamended carryover, but much in the sense that Stalin's system could not have come into existence except in the wake of the Revolution, as the embodiment of the last stages of that unfortunate process. One principle of the Revolution clearly was sealed into the Stalinist system—namely, the commitment to a socialized economy and the hatred of private property. This did not mean that Stalinism had to be a classless society, as its apologists maintained, but only that Marxism is wrong in suggesting property holding as the sole basis for class differences. Stalinist society is one variant of the worldwide trend toward the displacement of property owners as the ruling class by a new class of managers and manipulators, public or private, who owe their power and their rewards not to individual enterprise but to their function in and loyalty to bureaucratic organizations. In such processes of social evolution, if not in the political realm, one can indeed find support for the theory of "convergence" among all types of industrial societies.

Considering how far the Soviet system has gone in its postrevolutionary fusion of the old and the new, it would be surprising if the country's foreign relations did not reveal a corresponding amalgam of successive historical influences. Though the Revolution is central to the understanding of Russia's international presence and the world's response to it, the events of 1917 did not eradicate old historical continuities any more than they precluded the emergence of new challenges and new priorities. Russia is still the same vast country, and its revolution would have been of little moment to the outside world were this not true. As in imperial days, Russia continues to play the role of a world power, and it does so with cautious ruthlessness and a heavy commitment of its national resources. If the Communists have been more successful than the tsars, the difference is more readily accounted for by their material power and by weaknesses in the world around them than by some new compelling sense of mission. Soviet Russia has focused its efforts on the same areas of proximate geographical interest—eastern Europe, the Near and Middle East, the Far East—with markedly greater success only in the first of these. The Soviets, to be sure, have engaged in some far-flung ventures in recent times—in Latin America, Southeast Asia, Africa. Yet allowing for a half-century's change in communications technology and in political opportunities, it cannot be said that the Communists have done anything incompatible with tsarist aims and practices.

In its time, the Revolution appeared to friend and foe alike to have changed everything in Russia's external relations. It proclaimed an international crusade against capitalism, imperialism, and war—themes all echoed still by the Soviet leadership, and to good effect. It launched an international movement of revolutionary parties that still, in form, acknowledge this mission. It dug a political chasm between Communist and anti-Communist that has had incalculable ramifications in the internal politics of countries all over the world.

To some minds the Revolution, with its ideology of world proletarian upheaval, continues to account for all aspects of Soviet international behavior. But history did not stop with the Revolution, any more than it began at that point. New international challenges, along with the continuing internal transformation of the Soviet system, have added a thick postrevolutionary layer to the amalgam of policy influences in the minds of Russia's rulers.

Crucial among these recent changes was the polarization of power between the Soviet Union and the United States, as the two giants emerged from the carnage of the Second World War and faced off in the power vacuum created by the collapse of European and Japanese imperialism. Meanwhile Stalin's Russia had married the revolutionary program to traditional nationalistic interests. What appeared to the world at large as an epochal breakthrough by the new order of socialism was in fact permeated by old Russian modes of operating, whether they were continuations or revivals or only incidental parallels. In terms of the ultimate attractiveness of the philosophy of socialism, the fact that its initial victory occurred in Russia of all places is a burden from which it may never fully recover.

As the Russian Revolution recedes into the past, its unique impulse yields progressively to other policy determinants both more recent and more remote, fresher or more enduring in their impact on the nation's quest to succeed. The debate goes on among the Kremlin watchers: Is it ideology, national interest, or pure power lust that animates the makers of Soviet policy? But history defies such clear-cut choices. It is the total fabric of national experience, interests, and righteousness that governs what a country's leaders believe, intend, and attempt.

The contemporary relationship between the United States and Russia is unique in the history of the modern world. Two countries, vastly different in origins, traditions, and institutions, but without substantial points of conflict in the past, have emerged with the power between them to dictate the fate of the world or to destroy it altogether. Divided by principles of government that make each anathema to the other, they have nevertheless been able to establish a minimal modus vivendi. Unfortunately there is no guarantee that the relative good luck of the past will hold, and the historian can only advise that judgments deciding the future be made with a knowledge and understanding of past events.

What can awareness of this past-present connection do for outsiders—troubled citizens or beleaguered policymakers—who seek some formula for dealing with Russia? The United States cannot hope either to ignore Russia or to live comfortably in a world divided by American and Soviet power. But it may be able to avoid the self-defeating errors of simplistic thinking if it approaches the confrontation with the Soviets with a sense of history in lieu of the slogans of national anxiety.

History, of course, does not yield policy like a computer when all the correct buttons are pressed. Yet it can enhance the perception and judgment that contribute to realistic decisions. To recognize the actions of a foreign government as the outcome of its historical conditioning is not to dismiss or condone them, but only to render them intelligible and to restrain the cyclical Cassandra and Pollyanna attitudes so characteristic of public opinion in the United States. Historical perspective tempers both fears and expectations—the fear of the new and the expectation of the unfounded. It is my belief in the relevance of this perspective that inspires this work.

Tower of Ivan the Great in the
Kremlin, Moscow

Holy Russia

Compared with Russia, or with any major country of
Europe or Asia, the United States has hardly any history. Created scarcely two centuries ago by a trans-
plantation of European society and institutions to a
new land, the United States is an invention of modern

times, lacking the sense either of roots or of change that more truly historical nations must take for granted. Russia, by contrast, has been a national entity for more than a millennium, as long as any of Europe's modern states. Russia has been Russia since the dawn of recorded history in Eastern Europe.

Over this great span of time Russia's history followed a course entirely different from the path of the western European nations, whose past is more familiar to Americans as part of their own heritage. During most of its long struggle for existence, Russia remained isolated and backward. Until Peter the Great turned the nation's face toward the West at the beginning of the eighteenth century, Russia was really a different civilization, shaped by a unique set of harsh experiences. Since Russia's identity both as a nation and as an empire is rooted in those old days, it is not surprising that the country has preserved certain deep-seated traditions and assumptions that no amount of forcible modernization can entirely eradicate.

Most enduring of these ancient influences, perhaps, are Russia's assumptions about the outside world. Russia became committed to the proposition that military power was the country's supreme priority and that all of its energies and resources needed to be coordinated to that end through the agency of an all-powerful government. National security knew no natural limits: defense was best secured by expansion. But even while accumulating military successes, Russia was weighed down by a national inferiority complex when it confronted the material and cultural accomplishments of foreign civilizations. Russia never became sure of itself.

▪ The Phases of Russian History

It must not be presumed that Russia before the eighteenth century was completely static and uncivilized. The church maintained a significant cultural life, and the state carried on a successful military effort. But political and social change took place through historical traumas unknown to the West. Consequently, the natural dividing lines that set off the principal episodes in Russia's history do not, as might be supposed, coincide with the conventional ancient/medieval/early-modern/modern periodization in the more familiar history of Russia's neighbors to the west. Russia's destiny was shaped and reshaped by a unique set of forces, both material and cultural, impinging on it from the outside. It is these external impacts that have marked off the basic epochs of Russian history and shaped the primary features of each.

In its origins Russia was not, like Mediterranean Europe, the legatee of an older civilization extant in the same territory, nor was it created by the colonial extension of an existing culture. Russians—the East Slavic–speaking tribes in the woods of eastern Europe—created civilized life in their own land. They did this, to be sure, with the help of important foreign influence and examples, but without foreign conquest or rule until the invasion of the Mongols. This Russian civilization was an extraordinary human accomplishment: it is the only example in world history of the creation of a civilized culture and a territorial state under subarctic climatic conditions with a technology that was not only preindustrial but did not even know the fireplace and the brick stove.

As to the specific beginnings of politically organized society in Russia, there is still controversy among the scholars. Soviet texts carry the "history of the USSR" back to the Kingdom of Urartu, founded by the ancestors of the Armenians around 2000 B.C. However, this and other early outposts of civilization on the southern margin of present Soviet territory had no organic connection with the origin and development of civilization in Russia until these peripheral areas were annexed by the Russian Empire in comparatively recent times. Regarding the establishment of a state among the Russians themselves, the traditional view ascribes the decisive role to the Vikings (known as "Varangians" in Russia), who raided Russia and the rest of Europe during the ninth century A.D. and set themselves up as princes in fledgling city-states among the Slavs. The term "Russian" and the old name "Rus" by which the country was first known appear to be of Scandinavian origin, though the evidence is obscure. Russian nationalists, including the Soviets since Stalin, have preferred to stress the sketchy evidence favoring the formation of the state by native Slavic chieftains. In any case, the first strictly historical political entities on Russian territory—the city-principalities of Novgorod in the northwest and Kiev in the southwest—were populated by Slavic speakers, and the ruling dynasty, supposedly descended from the legendary Viking chief Riurik, was linguistically assimilated.

The center of Russian political and cultural life during the early Middle Ages was the city and principality of Kiev, and this epoch of cultural genesis is therefore known as the Kievan period. Under a line of vigorous princes—Sviatoslav (964–972); Vladimir (980–1015), the ruler who Christianized the country and was made a saint; Yaroslav the Wise (1019–1054)—Kiev successfully battled the nomads of the steppes and expanded its realm through the forest zone of the eastern European plain by spawning colony-towns and a network of satellite principalities. By the time of Yaroslav, Kiev's dominion extended from the lower Dnieper to the Arctic Ocean and from the province of Galicia, bordering Poland, to the upper reaches of the Volga. The princes of Kiev became part of the international community by marrying their sons and daughters to European royalty.

Kiev's preeminence in medieval times gave rise to the claim by some modern Ukrainians that Kievan civilization belongs to their history and not to that of the Great Russians, whose origins lay in the more barbaric region to the northeast. In reality there was at that time no distinction among the East Slavs corresponding to the present lines of language and nationality between Great Russian, Belorussian, and Ukrainian—differences that appeared only after the Mongol conquest. The Moscow region, settled and organized in the eleventh and twelfth centuries by princes and monasteries and their peasant retainers migrating from the Kiev area, drew its culture as much from Kiev as did the present area of the Ukraine.

Though politically independent under its grand dukes (in Russian, *velikii kniaz*—"great prince"), Kievan Russia was soon pulled into the cultural and religious orbit of what was in early medieval times the most opulent and impressive center of civilization between the Atlantic and India—namely, the Byzantine Empire, the Christianized Greek remnant of Rome centered on the great city of Constantinople. The decisive step was the acceptance of Constantinople's Eastern Orthodox Christianity by the Kievan princes in the tenth century, thereby orienting their subjects to the artistic forms and governmental styles of the Greeks. Soon afterward, as a result of the eleventh-century schism between Orthodox Constantinople and Catholic Rome, religion became a major obstacle for the Russians in the pursuit of cultural links with Catholic Western Europe.

The Kievan period of Russia's history was brought to an end by an externally inflicted disaster: the invasion of the Mongols under the descendants of Genghis Khan in the thirteenth century. Reducing the Russian principalities to the status of terrorized puppet states, the Mongols obstructed Russian contact with Europe even more, and caused the economic and cultural development of the country to stagnate for two centuries. Gradually a national resistance movement arose, led by the previously insignificant principality of Moscow (or Muscovy, as westerners called it). By the middle of the fifteenth century the Mongol domination was finally thrown off. Moscow emerged as the capital of a unified Russian national state, more or less confined at that point to the present Great Russian–speaking portion of the European part of the Soviet Union. The regions to the west and southwest, including Kiev, where Belorussian and Ukrainian are now spoken, were liberated from the Mongols not by Moscow but by the briefly powerful Grand Duchy of Lithuania. As part of the Lithuanian realm, these areas were shortly afterward merged with the Catholic and Western-oriented Kingdom of Poland. It was this divergent historical experience, extending until the late eighteenth century (and for the Western Ukraine until 1939), that gave the peoples of what are now the Ukraine and Belorussia the sense that they were a nationality distinct from the Great Russians.

The Muscovite period of Russian history extends from the unification of the state by Ivan the Great in the fifteenth century to the dramatic opening to the West by Peter the Great in the late seventeenth and early eighteenth centuries. It was a time of constant warfare, intermittent territorial expansion, autocratic consolidation, cultural isolation, and enserfment of the peasants. After the Turks overran the Balkans and captured Constantinople, Muscovy became the last independent bastion of the Eastern Orthodox faith, and the Russians acquired a lasting sense of suspicion and alienation toward the outside world.

The Westernization of Russia undertaken by Peter the Great—symbolized by his transfer of the capital from Moscow to the newly built seaport of St. Petersburg—appeared on the surface to shatter the old cast of mind and bring Russia into the community of European nations. This was true diplomatically and in the cultural Westernization of the upper class, but only in the most superficial sense did it apply to the inner workings of government, the economy, and the everyday life of the masses. In fact, a major theme of the St. Petersburg period, with its revolutionary denouement, is the internal tension stemming from efforts to remodel Russian society and institutions on the lines of the dynamic Western world.

Two watershed events within the St. Petersburg period were the Napoleonic Wars and the Emancipation of the serfs in 1861. After 1815, though Russia had proved its power in dealing with the West, it tried to arrest any further internal change on Western lines. With the Emancipation this stance was recognized as futile, and Russia once more tried to catch up, above all in the race to industrialize. But accelerated modernization proved in the end to be an invitation to revolution.

Running through all these epochs of Russia's history are certain commanding themes that link the travails of the prerevolutionary past with the burdens of the postrevolutionary present. Territorially, Russia is the outcome of a long and almost constant record of imperial expansion that created an empire covering one-sixth of the earth's land surface and embracing a host of national minorities. Politically, Russia developed under the tsars into one of the most centralized and coercive autocracies ever known before the dictatorships of the twentieth century. In terms of social structure, Russia evolved a rigid hierarchy of classes, all devoid of civil rights. Culturally, Russia was uniquely distinguished by its long, slow history of Westernization and by the national schizophrenia born of the conflict between native tradition and foreign models. Finally, the tension between tradition and accelerating modernization in the half-century before 1917 created a classic crisis of social transformation, setting the stage for the whole Soviet experience.

▪ Imperial Expansion

Russia has rarely known a peaceful national existence within stable and secure borders. Kievan Russia was plagued by princely feuds and by nomadic incursions from the steppes, culminating in disaster at the hands of the Mongols in 1237–1240. Moscow achieved its preeminence among the Russian principalities and its leadership of the resistance to the Mongols only through incessant warfare. When, finally, the Russians were united into a centralized national state by Ivan the Great, there was no obstacle of principle or practicality to the continuation of warfare for the greater glory of the realm. Russia thus passed directly from disunity and foreign overlordship to na-

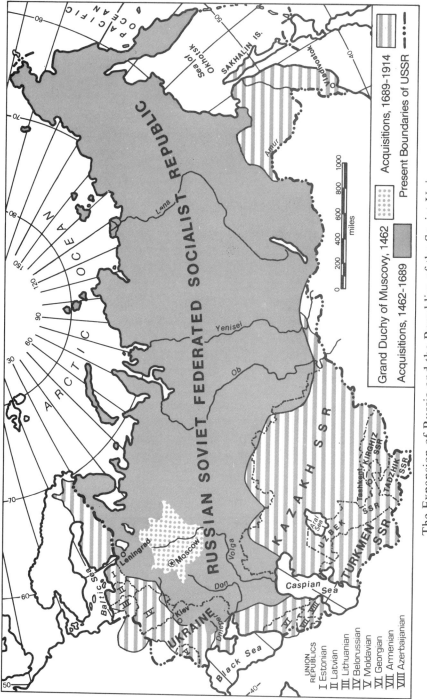

The Expansion of Russia and the Republics of the Soviet Union

Legend:

Grand Duchy of Muscovy, 1462	Acquisitions, 1689–1914
Acquisitions, 1462–1689	Present Boundaries of USSR

RUSSIAN SOVIET FEDERATED SOCIALIST REPUBLIC

PACIFIC OCEAN

ARCTIC OCEAN

Sea of Okhotsk

SAKHALIN IS.

Vladivostok

Amur

Lena

Yenisei

Ob

Volga

Don

Dnieper

Aral Sea

Caspian Sea

Black Sea

Baltic Sea

Leningrad

⊛ Moscow

Kiev

Tashkent

KAZAKH SSR

UZBEK SSR

KIRGHIZ SSR

TADZHIK SSR

TURKMEN SSR

UKRAINE

miles
0 200 400 600 800 1000

UNION REPUBLICS
I Estonian
II Latvian
III Lithuanian
IV Belorussian
V Moldavian
VI Georgian
VII Armenian
VIII Azerbaijanian

tional statehood, and on to aggressive expansion, sometimes frustrated but often successful, if neighbors proved too weak or friendless to resist.

The beginning of direct annexation of neighboring non-Russian peoples came in the reign of Ivan IV, better known as *Ivan Grozyny* —Ivan the Frightful, or Ivan the Terrible. Crowning himself in 1547, at the age of sixteen, with the new title of *tsar* (the Slavic corruption of "Caesar"), Ivan launched a stubborn campaign of military expansion toward both the west and the east. On the west he was beaten back by his Polish and Swedish adversaries in the decades-long Livonian War. On the east, however, he was successful against Russia's old enemies, the Moslem Tatars, heirs to the Mongol Empire but now mired in civil strife and militarily outclassed by the Russians. Ivan overwhelmed the Tatars of Kazan and pushed down the Volga to the Caspian Sea, making the inhabitants of this great region his involuntary subjects. Then he launched the venture of conquest and exploration across the Urals that was to culminate, in one of the world's great sagas of frontiersmanship, in the attainment of the Pacific Ocean in 1637 and Russia's annexation of the entire northern third of Asia. Through these successes, achieved even as central Russia was being torn by revolt and invasions, the imperial government attained nearly the territorial extent that it enjoys today and began to build a multinational empire.

From the mid-seventeenth century, well before the accession of Peter the Great, until the early years of the nineteenth, Russia's expansionist interests were directed toward the west, where the major victim was the large but disorganized Kingdom of Poland. In the 1650s, abetted by rebellious Cossacks, the Russians conquered the northeastern portion of what is now the Ukraine, up to and including the city of Kiev. The Ukrainians of this area had little sense of national identity, and were easily assimilated since their religion was also Eastern Orthodox. Next, under Peter, Russia defeated the Kingdom of Sweden (which then surrounded the Baltic) and won the site of St. Petersburg on the Gulf of Finland, together with what is now Estonia and half of Latvia, Lutheran in religion and Germanized in culture. Russia's new subjects included not only the Estonian- and Latvian-speaking peasantry but also the "Baltic barons," German descendants of the Teutonic Knights, who constituted the ruling class of the region and who went on to play, as a built-in Westernized elite, a disproportionately large role in the political and administrative life of the empire for the next century and a half.

New gains came in the late eighteenth and early nineteenth centuries at the expense of Russia's traditional enemies, the Poles, the Swedes, and the Turks. During the reign of Catherine the Great, in the course of the three partitions of Poland, Russia appropriated what is now Belorussia, the rest of Latvia, the remainder of the Ukraine (except for the western province of Galicia), and ethnic Lithuania. The new territory was a patchwork of nationalities and religions: Belorussian and Ukrainian followers of the Uniate Church, which had been formed in the sixteenth century as a Roman concession to the East Slavs; Catholic Lithuanians; Yiddish-speaking Jews in all towns; and a Catholic Polish aristocracy. Also under Catherine, Russia acquired the Black Sea littoral and the Crimean Peninsula from the Ottoman Empire, bringing under St. Petersburg the Tatars of the Crimea and opening the southern steppes to Russian settlement. During the Napoleonic period the Rumanian-speaking province of Bessarabia (the present-day Moldavian Republic) was seized from the Ottomans, and Sweden was compelled to cede the entire territory of what is now Finland. To absorb this substantial piece of the West, Emperor Alexander I recognized Finland as a constitutional grand duchy (with himself as the ruler) and allowed it to retain its own laws, currency, and representative institutions.

A similar constitutional experiment was attempted in the large portion of ethnic Poland, including Warsaw, that went to Russia in the Vienna peace settlement of 1814–15. However, the Poles, proud of their langauge, religion, and Western culture and embittered by their recent loss of nationhood, resisted any form of Russian domination. Twice they revolted, in 1830 and in 1863, only to be crushed by superior Russian force. All vestiges of Polish autonomy were eliminated after the second revolt, and the imperial government commenced a long though ineffective campaign of linguistic and cultural russification.

After the Napoleonic era, Russia's expansionist interests were directed again at its Asian frontiers. Between 1803 and 1828 what are now the Transcaucasian republics of Georgia, Armenia, and Azerbaijan, with their diverse languages and religions, were seized from Turkey and Persia. During the second and third quarters of the nineteenth century the Russians thrust across the deserts of Central

Asia, first to subdue the Kazakh nomads east of the Caspian Sea, and then to conquer the peoples now occupying the Turkmen, Uzbek, Kirghiz, and Tadzhik Soviet Republics. In the Far East, taking advantage of China's preoccupation with the great Tai-ping peasant rebellion, Russian forces seized the strategic though sparsely populated Maritime Province, including the present port of Vladivostok. It is noteworthy that the empire did not attain its greatest territorial extent until after the continental United States had assumed its present shape, and only a couple of decades before the Revolution.

■ Autocracy

The continental growth of a great state is relatively easy for Americans to understand in the light of their own history. It is much harder for them to appreciate the centuries-old legacy of autocratic rule under which Russians have labored, as bereft of personal freedom in their own country as any victim of colonial rule. Indeed, the American colonists' grievances against King George III seem insignificant when compared with the treatment that Russians of all classes have endured at the hands of their own government.

From the time it achieved national unity in the fifteenth century until a mere dozen years before the Revolution, Russia was governed as an absolute monarchy. A hereditary ruler embodied in his person, by the grace of God, total power over all his subjects. The Marquis de Custine wrote in his famous travelogue of early nineteenth-century Russia. "It can be said of the Russians, great and small—they are intoxicated with slavery. This population of automatons is like half a game of checkers, for a single man makes all the plays and the invisible adversary is humanity. One does not die, one does not breathe here except by permission or by imperial order."

Such an institutionalization of supreme authority was common in the history of continental Europe in the early-modern period (though not in the English tradition from which the United States sprang). But absolutism meant much more in Russia than in the West: not only did it develop earlier and last longer, but it was also much more complete and coercive. A monarch such as Louis XIV, though enveloped in all the pomp and majesty that a sophisticated culture could contrive, and possessed of an effective monopoly on political authority, found the actual scope of his power limited by an array of nongovernmental institutions and interests. The church was a distinct, international institution, supportive of the monarchy but immune to any encroachments on its own rights and property. The nobility was a corporate body of entrenched privilege and local hegemony. The cities enjoyed charters of mercantile self-government, with guilds regulating the various branches of the economy according to their traditional oligarchic powers and jurisdictions. Here were the three Estates of the realm, endowed by law and tradition with powers and privileges that the royal government challenged at its peril.

No such boundaries to the power of the sovereign existed in Russia. The church was a strictly national entity, subordinate to the state and incapable of playing an independent political role. The nobility were cowed and uprooted and reduced to serving as appointed officials and men-at-arms. The cities had no corporate existence apart from the government, which was chiefly responsible for supporting them as administrative centers. As the mid-nineteenth-century Russian historians of the "State School" recognized, "hypertrophy of the state," where political power determined the shape of economic and social development, was the key to Russia's history as an organized society. More recently, Karl August Wittfogel has elaborated the concept of "oriental despotism" to explain the power of government in a country such as Russia, where the state controlled the essential resource of arable land. In any event, Russian absolutism was more despotic, more centralized, and more oppressive than any contemporary counterpart in the West. Absolute power, its exercise, and the expectation of its enforcement became the basis of Russian political culture.

The concept of political culture is a useful notion in appreciating Russia's governmental background and its influence on the regime that issued from the Revolution. Broadly speaking, "political culture" denotes those aspects of a nation's traditions, habits, and assumptions that bear on the manner in which it allows itself to be ruled. As such, political culture may transcend particular ideologies and abrupt upheavals, to assert itself subtly in the long-run patterns of a country's institutions and behavior. At the same time it would be just as erroneous to regard political culture as an immutable part of the national character, frozen in form at the time of some archetypal experience, as it would be to attribute the nature of the Soviet experience solely to Marx's ideology or to Lenin's revolution. Political culture is a many-layered residue of successive historical influences in which the mix gradually changes as new experiences add to, sustain, erode, or revive the legacy of older events.

In the Kievan period, prior to the Mongol invasion, Russia had not yet developed its distinctive patterns of autocracy. As the historian Pavel Miliukov observed, the political constitution of the Kievan state was made up of three elements—the princely, the feudal, and the municipal, all more or less in balance. The grand duke in Kiev and his brothers and cousins of the Riurik line, among whom local leadership was parceled out after the time of Yaroslav, were essentially military chieftains. With their retainers, similar to the feudal knights of the medieval West, they rotated among the small commercial towns and fought one another for the nominal sovereignty over the whole country that was exercised at Kiev. Locally they had to share power with the town council, the *veche,* which usually represented the merchant oligarchy. The distribution of power thus resembled the decentralized feudal system of medieval Europe, though different elements tended to stand out in different parts of the realm. Novgorod, a virtually independent trading empire (though it accepted princes of the Kievan dynasty as its military leaders), was a city-state dominated by the merchants of the *veche.* In the western part of the country, following the Polish example, the feudal element prevailed. And in the northeast, where Muscovy arose, the local princes were paramount from the beginning of Kiev's colonization of the region.

This local bent toward one-man rule in the Moscow area was reinforced by the influence of Russia's primary model of civilized life, the Byzantine Empire. The infant Russian state, drawing its religion and its cultural models from Constantinople, also found its ideal of statecraft in the Byzantine pattern of bureaucratic despotism and universalistic pretentions. In particular, the Russian princes successfully emulated the Byzantine practice of subordinating the church to the state according to the notion of "caesaropapism"—that is, one man serving as caesar and pope, secular ruler and organizational (though not theological) head of the church. This is the Byzantinist interpretation of Russian autocracy.

Another explanation of the phenomenon is the influence of the Mongols. The argument has two facets: the destructive effect of the Mongol conquest on the Russian social structure, particularly the stifling of the towns and their representative institutions, and the forceful example of the Mongols' use of terror and centralized administration to mobilized the troops and collect the taxes needed for military power. Apart from the southern steppes, which they controlled directly from their capital of Sarai on the Volga, the Mongols ruled indirectly, granting the Russian princes of the Riurik line authority in their respective regions, provided they accepted the status of Mongol vassals. As such, the princes exercised more power over their subjects than in the days of independence. Moscow, recognized by the Mongols in 1328 as their preeminent Russian dependency, learned its overlords' lessons well and applied them in its campaigns to subjugate the other Russian princes and then to throw off the Mongol-Tatar domination altogether. By the time Ivan the Great had finished constructing the Russian national state, destroying all vestiges of autonomy in the former principalities and scattering the nobility throughout his realm, Moscow had already established the basis of the autocracy that was to distinguish the country throughout the modern era. "In the control which he exercises over his people," German visitor Baron von Herberstein observed of Ivan's son and successor, Vasili III, "he easily surpasses all the rulers of the entire world."

The autocratic principle in Muscovy was further reinforced by another factor, working throughout the epoch of state-building and imperial expansion. This was the constant danger to state and society posed by Russia's enemies, whether tribal nomads or hostile governments. In consequence, according to the frontier theory of the Russian historian Vasili Kliuchevsky, Moscow had to devote all of the country's energy to military defense—and, one might add, to offensive expansion when the opportunity presented itself. Because of the country's economic backwardness and cultural crudity, the unlimited state had to be accepted to enforce military priorities—that is, to collect the taxes and mobilize the needed armies. Otherwise the law of the survival of the fittest in international competition would have disposed of Moscow's aspirations to greatness.

Students of American history will note that the political effect of the frontier in Russia was the opposite of the United States, where according to the "Turner thesis" it promoted democracy and equalitarianism. The American outcome was the product of very different circumstances: the settlers had no autocratic institutions to begin with and enjoyed a decisive technological superiority over the Indians. Where the situation in Russia was more comparable—among

Russian frontiersmen who had escaped the authority of the center—the outcome was a rough-hewn democracy validating the Turner thesis. This was the society of the Cossacks, fugitives from justice or serfdom who settled the no-man's-land of the south Russian steppes in the fifteenth and sixteenth centuries. Only after many generations were the Cossacks brought under the effective authority of the tsar, to be employed as the imperial cavalry and border security forces.

Russia's embrace of autocracy contrasts with efforts in the West to resist the pretensions of royal absolutism, as in the English Revolution of the seventeenth century, which bequeathed America's most basic political institutions and assumptions. Hence, any comparative judgments about Russian and American political behavior even today must consider the four or five centuries of profound divergence between the two traditions—one despotic, centralized, bureaucratic, hierarchical; the other constitutional, decentralized, individualist, egalitarian (at least with respect to legal and political rights). It is hard to conceive of two more disparate lines of historical development.

Imperial despotism, to be sure, was not implanted in Russia without resistance, though the antibureaucratic forces were more narrowly based and hence less effective than corresponding movements in the West in the age of absolute monarchy. Localism had been smashed in the course of Moscow's consolidation of the Russian national state, and officials in the field were rotated to prevent the establishment of permanent local leadership (a custom followed not only by the Soviet government but by most modern bureaucratic organizations, in contrast to the highly localized basis of American political life). Resistance at the center erupted during the sixteenth century in a series of struggles between the princes and the upper nobility (the "boyars"), who fought to retain their role in the government. Two institutions dominated by the boyars showed some potential for curbing the autocracy: the traditional Boyar Duma, or council of royal advisors, and the *Zemsky Sobor* ("Assembly of the Land"), a broader body, periodically convoked by the princes, that was potentially analogous to the English Parliament or the French Estates General. Unfortunately for the cause of limited government, the Zemsky Sobor never became more than a political sounding board, and fell into disuse by the middle of the seventeenth century. The Boyar Duma, on the other hand, was converted into an appointive status group of rich magnates and officials, never with independent power, while the nobility as a whole contented themselves with competition for family rank and precedence in the hierarchical system of *mestnichestvo,* or "place holding." Ever since, the Russian political structure has maintained a visible body of all the top-status bureaucrats, extending from Peter the Great's *generalitet* (the top four grades in his Table of Ranks) through Alexander I's State Council. One is inevitably led to think of today's Supreme Soviet, the Central Committee of the Party, and the system of *nomenklatura* (placement of officials according to rank).

The climax of the struggle between the principles of aristocracy and autocracy came in the reign of Ivan the Terrible. Obsessed by suspicion of treason among the boyars (foreshadowing Stalin's purges), Ivan created a new governmental administration, the *oprichnina* ("exceptional body"), to cement his own power and purge the nobility. The tsar's new men, the *oprichniki* (likened to Stalin's secret police), waged a campaign of terror against the old noble families for half a decade, and destroyed their independent power in the old center of Muscovy just as Ivan III had done in the area of his new conquests.

Following Ivan IV, the dynasty fell on bad times. Ivan had killed his elder son and heir in a fit of rage, leaving the throne to his dimwitted son Fyodor in 1584. Real power devolved upon Fyodor's brother-in-law, Boris Godunov, the hero of Pushkin's drama and Mussorgsky's opera. According to legend, Boris had Fyodor's younger brother and heir, Dmitri, done to death, and seized the throne for himself when Fyodor died in 1598.

Godunov's accession was the first complete break in the hereditary line of the Riurik dynasty since its beginnings in Kiev. It inaugurated a period of political turmoil—the "Time of Troubles"—which was virtually a revolution, though ultimately abortive. The motive force behind this upheaval was similar to the crises experienced in those years in many Western countries: a combination of the nobility's resentment of the advancing autocracy, and the poverty and exploitation suffered by the urban and rural masses. Taking advantage of the break in the dynasty, the nobility revolted and found a pretender to the throne who claimed to be Ivan's son Dmitri, now grown up. With support from Poland, the rebels were at the point of driving Godunov from the throne when he died in 1605. False Dmitri was deposed and murdered in turn by anti-Polish boyars. By this time the habit of submission to authority had been so shaken that popular uprisings began to break out, particularly among the Cossacks and runaway peasants in the south. This extremist or social phase of the revolution found its leader in a new False Dmitri; so deep were the traditions of hereditary personalized rule that no protest movement could gain headway without claiming such legitimacy. Swedish and Polish intervention followed, abetted by some of the boyars who saw it as an alternative to anarchy and social upheaval. From 1610 to 1612, Wladyslaw, son of King Sigismund III of Poland, occupied the throne of Moscow. The Russian response was a broad national resistance movement, led by the church and the lower gentry, which culminated in the expulsion of the Poles and the election of a new dynasty—the Romanovs—at the last significant meeting of the Zemsky Sobor in 1613.

Paradoxically, the effect of the Time of Troubles was not to curb the autocratic trend but to intensify it. During the centuries that followed, the institution of absolute monarchy in Russia showed an extraordinary capacity to survive with undiminished power, despite incompetent monarchs and succession struggles. Every Russian reign between 1682 and 1917 was touched by revolutionary violence either at its beginning or at its end. But there was no social force or institution save the upper nobility that had the potential to take advantage of the monarchy's crises, and at these points resistance was undercut by the lesser gentry, the church, and the merchants, to whom the security of a strong regime outweighed the attractions of their problematic participation in the government.

Rebelliousness nevertheless persisted at all levels of Russian society—among the nobility, the army, the Moscow mob, the Cossacks, the serfs. By the nineteenth century Russians saw themselves as extremists, now cowed into sullen apathy, now flaring into anarchic violence. Two terrifying peasant uprisings took place, in the 1660s and 1770s, though neither had the organization to stand up to regular troops. Interestingly enough, the leader of the later revolt, the Cossack Pugachev, found it necessary (as had the False Dmitris) to assume the identity of the deposed Emperor Peter III in order to claim the legitimacy necessary to build a following. But the only successful revolts were palace conspiracies designed to change simply the ruler, not the system of rule.

Even Peter the Great, who strove to bring Russia into the orbit of Western culture and diplomacy, did not fundamentally change the

Russian system of power. If anything, Peter's efforts at administrative modernization and restaffing—considered a "revolution from above" by some historians—merely provided him with a more efficient instrument of autocracy, less inhibited by the family pretensions of the nobility and harsher than anything previous in dragooning the masses into its service. With his famous Table of Ranks—a system of civil service equivalencies for nobles, officials, and military officers—Peter succeeded only in bringing Western regularity into the old Russian system of hereditary and bureaucratic status. Like the Time of Troubles, though in a different way, the Petrine Revolution provides a model for the events of the Revolution of 1917: violent or abrupt attempts at change, which exacerbated the very conditions against which the impulse to change was initially directed.

Peter's death in 1725 ushered in the so-called Era of Palace Revolutions, a forty-year period of intrigue, conspiracy, and assassination involving various pro-Westernizing and anti-Westernizing court factions. Most of the time the throne was occupied by women— Peter's second wife, Catherine I (1725–1727); his niece, Anna (1730–1740); his daughter, Elizabeth (1741–1762); and finally his granddaughter-in-law, the redoubtable Catherine the Great (1762–1796)—yet the power of the autocracy remained undiminished. At one point, at the accession of Anna, the conservative nobility attempted to impose a set of semiconstitutional conditions on the crown, but a coup by supporters of the new empress disposed of this experiment. A measure of personal freedom was accorded the gentry when the deranged but ideologically enlightened emperor Peter III (grandson of Peter the Great and husband of Catherine the Great) emancipated them from compulsory state service. Before he could extend the same benefit to the peasants, he was murdered in the course of a palace revolution that put his German wife on the throne.

Catherine the Great brought Voltaire to St. Petersburg and fancied herself a child of the Age of Reason, but her plans for legal and administrative reform invariably came to naught. She exemplified the Russian tragedy of the autocrat who was intellectually capable of bringing justice to a suffering land but who always stopped short of any change that would compromise the power of the throne. Bureaucracy, according to the widely esteemed sociology of Max Weber, is supposed to be a facet of modernization, but in Russia bureaucracy antedated modernization. The entire first century of Westernization succeeded merely in grafting the forms of Western organization and rationality onto the old Russian roots of tyranny, begetting what the anarchist Mikhail Bakunin termed "the Germanic Empire of the Knout."

Russia's theoretical infatuation with enlightened despotism on the then-fashionable Western model came to an abrupt end with the outbreak of revolution in France in 1789. Fearing for the future of all established institutions and habits of obedience, the Russian government set itself firmly against any further flow of ideas from the West, even though it still tried (like the Soviet regime today) to avail itself of the practical fruits of Western science, technology, and education. The repression during Catherine's last years, felt particularly by Western-oriented members of the gentry, was continued under her son, Paul I (1796–1801), another royal psychopath (perhaps not a true Romanov but the offspring of Catherine's lover Grigori Orlov). Paul's capricious Germanophilism ended in his overthrow and murder in the last successful palace revolution before 1917, bringing to the throne his son Alexander I. Educated, like Catherine, in the spirit of the Age of Enlightenment, Alexander toyed with reform and even had his chief minister, Mikhail Speransky, prepare a scheme for constitutional monarchy. Unfortunately the Napoleonic Wars eclipsed these plans, except for their limited or abortive application in the two Western nations—Finland and Poland—annexed by Russia under Alexander.

The hopes and disappointments provoked by Alexander's erratic reform policy, coupled with the permeation of Russia's educated class by Western thought, caused an epochal parting of the ways between government and society. Society—or its articulate, critically minded component—could not accept the government; the government, distrustful of the most capable elements of society, suppressed criticism and resisted change. The result was the rise among the most consciously frustrated elements of society of a tradition of revolutionary thought and activity, destined to grow in strength until the Old Regime was ready to collapse in the early years of the twentieth century.

The first great manifestation of the new critical sentiment—and also the last of the classic palace conspiracies—was the Decembrist Revolt of 1825. Liberal army officers, plotting to establish a constitutional monarchy on English lines or a republic on the American model, seized the opportunity of Alexander's death in November 1825 (or, according to one version, his feigned death and retirement to a religious hideout) to claim the throne for the emperor's liberal brother, Constantine. The latter, however, had secretly willed his rights to the youngest brother, Nicholas, a reactionary of the post-1789 school. When the conspirators staged an uprising in December 1825, Nicholas easily put the attempt down and stifled further efforts at political change.

The reign of Nicholas I, the Iron Tsar (1825–1855), was the apogee of bureaucratic arbitrariness and police-state repression in prerevolutionary Russia, starkly contrasting with the contemporary example of representative government in England and North America and the ferment of liberal revolution in central Europe. Inspired by the slogan "Autocracy, Orthodoxy, Nationality," Nicholas perfected the system of secret-police controls and censorship, managed with un-Russian efficiency by Baltic German specialists in the "Third Section of His Majesty's Chancery." Thanks to this official intransigence, the cleavage between the authorities and the educated class became irreparable. Nevertheless, despite the censorship, Russia entered into one of the world's most glorious periods of literary creativity—from Pushkin and Gogol to Tolstoy, Dostoevsky, and Chekhov. During these same years the main lines of political and philosophical thought were propounded that were to guide Russian revolutionaries when tsarism finally began to crumble.

Nicholas I died just as Russia was suffering awkward setbacks in the Crimean War, leaving the government as well as the intelligentsia ready to open up to the modern world and accept change as the price of survival. Had a modernizing elite emerged on the model of Japan's contemporaneous Meiji Restoration, prepared to make constitutionalist concessions or otherwise absorb the most Westernized social elements into the power structure, Russia might have avoided revolution. And indeed, Alexander II, with the aid of some able and energetic ministers, did make his reign (1855–1881) the signal period of reform in Russia's prerevolutionary history. Proclaiming that "it is better to begin to abolish serfdom from above than to wait until it begins to abolish itself spontaneously from below," he freed the serfs in 1861, two years before Abraham Lincoln issued his Emancipation Proclamation. There followed a number of significant but still superficial reforms, aimed at modernizing Russia's institutional infrastructure—local government, the courts, the educational system, and the army. Civil restrictions on Jews and other ethnic and religious minorities were partially removed, and restraints on the free expression of opinion in the press and universities were relaxed. But despite an abortive plan for an advisory national assembly, Alexander II surrendered none of the basic power of the autocracy or of his police. The opportunity for gradual and peaceful change in the political system had been lost—and the opposition sensed it.

The irony of Alexander's reforms was that they whetted the appetite for revolution, as radical student groups conspired to assassinate the emperor and incite the masses. Poland, already put down by Nicholas I, again revolted unsuccessfully in 1863. This and an assassin's near-miss in 1866 confirmed Alexander's fear of further liberalization; in turn, he marked himself as the target for those elements now too frustrated to wait for change to percolate through the Russian bureaucracy. A terrorist's bomb mortally wounded the tsar-reformer in 1881—the same year in which President Garfield was murdered. The latter tragedy was a footnote to history; its counterpart in Russia signaled that the age of revolution had begun.

▪ Two-Storey Slavery

The overgrowth of the state in Russia's long history was matched by a corresponding deficiency, the underdevelopment of society. As late as the nineteenth century Russia knew little of the private or nongovernmental institutions, groupings, and undertakings that have always enriched life in the West since the Middle Ages. This imbalance in Russia contrasts diametrically with the American tradition relegating the government to management of the tariff and the apprehension of outlaws, while every private interest pursued its selfish advantage or enthusiasm. Between the two systems there is a chasm in historical experience which even today's political imagination still finds hard to bridge.

The weakness of nongovernmental society in Russia is rooted in many centuries of cultural and material poverty. Russia entered recorded history as a marginal agricultural society overawed by the splendor of the old civilizations that its raiders and traders encountered, and almost overwhelmed by the onslaughts of hostile neighbors on every frontier. From Kievan times, the princes took the initiative in everything from trade to religious conversion. The subsequent experience under the Mongols, with the commercial and cultural isolation that it entailed, left little capacity for group political action among either the nobility or the towns: everything fell into the hands of the princes.

Though some slavery existed in the Kievan and Mongol periods, Russian society did not then suffer from the kind of general bondage that came later. But after the consolidation of the national state under the Muscovite princes, the confrontation between ambitious government and amorphous society led inexorably to the shackling of both the upper and lower classes into a system of obligatory service. By purges and settlement the princes of the fifteenth and sixteenth centuries uprooted most of the noble warrior class from their hereditary holdings and replaced them with a humbler service nobility (*pomeshchiki*), who supported themselves on estates (*pomestia*) granted by the crown on condition that they continue to render military service. Through the successive political crises of the sixteenth and seventeenth centuries the *pomestie* system grew in scope, and by the Petrine era even the greatest landowners were the beneficiaries more of imperial favor than of hereditary fortune. Peter finally merged the hereditary and service landholders into one class of compulsory state servants, ranked by seniority and function.

Step by step with the conversion of the nobility into a dependent officialdom went the imposition of the bonds of serfdom on the Russian peasantry, who made up the great bulk of the population. Until about 1500, the peasants tilled the soil as free tenants of the warrior class or of the church. Thereafter they found their freedom of movement progressively restricted by debt and by princely decrees designed to make them a more reliable source of support for the nobility, on whom the state depended for service. Given the superfluity of land available after the Russian state began to beat back its nomadic enemies in the sixteenth century, coercion became essential to keep the peasants working for the benefit of the state's servitors and to prevent them from striking out on their own. The intensification of bondage culminated in the Law Code of 1649, which made serfdom universal and hereditary among the peasants. Thenceforth the serfs were the property of individual landlords, of the church, or, in the more sparsely populated locations, of the state itself. Thus did the open frontier under Russian circumstances work an effect opposite from its liberating influence in America. The entire course of development in Russia was doubly ironic because it was moving in a direction diametrically opposed to the social evolution of western Europe, where serfdom, a legacy of Roman slavery and early medieval chaos, had virtually disappeared just as it was being perfected in Russia. Peasants were enserfed in the West when the state was too weak to keep order; they were enserfed in Russia when the state became strong enough to deny them any alternative.

It is natural to try to compare Russian serfdom with the slave economy of the antebellum South. The two societies were alike as systems of forced agricultural labor for the benefit of the privileged estate-owning class. The abolitionist Cassius Clay, who served as U.S. ambassador to St. Petersburg in the 1860s, observed, "Russians of the higher classes are more like Southerners than the Southerners are like the Northerners." For the lower classes the analogy does not hold so well. Unlike the American slaves, the Russian serfs were racially and culturally the same people as the landlords, and they made up the great bulk of the population. They were not brought to the estates as an uprooted commercial commodity, but lived in their traditional villages where they had gradually been enserfed during the sixteenth and seventeenth centuries. Ordinarily they could not be sold apart from the land, though in the eighteenth century landlords gained virtually the power of life and death over them and could banish recalcitrant serfs to a lifetime of military service. The peasants maintained a tight patriarchal family system and managed village affairs through a direct democracy based on heads of households meeting as the village commune, the *obshchina* ("community").

The *obshchina,* also known as the *mir* (the "world"), was a closely knit, self-governing entity traditionally empowered to maintain order and settle disputes at the village level. It was also collectively responsible for the payment of taxes (by the state serfs) or of rent (by the private serfs, in cases where direct labor service had been commuted to money payments). Further, in the old Muscovite part of the country the *obshchina* had the traditional function of redividing the land among the peasant households according to need, once every generation. This custom gave rise to the notion among the intelligentsia in the nineteenth century that the Russian peasant was a natural socialist and an enemy of individualism.

The garrison mentality that gripped Russian society was scarcely relaxed at all during the first century of Westernization. Decrees by Peter removed all legal distinction between serfs and slaves, allowing the peasants to be exploited at will by private owners and even to be sold or put to work separately from the land. The nobility, too, found themselves under ever more coercive discipline as Peter sought to force Western standards of education, duty, and civilized life upon them. To be sure, thanks to the reforms of Peter III and Catherine the Great, the nobility were personally freed from obligatory service—which incidentally nullified the justification for serfdom—but private serf owning grew as vast tracts of state land and their inhabitants were awarded to court favorites or industrial entrepreneurs. From Catherine's time on, the state drew upon the nobility for voluntary service in the army and the bureaucracy, just as did the monarchies in continental Europe.

In their pursuit of military power and of gains in the European diplomatic game, Peter and his successors opted for the then-prevailing doctrine of mercantilism in economics. This was the philosophy (so irksome to the American colonists in the age of George III) that favored state regulation, protection, and subsidy of private business, all of which were designed to earn a favorable balance of trade and cultivate the technology and resources necessary for making war. Russia was reasonably successful with mercantilist principles in the eighteenth century, and never completely abandoned them: until the Revolution, the tsars were more deeply involved in the ownership or support of economic enterprise than any other government in the world. But in the nineteenth century, the Industrial Revolution in the West left Russia struggling to catch up once again. This was one of the reasons why the government of Alexander II felt it had to go through with the Emancipation and other reforms. But neither the nominal freedom accorded the peasants nor piecemeal liberalization of the governmental structure could satisfy the demand to overhaul Russian society that surged up in the last quarter of the nineteenth century, inspired by the West's example of progress. Alexander's murder left Russia squarely on the road to revolution.

▪ Cultural Schizophrenia

Some nations—the French and the English, especially—have for centuries basked in the assurance that whatever their vicissitudes in the competition for empire, their identity, uniqueness, and supremacy in the realm of culture were beyond challenge. This has not been so either with the United States or with Russia, though for very different reasons. The United States, of Europe but not in it, has nursed in popular circles a deep ambivalence about its European cultural origins, taking them for granted as a historical source but resentful of European pretentiousness as a "highbrow" antithesis to American democratic values. Abreast or ahead of their cultural progenitors in material and technological matters, Americans have consoled themselves with the conviction that these are the only areas of culture that really matter anyway. Russia, in Europe but not of it, has had to compete for centuries with a neighboring civilization stronger in all respects, material as well as intellectual, which the Russians have had to emulate as the price of survival however much this compromised their native values or their national pride. Russia has lived—and still lives—with an ineradicable inferiority complex vis-à-vis the culture of the West, and has been able to compensate for this only by messianic illusions and sheer military power.

From the outset, Russian culture has been unable to develop naturally. Higher civilization, beginning with the Byzantine Christian culture that came in with the Orthodox Church, has usually been a foreign import sponsored by the government. At the time of Russia's Christianization, not only doctrines and art forms but even church personnel had to be brought in from Constantinople. This dependence left Russian civilization highly vulnerable when first the Mongol invasion and then the fall of Constantinople to the Turks cut off the sources of cultural inspiration that had been channeled through the church. Thenceforth, until the time of Peter, isolation left Russia culturally stunted—no science, no universities, high illiteracy, little education outside the church, (even the hereditary village priests were often illiterate), virtually no artistic innovation or philosophical speculation or secular literature apart from folklore. The great European intellectual storms of the Renaissance, the Reformation, and the Scientific Revolution left Russia virtually untouched. Until the seventeenth century Russia was culturally hardly above the level of Europe in the Dark Ages between the fall of Rome and the rise of the great medieval civilization.

Throughout the pre-Petrine era the Orthodox Church played a key role in cultural life and indeed in the entire development of Russian national consciousness. As in the early medieval West, the church was the only repository of learning and literacy, and the only activities of an educational and social-service nature took place under its aegis. Firmly linked to the princes—and specifically to the princes of Moscow after 1326—the church under its Metropolitan (after 1589, the Patriarch of Moscow) inculcated loyalty and patriotism and a sense of Russia's exclusive virtue among nations. Sixteenth-century Russians found psychic consolation in the theory of the "Third Rome": Moscow was destined, after the fallen glories of Rome and Constantinople, to rise in its turn to dominant world power.

Since the church was so closely linked to the identity of the nation, Russia maintained a stronger and longer-lasting insistence on religious conformity than most of the countries of the West, perhaps with the exception of Spain's Catholicism. In both cases the tie to national identity made conformity of belief an imperative of the political culture. In each country religious conversion by members of ethnic minorities was sufficient to win admission to membership in the dominant nationality. The intensity of these feelings was underscored in Spain by the Inquisition, and in Russia by the church schism in the mid-seventeenth century, when certain liturgical corrections sponsored by Patriarch Nikon with the sanction of the government precipitated the traditionalist revolt of the "Old Believers." Decades of cruel persecution by the secular authorities followed, in a vain effort to bring these sectarians into line.

Russia's religious experience has no analogue in the American tradition, where the combined legacy of the English and American revolutions established a foundation of religious pluralism, a secular state, and an essentially private approach to matters of theological faith. It is as difficult for most Americans to appreciate the intensity of antireligious feeling that crystallized in the Russian revolutionary movement as it is for them to accept the idea of an official and exclusive church. During the nineteenth century, when Westernization shook the religious belief of many Russians, they went to the opposite extreme, to view the church as well as the state as the incarnation of evil and oppression, as an enemy to be eradicated. But in their deepest habits of thought they could no more dispense with theological certainty than with the coercive powers of government. Hence the absolutist reading they gave to the Marxist theory of revolution imported from the West, and the rigor with which the heirs of the Revolution have enforced this belief ever since.

The great watershed in Russia's cultural history, more so than in any other domain of life, was the reign of Peter the Great. In a reversal of national orientation unprecedented at the time, though paralleled by many modernizing governments more recently, Peter set his regime explicitly against the whole force of Russian tradition and custom. Infatuated with Western knowledge and technology, Peter imagined that he could transplant his country culturally into the domain of Western civilization and press upon his people Western modes in everything from dress and architecture to scientific method and the art of war. All this, moreover, he aimed to do without altering the fundamentals of Russian government and social structure. In fact, he resorted to the most un-Western methods of decree and coercion to initiate the cultural transformation of the realm.

Peter's impact was immense, but not, save for the superficialities, immediate. Change was resisted by old noble factions and ignored by the masses. The accoutrements of Western education and social graces, ranging from the admission of women into polite society to the introduction of handkerchiefs and knife-and-fork table manners, were initially confined to the land- and serf-owning nobility. Though Peter created an Academy of Sciences (staffed by foreigners), there was still no secular university, except for the old German-language University of Dorpat (now Tartu) acquired with the Baltic lands surrendered by Sweden. The first Russian university, in Moscow, was founded only in 1754, more than a century after Harvard. It was, rather, in the negative sense that Peter's impact was greatest, discrediting the old customs and transcending the ecclesiastical Orthodox culture. No longer could Russians draw their national self-confidence from their cultural purity and religious uniqueness; after Peter removed the barriers of cultural communication, the Russians were compelled by their own leadership to compete with the West on the West's terms. This challenge has caused a profound and continuing stress in Russian life ever since.

Enforced change in a nation's culture and way of life is a familiar story. Acculturation, as anthropologists term it, has occurred in countries all over the world during the last two hundred years, under the impact of modernization and Westernization. Russia's Westernization experience, in fact, is a prototype, and the nation's consequent tribulations should stand as an object lesson of what is to come as the forces of modernity emanating from the region of the North Atlantic impress themselves on other societies.

As Russia's case showed, acculturation usually begins with the adoption of technical and military elements—the attributes of the superior civilization that are easiest to copy and most useful for survival. But once contact has been established on these lines, it is impossible to keep out the influence of social values, lifestyles, art forms, and political ideas. A regime that attempts to bar these changes ultimately invites revolution—although one that sponsors them too enthusiastically runs the same risk, as the recent overthrow of the shah of Iran has shown. Inevitably, acculturation generates passions both for and against the process of change, dividing the nation into modernizers and nativists, neither of whom have an entirely rational foundation for their enthusiasm.

Peter's Westernizing program, inescapably shallow at first, had deeply affected Russian society by the end of the eighteenth century. The upper class, landholders and government officials, who had always been separated from the masses by legal status and privilege, were now, thanks to their Western-style education and orientation, distinguished culturally as well. Russian cultural life in the nineteenth century became an integral part of the European mainstream, making notable contributions in literature, music, and science, while the masses remained illiterate and superstitious. The nobility of the nineteenth century, as depicted by Tolstoy and Turgenev, could easily have been set down in English drawing rooms or Deep South mansions. But endowed with leisure and a Western outlook, they found little to do either in business or in politics that would challenge their abilities. The result was an extraordinary excursion by the Russian educated class into a world of pure theory and extremist action.

The social group that embodied this urge for self-realization in thought was originally an offshoot of the nobility, but came by the middle of the nineteenth century to be regarded as a distinct social class. This was the "intelligentsia" (a Russian word, derived originally from Italian). Members of the intelligentsia devoted themselves to the life of the mind, and espoused a set of attitudes, almost a new Orthodoxy, that derived from the intellectual stimuli they had been receiving from the West since the Enlightenment. They were rationalists, devotees of science and the scientific method; they were contemptuous of tradition, above all of Russian tradition before Peter; they were anticlerical and often avowedly atheist; they were all to some degree alienated from the entire institutional structure of

Russian society—state, church, serfdom, class structure. Their archetype was the radical critic Nikolai Chernyshevsky, whose utopian novel *What Is to Be Done?* had a powerful influence on Lenin. Scions of the privileged, the intelligentsia rejected the society that made their own existence possible. This was true even of the minority countercurrent among them, the Slavophiles and Pan-Slavists, who took the nativist course of anti-Western messianism. The intelligentsia formed the seedbed of revolution in Russia. Not only that: they left their mark profoundly imprinted on the regime that followed the Revolution, even though as a social class they almost ceased to exist.

3

Statue of Peter the Great ("The Bronze Horseman"), Leningrad

Imperial Power

Russia has been a power on the world scene far longer than the United States. Nearly a century before the United States even existed as an independent nation, Russia, thanks to the initiatives of Peter the Great, became a major player in Europe's game of diplomacy and war. Russia in its Soviet form is different but not new as a disturbing presence in international affairs. It is not so much change in Russia itself as in the world outside that has made the Soviet regime so influential and threatening in our own time.

It would be odd to suppose that centuries of a country's experience in the great-power arena could suddenly be swept aside, even by the tumultuous events of a revolution such as Russia's. Yet so electrifying was the impact of the Revolution and its ideological claims that everyone imagined for a time that Russia had been utterly transformed as an actor in international affairs. The Communists rejected their country's past; Russia's old allies were horrified by the country's present. Thus was established the premise, among both supporters and adversaries of the Soviet experiment, that its relations with other countries could be appreciated only in the new revolutionary terms of the twentieth century.

With the passage of time, more and more observers abroad began to detect parallels and even continuities between the Old Regime and the Communists in their conduct of foreign relations. Similarities were noted in strategic interest, in alliance making, in military doctrine and the use of force. The Soviets' revival of Russian nationalism and their return to past military and diplomatic strategies reinforced this view. Eventually a new school of Western thought took shape, arguing that the Soviet Union had subordinated its revolutionary commitments to its national interests and was behaving essentially like the imperial power it had been under the tsars.

Other observers have contended that Soviet policy has never lost its ideological core and its essentially revolutionary character, and that these distinguish it in kind from the tsarist experience despite superficial similarities. Although this ideological view was eclipsed during the era of détente, the issue remains fundamental: To what extent is the USSR's role in the world a perpetuation of traditional Russian behavior, and to what extent is it the manifestation of a still-vigorous revolutionary impulse?

▪ The International Context

The arena of power politics that Russia entered at the time of Peter the Great changed little in principle right up until the First World War. Europe was at the center, thanks to its economic, cultural, and military superiority. At the same time, Europe was permanently divided into highly competitive sovereign states, all amorally pursuing their interests by means of shifting diplomatic strategies, alliances, and wars. Some of the principal players in this game have remained significant powers ever since Peter's time—England, France, and the Kingdom of Prussia (the nucleus of the later German Reich). Another, the Hapsburg Empire of Austria, was destined to remain a counterforce in central Europe for as long as the monarchy lasted in Russia. But other once-great states were setting suns in the eighteenth century: the Netherlands, commercially and colonially outstanding but overshadowed by the great land powers; Sweden, a paragon of imperial administration in the seventeenth century, but likewise outclassed by its larger neighbors in the eighteenth; Poland, a vast multinational territory undermined by dynastic dissension and the self-centeredness of its nobility; Spain, feared in the sixteenth century, but moribund by the eighteenth; the immense empire of the Ottoman Turks, weakened by corruption and traditionalism—the "sick man of Europe." Three of these faltering giants were situated on Russia's borders: Sweden on the northwest, Poland on the west, Turkey on the south. They had all been grievous threats to Russia's peace and even existence, culminating in the Time of Troubles in the early seventeenth century when the Swedes and Poles occupied Moscow and schemed to reduce the country to satellite status. The decline of all three of these traditional foes in the eighteenth century gave Russia the opportunity to turn the tables. Thus Russia made its way into the world of European politics by pursuing its old border rivalries and continental expansion, previously aimed so successfully at the Tatars and the aborigines of Siberia.

It is of the greatest importance for Americans to appreciate how different was Russia's international environment from the circumstances of the young United States. Russia found itself in a world of hostile neighbors, the United States in secure continental isolation (apart from the British presence in Canada, neutralized after the War of 1812). Living under great threats and equally great temptations, Russia had developed a tradition of militarized absolutism that put the highest priority on committing its meager resources to meet those threats and exploit those temptations. The United States, once it had established its independence, could turn its back on the game of alliances and wars and proceed to exploit the economic potential of a continent. Russia, in different circumstances, with different traditions, accepted a different role and paid an infinitely higher price.

From all this it can be seen that much of the Russian and Soviet style of behavior in international relations, odious as it may be to Americans, stems neither from Asiatic barbarism nor from revolutionary scheming. It is only one instance, exaggerated and perpetuated, of the European tradition of unending power competition.

■ The Rise of Russian Power

Russia had become a national state by the end of the fifteenth century—earlier than most countries in Europe—despite unusually difficult conditions. Under the princes of Muscovy, Russia had to fight simultaneously for independence from the Mongol-Tatar yoke and for unity among the squabbling Slavic dukedoms, whom the foreign invaders had played off against one another. The formation of a centralized, independent national state, hailed nowadays by Soviet historians as much as by tsarist apologists of the nineteenth century, was also hindered by the country's vast geographical area, severe climate, technological backwardness, and cultural isolation. Success in these circumstances could be achieved only through brutality and chicanery, combined with single-minded self-sacrifice—qualities that have distinguished Russian governmental behavior to this day. Weakness begot delusions of grandeur: xenophobia and megalomania were combined in the theory of the Third Rome, which envisioned Moscow as the center of true belief wedded to invincible power.

Notwithstanding such messianic pretensions, for the first two hundred years of its national existence Russia was limited by its own weakness. Those centuries evidenced a pattern of expansive pressure that has characterized Russia ever since: cautious probes and dogged defensiveness when confronted by superior strength in one direction; swift and uninhibited application of force when faced by weak and unsupported neighbors in another quarter. The directions might vary—the push was eastward in the seventeenth century, westward in the eighteenth, southward and again eastward in the nineteenth, once more westward in the twentieth—but the basic pattern held: there were no limits of nature or principle to the growth of the empire, save superior power on its immediate borders.

Russia's westward expansion began in the mid-seventeenth century, in a series of exhausting conflicts with Poland from which the Muscovites gained the bulk of what is now the Ukraine. The great breakout came in the reign of Peter the Great, when Russia reached the Baltic Sea through Peter's "window on the West," his newly constructed capital of St. Petersburg. By virtue of Peter's military success against Sweden in the Great Northern War of 1700–1721, Russia joined the ranks of the recognized European powers and became a regular participant in their wars.

Russia in the eighteenth century, once the then-available technology of musketry and navigation had been assimilated along with Western models of military organization and command, was the war-making peer of any European power. Of the fundamental constituents of national power—population base, strategic location, economic and cultural resources, and political organization—Russia enjoyed all but cultural resources on a plane equal to or above any European rival. In population Russia passed France (until the eighteenth century Europe's most populous country), and by the early nineteenth century, thanks both to territorial annexations and to a remarkable and still-unexplained population explosion among the enserfed masses, it overshadowed all other European states in demographic weight. Russia had the geographical asset of vast open territory, exposed on many frontiers but serving to entrap invaders from Charles XII through Napoleon to Hitler. With the bureaucratic administration fashioned by Peter and his successors, Russia had the political organization to mobilize the country's human and economic resources and the will to throw them into the cause of national success and expansion. Only lacking were the qualitative factors of economic, technological, and cultural development, and it was to this area that tsars and commissars alike have bent their greatest efforts from Peter's day to this, in a most despotic and un-Western way, racing to overtake and surpass the West. "They wish to rule the world by conquest," wrote the Marquis de Custine. "They mean to seize by armed force the countries accessible to them, and thence to oppress the rest of the world by terror."

▪ Russia in the Age of Alliances

For two hundred years, starting with Peter the Great and continuing to Nicholas II, Russia was a successful participant in the European power game, with premises no different from those of any other continental monarchy. Russia fought in all the major eighteenth-century wars of dynastic rivalry—in the War of the Polish Succession (1727–1732); in the War of the Austrian Succession (1742–1748, known as "King George's War" in the American colonies); and above all in the Seven Years War (1756–1763, in America the French and Indian War), when Russian intervention had almost brought Frederick the Great of Prussia to his knees before the death of Empress Elizabeth and the accession of her mad German nephew Peter III caused St. Petersburg to change sides and assure the status quo. During the American Revolution, internationalized by French and Spanish intervention against Britain in 1777, Russia led the so-called League of Armed Neutrality, leaning toward the anti-British allies. Thus began the strange tradition of diplomatic cordiality between Washington and St. Petersburg, the two most dissimilar governments on earth.

Meanwhile Russia successfully continued its continental expansion at the expense of its faltering neighbors, the Swedes, the Poles, and the Turks. Three wars with Sweden culminated in 1809 in Russia's complete annexation of Finland. Poland was partitioned in 1772, 1793, and 1795, and thereby obliterated as a nation. Against the Turks the Russians were victorious three times in the eighteenth century and twice in the first third of the nineteenth. They won control of the northern shore of the Black Sea and, with the annexation of Bessarabia and Transcaucasia, established Russia's present borders in that part of the world.

The outbreak of revolution in France in 1789 cast international relations in an entirely different light. For the first time since the religious wars between Catholics and Protestants, Europe was divided, among and within the various states, on lines of philosophy rather than of simple *raison d'état.* After the interventionist armies of Austria and Prussia were defeated by the popular forces of revolutionary France, adherents of the traditional order all over Europe looked to Russia, unshaken by any revolutionary agitation save a handful of easily silenced intellectuals, as their savior from the Jacobin madness. (The analogy with Western Europe's turn to U.S. protection in the face of the Soviet threat after World War II is intriguing.) Russia willingly assumed the counterrevolutionary world leadership, and bore a major share in the wars against Napoleon from 1798 to 1814 (allowing for the uneasy truce of 1807–1812, often likened to the Stalin-Hitler pact of 1939, when Russia faced a continent almost completely dominated by the French). Victorious in the "Great Patriotic War" against Napoleon after his ill-fated drive to Moscow in 1812, Russia emerged as Europe's strongest single power in the "War of Liberation" that put an end to the French Empire and restored the traditional dynasties all over the continent. Inspired by the call of nationalism, serfs fought and died by the thousands in the "Patriotic War" to preserve the power of their rulers, just as their descendants did for Stalin in the second "Great Patriotic War" of 1941–1945.

As arbiter of Europe's destiny after the fall of Napoleon, Russia was guided by the personal visions of Tsar Alexander I, enigmatic and contradictory in his foreign policies as much as in his domestic rule. Imbued with a mixture of Western liberal philosophy and religious mysticism, Alexander toyed with schemes of internal and international reform, while assuring himself that there would be no diminution of his actual power either at home or abroad. A sort of monarchical Woodrow Wilson, he gave a nod to constitutionalism and self-determination when he brought the Finns under his control in 1809 and the major portion of the Poles in 1815, by granting both peoples parliamentary governments. Wilsonianism was further heralded in Alexander's scheme, proposed at the Congress of Vienna, for an international league of powers to keep the peace and guarantee the traditional order—a "Holy Alliance." England, like the United States when it was faced with the League of Nations in 1919, rejected the Holy Alliance as too reactionary and entangling; rulers in other European countries were happy to accept Russian leadership and support as they confronted the spreading waves of liberal revolutionary sentiment generated by the events of 1789. In 1848 and 1849, when liberals revolted all over Europe, Russia—still unshaken—was the spoiler, backing the monarchies and intervening directly to suppress nationalists in Hungary and save the tottering throne of the Hapsburgs in Vienna.

That was the high point in Russia's role as international arbiter. Within a generation, the economic and political transformation of western Europe brought about by the Industrial Revolution left Russia both ideologically isolated and technologically outclassed, to a degree that had not been evident since the time of Peter the Great. The East-West gap in industrial accomplishment and technical facility rapidly reopened, leaving Russia only its traditional strength of numbers. Defeat at the hands of the British and French in the

Crimean War of 1853–1856 checked Russian pressure on the Ottoman Empire and underscored the inadequacy of Russia's power base. Nevertheless, Russia kept trying to exploit Turkey's weakness and invoked the rationale of "Pan-Slavism"—that is, the mission of liberating the Slavic-speaking peoples from Turkish or Austrian rule and bringing them into a new federation under Russian aegis. (Interestingly enough, the sphere of Russian influence envisaged by the Pan-Slav theorists coincided almost exactly with the zone of Communist satellite states established under Soviet domination at the close of World War II.) When the Serbs and Bulgarians revolted against Turkish rule in 1875–76, Russia successfully intervened, but its ambitions were again thwarted at the Congress of Berlin in 1878, when the European powers forced Alexander II to abandon his plans for a Balkan sphere of influence. Meanwhile the evolution of central Europe toward constitutionalism had eroded the ideological basis of international monarchical cooperation, and had cast a cloud of liberal suspicion over the unregenerate colossus of the East. Karl Marx reflected the opinion of many Europeans when he warned, in his dispatches to the *New York Tribune,* of Russia's counterrevolutionary threat to Europe: "The Russian bear is certainly capable of anything, so long as he knows the other animals he has to deal with to be capable of nothing."

The Russians' frustration in the West did not deter them from pursuing their imperial ambitions in the East. After annexing Transcaucasia during the first quarter of the nineteenth century, St. Petersburg had to wage counterinsurgency warfare for another two decades against the Moslem mountaineers of the North Caucasus— the Circassians, backed by the British and made famous by the literary accounts of Lermontov and Tolstoy. In mid-century, while the British, French, and Germans were preparing to partition Africa and establish their sovereignty on the last unclaimed islands of the South Seas, the Russians undertook the systematic occupation of Moslem Central Asia, culminating in the conquest of the ancient Turkic khanates along the mountain rim of Persia, Afghanistan, and the Chinese Empire. Tashkent, the largest city of the region, fell to Russian troops in 1865, and by 1884 the authority of the tsar had been extended to the present Central Asian boundary of the USSR, to be contained there only by the presence of British power in India.

In this vigorous southward thrust there was nothing incompatible either with Russia's expansionist tradition or with the contemporary imperialism of the major Western powers. The late nineteenth century was, after all, the heyday of colonial land grabbing, international commercial expansion, and the "white man's burden." Only the particular circumstances differed for Russia: instead of seizing overseas territories and spheres of influence, Russia moved directly into foreign regions along its own frontiers.

Some of Russia's acquisitions in Central Asia involved territory claimed by the moribund Chinese Empire. More direct advances at the expense of China came simultaneously in the Far East, beginning with Russian occupation of the Vladivostok region in 1860. Next the Russians penetrated China's northeastern region of Manchuria and the satellite Kingdom of Korea. They moved into Mongolia after revolution had disrupted the effective authority of Peking, and set up a Russian-sponsored regime in 1916. The legacy of these moves is all too apparent today: critical Russian involvement in the Far East; Mongolia's status as a Soviet satellite; and a profound bitterness between the Soviet Union and China, where the consequences of Russian imperialism have undermined the bonds of common revolutionary ideology.

■ The Road to Catastrophe

Minor setbacks notwithstanding, Russia's record in international politics up to the turn of the century was a tale of steadily growing strength, success, and influence. Few people sensed the underlying weaknesses in Russian society or even the scope of Russia's technological deficiencies while the major powers of the West were developing the industrial foundations of their national power. No one, not even the revolutionaries, anticipated the fateful turning point of the First World War.

The outbreak of the war has been the subject of more meticulous investigation than almost any other historical event. Yet the causes usually cited are insufficient: nationalist animosities, commercial greed, dynastic pride—none of these can fully account for the four years of mindless bloodletting that brought to grief most of the governments responsible for the carnage. The war, all viewpoints agree, was the precipitating cause of the Russian Revolution. Indeed, Lenin thought that it would ignite the world revolution, made imminent by the global forces of imperialism that in their insatiable competition for resources, markets, and investment outlets drove their respective governments inevitably toward an armed resolution of the contest. But Lenin's theory of imperialism, for all its later attractiveness to the world's disaffected, has been discounted by most non-Marxist commentators as a shallow and one-sided—as well as unoriginal—conception of the phenomenon.

A much more insightful explanation of imperialism has been suggested by the Austrian-American economist Joseph Schumpeter. Schumpeter maintained that imperialism did not stem primarily from capitalism but rather from the feudal-aristocratic elements still prominent in many capitalist countries in the nineteenth century, elements whose usefulness and status depended on the priority given to military concerns and periodic warfare. This social force was still very influential in Germany, Austria-Hungary, and England; less so, but not absent in France and Italy; and dominant in the political life of Russia. In America, of course, aristocracy had been excluded on principle by the revolution of 1776, though a surrogate of sorts was represented by the Southern gentry, whose militarist ethic survived the Civil War and contributed disproportionately to the hawkish side of every foreign-policy issue from 1898 to the present.

Russia, viewed in the light of Schumpeter's thesis, was by virtue of its social structure a major contributor to the military disaster that destroyed that same social structure. The Great War—or at least Russia's involvement in it—flowed from the basic character of the Russian state. Thus, though it is correct to stress, as many anti-Communist historians do, the disruptive effect of the war in setting up the opportunity for revolution, the war was no externally imposed aberration but a fate invited by the nature of Russia's Old Regime.

The Russian Empire was committed by its feudal social structure and hereditary autocracy to the pursuit of military power and imperial expansion. Absolute monarchy can no more abstain from war than a jungle cat from its prey—it is the nature of the beast. But an aggressive role was never easy for Russia, despite its size; the problem of cultural and technological backwardness was never fully overcome, and during the nineteenth century Russia lagged ever further behind the industrializing West. Fiscal and human resources were always overcommitted to military purposes, which further impeded the effort to catch up economically. Strained and threatened, St. Petersburg became increasingly prone to take risks to uphold the honor of the dynasty.

The reality of Russia's inferior position was driven home by a series of foreign-policy failures in the latter part of the nineteenth century and the early years of the twentieth. Russian efforts to make the Balkans a satellite zone were frustrated repeatedly from the time of the Congress of Berlin in 1878 to the great Balkan Crisis of 1908, when Vienna stole a march on St. Petersburg by annexing the Turkish province of Bosnia-Herzegovina. Russian expansion from Central Asia south to the Indian Ocean was balked by the British, Afghanistan was preserved as a buffer state, and Persia, in 1907, was partitioned into British and Russian spheres of influence. Most humiliating of all was Russia's setback in the Far East in the Russo-Japanese War of 1904–5, when the Empire of the Rising Sun attacked Russian positions in Manchuria and forced the Russians ignominiously to the peace table. Continuation of hostilities was impossible for the St. Petersburg regime, given the internal political crisis of 1905 and the intercession of President Theodore Roosevelt, who feared Russia's threat to the "Open Door Policy" governing U.S. trade with China. The terms of peace compelled the Russians to accept the loss of most of their bases and railroad interests on Chinese territory, and thereby opened the way to the new Far Eastern imperialism of a Westernized Asian power aping methods of the European dynasts.

Outpaced in modern arms, universally distrusted, and balked in all of its expansionist probes, Russia at the end of the nineteenth century was faced with diplomatic isolation and the reputation of a loser in international competition. The response was a diplomatic revolution presaging a similar breakout by means of the Popular Front in the mid-1930s: Russia gave up its strained ties with the central European monarchies and, in defiance of all ideological affinities, concluded a military alliance with the most democratic power on the continent—the Third French Republic. This was a classic marriage of diplomatic convenience, based solely on the principle that "the enemy of my enemy is my friend." The German Empire, allied with Russia's Austrian rivals in the Balkans, had to be written off as a potential foe; France, smoldering after the defeat of 1870, nursed hopes of revenge against the Germans, and therefore offered the Russians a logical partnership. A formal military alliance was initiated in 1891.

Russia's alliance with France was the first link in a chain of events destined to set off the conflagration of 1914 and the Revolution of

1917. Both the German-Austrian and Franco-Russian partnerships sought additional allies to bolster their respective positions and provide a shield for the continued pursuit of their imperial ambitions. Berlin and Vienna drew Rome into the "Triple Alliance." Britain was left, as it often was, in a position to swing the balance of power; but threatened by Germany's growing sea power, London resolved to compromise its colonial rivalries with the French and its old Middle Eastern standoff with the Russians. In 1907, having had the satisfaction of seeing the Great Bear checked by the Japanese in the Far East, and upon agreement with St. Petersburg on respective spheres in Persia, Britain joined France and Russia to form the "Triple Entente." Two great armed camps now confronted each other, waiting for the moment when some friction between any of their members would produce a situation where neither side could retreat.

General war between the two great-power teams was barely averted in the Balkan Crisis of 1908 and in the Moroccan Crisis of 1911. However, the entire international equilibrium was destabilized by the deterioration of both the Austrian and the Ottoman empires, torn in each case by minority separatism. With Russian encouragement, the newly independent states of Bulgaria, Serbia, and Greece conspired to attack the Turks and drive them out of their remaining European provinces. This was easily accomplished in the First Balkan War of 1912–1913. There followed a squabble for the spoils in which Rumania and the Turks joined Serbia and Greece in the Second Balkan War to deprive Bulgaria of most of its gains. Meanwhile Serbian nationalists hoped to exploit dissension among the southern Slavs within the Austrian Empire and achieve the dream that ultimately materialized as Yugoslavia. The knowledge that Russia was backing Austria's enemies emboldened them: "We and the Russians are a hundred and forty million strong," said the king of the lilliputian Slavic country of Montenegro. These were the circumstances that led to the assassination of the heir to the Austrian throne, Archduke Franz Ferdinand, in Sarajevo on June 28, 1914, by Serbian fanatics who feared that the archduke's conciliatory attitude toward his minority subjects would short-circuit the Greater Serbian idea.

The sad tale of diplomatic failure leading from Franz Ferdinand's death to the Guns of August is familiar to all readers of history. A confrontation between the Austrians and the Serbs automatically involved all the parties in the great alliances, and none would back down for fear of losing credibility. The Russian government, after its recent humiliations and frustrations in the Balkans, was the least willing to make concessions, despite the woeful state of its readiness for general war. Russia's industry and finances could not support the kind of arms buildup that the Western powers had been pursuing; in fact, the government of Nicholas II had taken the initiative in the Hague disarmament conferences of 1899 and 1907 in the hope of alleviating the economic burden of the arms race. Russia's rail network—the key to military deployment in 1914—was inadequate. Mobilization—the call-up of reservists and the deployment of forces on the frontier (actions that represented the early twentieth-century equivalent of having one's bombers in the air before an enemy attack)—was easy for the Western powers but slow and difficult for the Russians. After the tsar ordered mobilization on July 30, it could not be called off in response to Germany's ultimatum. Two days later the German Empire mobilized and declared war on Russia, setting in train the general conflict between the rival alliance systems.

For many antimonarchists and antimilitarists around the world, ranging from American democrats to Russian socialists, the war of 1914 was an insane manifestation of Europe's old imperialist game, of no purpose to the peoples who had to contribute the requisite blood and treasure. American neutralism was paralleled by the efforts of the Socialist International to mediate the crisis. But so powerful were the emotions of national pride and national anxiety among all of the nations dragged into the war that the pacifist traditions of the socialists went almost for naught. French and British socialists rallied to their respective flags to fight againt German autocracy. German socialists fell in behind the imperial government and voted the emergency appropriations on the ground that Germany was fighting for a more democratic future, against Russian autocracy. Russian socialists—some of them—argued that the future of democracy depended on defending the homeland and supporting the cause of Russia's democratic allies against the Central Powers. But the hatred of tsarism that was so ingrained in the West made the Russian alliance a political embarrassment to England and France, and helped deter the United States from committing itself to the Allied cause until the February Revolution of 1917 had removed the offending symbol of autocracy from the scene. Among Russians themselves, animosity toward the regime was sufficient to drive a majority of the socialists to antiwar protest and even outright defeatism. Lenin quickly achieved fame and influence as the chief apologist for this position. It was not long before the losses and privations of an incompetently conducted war caused disaffection to spread throughout all strata of the Russian population. Thus did the Old Regime's foreign ventures set the stage for disaster.

■ The United States and the Tsarist Government

Of all the nations that jockeyed for power in the eighteenth and nineteenth centuries, none of any significance had less in common or fewer points of contact than the United States of America and the Empire of St. Petersburg. Geographically separated, neither competitive nor complementary in economics, preoccupied with their respective continental aspirations, the United States and Russia were of little concern to each other diplomatically. It is therefore impossible to trace the Soviet-American antagonism of the twentieth century to the experiences and traditions of the past. Indeed, some of the frenzy of the recent confrontation on both sides may be attributable to the unfamiliarity of each nation with the habits, assumptions, and interests of the other.

Historical tradition, backed by much contemporary expression of amicable sentiment, holds that the United States and the Russian Empire were steadfast allies from the creation of the American republic to the beginning of this century. John L. Gaddis has called it "the most consistently friendly relationship the United States would have with a major European power in the nineteenth century." But it was the tenuousness of the connection, allowing little opportunity for disappointment on either side, that made possible a history of cordiality between such dissimilar friends. The diplomat-historian John Lothrop Motley wrote to Oliver Wendell Holmes in May 1872, "I do not know that I appreciate very highly that affection which is supposed to exist between Russia and America. At any rate, it is a very platonic attachment. Being founded, however, on entire incompatibility of character, absence of sympathy, and a plentiful lack of any common interest, it may prove a very enduring passion." Where there are no expectations there can be no disappointment.

There was one mutual concern that encouraged the two governments to offer modest support to each other during the first century of American independence. This was their common hostility to Great Britain, demonstrating again the diplomatic law of amity with the enemy's enemy. For the United States, anti-British sentiment was rooted in the revolutionary experience, confirmed by war in 1812, and expressed in numerous border and maritime controversies thereafter. For Russia, Britain was a major imperial rival, contributing to the frustration of Russia's expansionist ambitions everywhere from the Balkans to the Pacific.

The anti-British alignment of Russia and America dates from the American War of Independence, when Catherine the Great formed her League of Armed Neutrality. Her motive appears to have been shrewdly calculated: to hasten the disentanglement of the British from America so that they could counterbalance the French in Europe, and simultaneously to support the emergence of a new maritime power that would counterbalance the British at sea. Formal recognition of the United States by Russia did not come, however, until 1809, when St. Petersburg again wanted a counter to the British at sea during its brief alliance with Napoleon. Thereupon the future president John Quincy Adams took up his post as the first U.S. minister to the court of the Romanovs.

Russian policy continued in a similar vein during the War of 1812, when St. Petersburg endeavored to mediate, with the dual objective (as during the revolutionary war) of disengaging the British and simultaneously supporting the American counterweight to British maritime power. Long afterward, in the closing months of the Second World War, the anti-British attitude embedded in the populist-isolationist strand of American foreign-policy thinking surfaced again in the notion that the United States and Russia might have to band together to curb the unextinguished imperial ambitions of Churchill's England.

Early nineteenth-century Russian-American relations were more direct and correspondingly less cordial over one particular issue: Russian colonial expansion in the northwest sector of the North American continent. Russian America (present-day Alaska) had been claimed by Russian explorers crossing from Siberia in the eighteenth century and marginally exploited by an official trading monopoly, the Russian-American Company. Russian penetration down the coast of the present Pacific Northwest, over territory already disputed by the United States and Britain, was one of the circumstances prompting the enunciation in 1823 of the Monroe

Doctrine: any extension of European colonial rule in the New World would be resisted. The Northwest issue coincided with Russia's active role in the Holy Alliance and the specter of European monarchs intervening against the new Latin American republics that had just revolted successfully against Spanish rule. *Realpolitik* prevailed for Russia, however, and confrontation was avoided. St. Petersburg agreed by treaty in 1824 to pull back to Alaska, and removed its last post from the territory of the present forty-eight contiguous states in 1844.

The potential for dissension on ideological grounds was never entirely absent from Russian-American relations, though it arose more from American perceptions of Russia than from the reverse. Then, as later, it was the democracy that responded more sensitively to events and their emotional repercussions, while the autocracy calculated its interests primarily in terms of the global power game. Revolts in Europe in 1830 and 1848, involving Russian suppression of the Poles in the first instance and intervention in Hungary in the second, stirred an impassioned response in the United States. American representatives to the court of Nicholas I were appalled, like their West European contemporaries, by what minister James Buchanan in 1832 called "the calm of despotism," and by the secretiveness and deviousness recorded in the 1850s by minister Neill S. Brown in dispatches rivaling the account of the Marquis de Custine. "A strange superstition prevails among the Russians," Brown wrote to Secretary of State Daniel Webster in 1852, "that they are destined to conquer the world." Culling impressions of this order, the future Maryland congressman and abolitionist Henry Winter Davis published in 1837 a remarkable book, *The War of Ormuzd and Ahriman in the Nineteenth Century,* foretelling an American-Russian struggle for world power. He spoke of Russia in terms indistinguishable from today's rhetoric: "Her interest, her ambition, her hate, the principles of her Czar, the proud hope of taming Europe to the yoke of absolute power, all combine to impel her into active hostility against this republic . . . She only waits the auspicious solution of the European problem to seize the first invitation of internal discord or foreign embarrassment, to begin the plot that is to end with our ruin."

The pragmatic alignment of the United States and Russia was restored at the outbreak of the Crimean War in 1853, due to the anti-British interests of both countries. The tie was further cemented during the American Civil War, when Russia helped deter possible

British and French intervention on the side of the Confederacy. When Russian warships assembled at New York and San Francisco in 1863, they won enduring American gratitude, though the chief Russian motive seems to have been to keep the fleet from being bottled up in home waters during the crisis over the Polish revolt that year.

In 1867 the issue of Russian colonialism in North America was finally resolved when the Russian government sold Alaska to the United States for $7.2 million in gold. To the Russians, Alaska had proved an economic liability and a strategically precarious holding. In the post-Crimea mood of consolidation, Russian policymakers judged that the area was too vulnerable to seizure by the British or by the Americans; sale to the latter seemed the most effective way to check the former. Secretary of State William Seward, dreaming of a Pacific empire, lobbied the deal through a reluctant Congress with the help of Russian bribes. Neither seller nor buyer could have predicted the strategic implications of this transfer.

The year 1881, when the murdered Emperor Alexander II was succeeded by his antireform son, was a watershed in Russian-American relations. Again, the democracy reacted to the monarchy's domestic oppressiveness, as Alexander III stepped up the persecution of religious and national minorities and unleashed the pogroms against Russia's Jewish population. American revulsion over these developments, shared by most Europeans, was intensified in the years that followed by growing awareness of the police and penal practices of the tsarist regime, especially as revealed by George Kennan's *Siberia and the Exile System,* published in 1891. (There is an obvious parallel here with present-day Western reactions to the Soviet treatment of dissenters and minorities.) Meanwhile, American democracy offered itself as a model of freedom and justice to Russian intellectuals, from the Decembrists of 1825 to the advent of Marxism near the end of the century. Russian radicals, like Karl Marx, regarded the victory of the Union in the American Civil War as a great triumph for democracy and progress.

The first real power clash between America and Russia came at the turn of the century, as the Chinese Empire was collapsing and all the imperialist nations were competing for bases in the Far East. America's position, formulated as the Open Door Policy by Secretary of State John Hay in 1899, was to forestall as far as possible the carving out of private preserves in Chinese territory by any of the other contenders who might thereby constrict American commercial opportunities in Peking's realm. Russia, bent on dominating Manchuria, was the most direct threat to the Open Door. Therefore, the United States, newly endowed with its own Far Eastern colonies thanks to the Spanish-American War, threw its weight to the side of the lesser evils, Britain and Japan. The Russians were diplomatically isolated when the Japanese attacked and defeated them in the lightning war of 1904–5, with the United States helping to bring the Russians to the peace table in Portsmouth, New Hampshire. None of the old Russian-American cordiality was left when war came in 1914, and the tsar's participation in the anti-German alliance constrained the U.S. government as it turned against Germany, until revolution finally put an end to the throne of the Romanovs.

None of these oscillations in U.S. opinion and policy toward tsarist Russia were informed by more than the amateur impressions of diplomats and travelers. There was no academic study of Russia or the Russian language in the United States until after the turn of the century, when men such as Archibald Cary Coolidge at Harvard and Samuel N. Harper at the University of Chicago first ventured into this exotic field. Myth, presupposition, and a few horror stories were virtually the only basis for American judgments of Russia, until the Revolution injected a new set of myths, presuppositions, and horror stories that long outweighed reasoned knowledge about the Russian enigma.

▪ America and the Peoples of Russia

In human terms Russia has always impinged on the American psyche as a specter of cruelty and repression, the "prison of the nations." In the nineteenth century this perception focused on a particular aspect of the Russian system, the minority peoples who had been incorporated into the Russian Empire during its centuries of expansion. These minorities, in turn, saw the United States as a beacon of liberty, and as an actual refuge when awareness of migratory opportunity and the economics of transportation combined in the last two decades of the nineteenth century to make large-scale emigration from the Russian Empire a reality. Subsequent periods of political calamity broadened the emigrant stream, to include dissident and persecuted Russians as much as the minorities. America's perception of Russia was deeply influenced by the migrants and the political and ethnic woes they brought with them.

American sympathy for the peoples of the Russian Empire was first aroused by the tribulations of the Poles. During the American Revolution, Polish general Tadeusz Kosciuszko won the admiration of the patriots for his exploits on their behalf, before returning to his homeland to lead a futile resistance against the Russian occupiers in the 1790s. The Polish Revolt of 1830 and its suppression by Nicholas I again aroused great American indignation. More dimly perceived were the efforts at russification in Poland, Finland, the Ukraine, and the Baltic provinces under Alexander III; what especially captured the attention of Americans were the anti-Jewish pogroms. Sympathy for the oppressed minorities was the outstanding emotional and, one might say, ideological factor in American antipathy toward the Romanov monarchy in the generation preceding the Russian Revolution. It was the same sentiment that has been uppermost in American anti-Soviet feeling in the late twentieth century.

Large-scale emigration from the Russian Empire to the United States began only after Alexander III ascended the throne in 1881 and reversed his father's modest liberalism toward Jews and non-Russian nationalities. This worsening of the political climate coincided almost exactly with the introduction of relatively quick, cheap, and safe transatlantic transportation by steamship. It was in this period that the great wave of European migration reached the shores of North America, drawing its flow increasingly from central, southern, and eastern Europe. Although the availability of free land and open settlement in the American West was closing off in these same decades, that fact did not deter the stream of immigrants, who now sought employment in the burgeoning industrial centers. Migration from Russia to the United States was thus just one current in the great worldwide shift of population from rural to urban areas that commenced with the Industrial Revolution and continues today.

The flow of migrants from Russia grew steadily from the 1880s to the eve of World War I. The peak, according to records of the U.S. Immigration Service, came in 1913, when nearly 300,000 individuals arrived from territories under the jurisdiction of the tsar. (The Immigration Service counted newcomers not by nationality but by country of departure.) This compared with a total European influx of a little over a million that year, just short of the record 1.2 million in 1907. Altogether, between 1880 and 1914, more than 3 million Russian subjects entered the United States.

This human outflow from the Russian Empire consisted overwhelmingly of members of its ethnic and religious minorities, above all Catholic Poles and Lithuanians, and Jews. Of the approximately 10 million inhabitants of Russian Poland (that is, the old Congress Kingdom, almost entirely Polish speaking), perhaps half a million left for the United States or other destinations during the thirty-five years of the Great Migration. Of a Jewish population of perhaps 3 million in 1880, still living mainly as a minority among minorities in the Polish, Lithuanian, Belorussian, and Ukrainian areas, at least a million departed in the same period, mainly though not exclusively for the United States.

People emigrated for a mixture of reasons: the quest for a better life, the desire to evade military service, resentment of political and religious oppression, fear for their personal safety and even their lives. However, these were old motivations for the minorities of Russia. What was additionally required to set off such a movement was the opportunity to leave, travel, and be received in an open host country; they needed to be aware of these possibilities and to have the initiative to exploit them. In this respect there were great differences among the various nationalities of Russia, depending on the extent to which modernization had affected their lives. The response correlated with religion: Catholics and Jews emigrated in the greatest proportion, together with Lutheran Finns. Far fewer, proportionately, of the Orthodox left the country; they made up less than 10 percent of all emigrants. After Emancipation they had the option, unavailable in any other European state, of moving to new land within their country—that is, to Siberia; as many as seven million people took this direction. Moslems and other nationalities of the East were hardly affected at all. Ukrainians, to be sure, did emigrate in large numbers, particularly to Canada, but most of them were of the Uniate Church from the Austrian Ukraine (Galicia), or else religious dissenters such as the Dukhobors. Not until the Revolution were large numbers of Orthodox ethnic Great Russians thrust from their homeland.

Much has been written about the immigrants in American society, the difficult lives of the new arrivals in ethnic ghettos, and their gradual assimilation into the mainstream of American economic, political, and cultural life. I will not attempt to retell this story, except to note certain ways in which the experience of immigration affected American perceptions of Russia and the future premises of American-Russian relations. In the most direct sense, as noted here already, immigration was a symptom of everything in Russian political life that was antithetical to the American political tradition. The message of the immigrants did much to undermine the pragmatic diplomatic friendship that had existed between the two countries for most of the nineteenth century. But another significant current was the tradition of political dissent brought by many of those escaping from tsarist rule—in particular, ideas about socialism and notions of direct action. Recent arrivals from Russia contributed substantially to the proliferation of political sects in the United States around the turn of the century, ranging from the Socialist Party to the Anarchists. An especially vigorous form of socialist trade-unionism came with the Jews of Poland and western Russia, organized in the Social-Democratic Bund. When the American Socialist Party, like its larger counterparts in Europe, had to confront the issues of the Russian Revolution, the radical wing that split off to form the Communist Party was composed mostly of first-generation immigrants from the Russian Empire and adjacent areas of Eastern Europe who brought their radicalism with them from the old country and now responded like the people they had left behind.

The politics of immigration were not entirely a one-way matter. After a taste of the class struggle in the land of the robber barons, some immigrants returned to Russia more radical than ever. Among the future Communist luminaries who spent time in the United States were Leon Trotsky and Nikolai Bukharin, both of whom were living in New York when the Revolution broke out.

The effect of the Great Migration on Russia has never been well calculated. It obviously drained off a large number of working-age people, while at the same time serving as a political safety valve. Creating a sense of the possibility of personal improvement, the phenomenon of emigration meant a rise in expectations for those who had not yet left as well as for those who had. Then war and revolution suddenly closed off the opportunity to leave. The ferment of the revolutionary years and the movements of national self-determination among the minorities were all the stronger in consequence.

The later history of migration from Russia to the United States is closely intertwined with political events. Of the great "White Russian" emigration of upper and middle class anti-Communists following Bolshevik victory in the civil war, the United States received only a trickle until the displacements of World War II drove hundreds of thousands of these unfortunates from their temporary homes in western and central Europe. Then, almost simultaneously, came the "Second Emigration," representing every Soviet nationality, detached willy-nilly from Soviet control by the German occupation and after the war left free to migrate if they escaped the forced repatriation of Soviet citizens. Finally a "Third Emigration" began to arrive, once again consisting largely of ethnic and religious minorities, especially Jews, as the Soviet Union was persuaded in the years of détente to loosen emigration restrictions. With each of these postrevolutionary waves of emigration, disproportionately drawn from the more highly educated and Westernized elements of the population, Russia's loss was the Western world's gain. If only as a trickle, the outflow has continued into the 1980s, as the Soviet regime tries vainly to curb dissent and defection among its most talented citizens.

4

Villagers fleeing famine

The Road to Revolution

Contemporary Russia is the product of one of the most profound and violent upheavals in world history. Revolution was the most sensational manifestation of this change, though not its only component. Socially, economically, and psychologically, Russia has undergone since the 1880s a wrenching transformation embodying in a particularly intense form the universal experience of modernization and Westernization. This makes Russia's recent history a model for comprehending the way in which these forces are transforming much of the world in our time.

Modernization is a loose but vital concept in contemporary social science that designates the whole series of interconnected changes in mankind's way of life since the seventeenth century—the rise of science, secularism, education and literacy, urbanization, industrialism, the technological revolutions in transportation and communication, and the advent of democratic and nationalist ideologies in the political sphere. "Westernization" is shorthand for the extension of these developments from their source in Western Europe and North America to other parts of the world. In Western and non-Western countries alike, the political expression of modernization has more often than not been revolution.

It is not easy for Americans to grasp the impact of modernization, Westernization, and revolution in other parts of the world. To be sure, beginning even before Independence, the United States went through the experience of modernization, but only in the gradual form characteristic of a society in the forefront of such change. America knew no real revolution; in 1776 the colonies already enjoyed internal representative government, in keeping with the English tradition. As a leader in the industrial and technological transformation of the nineteenth century, the United States did not have to absorb a cultural transformation imposed by outside pressure; instead, it contributed to the great force of Westernization exerted by the North Atlantic societies on the rest of the world. Except in the slave society of the South, Americans did not have to traverse the cultural distance faced by most Russians on the brink of modernity. Russians are in a much better position than Americans to understand what the third world is going through. Correspondingly, there is an intuitive sympathy among third-world political movements for the Russian method of modernization.

Most changes in history are matters of degree rather than of kind. The United States underwent rapid industrialization in the nineteenth century, with great problems of social adjustment and economic inequity, including the armed attempt of the Southern slave-owners to secede from the modern world. Nevertheless, there was no revolutionary breakdown of the national government. Why, then, did modernization in Russia lead to total revolution? Could Russia, without the First World War or misguided conspirators, have evolved gradually toward a constitutional government and a capitalist economy? Or was the modernizing experience so sudden, intense, and rapid, beyond any Western parallel, as to lead inexorably to revolution of an extraordinary intensity?

This issue raises the question of the nature of revolution in general. Is a revolution the result of circumstances or of deliberate action? Antirevolutionaries have always inclined to the conspiracy theory: they see the Russian Revolution as an extraneous evil imported by traitors and imposed on a hapless nation. Apologists for revolution, on the other hand, often contradict themselves in an effort to demonstrate the historical necessity of the process and at the same time glorify the role of activist revolutionary leaders. This is the contradiction in which Marxism finds itself. Neither side usually considers whether the outcome of a revolution corresponds with the original aims of the revolutionaries, or whether it may be governed blindly by the same circumstances that made revolution likely and possible in the first place.

▪ Modernization and Revolution

Revolutions do not commonly occur in static, traditional societies. Like Russia in the eighteenth century, such societies are subject at most to palace coups and revolts of desperate villagers, neither of which threaten the basic structure of authority. True revolutions, involving the collapse and replacement of the whole system of political and social power, occur only in times of rapid social change—change that collides with an excessively rigid set of political institutions.

Russia faced exactly this kind of impasse in the early years of the twentieth century. Western intellectual influence had, ever since Peter's time, undermined not only confidence in the monarchy but the sense of its legitimacy, as doubts spread even to the ranks of officialdom. The legal and administrative reforms of the 1860s had smoothed the way for economic development without assuring that the political structure would be responsive to the new social forces thus generated. In fact, under Alexander III and Nicholas II, the imperial regime turned firmly against further political reform, including any concessions to the idea of representative government.

At the same time, a more educated country, in its upper and middle
strata, was becoming a less patient country, as shown by early revolutionary activity among the intelligentsia. Then, with political
stability already in doubt, came the massive onslaught of industrialization.

Russia's industrial revolution was almost literally a revolution.
Between the 1870s and 1914 urban Russia was transformed, as factories sprang up, cities burgeoned, rail, telegraph, and telephone
networks spread around the country, natural riches were exploited,
and cadres of engineers and businessmen emerged from Russia's
Western-style institutions of higher education to administer the
physical metamorphosis of the nation. A few statistics tell the story
more graphically than words: pig iron output, a traditional index of
industrialization, rose from a mere 400,000 metric tons in 1870 to 4.6
million tons in 1913, putting Russia well into the ranks of the major
industrial powers. Compare this with a 1913 output of 31.5 million
tons for the United States, 10.4 million for England, 19.3 million for
Germany, and 5.2 million for France (see W. S. Woytinsky, *World
Population and Production*). This impressive expansion, concentrated in the Donbas region, was complemented by the exploitation
of coal resources (output 1 million tons in 1870, 25 million in 1910)
and the development of a petroleum industry around Baku on the
Caspian Sea (Russia in 1914 ranked second after the United States
among the world's producers). Railroad mileage grew from 6,000
miles in 1870 to nearly 50,000 in 1910, compared with 240,000 in the
United States (see Peter Lyashchenko, *History of the National Economy of Russia to the 1917 Revolution*). St. Petersburg and Moscow
both became major industrial centers, one concentrating on machinery, the other on textiles. St. Petersburg's population rose from
approximately 700,000 in 1870 to nearly 2 million in 1910; Moscow's in the same forty-year period increased from 600,000 to 1.5
million. The nationwide total of industrial workers grew almost tenfold in the half-century preceding the war (see William Blackwell,
The Industrialization of Russia).

Russia's industrialization was distinguished by several factors that
help explain its speed and intensity. One was the role of the government, which increased after Alexander III ascended the throne in
1881. A series of able finance ministers, trained in economics and
banking, superintended the effort. (The most notable were Nikolai
Bunge, 1881–1887, and Sergei Witte, 1892–1903, both of Baltic

German descent.) Though it was ironic for an avowedly reactionary regime to promote such precipitous economic change, Russians had had a predilection for the mercantilist philosophy ever since Peter's time. They believed that it was proper for the state to guide and promote economic development rather than leave it to the vagaries of free trade and the free market, as prescribed by the laissez-faire philosophy dominant in the West in the nineteenth century. The Russian state, striving to keep up militarily, not only resorted to the usual protectionist devices of protective tariffs and subsidies but entered directly into business activity where, as in the communications infrastructure, development was vital to the national interest. As in continental western Europe, most of the new railroad system was built or acquired by the state, including the famous trans-Siberian project pushed through between 1891 and 1904.

Another major force in Russia's economic development was foreign capital. Contradicting the Marxist dictum that capitalists must seek colonies as investment outlets, European investors—English, French, Belgian, and German for the most part—poured funds into Russia's new industrial and extractive enterprises, taking advantage of cheap labor and new markets. By 1914 almost half of Russia's industrialization had been financed by foreign loans and investments, and the new plant was largely equipped with foreign machinery purchased with those funds. French capital dominated the Donbas; the British funded the Baku oil fields; and everyone invested around St. Petersburg. Only the textile industry of the Moscow region was built with largely native capital. The Russian government fell heavily into debt to foreign lenders, private and governmental (especially France), in the effort to finance its railroad building and its armed forces.

No such rapid economic growth, whatever the sources of funding, would have been possible without the great reserve of surplus labor in the Russian countryside. Liberated from personal bondage but still prevented from improving themselves by the authority of the village commune, many impoverished peasants, like the serfs before them, moved to the towns to find a better living than was possible on their poor plots of land. This movement was part of the great rural-urban migration of Russia's industrial revolution, paralleling earlier population shifts within the major European countries and the vast transatlantic flow of European peasants to factory towns and cities of the United States.

The transplanted Russian peasant met with all the miseries of early industrialism—dawn-to-dusk factory discipline, exploitive wage levels, and slum housing—while laboring in large modern enterprises. The Russian worker, a subject of the autocracy, was allowed to do nothing on his own to improve his condition. Until 1905 trade unions and strikes, not to mention political organizations, were illegal, while the government's decrees on hours and working conditions were universally ignored. Usually literate, thanks to instruction received during his compulsory service in the reformed army, the Russian worker by the turn of the century was receptive to the message of the revolutionary intellectuals.

The peasants who remained in their villages were likewise affected by Russia's late nineteenth-century modernization. Commercialization of agriculture in the south and around the major towns, the land hunger of a growing rural population, increasing literacy among men who had served in the military, the influence of city workers who kept their family ties with the village—all combined to create a mood for change. Though they had been granted land at the Emancipation (a more enlightened step than in the United States, where "forty acres and a mule" became a Reconstruction joke), the villagers were obliged to make redemption payments to the landlords, and this burden became an acute source of resentment. Some peasants were able to raise themselves above the subsistence level to become more or less commercial farmers. Growing numbers resettled in Siberia or southern Russia, an analogue of the American frontier, which was just then coming to a close. These more successful individuals were the kulaks (their label derives from the Russian for "fist," because they were often tight-fisted village moneylenders). Their success left the majority even more resentful—a potential for political violence far greater than anything remaining in the West since the French Revolution.

Perhaps the most important response to modernization in Russia was a sociopolitical development long known to western Europe and the United States—namely, the rise of a middle class and a cadre of professionals. Historically the Russian merchant class, caught between the nobility and the populace, had lacked both power and prestige. Indeed, prejudice against the *meshchanstvo* (the petty bourgeoisie) among both the intelligentsia and the masses seems to have come into play at critical moments during the Revolution and under the Soviet regime to support the condemnation of individual enterprise, whatever its economic rationality. But the growth of industry and the modernization of the country's educational and professional establishment at the end of the nineteenth century rapidly generated a new middle class, oriented more toward public service than to small business. They were particularly interested in local government—the rural councils (*zemstva*) and the urban councils (*dumy*) created under Alexander II, which were responsible for bringing education, health care, and economic improvement to the masses. Unfortunately these civic-minded people were excluded almost as much as the workers and peasants from any real political power, which remained the preserve of the tsar and his bureaucracy and police.

Russia by 1900 exhibited most of the signs of a classic prerevolutionary situation, in which the irresistible force of economic and social change meets the immovable object of absolute monarchy. Progress had made most classes aware of greater vistas—the revolution of rising expectations. Yet all the newly conscious, resentful, and frustrated elements of Russian society were denied a voice in the country's affairs, a perfect case of what Lyford Edwards described as the "cramp" typically preceding revolution. Furthermore, there was no lack of interest in exploiting this mood: Russia, unlike other revolutionary societies, had been the scene of revolutionary plotting and agitation long before the masses had become ready to receive the message.

▪ The Russian Revolutionary Movement

Revolutionary talk, punctuated by outbursts of violent if ineffective action, was a tradition in Russia from the Decembrist uprising of 1825 to the Revolution. Although sporadic and fruitless revolts by the downtrodden had been endemic in Russian history, no serious challenge to the legitimacy of the system as a whole was articulated until a few brave members of the privileged class tried, at the end of the eighteenth century, to speak out against the immorality of despotism and servitude. The best-known of these was Alexander Radishchev, who incurred the ire of Catherine the Great with his exposé of serfdom and autocracy in his book *A Journey from St. Petersburg to Moscow*. Such critics were forthwith suppressed, as were the liberal officers who tried in 1825 to apply some of the constitutional ideas they had acquired from France, England, and the United

States. Nevertheless, a tradition of criticism and conspiracy was established among the more conscientious members of the educated elite, who felt guilty about their own privileges and ashamed of the political backwardness of their country.

The revolutionary movement was thus just as much moral as political, with overtones even of a religious nature, however much the revolutionaries found themselves at odds with the established church. Applying the critical norms of rationalism and science, they found the existing political and social structure unjust and illegitimate. By the middle of the nineteenth century, the fashion was to believe in nothing that was not scientifically demonstrable—no faith in religion, national tradition, inherited privilege, or custom. Hence, the term "nihilist" was often applied to radical circles from the 1850s to the 1870s. But this radical outlook itself rested on a new faith in science and philosophical materialism. This world view, ingrained in the Russian intellectual tradition, has remained one of the ideological foundations of the Soviet system, to the extent that the system dogmatically rejects not only religion but any philosophical questioning that smacks of "bourgeois idealism."

As rationalists and antitraditionalists, the revolutionary intellectuals were squarely opposed to received religion. For the anarchist Bakunin, God was just as much the enemy as the state. Although a few literary and philosophical figures looked for a modernization or a deinstitutionalization of religion (notably Leo Tolstoy, with his Christian anarchism), no significant church-backed reform movement ever developed. Conversely, the reformers' views of the church varied only in the degree of their repugnance for it. Thus, the antireligious current in Communism, so strident and senselessly cruel as it has been, has its roots not only in Marxism but in the Russian intelligentsia's biases that predated Marxism and prepared the ground for it.

The intelligentsia early absorbed the premises of socialism—a Western notion again, blossoming in the second quarter of the nineteenth century into diverse schools of thought. The Russians, starting with the exiled Alexander Herzen, knew they were socialists more clearly than they knew what socialism was, and the vagueness of the concept lent itself to a variety of interpretations in Russia from the middle of the nineteenth century to the Revolution and even beyond. Generally, socialism was understood in the utilitarian sense as a commitment to the well-being of the masses, whom the intelligentsia were inclined to worship more than understand. It clearly meant an antipathy to capitalism—that is, to individual profit-making enterprise—which intellectuals identified with the despised merchant class. Here again, a native Russian bias was firmly established prior to the influence of Marxism. The peasants were perceived as natural socialists who wanted only to see the government and the landlords lifted off their backs. It is debatable whether the tradition of village communes and land redistribution facilitated collectivization under the Communists; nevertheless, in the center of European Russia, where agriculture was traditionally both poorer and more communal, the collectives were accepted with relatively little resistance; in other regions, where there was less of the communal tradition, they were bitterly fought.

Rationalist, antireligious, and socialist, the intelligentsia saw itself as a distinctive and self-motivating force devoted to the transformation of Russian society. There were great differences in tactics, as well as in degrees of commitment to activism, but there was general acceptance of deliberate action by organized groups of the educated elite, necessarily conspiratorial under the police state, whether the aim was to enlighten and arouse the masses or to attack the living symbols of authority by outright terrorism. The young Sergei Nechaev (prototype for a character in Dostoevsky's antirevolutionary novel *The Possessed*) created a scandal with his "Catechism of a Revolutionary": "Merciless toward himself, he must be merciless toward others. A single, cold passion for the revolutionary cause must suppress within him all tender feelings for family life, friendship, love, gratitude, and even honor. For him there exists only one pleasure, one consolation, one reward, and one satisfaction—the success of the revolution." Although this harbinger of Bolshevik party discipline was extreme for its time, all early currents of revolutionary thought accepted the underlying doctrine, articulated by the social philosophers Pyotr Lavrov and Nikolai Mikhailovsky in the 1870s and 1880s, of the "critically thinking individual." Such a person, undertaking out of moral conviction and personal enlightenment to lead the masses, was presumed to be the moving force in history. Implicitly this was the philosophy that Lenin followed when he organized his revolutionary party.

All this—the tactics of elitist conspiracy, the socialist faith in the peasant masses, the revolutionary rejection of everything else in the Russian past—came to be subsumed under the label "Populism" (*narodnichestvo*). Populism in the Russian context was a much more radical philosophy than the democratic reformism that went by the same name in late nineteenth-century America, though a focus on justice for the rural majority characterized both movements. Russian Populism was a distinctive contribution to the international panoply of socialist theories, and until the 1890s it was, in one version or another, received doctrine for the great majority of Russian intellectuals and students. Its assumptions, if not its specific terms, continued to exert an influence in revolutionary Russia through the Bolshevik Party, despite the ostensible triumph of the rival ideology of Marxism.

■ Marxism in Russia

What most of all distinguishes and legitimizes the heirs of the Russian Revolution in their own eyes is the philosophy of Marxism. It is also Marxism that in most Americans' responses to Russia defines and explains the evil that they fear. Obviously, it is impossible to understand Soviet Russia without recognizing the meaning and influence of Marxist ideas and the way they were intertwined with the country's revolutionary and postrevolutionary politics.

Marxism, to begin with, was not the sole source of Russian revolutionary behavior. Even before Marxism became widely known among Russian thinkers, they were heavily committed to the necessity of revolution of some sort, usually by a conspiratorial organization. Russian radicals were already materialist, antireligious, and anticapitalist, even if the socialist alternative to capitalism often seemed vague and unrealistic. In short, the Russian intelligentsia independently anticipated the philosophical and political framework of Marxism, which explains how they could be converted to Marx's propositions so quickly and intensely.

What Marxism added to the Russian revolutionary outlook, when Georgi Plekhanov and his followers in the "Liberation of Labor" movement started to popularize it in the 1880s, was a scientific rationale for revolution. Marxism offered a theory of economic development that set Russia in the context of industrialization and charted the stages that would presumably lead to the end of tsarism and the victory of the working class. The key text was Marx's introduction to his early version of *Das Kapital*, published in 1859 as *A Contribution to the Critique of Political Economy*. He wrote: "At a certain stage of their development the material forces of production in society come into conflict with the existing relations of production . . . From forms of development of the forces of production these relations turn into their fetters. Then comes the period of social revolution." But, he warned, "No social order ever disappears before all the productive forces for which there is room in it have been developed, and new, higher relations of production never appear before the material conditions of their existence have matured in the womb of the old society." This applied to all the phases—"the Asiatic, the ancient, the feudal, and the modern bourgeois methods of production"—which together constituted the "prehistoric stage of human society."

Unlike Russian Populism, whose antiurban socialism was thrown into confusion by the country's industrial transformation, Marxism accepted capitalist industrialization and even credited it with a progressive role: it would develop a country's productive forces and prepare for the day when a socialist revolution could usher in a society not of bucolic austerity but of high-technology abundance. Some Russians, though interested in Marxism, questioned whether Russia would have to go through the capitalist phase to reach socialism. To find the answer, they simply wrote to the prophet himself. Marx replied, in one of his last letters before his death, that his theory was binding only for western Europe. Nevertheless, Plekhanov insisted on the deterministic and unilinear theory that prescribed a capitalist stage in Russia. This reading of Marxism quickly appealed to legions of Russian intellectuals, no less than to literate activists among the new working class, as a rationale for accepting capitalism and its temporary benefits, while looking ahead to a socialist revolution when the forces of the working class had sufficiently grown and matured. Lenin himself in his economic treatise *The Development of Capitalism in Russia* (1899) commented on "the progressive historical role of capitalism," based on "increases in the productive forces of social labor, and the socialization of that labor."

Acceptance of Marxism did not answer all of the potential questions about revolution. There were not only disagreements over how to apply the doctrine to Russia, but also inconsistencies in Marx's and Engels' writings that were just at this time provoking serious cleavages within the Marxist movement in the West. Marxism was initially couched, as in the Communist Manifesto of 1848, in terms of violent revolutionary opposition to the existing capitalist society.

By the time its founders died (Marx in 1883 and Engels in 1895), they saw socialism as something evolutionary and automatic. Both at the end acknowledged the possibility of a bloodless democratic transition to proletarian rule in certain countries, including Britain and the United States. Most of their followers in the rising Labor and Social-Democratic parties of western Europe in the last quarter of the nineteenth century moved in the same direction, differing only as to whether the intrinsic crisis of capitalism would beget a sudden socialist takeover (the "Orthodox" view), or whether the workers should pursue incremental gains through trade unions and the parliamentary process (the "Revisionist" view). By 1914, outside Russia only a few ultra-radical Marxists still believed in violent revolution, along with the Anarcho-Syndicalists (who were not Marxists but adherents of the direct action preached by Bakunin and Georges Sorel).

For Marxists in Russia, at least until 1905, it was not so easy to surrender the revolutionary perspective, given the persistence of the tsarist autocracy. In fact, they predicted two revolutions. The first would be the "bourgeois-democratic" revolution, which would overthrow the autocracy and permit the capitalists to develop the economy. The second, the actual proletarian revolution, would take place only after mature industrialism had generated a sufficiently large and class-conscious working class. Only thus could the backward situation in Russia be squared with the Marxist dictum that socialist revolution was the outgrowth of capitalism where it was most developed and ripe for terminal crisis.

Although Marxism attracted Russian revolutionaries with its aura of scientific inevitability and technological modernism, it ran into a political difficulty not posed by Populism when it put off the socialist goal to the distant future. Some Marxists, such as Pyotr Struve, could accept this perspective and meanwhile expound Marxism as an apology for capitalism. They were the "legal Marxists," so called because the censors tolerated their views. Some gave up on revolution and dedicated themselves to the practical struggle for workers' economic benefits, on the model of the western Revisionists; these were known as the "Economists." The Orthodox, following Plekhanov, held to the two-stage outlook, but the more radical and impatient among them found a long-delayed proletarian revolution unacceptable. Though Marxism predicted that socialism would follow the exhaustion of capitalism, the radicals began to seek a rationale for a workers' revolution at an earlier date. Here was the basis for the split in Russian Marxism and the rise of the Bolsheviks.

The Bolshevik faction of the Russian Marxist movement was essentially the creation of one man, Vladimir Ilyich Ulyanov, better known to history by his revolutionary pseudonym, Lenin. (In the English-language literature Lenin has often been called "Nikolai," an imaginative error of some early British Communists who tried to spell out the signature "N. Lenin." "N.," actually standing for "nothing," was merely the sign of an alias.) Born in 1870, the son of a provincial school administrator, Lenin followed the typical path of the educated elite into revolutionary thought and action. For him, as for so many others, this was a matter of choice, not constraint; with his drive and training, Lenin could have become a corporation lawyer or a shaper of the new capitalism. But events—his brother's revolutionary involvement and ultimate execution, his own expulsion from the University of Kazan—combined with the intellectual climate to impel Lenin toward the career of professional revolutionary and a very different place in history. Lenin's biography is a case study in the autocracy's self-destruction.

Like so many of his contemporaries, Lenin was early converted to Marxism, and his first major piece of writing ("What the 'Friends of the People' Are and How They Fight the Social-Democrats") was a polemic aiming to show how Russian industrialization refuted Populism and sustained the Marxist approach to revolution. But the idea for which Lenin was most famous, the idea that colored the whole nature of his revolutionary work, came later, crystallizing in his mind during his imprisonment and Siberian exile from 1897 to 1900. This was his concept of the political party as an instrument for making revolution. Rejecting the Western notion of the party as a loose movement of like-minded followers, he called for a tightly knit conspiratorial organization of professional revolutionaries like himself, "a small, compact core of the most reliable, experienced, and hardened workers," dedicated to the overthrow of both tsarism and capitalism. Lenin launched this idea in his most important work, the 1902 pamphlet "What Is to Be Done?"

Lenin's conception of political organization and tactics was hardly novel, except in the Marxist context. What he had really done was resurrect the Russian conspiratorial tradition of the 1860s and 1870s, detach it from Populism, and graft it onto the Marxist theory of proletarian revolution. "Give us an organization of revolutionaries," he wrote, paraphrasing Archimedes, "and we shall over-turn Russia." Russian Marxist leaders, as well as Westerners, were appalled by Lenin's authoritarianism and military style. As a result of the organizational issue that he posed, the Russian Marxist party broke apart at the very moment of its birth.

An abortive attempt had been made by Russian Marxists in 1898 to set up a "Russian Social Democratic Workers Party," at the same time that the Populists were taking steps to organize a modern-style "Party of Socialist Revolutionaries" (known by all as the SRs) and the liberals were setting up a "Constitutional Democratic Party" (known as "Kadets," from the Russian initials K and D). But the first real congress of Russian Marxists, or Social Democrats, came only in 1903, opening in Brussels and closing a couple of weeks later in London, where it was forced to move by the nervous Belgian authorities. This "Second Congress" split irretrievably on the organizational question. Lenin, seizing the occasion of one favorable vote, called his faction "Bolsheviks" (meaning "majority people") and labeled the rest, who favored a Western-style mass party, as the "Mensheviks" ("minority people"). History has allowed these terms to stick, though the Menshevik current was much the stronger until 1917.

The differences between the Bolsheviks and the Mensheviks went beyond details of organization and tactics. Lenin's people were younger and more intemperate, and the implications of their stand went deeply into the nature of revolution and Russia's prospects for it. In 1905 Lenin articulated their impatience in a work called "Two Tactics of the Russian Social Democracy," in which he addressed the presumably impending bourgeois-democratic revolution. Would the Russian workers and the workers' party let the bourgeoisie carry out this revolution and hold power for generations while capitalism matured, or would they seize power themselves to assure the most rapid progress toward socialism? "The proletariat must carry to completion the democratic revolution, by allying to itself the mass of the peasantry in order to crush by force the resistance of the autocracy and to paralyze the instability of the bourgeoisie." Thus did Lenin resolve the logical paradox of Russian Marxism, which envisioned a utopian future but put this goal off to a remote time. Discounting the revolutionary capacity of the Russian bourgeoisie, Lenin proposed an immediate role for the self-styled representatives of the working class: they should carry out the bourgeois revolution themselves, eradicate tsarism, and institute a "democratic dictatorship of the proletariat and the peasantry" presided over by the Marxist party. They would be guided and steeled in this effort by their firm commitment to Marxist ideology, and would raise the workers to true revolutionary consciousness.

Most of Lenin's program was fully compatible with the Russian revolutionary tradition—willful action by a dedicated elite, a passion for socialism, reliance on ideological if not moral guideposts, and conspiratorial organization. But it was hard to reconcile with Marxism the implication that if these Russian-style efforts were not made, the working class would lose its revolutionary fervor and the proletarian revolution would be delayed indefinitely. Lenin, though he held to the letter of Marxism like a born-again believer, in practice had little faith in the spontaneous workings of history to generate revolutionary potential among either the bourgeoisie or the proletariat. It was strange Marxism to suggest that the revolution embodying the aims of one class (the bourgeoisie) had to be accomplished by the party representing another class (the proletariat) and that even the workers would fail to act as a revolutionary force without a dedicated vanguard to rouse them. Although Lenin did not admit it, his thinking was close to that of the Populist Pyotr Tkachev, who in the 1880s called for a seizure of power to prevent the successful development of capitalism—an outcome that might preclude the morally superior socialist order altogether. For a revolutionary in Russia, Lenin's program may indeed have been more appropriate and even more realistic than the deterministic premises of Marxism; the problem was Lenin's insistence that his program *was* Marxism and that any who questioned this identity were "petty-bourgeois" deviators, virtual heretics. At this point, Lenin's ideology became dogma. This would prove to be a devastating influence after Bolshevism succeeded in winning power.

▪ The Uprising of 1905

The Russian Revolution had its true beginnings in 1905—a year of demonstrations, strikes, mutinies, and peasant revolts that shook the imperial regime to its foundations. Russians who had theorized in a vacuum for generations were suddenly confronted with their country's real potential for revolution. It was, thanks to two decades of intense economic and social change, a potential needing little of the agitation and conspiracy that were thought essential by the intellectuals, Lenin included, to set the masses in motion. The events of 1905 testified to the spontaneity of the revolutionary process.

Since they failed to terminate the monarchy, the events of 1905 are often regarded as a mere curtain raiser to the drama of 1917. They assume much greater significance when the entire course of revolution in Russia is viewed against the background of other major revolutions. In France, Louis XVI was not removed after the storming of the Bastille, though he had to concede the principle of constitutional limitations on the monarchy—and this is exactly what happened to Nicholas II as a result of the St. Petersburg general strike in October 1905. After that retreat, the Russian government managed to restrain the forces of protest for another ten years, whereas Louis XVI was deposed just three years after the fall of the Bastille. But temporary stabilization did not mean in any sense a return to the status quo in Russia; the mystique of authority on which all despotic regimes rely had been irretrievably dispelled. Russia's mood in the following decade resembled that of the American colonies between the Stamp Act protests of 1765 and the outbreak of war at Lexington and Concord: the country had become aware of its collective hostility to the Old Regime and of its capacity to organize and act for political change.

Ironically, 1905 began with an incident unforeseen by any of the liberal or socialist activists who had been clamoring for a change of regime. The war launched by Japan in the Far East in 1904 had been a series of disasters for Russia. Sensing a crisis of morale, the government had hinted at concessions, then denied them—the greatest folly for any leadership threatened by popular protest. A certain worker-priest, Gapon by name, had been encouraged by the police to organize among the St. Petersburg proletariat so as to divert them from the blandishments of the Marxists. In January 1905, to petition the tsar for redress of their economic grievances, he led his flock in a demonstration at the Winter Palace. The Cossacks on guard, fearing they had lost control, charged the crowd and butchered several hundred.

Revolted by this "Bloody Sunday," the nation lost all confidence in the government and turned to every form of defiance. The middle class went to reform dinner meetings and demanded constitutional government; the workers struck for the eight-hour day and trade union rights; peasants in land-hungry central Russia began seizing the estates. Here and there, military units defied discipline, notably the crew of the battleship Potemkin, who mutinied at Sevastopol, threw their officers overboard, and sailed to Rumania (the event is celebrated in Sergei Eisenstein's film *Potemkin*). In October, in the teeth of the general strike led by the "St. Petersburg Soviet [council] of Workers' Deputies," Nicholas II acceded to the advice of the pragmatic Count Witte and promised Russia a constitution.

Nicholas' October Manifesto more or less satisfied the middle-class liberals and split them from the proletariat. Marxist-led workers vainly prolonged their defiance, culminating in a bitter but futile armed uprising in Moscow. The St. Petersburg strike leaders—including the young Lyov Davydovich Bronstein, alias Leon Trotsky—were arrested, and the restive peasants were firmly put down with the help of regular troops returning from the Far East. By the time the newly promised constitution went into effect, the imperial military and police were again in full control, and the revolutionary process had been halted—a significant achievement, in view of the fact that obedience to the Old Regime had almost completely evaporated.

Although the Russian revolutionary tradition extolled organized leadership, the upheaval of 1905 was largely beyond the direction and control of any of the radical parties. Many revolutionary intellectuals returned from exile to take advantage of the temporary advent of political freedom and to try to regain their popular following. But events had outrun any strategy they could devise.

This circumstance seems especially paradoxical for the Marxists, in view of their "scientific" theory of revolutionary politics. Yet Marxism, stressing the class theory of the causes of revolution, lacks an adequate explanation and interpretation of revolution as a political process. Placing its faith in the overthrow of the bad class by the good one, it ignores the characteristic stages of a revolution: the collapse of the old authority, the failure of moderate reformers, the accession of extremists, the indulgence in utopian fancy, the encounter with the practical demands of survival, the retrenchment of ideals, and the consolidation of a practical system of postrevolutionary rule. This process, graphically depicted in works such as Crane Brinton's *Anatomy of Revolution* as well as in the actual events of 1905 and 1917, has never been directly addressed by the Russian

Marxists. The one indirect attempt by a Marxist at a process theory of revolution was eventually rejected by the Communists because it came from the pen of the ultimate heretic, Trotsky.

Sentenced to prison for his part in the St. Petersburg strike, Trotsky had time to theorize about the meaning of the 1905 episode. Though not yet a Bolshevik, he agreed with Lenin that the Russian bourgeoisie—that is, the revolutionary moderates—were too weak and irresolute to carry the "bourgeois" revolution to the point of destroying tsarism. However, he recognized that owing to a "law of combined development," urban Russia was approaching industrialized modernity while rural Russia was still struggling to overcome its feudal legacy. This meant that the workers in the big cities represented a potential for proletarian revolution and socialism, even though the bulk of the population had only petty-bourgeois aspirations for individual rights and property ownership. Consequently, argued Trotsky with the hindsight of 1905, when the government succumbed again to revolution, the upheaval would move in a unbroken, continuous, "permanent" development from the bourgeois phase to the proletarian phase—in other words, from the moderate to the extreme stage—in a matter of months. The workers would take over in the major industrial areas and attempt, as long as they held power, to establish socialism. But sooner or later they would face a petty-bourgeois backlash. However, outside aid would be guaranteed, Trotsky argued, by the international extension of the revolution, which he likewise expected to proceed in a continuous or permanent manner. The Russian workers, given an early chance to grasp power because tsarism balked middle-class reform, would by their example inspire the proletarian revolution that was supposed to be imminent in the advanced capitalist countries of the West. In turn, workers' governments in the industrialized countries would come to the aid of their Slavic confreres and help avert a "Thermidorean Reaction" such as befell Robespierre when he was deposed and executed in July 1794. (The date fell in the month of "Thermidor" according to the French revolutionary calendar.) All this came to be known as Trotsky's "Theory of Permanent Revolution." Under Stalin the theory was condemned as heresy, but in 1917 it was the guiding premise of Bolshevik Party strategy.

While Russian radicals smarted from the defeat of 1905 and theorized in jail or pursued the petty politics of exiled factions, the supporters of constitutionalism found their hopes disappointed by the constitution that the imperial government put into effect in 1906. It was much nearer the sham constitutionalism of the kaiser's Germany than what Americans or Britons think of as a constitution. To be sure, legal rights and political freedom were promised, and an assembly, the Duma, was to be elected by universal male suffrage. However, the power of the popular will was narrowly circumscribed: the bureaucratically appointed Council of State was kept on as an upper house with veto power, and the executive, military, and police functions of government remained independent of parliamentary regulation. Moreover, representation in the Duma was biased in favor of property owners and against non-Russian minorities. After 1907, when prime minister Pyotr Stolypin decreed an extralegal revision of the electoral system, the Duma was controlled by a docile, reactionary majority of progovernment landowners. On the other hand, the Duma did provide small minorities of dissidents, including even a few Bolsheviks, with a legal sounding board that they could use to publicize their philosophies and badger the government. In addition, censorship and the ban on trade unions were nominally relaxed. Russia began to experience at least some of the aboveground political life and exchange of opinion taken for granted in the major democratic states.

The great question about Russia's semiconstitutional regime of 1906–1917 is whether it might have made possible Russia's gradual evolution into a modern constitutional monarchy on the British model. One school of thought contends that had it not been for the shock of the First World War, Russia could readily have progressed toward democratic politics and a capitalist economy. This implies that 1905 had achieved all the revolutionary loosening required to free the Russian body politic for further improvement, without unleashing the catastrophic violence of a complete social revolution. Such a view probably expresses more the wishful thinking of Western constitutionalists than a realistic appraisal of modern Russia and of the nature of revolution. The autocratic behavior of Russian rulers before and since calls into question the country's ability to manage democratic institutions under any circumstances. Furthermore, the trend toward right-wing dictatorship in most of central and eastern Europe in the first half of the twentieth century suggests that this, rather than constitutionalism, may have been Russia's path had not the Revolution of 1917 intervened. In any case, the events of 1917 were not disconnected from those of 1905. Abortive though it was, the revolution of 1905 initiated the defiance and struggle that in 1917 developed rapidly into the most extreme forms of revolutionary violence.

Lenin and his sister

The Revolutions of 1917

The year 1917 has become one of those epochal dates that cleave human experience into a past that can never be recovered and a succeeding era that can never turn back. Russia's revolutionary upheaval revealed to the entire world new horizons of hope, fear, and hatred that transcended most old ideas about the nature and potential of politics. Indeed, 1917 culminated, as the Soviet expression has it, in "a revolution that opened a new era in human history"; they do not add, "for better or for worse."

The Russia of today is inconceivable apart from its revolutionary origins. This does not mean that the shape of the Soviet system was immutably cast in 1917, but simply that the Revolution was the event from which all subsequent Soviet development has proceeded and from which the essential premises of Soviet thinking are still derived. The Revolution necessarily remains the centerpiece in any attempt to understand the evolution of the USSR.

The violence and cruelties of the Russian Revolution had an impact on Americans far surpassing that of earlier episodes of Russian despotism. Although the United States, too, was born of a revolution and benefited indirectly from the English Puritan Revolution of the seventeenth century, no one—not even the most ardent Bolshevist sympathizers—supposed that the Russian Revolution had anything in common with the American. Quite the contrary: it has been the fashion among political commentators—Hannah Arendt and Dennis Brogan, for example—to draw invidious comparisons between the moderate American Revolution, which fought for political liberty and the rule of law, and the violent Russian Revolution, which turned society upside down and imposed a ruthless despotism on the wreckage. But there are vast differences between the circumstances of the two events that make even such an exercise in comparative moralism futile. The American Revolution was not a true revolution, since it did not lead to a complete breakdown of authority and to general social strife; it was primarily a struggle for national separation from a foreign authority, during which internal institutions and social relationships were not seriously disrupted. America had lived under no absolute monarch but only under the shared authority of the British Parliament and colonial constitutions, both part of the legacy of the revolutionary struggles in seventeenth-century England. The American Revolution never left the phase of moderate constitutionalism; it engendered no dictatorship and little terror. It left no tradition by which Americans might comprehend the bloodthirsty fanaticism of true revolutions. Worse, by bequeathing the standard of a "good," American-style revolution, it encouraged the search for some diabolical power to account for the horrors of revolutions elsewhere.

▪ The Setting

"A revolution," said the ex-emperor Napoleon, "cannot be made; neither can it be stopped." Although revolutionaries and antirevolutionaries alike are tempted to attribute revolution to the schemes and plots of radical activists, Russia's history, like that of many other countries, makes it clear that revolution—as distinct from a mere coup d'état, which changes only the personalities in power—cannot be launched at will, nor can it simply be steered toward a chosen goal. A revolution, when it occurs on a grand scale, means the complete breakdown and reconstruction of a country's system of rule. This is not an event but a process, as one crisis leads to another, that takes years to work itself out. Revolution is a convulsion of the whole social system and it proceeds according to its own laws, however much revolutionary leaders may claim to be in command of events.

There is no particular point in the evolution of a society at which revolution breaks out—it is only a matter of the requisite rigidities and upsets. Certainly the history of Russia does not bear out Marx's proposition that a social system will not be overthrown until it has exhausted all the possibilities of its development. Capitalism had the misfortune in Russia of arriving on the scene before monarchy had given way to representative government. When revolution broke through the old structure, it quickly became as much anticapitalist as antimonarchical, even though Russia was only beginning to approach full industrial development. Furthermore, the anticapitalist revolution contradicted the Marxist belief that socialism required the prior development of industry and the concentration of individual producers, rural and urban, into factory-scale enterprises. Consequently, the problems and tasks facing the victorious revolutionaries in a Russia of half-built industry and poor peasants were not the ones their doctrine was prepared to address.

After the disorders of 1905 were quelled, Russia for a time did appear to be on the road of constitutional and capitalist evolution. With foreign investment growing, industrial development surged ahead and more and more took the form of modern corporate enterprise. The agrarian problem was addressed first by canceling the redemption payments still owed by the peasants for the land received at the Emancipation. Then Prime Minister Stolypin's land reform broke the grip of the village commune and allowed its more ambitious members—"the strong and sober," he called them—to trade their scattered strips of land for compact, permanent, individual farms. But population growth had intensified the land hunger of the peasants, who coveted what large estates still remained (particularly in the overcrowded central part of European Russia). In the cities, industrial expansion had done little to lessen the exploitation and alienation of the growing working class. In 1912, after a half-decade of quiescence, the labor and revolutionary movements were incited to new protests by the massacre of striking miners in the Lena gold fields in Siberia. Only the outbreak of war in 1914 put a temporary damper on this wave of agitation, leaving the underlying tensions unabated.

All the while the imperial government was in a state of near-paralysis. Here the effect of individual personalities was crucial, as it has been on the eve of most revolutions. Nicholas II was an amiable incompetent, a believer in absolute power but incapable of exercising it decisively. Like Louis XVI, he was heavily influenced by his headstrong foreign-born consort, the Empress Alexandra, daughter of a German prince and granddaughter of Queen Victoria. The family tragedy is a familiar story: the young heir to the throne, Alexei, born late to the marriage, was soon found to be afflicted with hemophilia, and this misfortune made possible the bizarre role of the peasant-adventurer Grigori Rasputin. It was in the troubled year 1905 that Rasputin began to worm his way into a favored place at court, by practicing his gift for hypnotism on the tsarevich. He soon became the power behind the throne, and, through his influence on the empress, was able to make and break ministries at his whim.

In 1911 the last effective imperial executive, Stolypin, was shot to death in a Kiev theater, one more victim of the terrorism that had marked the entire previous decade. In this case the circumstances were most peculiar: his killer proved to be a double agent, an anarchist and at the same time an employee of the secret police. The surmise is that Stolypin was too much the modernizer for the reactionaries in the bureaucracy, and that the tragedy was allowed to happen. From then on, through the war years to the Revolution, the Russian government played ministerial musical chairs, as the empress and Rasputin shifted their blessing to bureaucrats whose integrity was low enough to curry such favor and whose competence was low enough to need it.

The First World War was the ultimate and impossible test of the Old Regime, as Russia met with a series of catastrophic defeats at the hands of the Germans. Tempted to invade German territory while the kaiser's forces were concentrating to crush the French, the Russian army was routed with enormous losses at Tannenberg and the Masurian Lakes in East Prussia, battles that have been chronicled by Alexander Solzhenitsyn in his novel *August 1914*. The following year, repulsed in the west, the German High Command threw its best forces against the Russians, overwhelmed them on the plains of Poland, and drove the tsar's army back nearly to Russia's old boundary prior to the partitions of Poland in the eighteenth century. Here, resisting the temptation to push deeper into Russia, the Germans and Austrians allowed the front to stabilize, while the Russians nursed their wounds and endeavored, in vain, to modernize their economic base for war. Too late: the entire spectrum of well-meaning moderates and reformers, not to mention the suffering masses, had lost confidence in the government, just as they had in 1905. The economy was overstrained and transportation broke down. Inflation, exacerbated by the prohibition on liquor and the consequent loss of the state's vodka revenues, ran out of control. Conscript troops, raised in numbers that drained the villages of male labor but could not be deployed or supplied at the front, languished in garrison centers and listened to the frightening tales of the returning wounded. Loyal reform efforts urged by the businessmen's War Industries Committees and the local governments were brushed aside by reactionaries in the central administration. Freemasonry, an old Russian interest, was revived as the umbrella organization for a drawing-room conspiracy of upper-class liberals. Discredited by the intrigues of Rasputin and the empress, the court became an object of hatred and derision.

These grim conditions were described in an extraordinary secret police report in the fall of 1916:

The systematically growing disruption of transportation; the unrestrained bacchanal of free-booting and robberies by a novel kind of shady operators in various branches of the commercial, industrial and social-political life of the country; the unsystematic and mutually contradictory assignment of representatives of the governmental and local administration; the lack of conscientiousness on the part of the secondary and lower agents of authority in the provinces; and, as a consequence of all the foregoing, the unequal distribution of food supplies and items of prime necessity, the incredibly rising cost of living and the absence of sources and means of feeding the presently starving population of the capitals (Petrograd and Moscow) and the major social centers ...; all this, taken together, characterizing in bright, comprehensive colors the result of neglect of the rear, as the basic source and cause of the serious sick condition of the internal life of the vast state organism, at the same time definitely and categorically indicates that a terrible crisis is already ripe and must necessarily be decided in one direction or the other.

From which the conclusion followed:

It is necessary to recognize as unconditional and indisputable, that the internal set-up of Russian governmental life at the present time finds itself under the severe threat of immediately impending serious shocks, brought on and explained exclusively by economic motivations: hunger, unequal distribution of food supplies and objects of prime necessity, and the fantastically rising cost of living ... It is only necessary for this movement to be cast in some concrete form and to be expressed in some definite act (a pogrom, a major strike, a massive clash of the lower orders of the population with the police, etc.), and it will at once and unconditionally become purely political.

In December 1916 Rasputin was assassinated by a group of young noblemen (including the emperor's cousin), who hoped that their act would cure the sickness of the Old Regime. This should have indicated that Russia's impasse was likely to be resolved very soon by violence; but some observers were not so sure. Said Lenin in Zurich in January 1917, "We of the older generation may not live to see the decisive battles of this revolution."

▪ The February Revolution

The Revolution of 1917 was started by women. On International Women's Day, March 8 (February 23 by the unreformed Russian calendar), women factory workers and housewives staged a mass demonstration in the streets of the capital to protest the food shortage. By chance, the Putilov locomotive and machinery works—one of Russia's marvels of modernization—decided the same day to teach its restive employees a lesson by locking them out. The men joined the women's demonstration and drew others in turn: by that evening a hundred thousand workers had spontaneously walked off the job. On March 9 and 10 the protests grew, still without evidence of any centralized initiative or direction. By Saturday evening, March 10, Petrograd (as St. Petersburg had been renamed in 1914) was in a state of general strike unparalleled since 1905.

As crowds overwhelmed the police and defied the wavering Cossack cavalry, Nicholas II telegraphed from his headquarters at the front to demand the restoration of order. General Khabalov, commander of the Petrograd Military District, thereupon called out the reserve infantry regiments garrisoned all over the city, and gave them orders to shoot if necessary. On Sunday, March 11 (February 26, Old Style), as the crowds grew even larger, some units actually did fire, causing hundreds of casualties. But then occurred the decisive psychological break that spells the doom of any government relying on force: the troops, mostly raw conscripts, felt themselves at one with the people opposing them, and a wave of disgust at their mission ran through the ranks. That afternoon a company of the Pavlov Regiment mutinied and refused to shoot. Troops of the Volhynsky Regiment debated their orders during the night, and, when morning came, shot down one of their officers who had attempted to force them to obey. This act marked the point of no return. The Volhynsky troops scattered to the other barracks, and their appeals immediately produced a general mutiny of the entire garrison. Sensing the end of effective authority, the people ran wild, sacking police stations and storming the prisons.

One of the most graphic accounts of this incredible day was written by the U.S. ambassador, David Francis, in his dispatch to Washington:

About ten A.M. today a regiment of 1000 to 1200 men stationed in barracks about two blocks from the Embassy mutinied and according to reports killed their commanding officer because he would not join them.

At 11:30 A.M., Mr. Miles phoned me from the Second Division in the Austrian Embassy [under U.S. care prior to American entry into the war] that some of the mutineers accompanied by many revolutionists had visited the munition factory adjoining the Austrian Embassy; had killed the officer in command there, and had ordered the men to quit work; that many of the employees had come into the Austrian Embassy, and one lieutenant, in order to conceal themselves from the angry crowd. Mr. Miles said that he had and was at the time he phoned endeavoring to prevent more employees from entering the Embassy but fearing that the crowd might learn that the Embassy was being used as a refuge he called me up and requested that an additional guard should be requested immediately. I phoned to the Foreign Office and was assured that the guard would be strengthened if possible, but it mut be done by the War Department or General Staff, with which the Foreign Office would immediately communicate by phone. That was the last communication I have had with the Foreign Office and this dispatch is written at 8 P.M. For four or five hours past there have been crowds on the Liteiny which is the most frequented thoroughfare in this section of the city, and Secretary Bailey who came into the Embassy from his apartment at about 3:30 P.M. reported that he had seen four dead men lying on Liteiny and there were also five wounded men. Within one hour thereafter many of the mutineers were seen walking on Furshtadtskaya in front of the Embassy, some with guns and some without, and there marched by the Embassy in the roadway a body of about one hundred men in citizens' clothes who carried muskets but observed no order of marching and appeared to have no commanding officer. During this hour, from 4 to 5 P.M. there also passed in front of the Embassy a number of motor cars filled with soldiers with guns, but in every car there were some citizens or men in citizens' clothes who were no doubt revolutionists. About this hour the Embassy was informed by telephone that the Duma had been dissolved or prorogued until about the middle of April—I heard later that this order was issued yesterday afternoon but as there have been no newspapers for two days past it was not known until the hour for the Duma's assemblage, and I suppose the members were ignorant of it until they went to the hall of the meeting. At about six o'clock P.M., Captain McCully, the Naval Attaché of the Embassy, who had left for his apartment about 5 P.M., phoned that in his walk from the Embassy to his apartment, a distance of over a mile, he had seen no policemen nor any soldiers who acknowledged fealty to the Government but he had observed a thousand or more cavalrymen riding quietly toward the [river] Neva and abandoning the streets of the city to the mutineers and revolutionists.

The abrupt evaporation of the tsar's authority, as the whole empire emulated Petrograd's defiance, testifies to the profound alienation that had taken hold of the country as a result of the war, its mismanagement, and the conviction that power was held by a corrupt and incompetent clique. But as the Old Regime gave way, there was no automatic replacement to guide Russia's political future. Russia had nothing comparable to the American state legislatures and Continental Congress, which led protests before the Revolution and steered the ship of state afterward—nothing comparable even to the French Estates General or the English Long Parliament, which represented some continuity of legitimate authority during the early phases of revolution. The Duma, unrepresentative though it was, was given no chance to try its hand at revolutionary leadership: the last act of the tsar's last prime minister, Prince Golitsyn, on the evening before the collapse, was to dissolve the Duma and end negotiations aimed at establishing a ministry responsible to the deputies.

There was, to be sure, a tenuous though extraconstitutional link between the Duma and the new regime that attempted to fill the political vacuum. On the afternoon of the great revolutionary day, March 12, the Duma deputies met informally and authorized the creation of a "Temporary Committee" headed by Duma president Mikhail Rodzianko. This committee was established ostensibly to maintain public order, but by the following day it was acting like a government, taking over ministries and arresting members of the old administration. Two days later it legitimized its role by announcing the formation of a "Provisional Government" and by promising democratic liberties and amnesty for political prisoners.

The Duma's efforts were paralleled by a flurry of activity among all those political activists still at large in Petrograd or just released from jail who aspired to represent the working population. Almost at the same hour as the Temporary Committee, labor leaders and radical Duma deputies gathered at the Duma's meeting place, the Taurida Palace, and announced the revival of the 1905 idea of the soviet, this time to be called the "Petrograd Soviet of Workers' and Soldiers' Deputies." The lawyers and pamphleteers of the revolutionary parties—primarily Mensheviks and Socialist Revolutionaries, with a few Bolsheviks on the left and semisocialists on the right—scattered to the factories and barracks to get themselves elected to the soviet. That very evening the reconstituted soviet held its first meeting to begin reorganizing public services and guarding the gains of the Revolution. That the events of that day were indeed a revolution was now recognized by almost everyone.

Everyone, that is, except the emperor and his entourage at Army Headquarters in Mogilev. Brushing aside suggestions of constitutional concessions, Nicholas ordered loyal troops to march on Petrograd, and set off himself by train for the capital on March 13. By the next day, as a result of disorders along the line, he had gotten no further than Pskov, headquarters of the Northern Front. Meanwhile the supposedly loyal troops had defied their orders and joined the Revolution, like their counterparts in Petrograd. The military command, together with Rodzianko and the Temporary Committee, determined that if the monarchy were to be saved there was no alternative except to insist on the tsar's abdication in favor of Tsarevich Alexei. On the following day, March 15, Nicholas gave in but only on condition that he might abdicate in favor of his younger brother, Grand Duke Mikhail, rather than suffer separation from his invalid son. Mikhail, visited in Petrograd by the Temporary Committee, was not satisfied that his own safety could be assured and refused the proffered crown. A week later Nicholas was placed under house arrest at his palace in the Petrograd suburbs. So ended the reign of the Romanov dynasty, by default.

■ The Provisional Government

It is the great tragedy of the Russian Revolution that the February hopes for peaceful constitutionalism were ultimately crushed by revolutionary terror and civil war. Lenin and the Bolshevik Party are often cast as the villains, but the Revolution's violence cannot be ascribed simply to the agitation of a few fanatics. It is, sadly, in the nature of revolution that moderate beginnings cannot usually be contained. The forces unleashed by the fall of an oppressive government—the hopes, hatreds, and demands that people allow themselves to act upon once the power of the old regime has been broken—precipitate the most bitter struggles over the nation's destiny, struggles that usually can be resolved only by a new despotism. The fall of the tsar had for Russia the same effect as did the storming of the Bastille in France: it signified the end of effective authority and the beginning of an era in which only force could arbitrate among the disparate segments of society.

The moderate politicians who emerge from the more or less loyal opposition and try to take charge in the early phase of a revolution do not understand the dilemma between demands for change and hopes for order, even though the circumstances that brought them to power are by definition already immoderate and illegal. The government of aristocratic and bourgeois liberals that was formed by the Temporary Committee on March 15 was no exception. For prime minister they chose the former head of the association of provincial governments, the kindly but ineffective Prince Georgi Lvov. The real strongman was foreign minister Pavel Miliukov, historian and leader of the Constitutional Democrats in the Duma, who was a proponent of constitutional monarchy and "national honor." Only one member of the new cabinet had connections with the popular forces represented in the soviet: he was Alexander Kerensky, the minister of justice, a flamboyant lawyer and Duma deputy of vaguely socialist persuasion whom the workers liked because he had defended the Lena gold-field strikers before the war.

Conscious of the lack of a popular mandate, the framers of the Provisional Government sought support from the leaders of the Petrograd Soviet. The soviet, for its part, was dominated by orthodox Marxists of the Menshevik faction, who could foresee only a bourgeois revolution and held back from claiming power in the name of the workers. They deferred to the de facto authority of the conservatives in the cabinet and extended their conditional endorsement to the new regime, "insofar as" it respected the democratic gains of the Revolution. Both the cabinet and the soviet agreed that their respective roles would be only temporary, until such time as elections could be held for a Constituent Assembly to draft a constitution.

Hopes for such a peaceful and legal determination of the country's future began to dim almost at once. The immediate issue was the war with Germany and the Central Powers: whether to prosecute it, end it, or seek a negotiated settlement in conjunction with Russia's allies. Though the Germans had allowed the eastern front to fall dormant while they awaited the outcome of Russia's turmoil, the Provisional Government under Miliukov's guidance reaffirmed its treaties with the Allies and pledged to fight for victory.

Miliukov's commitments, made known in April, triggered new mass protests and precipitated the first cabinet crisis of the Provisional Government. Caught off guard by the demonstrations of the "April Days" (May 3 and 4 by the Western calendar) and the soviet's call for a "democratic peace without annexations or indemnities," the Provisional Government ousted Miliukov and negotiated with the soviet to form a coalition cabinet. Five soviet leaders, including the Menshevik Irakli Tsereteli and the Socialist Revolutionary Viktor Chernov, overcame their compunctions about collaborating with the bourgeoisie and joined the government in the hope of preserving order and negotiating peace. The dominant figure in the new leadership was Kerensky, now minister of war, standing politically midway between the old Duma forces and the new movement of the soviets.

The Petrograd Soviet, operating as a purely democratic body, had meanwhile been emulated all over the country, not only in the cities but also by peasants in the villages and districts. In many areas the soviets quickly assumed responsibility for public administration, succeeding the old class-biased local councils. Everywhere the spirit of autonomy made it difficult to exercise any centralized authority. The only national institution with any moral authority was the Congress of Soviets, convened in June and made up of delegates from local soviets all over the country. The congress ineffectively debated the country's enormous political problems and created a Central Executive Committee to sit in permanent session in Petrograd to safeguard the Revolution after the delegates returned home. But the war, the state of the economy, and the erosion of revolutionary hopes by legalistic quibbling were radicalizing opinion so rapidly that not even the soviets, let alone the Provisional Government, could keep up with the political mood of the people.

It is often claimed that the Russians lost their chance at constitutional freedom in 1917 because they did not really understand democracy, but this is unfair. In fact, they understood democracy all the better because of their experience under arbitrary rule. Their problem in 1917 was not their failure to apply democracy but their passion to carry it to excess—to extend it to areas (such as the economy and the military) where liberal regimes of the West did not dare to venture. The year 1917 was an orgy of democracy: in government, through radical decentralism in the soviets and the practice of instant election and recall of representatives; in industry, through the efforts of factory committees to impose control over factory management; in the army, through the abolition of the prerogatives of rank and the subordination of the chain of command to a panoply of debating committees; in the rural sector, through the democratization (by direct seizure) of the ultimate resource, the land. The democratization of institutional relationships and of the management of resources proceeded so fast and so far that it threatened to shatter the country's political and economic structure. At the same time it made it impossible for any central authority to reconcile all the conflicting demands of the diverse sectors of society, each of which undertook to realize its goals by direct action.

Russia's urban working class, strengthened numerically by wartime industrial expansion but beset by inflation and food shortages, was a paragon of Marxist virtue. Thanks to their experience of the previous two decades, the workers were organized, militant, and class-conscious, ready to join the ranks of the socialist parties. The fall of tsarism, for them, signaled the opportunity to achieve old demands—an eight-hour workday, a living wage, and an end to the arbitrary power of the employer. Strikes mounted throughout the country and the workers became ever more politicized, as inflation outstripped their wage gains. Factory committees demanded workers' control over the decisions of management; on occasion, managers were bodily ejected from the factories. The workers of Petrograd, the most sophisticated and the most militant, became the decisive force in the revolution.

For the peasants—more numerous than the workers, but slower to react politically—the Revolution meant above all an end to their age-old land hunger, still acute in the central and south-central portions of European Russia, where as much as half the arable land still remained in the possession of landlords. The provisional Government, hoping to keep land reform within legal channels by compensating the owners, set up a maze of local land committees but left final resolution of the problem to the anticipated Constituent Assembly. The peasants thereupon took the law into their own hands, as they had tried to do in 1905: during the summer and fall of 1917 a wave of violent seizures of landlord estates spread through the country. In many areas, the authority of the Provisional Government was reduced to a fiction.

The political force of the peasants was at first most clearly felt in the army, largely recruited from the villages. The rank and file in the armed forces, as in other segments of Russian society, took the fall of the tsar to mean the end of all forms of hierarchical command and humiliation. This was confirmed when, on March 14, regimental representatives to the fledgling Petrograd Soviet issued the celebrated "Order Number One," annulling the prerogatives of rank and authorizing the election of rank-and-file committees throughout the army and navy. As in civilian life, the reflexes of obedience vanished, and in some instances, especially in the navy, class grudges were vented in the lynching of officers. Weary of fighting and fearful of being sent into renewed combat, the troops anxiously awaited a decision on war and peace.

Kerensky, as minister of war, undertook to restore the army's fighting spirit by ordering an offensive on the southwestern front in June. Initial success against the Austrians soon collapsed in the face of counterattacking German reinforcements. Thereafter the Russian army was finished as a fighting machine; throughout the summer and fall soldiers deserted in droves, returning to their villages to share in the land seizures.

The breakdown of central authority suddenly liberated the non-Russian national minorities of the empire, who had all (except the Finns) previously been denied any form of local self-government. In these areas the soviets (or their local equivalent) automatically became organs of national autonomy, anticipating home rule in a loose Russian federation. Finland, with its own century-old institutions of government, quickly began to act like an independent country, and it was a short step for the new Soviet government to approve this status after the October Revolution. Elsewhere there was little outright talk of independence, the most restive part of the empire, Russian Poland, having been under German occupation since 1915. Potentially the most serious problem was the Ukraine, where nationalists in the *rada* (Kiev's equivalent of the soviet) demanded a degree of autonomy that the Petrograd cabinet refused to grant.

The radicalization of the country and the division of opinion over the war had already made the survival of the Provisional Cabinet dubious, when in mid-July a split over Ukrainian autonomy prompted the conservatives to resign and brought on the second major crisis in the Provisional Government. This was the signal to rebellious workers, soldiers, and sailors in Petrograd and its environs to stage armed demonstrations against the war and the government. For two days the tumult in the city's streets resembled that of the February Revolution. The Bolsheviks were suspected of planning a coup d'état, but they exerted no determined leadership, and the Provisional Government was finally able to bring in reliable troops from the front and put an end to the disturbances. In the midst of the crisis the government published charges—not without some basis—that the Bolsheviks were being subsidized by the Germans, and the party was outlawed. A couple of days later, just as the Germans were counterattacking decisively, Prince Lvov resigned the prime ministership and Kerensky took over.

Although it had weathered the storm from the left during those "July Days," the Provisional Government soon had to face the ire of the military command and the propertied classes, who feared the disintegration of all order and authority. Calling for a restoration of military discipline and reinvigoration of the war effort, conservatives found their champion in the chief of staff, General Lavr Kornilov, a career officer of humble origin. What then transpired is unclear, but it appears that Kornilov proposed to Kerensky that the soviets and the army committees be forcibly suppressed. Kerensky misunderstood or objected, and put him off. Kornilov then attempted to move his troops on Petrograd and disband the soviet, with or without Kerensky's blessing. But when the troops moved, there occurred a replay of the events of March: the soldiers fraternized with delegations from the city, defied orders, and dispersed. Kerensky, obliged to call upon all the left-wing elements in Petrograd to save his government, put Kornilov under arrest, but by this time (mid-September) the authority of his government had wholly dissipated. Left and right alike sought the first opportunity to remove him.

▪ The October Revolution

Candidates were not lacking to take the place of the Provisional Government as it faltered and splintered. Revolutionaries of every description had taken advantage of the amnesty to surface from the underground or to return from exile in Siberia or abroad. Few of them, even Bolsheviks, thought they could go much beyond the Provisional Government, but Lenin (in Zurich) and Trotsky (in New York) immediately realized that February was only the beginning of their revolutionary opportunity.

Seeing that a bourgeois leadership could actually take power in Russia, Lenin borrowed several leaves from Trotsky's book (without attribution). In line with the theory of permanent revolution, he now predicted that the workers would overthrow the "imperialist" Provisional Government, install the soviets in power, and sound the tocsin for world proletarian revolution. Whisked back to Russia with the connivance of the kaiser's government (Berlin was naturally eager to see the enemy politically destabilized), Lenin astounded the nation with a speech delivered upon his arrival in Petrograd at the Finland Station: "The specific feature of the present situation in Russia is that it represents a *transition* from the first stage of the revolution—which, owing to the insufficient class-consciousness and organization of the proletariat, placed the power in the hands of the bourgeoisie—*to the second* stage which must place the power in the hands of the proletariat and the poorest strata of the peasantry." So he declared in his "April Theses," setting the revolutionary direction for his party.

Week by week, as the masses grew more radical and confidence waned in the government's peace efforts, the influence of the Bolshevik Party grew. By summer, the Bolsheviks had won control of the Factory Committee movement and a strong place in the soviets (taking advantage of the workers' and soldiers' right to recall deputies and replace them with more radical representatives). Meanwhile a special Military Organization set up by the party established a following among the army committees. Secret funding from Germany helped the party build a mass-circulation press and a network of paid militants.

To be sure, the Bolsheviks suffered a setback during the July Days, when their headquarters and press were closed down and Lenin was forced into hiding. The Kerensky government did not fail to recognize its enemies or hesitate to take action against them. Unfortunately for the cause of moderation, the mood of the country, particularly of the urban workers and the army, was by this time more in tune with the extremists than with the government. Lenin's slogans—"Bread, Land, and Peace" and "All Power to the Soviets"—inspired multitudes. The swing to the left was accentuated by the Kornilov fiasco, so much so that in mid-September the Bolsheviks won majorities in the key Petrograd and Moscow soviets. Trotsky, formally joining the Bolshevik Party after making his way back from North America (he had been seized by the British in Halifax and briefly interned), became the new chairman of the Petrograd Soviet.

At this point Lenin was still hiding in Finland and working on *State and Revolution,* his manifesto against parliamentary democracy. Abruptly he decided that the time had come for the Bolsheviks to take power by an armed uprising in the name of the soviets. He wrote to his lieutenants in Petrograd: "The Bolsheviks, having obtained a majority in the Soviets of Workers' and Soldiers' Deputies of both capitals, can and *must* take state power into their own hands ... It would be naive to wait for a 'formal' majority for the Bolsheviks. No revolution ever waits for *that* ... History will not forgive us if we do not assume power now." Finding that the Bolshevik Central Committee was reluctant to take any precipitate action prior to the upcoming Second Congress of Soviets, which they expected to control, Lenin returned secretly to Petrograd to demand endorsement of his insurrectionary line. This he secured in an all-night meeting of the Central Committee on October 23, by a vote of ten to two (the two opposed were, ironically, his old lieutenants Grigori Zinoviev and Lyov Kamenev). The resolution set no specific date but merely "placed the armed uprising on the agenda."

The assumption of power by the Bolsheviks was quickly mythologized as the historic centerpiece in a secular state religion. The official version, accepted by most enemies of the Revolution as well, is that the Bolshevik Party overcame "strikebreaking" by Zinoviev and Kamenev and sabotage by Trotsky; drew up a plan of attack inspired by Lenin's genius; and at the decisive moment, on the eve of the Second Congress of Soviets, seized the city of Petrograd and overthrew the Provisional Government in order to present the soviet delegates with a fait accompli. In fact, the Central Committee, fearing a new Kornilov-style right-wing plot possibly involving the surrender of Petrograd to the Germans, never took the actual decision to seize power. Most of its members (including Trotsky and Stalin) were waiting for the Congress of Soviets to decide the issue, which was exactly what Lenin did not want. No record of any plan of attack has survived, but only the evidence of last-minute efforts to win control of the garrison for the defense of the Petrograd Soviet and the Congress. This was accomplished by the "Military Revolutionary Committee," which the soviet under Trotsky's direction had established to act as a center of command.

An uprising prior to the Congress did, however, take place, as the result of an unexpected incident. Kerensky, tired of negotiating with the soviet over control of the garrison, ordered officer cadets to close down the Bolshevik newspapers early on the morning of November 6 (October 24, Old Style), just a day before the Congress was set to convene. The Bolshevik Central Committee and the Military Revolutionary Committee, perceiving this as the first step in the long-feared counterrevolutionary conspiracy against the soviet, called out all their supporters in the garrison and among the workers' Red Guards. To everyone's surprise, the whole city fell into the hands of the Bolsheviks with scarcely a shot being fired. As Lenin said, "We found the power lying in the streets, and we picked it up." Both sides had overestimated the government's political and military strength. When the critical moment came, hardly anyone fought for Kerensky. Power was virtually won for the soviets before Lenin, still in hiding, even learned of the event. Late in the evening on November 6, he made his way by streetcar and then on foot to soviet headquarters at the Smolny Institute to find out what was really happening, and then to take command as the soviet consolidated its power.

The last act, on November 7, was an anticlimax: the so-called storming of the Winter Palace of the tsars, where the Provisional Cabinet held out while Kerensky fled in an American Embassy car to seek loyal troops at the front. The actual event (there are no photographs of it, only paintings that show it as it is supposed to be remembered) was more a mob scene than a military action. Revolutionaries surrounded the building and pressed inside, to the accompaniment of blank artillery fire, and the defending units—officer cadets and the Women's Battalion of Death—threw down their arms. There were few casualties on either side, and no recorded martyrs' deaths among the Bolsheviks at all. The ministers were found in the imperial dining room and arrested, and Russia's brief experiment in constitutionally inspired if not legitimized government came to an end. John Reed, the radical American journalist, described the scene in *Ten Days that Shook the World:*

Just as we came to the Morskaya somebody was shouting: "The *yunkers* [cadets] have sent word they want us to go and get them out!" Voices began to give commands, and in the thick gloom we made out a dark mass moving forward, silent but for the shuffle of feet and the clinking of arms. We fell in with the first ranks.

Like a black river, filling all the street, without song or cheer we poured through the Red Arch, where the man just ahead of me said in a low voice: "Look out, comrades! Don't trust them. They will fire, surely!" In the open we began to run, stooping low and bunching together, and jammed up suddenly behind the pedestal of the Alexander Column.

"How many of you did they kill?" I asked.

"I don't know. About ten . . ."

After a few minutes huddling there, some hundreds of men, the army seemed reassured and, without any orders, suddenly began again to flow forward. By this time, in the light that streamed out of all the Winter Palace windows, I could see that the first two or three hundred men were Red Guards, with only a few scattered soldiers. Over the barricade of firewood we clambered, and leaping down inside gave a triumphant shout as we stumbled on a heap of rifles thrown down by the *yunkers* who had stood there. On both sides of the main gateway the doors stood wide open, light streamed out, and from the huge pile came not the slightest sound.

Carried along by the eager wave of men we were swept into the right hand entrance, opening into a great bare vaulted room, the cellar of the East wing, from which issued a maze of corridors and stair-cases. A number of huge packing cases stood about, and upon these the Red Guards and soldiers fell furiously, battering them open with the butts of their rifles, and pulling out carpets, curtains, linen, porcelain plates, glassware. . . . One man went strutting around with a bronze clock perched on his shoulder; another found a plume of ostrich feathers, which he stuck in his hat. The looting was just beginning when somebody cried, "Comrades! Don't touch anything! Don't take anything! This is the property of the People!" Immediately twenty voices were crying, "Stop! Put everything back! Don't take anything! Property of the people!" Many hands dragged the spoilers down. Damask and tapestry were snatched from the arms of those who had them; two men took away the bronze clock. Roughly and hastily the things were crammed back in their cases, and self-appointed sentinels stood guard. It was all utterly spontaneous. Through corridors and up stair-cases the cry could be heard growing fainter and fainter in the distance, "Revolutionary discipline! Property of the People . . ."

After the capture of the Winter Palace, the Congress of Soviets needed only to recognize the fait accompli that Lenin had hoped for, and to proclaim itself along with the network of local soviets the sovereign government of Russia. This it did, as the moderate minority of Mensheviks and Socialist Revolutionaries walked out to protest the Bolsheviks' forcible overthrow of the Provisional Government. Interim legislative authority was vested in the Central Executive Committee of the Soviets, reconstituted with a pro-Bolshevik majority, while a new executive authority was proclaimed—the Council of People's Commissars. (The term "commissar," borrowed from the French republican tradition, was already widely used to mean an agent of the soviets.) Lenin naturally assumed the chairmanship of the new council, a post equivalent to prime minister, and Trotsky became commissar of foreign affairs. A committee took charge of the military, and a little-known professional revolutionary from Georgia, Joseph Dzhugashvili, alias Stalin, the Man of Steel, was made commissar of nationalities. Sweeping decrees, drafted mainly by Lenin, were forthwith issued to herald the conquests of the revolution: a decree on peace, calling on all warring governments to end hostilities; a decree on the land, abolishing private ownership and ratifying possession by the tillers of the soil; a decree on the right of self-determination, promising minorities the right to choose independence; and a decree on workers' control, ratifying the power of factory committees over business enterprise. All the forces that made the Bolsheviks' triumph possible—the workers, the peasants, the soldiers, the minorities—seemed to have achieved their most ardent demands.

Like the displacement of the tsar by the Provisional Government, the transfer of power to the soviets was quickly accepted almost everywhere in the country, with relatively little violence. Only in Moscow did the local military try to hold out against the soviet forces. Bitter fighting raged around the Kremlin for several days, with atrocities on both sides, until the beleaguered anti-Bolsheviks capitulated. Simultaneously Kerensky tried to fight his way back into Petrograd with a few thousand loyal troops, timing their arrival to coincide with an uprising by the cadets in the Officer Candidate Schools scattered through the city. The outcome was no different from that of the earlier attempts to move on the revolutionary capital in March and August. After brief fighting, Kerensky's forces dispersed or surrendered, and the deposed prime minister was compelled to go into hiding for the next several months until he was able to arrange his escape to England, and eventually to America. But the Revolution had now had its baptism of blood.

It remained to be seen how the Bolsheviks would wield and defend their newly won power. Some of them wanted to form a coalition government with the moderate minority in the soviets, but the moderates—the Mensheviks and the right wing of the Socialist Revolutionaries—refused to cooperate unless Lenin was excluded from the cabinet. Finally three representatives of the left wing of the Socialist Revolutionaries (the Left SRs) joined the Council of People's Commissars, where they remained until the crisis over war and peace in March 1918. As to other political rivals, Lenin showed his hand early by ordering the suppression of "bourgeois" newspapers and by creating, in December, the "All-Russian Extraordinary Commission to Combat Counterrevolution," commanded by the fanatical Polish Bolshevik Felix Dzerzhinsky. This body, known (from its Russian initials) as the "Cheka," was in fact a revived secret police and the ancestor of all the subsequent forms of this key totalitarian instrument.

The most ominous indication of the future direction of Soviet politics was the fate of the Constituent Assembly. As promised by the Provisional Government and demanded by the Bolsheviks, the Constituent Assembly was duly elected according to a law adopted under Kerensky but not implemented until after the October Revolution. Despite this timing, the elections were relatively free and honest, as shown by the fact that the ruling Bolsheviks placed only second in the count, behind the Socialist Revolutionaries with their vast peasant majority. The Bolsheviks were clearly the choice of urban Russia, but no more than that, and the party thus found itself in the dilemma anticipated by the theory of permanent revolution: the workers, sweeping into power in the key population centers, would have to confront the petty-bourgeois masses of the countryside. Lenin's answer was unequivocal: "To relinquish the sovereign power of the soviets, to relinquish the Soviet republic won by the people, for the sake of bourgeois parliamentarism and the Constituent Assembly, would now be a retrograde step and cause the collapse of the October workers' and peasants' revolution." Accordingly, after permitting the Constituent Assembly to convene in January 1918 for one day, under the presidency of the Socialist Revolutionary Chernov, Lenin ordered it dissolved. From that day forth, the Bolsheviks were committed to one-party dictatorship, whatever the cost in civil strife.

▪ The Legacy of Revolution

The future of Soviet Russia was not yet cast in iron by the October uprising. History still had great changes in store for the new system—changes that stemmed from the nature of revolution, the conditions of Russian life, and the personalities who were destined to place their stamp on the brave new world. Yet the violence of October, dividing victors from vanquished, was a giant historical step that could never be retraced. Having won power by means of force that was unplanned but not unintended, the Bolsheviks would not yield to any other method of political change. Although, oddly enough, they had lacked an explicit one-party philosophy before they took power, they were quick both to enforce and to justify the monopoly that success had conferred upon them. Claiming that their government was the embodiment of working-class rule, they denied political legitimacy to any other party and condoned the use of all forms of coercion and even terror to sustain their position.

The Bolshevik Revolution was a socialist revolution. Herein lay the key to the loyalties and enmities it aroused, foreign as well as domestic. The Bolsheviks and their followers were profoundly committed—whether by Marxist doctrine, Russian radical tradition, or personal experience—to destroy the role of private property in economic life. They thus departed radically from the American revolutionary tradition, not only in methods but in goals. It eventually became obvious that the Bolsheviks were ready to defend socialism by any means and to any extreme; halfway measures were to them only temporary tactical concessions.

In their commitment to socialism, the Bolsheviks went beyond the Marxist determinism that constrained their Menshevik cousins to withhold promises of radical economic change, however popular. They forgot that Marxism had prescribed industrial productivity as a precondition of socialism and had assigned capitalism the role of forcing inefficient private producers into a factory-style proletariat. The Bolsheviks tried to socialize everything, large and small, disregarding the unreadiness of Russian economic life for such a reordering. The result was not progress but retrogression: after smashing the unfinished structure of capitalism, the Bolsheviks found that their only institutional resource was the Russian tradition of centralized despotism.

The Bolsheviks were extremists in thought and action. They won and kept power because they were ready to use the methods that a society in the radical revolutionary phase would recognize and respect. Had they been less violent, more democratic, more legalistic, they would not have been Bolsheviks, and they would not have gained or held power at the critical moment. As the social strife of revolution peaks, democracy becomes more and more difficult to sustain. Moderates disqualify themselves from rule precisely because of their moderation. Typically only a party that is prepared to be violent and dictatorial can resolve the political crisis, put down its enemies, curb unruly elements, and direct the country toward stability—whether it looks ahead toward a new social order or backward toward the old.

No government, however, can rule through terror and fanaticism alone, and the Bolsheviks found before long that they would have to adjust their methods and their aspirations to the ebbing of revolutionary elation and to the ongoing realities of Russian life that still remained. And adjust they did, in a manner unique among revolutionaries, so successfully that the rule of their party has survived to this day. With this success came a singular burden: the Communists have had to defend the rule of a revolutionary movement after the revolution has ended, to reconcile utopian urges with the requirements of domestic and international power, and to explain to themselves, their children, and the world how this enterprise still embodies and justifies its origins. Russia's history since 1917 is the history of a revolutionary mystique that has lost its raison d'être but still commands the resources of one of the most powerful nations on earth.

6

Allied troops in Vladivostok

War, Intervention, and International Revolution

The Bolshevik Revolution of 1917 was a watershed in world politics as much as in the internal history of Russia. This was recognized immediately by the Revolution's leaders as well as by its enemies, though for reasons that in retrospect appear hysterical, peripheral, or misconstrued on both sides. Soviet Russia was condemned by the Allied powers because it betrayed their cause in the First World War. Virtually every foreign government shunned the Bolsheviks as instigators of world proletarian revolution, and Western leaders vented their moral outrage over the atrocities of the Soviet dictatorship and its repudiation of religion. But the major international impact of Russia's transformation was less exotic: a new Russian commitment to build unchallengeable national power. Soviet Russia defied the entire system of world politics and world economy, initially in the name of revolution, then in pursuit of national security against the "capitalist encirclement," and ultimately as the leader of a "socialist camp" that was to divide the world in competition with the capitalist West.

The Russian Revolution set up the confrontation between the United States and the Soviet Union that has dominated international politics in the second half of the twentieth century. To be sure, almost three decades elapsed before the bipolarity of the Cold War clearly emerged. Since then no country, no movement, no event has been unaffected by the state of relations between Washington and Moscow.

▪ World War and the Provisional Government

Neither the passions of the Russian revolutionaries nor the fear and anger that they inspired in Americans can be fully understood apart from the Revolution's wartime context. War set the stage for the events of February 1917, as it had in 1905. By its ineptitude and obtuseness, the Old Regime had dissipated the fund of patriotism that had inspired its citizens at the outbreak of war in 1914. Mismanagement of the war and military setbacks had caused a crisis of confidence among all social classes, a situation where casual riots could trigger the collapse of the government.

The fall of the monarchy did not end the question of the war. There were those who felt that Russia was now freer to prosecute the war in cooperation with its allies. Many others believed that the Revolution offered the opportunity for a negotiated peace. And there were a few who saw the war as a way of discrediting the Provisional Government and paving the way for a new revolution.

Initially, foreign minister Miliukov and the Provisional Government took the view that the end of tsarism made it all the more legit-

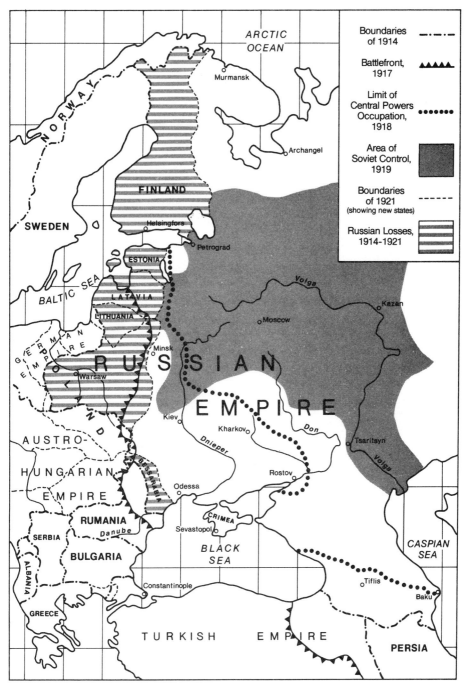

World War I and the Russian Revolution

imate for Russia to pursue its war aims, particularly the conquest of the Bosporus and the Dardanelles. Convinced that the war would generate enthusiasm for the new regime and vice versa, they proclaimed on March 7: "The government believes that the spirit of lofty patriotism, manifested during the struggle of the people against the Old Regime, would also inspire our valiant soldiers on the field of battle."

The overthrow of Nicholas II immediately improved Russia's relations with its democratic allies, now relieved of the burden of apologizing for their despotic partner. The U.S. government, still debating whether to intervene in the war against Germany, was the first to recognize the new regime in Petrograd. In his war message to Congress, President Wilson hailed the end of Russian autocracy: "Does not every American feel that assurance has been added to our hope for the future peace of the world by the wonderful and heartening things that have been happening within the last few weeks in Russia?" To the British and French, far from certain of victory at that point, even with the promise of American reinforcements at some future date, the new Russian regime meant first and foremost an invigoration of the war effort. Unfortunately, the Allied governments failed to foresee the ultimate cost to Russia of the Provisional Government's commitment to prosecuting the war.

From the outset, the Petrograd Soviet wanted to limit the international undertakings of the Provisional Government. Rejecting the legacy of imperialist ambition, the soviet borrowed a line from Wilson and called for a "democratic peace without annexations or indemnities." On March 14 it issued an "appeal to the people of the world," announcing that "the Russian democracy . . . will, by every means, resist the policy of conquest of its ruling classes, and it calls upon the people of Europe for concerted, decisive action in favor of peace." In the meantime, however, the soviet affirmed the defense of Russia against any attempt by the Central Powers to take advantage of the country's internal turmoil—a position that came to be known as "revolutionary defensism." Initially the Bolshevik Party was not opposed to this stance, and even Stalin supported it when he first returned from exile. It remained for Lenin to correct his followers in his April Theses: "In our attitude toward the war, which also under the new government of Lvov and Co. unquestionably remains on Russia's part a predatory imperialist war owing to the capitalist nature of that government, not the slightest concession to 'revolutionary defensism' is possible."

Political troubles commenced scarcely a month and a half after the February Revolution over the definition of Russia's obligations to its wartime allies. Pressured by the soviet to transmit its declaration on peace as an official note to the Allied governments, Miliukov persuaded the cabinet to add an "explanation" confirming Russia's continuing obligations. It was the release of this comment by the press on May 3 (April 20, Old Style) that precipitated the April Days and the reorganization of the government. Miliukov was replaced as foreign minister by liberal businessman Mikhail Tereshchenko, leaving Russia's foreign policy clouded with ambiguity.

Growing sentiment in favor of a negotiated peace prompted Allied efforts to revive the war spirit in Russia. Socialist members of the French and British governments traveled to Russia for this purpose, and in mid-June an American mission headed by former secretary of state Elihu Root reached Petrograd via Vladivostok and the Trans-Siberian Railway, bearing assurances of American support. Secretary of State Robert Lansing was candid with Wilson about the purpose of the visit: to "prevent the socialistic element in Russia from carrying out any plan which would destroy the efficiency of the Allied Powers." Meanwhile, socialists from neutral countries proposed a peace conference in Stockholm—a move that was publicly endorsed by the Petrograd Soviet. The anxious Allied governments at first temporized, but then, following the example of the United States, denied passports to their respective socialist party leaders and thus destroyed all prospects for the meeting. Ironically, the Allies' obstruction of such peace efforts helped undermine the friendly government in Russia, and contributed to what was from their point of view the diplomatic disaster of the Bolshevik Revolution.

Although support for a negotiated peace was increasing, the Provisional Cabinet and war minister Kerensky revived Miliukov's theory that the war would rebuild national morale. It was a fatal mistake. The collapse of Kerensky's offensive undid all his gains and accelerated the disintegration of the Russian army. Thereafter, all efforts to restore military discipline, especially the abortive putsch by General Kornilov, simply played into the hands of the extreme left.

By the fall of 1917 the issue of war and peace had provoked a crisis of confidence almost as severe as the reaction against the tsar. The Bolsheviks exploited this mood vigorously and successfully. As William Henry Chamberlin wrote in *The Russian Revolution: 1917–1921,* "By refusing to give up the utopian formula 'war to the victorious end' the Russian propertied and middle classes assured themselves revolution to the bitter end." Long afterward, Kerensky himself recognized that it had been a mistake to prosecute the war and blamed the Allies for failing to realize that revolutionary Russia would not support the old war aims. The Russian-American historian Michael Florinsky captured the irony of this when he wrote in *Russia: A History and Interpretation* that if Kerensky "had made immediate peace and given all land to the peasants, it is possible that Lenin would never have come to the Kremlin. Such a program, of course, *was* Bolshevism in 1917, and would have been vehemently opposed by the allies and by liberal Russians."

■ The Bolsheviks and the World

The beneficiaries of the Provisional Government's embarrassment over the war had long prepared themselves for their role. As Marxists and participants in the prewar Socialist International, the Bolsheviks were internationalist, anti-imperialist, and antimilitarist. In the shadow of war in 1914, socialists all over Europe thought they were strong enough to keep their governments from the precipice. They were more naively antinationalist then Marx himself, who, despite his famous dictum that the workers have no fatherland, played his favorites among the nations, disdained the Slavs, and hated Russia. When hostilities actually broke out, the leading members of the Socialist International opted to support the war efforts of their respective countries, and the international movement was left in ruins.

The war and the breakup of the Socialist International gave Lenin his chance for national and international notoriety. Finding a haven in neutral Switzerland, he wrote and organized furiously to discredit Europe's prowar socialist leaders and to lay the foundation of a new international organization rejecting the democratic tactics as well as the patriotic loyalties of socialism's old guard. Lenin was convinced that the war's carnage would soon turn the masses on both sides against their bourgeois governments and initiate the world proletarian revolution. He openly advocated the defeat of the imperial Russian regime: "For us, the Russian Social Democrats, there cannot be the slightest doubt that from the standpoint of the working class and of the laboring masses of all the nations of Russia, the lesser evil would be the defeat of the tsarist monarchy, the most reactionary and barbarous of governments." For workers everywhere, his slogan was "Transformation of the International War into a Civil War."

In 1916 Lenin amplified his revolutionary reasoning in the polemical work *Imperialism: The Highest Stage of Capitalism.* He argued that concentrated monopolies and competition among capitalist governments for markets and colonies would inevitably end in a war to the death—a safe prediction, since the anticipated war was already in progress. The war, Lenin held, presaged the end of capitalism and set the stage for the general proletarian revolution. This argument was not particularly original, but it ultimately became the most influential of all Lenin's doctrines. By the 1950s the theory of imperialism had become the ideological link aligning revolutionaries in the third world with the Soviet Union, simply because it identified capitalism with the old enemies of their nationalist aspirations.

Marxism's appeal as a vehicle for anti-Western nationalism is doubly paradoxical, in view of its Western origin and its internationalist principles. Many have mistakenly supposed (as did Americans with regard to Vietnam) that Marxists must necessarily be opposed to nationalism and that their doctrine admits of no end but Russian world domination. In fact, it is nationalism in many cases that has led people to Marxism via Lenin's theory of imperialism, and hence to the assumption that the Soviet Union ought to be their natural ally in the struggle against capitalist imperialism, colonialism, and neocolonialism. But even the Soviet Union has not been immune to nationalism and to motives of an imperialist character. In the Sino-Soviet schism, nationalism has actually proved capable of setting two major Marxist powers against each other.

If nationalism has played such a role as this in the Marxist movement, what is the meaning of the Marxist doctrine of world revolution? Contrary to widespread American belief, particularly in the early Cold War period, Marxism is not a prescription for world revolution by conquest. World revolution is only a prediction, still nominally subscribed to by the Soviets, of a movement that will emerge someday as a consequence of the economic contradictions of

imperialistic capitalism. Until 1917 Marxists expected this movement to begin not in Russia but in the most industrialized capitalized countries. Confronted at that point with the unexpected
opportunity (as they thought) to lead the way to socialism, Lenin
and the Bolsheviks adopted world revolution as the doctrinal rationale for their attempt to seize power prematurely in a relatively
backward country. In October, Lenin wrote, "There is no room for
doubt . . . We are on the threshold of a world proletarian revolution." In line with Trotsky's "permanent revolution," Russia was
supposed to inspire others with an armed uprising. "To 'wait' for the
Congress of Soviets, etc., under such conditions," Lenin went on,
"means *betraying internationalism,* betraying the cause of the international socialist revolution."

Some of Lenin's lieutenants, convinced after the victory that their
newly won power in Russia made no sense apart from the international revolution, took the doctrine further than their chief cared to
go. Under Bukharin's leadership these "Left Communists" resisted
peace with Germany and took the chance of jeopardizing the Soviet
regime by calling for "revolutionary war," not in the expectation of
conquest but as a rallying cry for the expected uprising of workers
all over Europe. Lenin's choice—to make peace with Germany and
forgo the dubious opportunity for world revolution at that risky
point—set the tactical priorities that the Soviet government has observed ever since: the security of Communist power in Russia took
precedence over any particular opportunities to advance the cause
of international revolution, unless the circumstances were such that
the two interests coincided. For some time, however, the Communists continued to believe both that world upheaval was imminent,
and that socialist revolutions were necessary in advanced countries
to assure the continuance of their own regime in Russia. The way
in which they adjusted, materially and ideologically, to a world
where they had to depend on their own power for survival proved
crucial in shaping the subsequent character of the Soviet system.

▪ Russia Leaves the War

One of the keys to the Bolsheviks' victory in 1917 was their ability to
identify the Provisional Government with the tsarist regime in its
pursuit of an imperialist war, and to establish themselves in the

public mind as the natural leaders of the antiwar movement. The Provisional Government counterattacked, for a time effectively, with the charge (published during the July Days) that Lenin and the Bolsheviks were German agents. This accusation was for years a major subject of contention between apologists and enemies of the Soviet regime. In retrospect, it is preposterous to consider Lenin anything but a determined revolutionary for whom the German government was as much an enemy as the Russian. Nevertheless it is apparent that Germany in 1917 was using what today would be called destabilizing tactics, to subsidize Russian revolutionaries and weaken the Provisional Government, which was, after all, its wartime enemy. Despite the flimsiness of the evidence cited by Kerensky's Ministry of Justice, the German archives that came to light after World War II reveal that substantial amounts of money had in fact reached the Bolsheviks and presumably other Russian radical groups by secret channels. After July 1917 the archival evidence dries up, suggesting that once the connection had been brought out into the open, the German government preferred to curtail the relationship.

Shortly after the July Days the Germans captured the Baltic city of Riga, and this combined with the Kornilov affair to create a state of hysteria among the revolutionaries in Petrograd. Just as in Paris in 1792, when the Bourbons were finally dethroned, it was fear of the outside enemy as an accomplice of counterrevolution that, more than any other factor, enabled the Bolshevik-led soviets to establish their influence over the garrisons in Petrograd and other major cities. At the same time, what were taken to be revolutionary rumblings in Germany, in the factories and in the navy, served Lenin as his main justification in calling for the Bolshevik seizure of power.

Consistent with his plan for exploiting the war to promote revolution, Lenin issued his Decree on Peace the very day after taking power: "The workers' and peasants' government . . . calls upon all the belligerent peoples and their governments to start immediate negotiations for a just, democratic peace." He obviously expected that the various imperialist governments would refuse to respond and would thereby invite internal revolution. But to the Allied governments and most opinion makers in the West, the Bolsheviks were mad anarchists and traitors, doomed to defeat in a matter of days. The Allies not only ignored the Soviet peace appeal but instructed their diplomatic missions in Petrograd to avoid any contact with the usurpers that might imply recognition. Warned Secretary of State Lansing, "If we should recognize them in Russia, we would encourage them and their followers in other lands."

Two weeks into the new regime, Trotsky formally invited the Allies and the Central Powers to initiate armistice negotiations. He also bgan publishing the wartime secret treaties, with all their imperialistic deals. The Allies, naturally, were shocked by what they regarded as Russia's desertion from their cause. Lansing called Trotsky's invitation "an appeal to the proletariat of all countries, to the ignorant and mentally deficient who by their numbers are urged to become masters." The Central Powers, on the other hand, jumped at the opportunity to negotiate a separate peace with Russia and thereby revive their hopes for victory in the West. An armistice along the generally dormant Eastern front was quickly arranged, and the two sides commenced peace negotiations at the town of Brest-Litovsk in German-occupied Russian Poland.

The Russian delegation to Brest-Litovsk engaged in a highly unconventional brand of diplomacy. Led by Trotsky as commissar of foreign affairs, they tried to use the negotiating table as a platform for revolutionary propaganda, hoping to arouse sympathy abroad. The representatives of the Central Powers impatiently pressed sweeping territorial claims upon the Russians and threatened to resume the conflict if their demands were not met. At this juncture, on January 20, 1918, two days after receipt of the enemy terms and the day after closing down the Constituent Assembly, Lenin astounded his lieutenants in the Bolshevik Party by suddenly and radically reversing his position on Russia's international relations and the peace negotiations with Germany. He came out solidly in favor of capitulating to Germany's imperialist demands and paying the price in territory to buy time and secure a "breathing space."

Lenin's "theses on peace" repelled most of the Bolshevik Party leadership, and bitter controversy ensued over acceptance of the German terms. Lenin argued pragmatically that the Bolshevik regime was doomed if it tried to continue the struggle. His more orthodox opponents, including Trotsky and Bukharin (then leader of the party's left wing), believed that Soviet Russia had to continue the war at all costs, no matter what the odds, in order to use it to revolutionize Europe. At Brest-Litovsk, Trotsky proposed the formula "No War, No Peace," defying the Germans to resume their advance in the face of world opinion. Bukharin, even more radical, called for guerrilla warfare, if need be falling back to the Urals and risking the very existence of the new Soviet regime in the hope of evoking a world revolutionary response. For these purists, revolutionary power in Russia meant nothing in the absence of international support, since they reasoned that if the revolution were confined to Russia alone, a workers' government in an overwhelmingly peasant country had little chance of survival and no chance of maintaining its proletarian character. But Germany soon forced the issue by suspending negotiations and attacking in the Baltic provinces. The Russian army could offer virtually no resistance, and, faced with the likely fall of Petrograd, Lenin prevailed. On February 23 the Bolshevik Central Committee accepted the German terms by only seven votes against Bukharin's four, while Trotsky's bloc of four abstained.

The Treaty of Brest-Litovsk, signed on March 3, 1918, was regarded at the time as truly Carthaginian. Russia had to concede German control of occupied Poland and of the Baltic provinces, and to recognize the independence of a German-dominated government in the Ukraine. Transcaucasia, with its oil resources, was surrendered to German and Turkish occupation. Having already conceded independence to Finland the previous December, Russia was now reduced to its borders before the time of Peter the Great, with the exception of the narrow window on the Baltic at Petrograd. This was the first major territorial setback suffered by Russia in almost four centuries. What was worse, from the standpoint of many Bolsheviks, was that Russia had to cease all revolutionary propaganda directed at the population of the Central Powers.

The Peace of Brest-Litovsk was opposed not only by Bukharin's group of Left Communists but also by the Bolsheviks' coalition partners, the Left Socialist Revolutionaries, and by practically all other political elements in Russia who were still at large. With this evidence of willingness to continue the war despite the odds, why did Lenin nevertheless insist on the peace? The Allied governments saw the obvious connection between the pre-October charges that Lenin was a German agent and his eagerness to meet Germany's conditions for peace. But alternatively, Leonard Schapiro has argued that Lenin favored the peace in order to distance himself from other political elements in the country, and thereby justify the dictatorship that he felt the revolutionary cause demanded.

■ Civil War

The breathing spell gained at Brest-Litovsk lasted scarcely two months. By May the civil war feared even by some Bolsheviks had become a reality, and two and a half years were to pass before armed resistance to Soviet rule ceased on Russian territory. Most of the formative period of the Communist regime, in which the early lines of internal and external policy were established, was a time of desperate struggle.

Even as the Brest-Litovsk Treaty was being debated, the revolutionary leaders took two symbolic steps that served further to mark the future off from the immediate past. They moved the capital of the country from exposed Petrograd back to inland Moscow where it had been before the era of Westernization, and, harking back to Marx's first revolutionary organization, the Communist League, they adopted the name "Communist" for the ruling party. Ever since, "Communism" with a capital *C* has denoted Lenin's methods of revolution and dictatorship in the service of extreme socialism, not to be confused with "communism" with a small *c*, meaning Marx's theoretical ideal of a communal society.

Civil war in Russia was a very different matter from civil war in the United States, in which one part of a sovereign state fought for independence. The Russian civil war resembled the English civil war of the seventeenth century and the Chinese civil war of the 1940s, as an armed struggle waged by rival political movements for control of the entire country. In England civil war erupted in the first stage of revolution, between the parliamentary camp and the adherents of the Old Regime who rallied around the king. In China it came at a later stage, and represented the path by which the revolutionary extremists—the Communists—fought their way to power. In Russia the extremists were already in power, controlling the capital and what there was of a central government, when a broad counterrevolutionary military effort was launched against them.

In a sense Russia was in a state of civil war from the first day of the October Revolution, since the enemies of the Bolsheviks—collectively known as the "Whites," in opposition to the "Reds"—never recognized the forcible takeover. Some areas were not brought under Bolshevik control until the civil war had ended. Though the power of the soviets was quickly asserted over most of the country following the Bolsheviks' victories in Petrograd and

Moscow, the new regime met stiff opposition in the Cossack region around Rostov-on-Don, and it failed to extend its authority to most national minority areas, including the Ukraine and Transcaucasia. Here the presence of Germany and its allies, still fighting the Soviet government until March 1918 and then vested with extensive occupation rights until the First World War ended in November, sufficed to block the consolidation of Communist control. Under the terms of the Treaty of Brest-Litovsk, Soviet Russia had to acknowledge the independence of a non-Communist Ukraine and of the three Transcaucasian regions of Georgia, Armenia, and Azerbaijan; Poland and the Baltic provinces were left under indefinite German occupation. In the meantime, numerous officers of the old Russian army, headed by General Kornilov, made their way to the Cossack region on the Don and organized a small "Volunteer Army," which managed to hold out against the motley units of sailors and Red Guards that the Soviet authorities sent against them.

The fortunes of the already troubled Soviet government took an abrupt turn for the worse in May 1918, when a curious incident precipitated the sudden expansion of civil war. Military units of Czech and Slovak troops, who had been captured while serving with the Austrians and organized to fight for the Allied cause, were being shipped out of the country via the only available route, the Trans-Siberian Railway to Vladivostok, so that they could sail to France and continue in the war. They were strung out in slow-moving trains all along the line from the Volga to the Far East, when at the station of Cheliabinsk in the Urals a clash occurred between the Czechs and some Hungarian prisoners who were being repatriated westward. Alarmed by Moscow's orders that they be disarmed, the Czechoslovaks took over every principal point along the railroad, and presented the anti-Communists throughout this vast and conservative area with the opportunity to overthrow the local soviets. At one stroke, Moscow lost control of more than half of Russia and had to prepare for a possible military threat from Siberia, while the Allied governments embraced the chance to sponsor an alternative to the Communist regime that would bring Russia back into the war against Germany. New anti-Communist governments, legitimized by the presence of Socialist Revolutionary members of the defunct Constituent Assembly, were quickly organized in the territory removed from Soviet control. Small but determined forces of anti-Communists and Czechs linked up and drove toward Moscow, reaching the key city of Kazan at the great bend of the Volga early in August. It was in the course of this advance that the Soviet authorities guarding the tsar and his family in the city of Yekaterinburg (now Sverdlovsk) in the Urals received authorization to execute them in order to forestall their rescue by the Whites. (The story that the youngest daughter, Anastasia, survived the massacre and escaped abroad has been neither proven nor refuted definitively.)

Faced with a mortal challenge, the Soviet government took drastic steps. To replace the imperial army, it recruited a new "Workers' and Peasants' Red Army," organized by commissar of war Trotsky (who had quit the Foreign Commissariat to protest the Brest-Litovsk treaty) on lines of strict military discipline and command. As if this were not enough to shock the purists in the Communist Party, Trotsky employed former imperial officers to fill the leadership vacuum—often by threatening their families, always by offering preferential pay—and then installed loyal Communists as "military commissars" alongside the unit commanders to ensure their political reliability. (This was the origin of the present system of political control over the military.) At the same time, compulsory military service was reinstated to build the rank and file of the new Red Army. Surprisingly, the system worked: it provided the force that stopped the first drive on Moscow and ultimately secured victory for the Reds over the Whites.

Civil war is one of the most vicious of human experiences, when all order and trust disappear and the most barbaric atrocities are committed on neighbors and countrymen. An assassination attempt in August 1918 left Lenin wounded and the Petrograd Cheka chief dead. This triggered systematic "Red Terror" against actual or suspected enemies of the Soviet regime, with summary executions and the shooting of hostages. The Whites replied in kind, hunting down suspected Bolsheviks in areas they controlled and again inciting anti-Jewish pogroms.

None of this is surprising to people who have survived three-quarters of the twentieth century and witnessed the behavior of revolutionaries and counterrevolutionaries around the world. When revolution leads to civil war, the chances for the decent politics of democratic moderation are reduced to nil, while the extremes of left and right engage in a death struggle. So it was in Russia, as the Communist swing to the fanatical left was matched by the exclusion of all but confirmed counterrevolutionaries from the leadership of the Whites. By the end of 1918 the Right Socialist Revolutionaries who had initiated the anti-Communist regimes were eliminated in favor of what amounted to proto-fascist military dictatorships—enemies not only of the workers' revolution but of the peasants' and national minorities' revolutions as well. In November, with the Allies' blessing, Admiral Alexander Kolchak (former commander of the Black Sea Fleet) ousted the democratic elements from his government in Siberia and proclaimed himself "Supreme Ruler" of Russia. Meanwhile, the Mensheviks, who tried to hold the middle ground and never overtly joined the counterrevolution, were victimized by both sides.

In the fall of 1918 the Soviets gained a brief respite when Germany capitulated to the Western Allies and the Treaty of Brest-Litovsk was annulled. The winter and spring of 1919 were a time of revolutionary upheaval throughout the territories of the defeated Central Powers, and it seemed to Moscow that the hour of world proletarian revolution had struck after all. In March 1919, the Russian leaders challenged the whole capitalist world by creating the Communist International, while the Allies stepped up their intervention in the civil war with the direct aim of helping the Whites destroy the Bolshevik menace.

The most serious threat to the Soviet regime came in the spring and summer of 1919, when the White forces again took the offensive, with Allied financial and logistical support. The Soviet-held heartland of European Russia was assaulted by Kolchak's forces pushing west from Siberia, by the Cossacks and the Volunteer Army (commanded by General Anton Denikin after Kornilov was killed in action) striking from the south, and by a British-supported force which had been mobilized in Estonia under General Nikolai Yudenich in an effort to take Petrograd. Fortunately for the Red Army, it was operating on interior lines against widely separated enemy armies, and hence could concentrate its counterthrusts against one segment of the adversary at a time. By early summer the Red Army had thrown Kolchak back into Siberia; early in 1920 he was captured and executed in Irkutsk. Meanwhile, Yudenich was repulsed twice in his efforts to reach Petrograd, but Denikin's forces surged over southern Russia and the Ukraine and struck northward, in the fall of 1919, to within two hundred miles of Moscow. The Red Army, with General Budenny's legendary cavalry in the lead, coun-

terattacked, broke Denikin's overextended front, and sent the
Whites into a rout from which they never recovered. The remnants
of Denikin's army regrouped in the Crimea early in 1920, where the
command passed to Baron Pyotr Wrangel. Distracted for the next
few months by hostilities with the newly independent Republic of
Poland, the Red Army turned back in the fall to dispose of Wrangel.
His army, and the thousands of civilian refugees who accompanied
it, successfully evacuated the Crimea and dispersed throughout Europe to join the White Russian emigration. This marked the end of
the civil war.

In retrospect, the failure of the Whites is easy to explain. It was
impossible to connect their various zones of control, and this weakened them strategically. They were beset by political divisions as
well—among the parties ranging from moderate left to far right, between the politicians and the military, and, most serious of all, between the White governments and the populations under their
control. The dominant military faction repudiated every one of the
conquests of the Revolution: the soviets, the breakup of the estates,
the separation of church and state, the rights of religious minorities,
the autonomy and equality of national minorities, not to mention
the socialized economy and workers' control. The ardent Russian
nationalism of the Whites made their position particularly awkward
because many of their base areas were inhabited by non-Russians;
at the same time, their appeal to rank-and-file Russians was compromised by their identification with foreign intervention. As in
1917, the Communists owed their victory less to their own strength
than to the weaknesses of their enemies.

The civil war cost Russia dear, not so much in battle casualties,
because the numbers involved in combat were relatively small, but
in economic dislocation and in the violence done to the whole social
fabric. Hundreds of thousands of people died (more often by summary execution than in battle) or were left homeless or orphaned.
The transportation network was a shambles, large-scale industry
had virtually ground to a halt, the currency was worthless, city
dwellers were starving, and the peasants were enraged by the practice of grain requisitioning. Some two million "class enemies" were
forced to flee the country, ridding it of the most ardent opponents of
the Revolution but at the same time depriving Russian society
of many of its most educated, Westernized, and creative people.
Even the proletariat was decimated: the most politically aroused

workers joined the government (if they had not already fallen on the battlefield), and many of the others drifted back to their ancestral villages.

▪ Allied Intervention

The intervention of the Allied powers in the Russian civil war has been the subject of unending controversy. In the Soviet view, naturally, it was a conspiracy to put down the revolutionary threat to capitalism and rescue Western stock- and bondholders. Admittedly such motives were present in the minds of many Allied leaders, notably Georges Clemenceau and Winston Churchill. Yet as George Kennan and others have demonstrated, intervention cannot be understood without reference to the war with Germany.

Gripped by a sense of betrayal when the new Soviet government called for peace, and fearful that Germany could win the war by throwing its forces to the western front before U.S. troops arrived in strength, the Allied governments immediately looked for ways to support anti-Bolshevik Russians, in order to keep Russia in the war and restore the eastern front against Germany. American skepticism discouraged the earliest projects proposed by the French, British, and Japanese, except for financial aid to the Cossacks resisting Soviet rule.

Soviet repudiation of Russia's international debts in December 1917 had surprisingly little documented repercussion. At the time, the war and the Brest-Litovsk negotiations overshadowed all other concerns among the Allies. The U.S. government declined to make an issue of Russia's default on bonds that had been sold to Americans before the United States entered the war, and the old Russian Embassy was able to continue to meet the interest due for more than a year by dipping into funds that Washington had loaned the Provisional Government. Not until February 1918 did the Allies formally protest the debt default—to no avail.

At this point, when the breakdown of the Brest-Litovsk negotiations led to the resumption of hostilities by Germany, Allied officials momentarily thought they might collaborate with the Soviets. The latter quickly made known their readiness to accept the help of the capitalist devils if it meant survival against the Germans—or even the opportunity to frustrate Japanese designs on Siberia. Even after the peace treaty had been signed but prior to its formal ratification, Trotsky asked the unofficial American go-between, Red Cross representative Raymond Robins, if American aid might be forthcoming. Ambassador Francis supported the approach. But for reasons that were never determined, the military attaché who had been entrusted with the dispatch of Trotsky's note to Washington failed to cable it until days had passed; hence, there was no timely reply from Washington and no cause for Lenin, had he so chosen, to hold up ratification of the treaty. Nevertheless, Washington remained apprehensive about intervention, and particularly about the Japanese. To the Congress of Soviets assembled to ratify the treaty, President Wilson telegraphed a reaffirmation of the commitment to self-determination he had just expressed in January in his famous "Fourteen Points." He offered "the sincere sympathy which the people of the United States feel for the Russian people at this moment when the German power has been thrust in to interrupt and turn back the whole struggle for freedom and substitute the wishes of Germany for the purposes of the people of Russia." But he continued to avoid the issue of cooperating with the Bolsheviks. The congress replied defiantly by calling upon "the toiling masses of all bourgeois countries" to "throw off the yoke of capitalism."

Intervention had begun, meanwhile, at the northern port of Murmansk, where, with the acquiescence of the Soviet government, the British landed marines to prevent the Germans from seizing Allied war materials accumulated at the port. A harbinger of a more serious situation was the landing of a Japanese contingent in Vladivostok in April, on the pretext of protecting Japanese nationals. The Western Allies made other efforts to secure the Soviets' permission to intervene against the Germans, but these came to naught, due to growing mutual suspicion and the establishment of Soviet-German diplomatic relations pursuant to Brest-Litovsk.

The uprising of the Czechoslovak Legion and the eruption of widespread civil war in Russia in May 1918 made intervention a far more serious enterprise for the Allies, who were now no longer concerned about obtaining Soviet approval. The Soviet government has always maintained that (in the words of the official *History of Soviet Foreign Policy*) "the anti-Soviet revolt of the Czechoslovak Corps was part and parcel of the Allied intervention in southern Russia . . . The Corps command made a criminal deal with Entente representatives to start an anti-Soviet revolt." This may have been a logical presumption at the time, but it is not supported by the facts. To be sure, as early as March the Allied War Council had entertained the idea of somehow using the Czechs against the Germans, but would have done so only with Moscow's concurrence; and in fact the Soviet government agreed early in May to a plan (never implemented) to redeploy some of the Czech troops to protect the northern ports. It was because of Moscow's reluctance to let them pass quickly to Vladivostok and join the Japanese that the Czechs found themselves extended along the Trans-Siberian Railway in a manner that made no sense militarily. However, they still had some of their weapons, and their anti-Communist command structure was still intact; amid the general confusion they were the most respectable fighting force in Russia. They knew that they might have to fight their way out, and had already made contact with anti-Bolshevik officers in Siberia when the Cheliabinsk incident of May 14 and Moscow's reaction forced their hand and precipitated the general uprising.

In respone to the Czechs' success, the Allied governments took up the idea of intervention in earnest. At the moment, the massive German offensive on the western front had cast London and Paris into a desperate mood, and the Allied leadership grasped at the notion of reestablishing a battle line somewhere in Russia to contain the Germans in the east. Funds were scattered by the British and French among various anti-Communist groups. The first major step came in the north, when the British, alarmed by the victory of the German-supported counterrevolutionaries in Finland and the presumed threat to Murmansk, asked the United States to reinforce the small garrison there. On June 1 Wilson agreed to do this if the troops could be spared. One hundred fifty marines from the cruiser Olympia landed on June 11, followed by British reinforcements later in the month, all with the approval of the local soviet. Allied activity in Murmansk was strongly protested by the Germans as a violation of their peace treaty with Russia, and Moscow then tried to assert its authority by force. This occasioned the first armed clash between the Allies and the Russians, when Soviet units encountered the British south of Murmansk on June 27 and were forced to retreat.

Broader action was not long in coming. On July 2, as the Germans were pressing their final drive toward Paris, the Allied Supreme War Council formalized the policy of intervention in a final appeal to President Wilson: "The Supreme War Council consider that since its last meeting a complete change has come over the situation in Russia and Siberia, which makes Allied intervention in these countries an urgent and imperative necessity." The Czechs' success and the deterioration of the Bolsheviks' position left intervention as the only means "to save Russia from the establishment of autocracy supported by German bayonets" and "to shorten the war by the reconstitution of the Russian front." Already agonizing over the situation in Russia, Wilson responded to the Allies on two levels: he would reject intervention in principle, but cooperate in practice. "It is the clear and fixed judgment of the Government of the United States," he wrote on July 17, "that military intervention . . . would add to the present sad confusion in Russia rather than cure it, injure her rather than help her, and that it would be of no advantage in the prosecution of our main design, to win the war against Germany. It cannot, therefore, take part in such intervention or sanction it in principle." But Wilson believed that the United States was obligated to help the Czechs, as well as to guard the munition dumps, and concluded, "The Government of the United States is glad to contribute the small force at its disposal for that purpose."

With American acquiescence assured, the Allies immediately implemented their plan for intervention around Russia's periphery. Their moves came at the most critical point in the Russian civil war, when the Whites, with Czech aid, captured Kazan and were about to push on to Moscow. Almost simultaneously, in early August, the British occupied Archangel and rushed a small force via Persia to Baku in a vain effort to forestall Turkish occupation of the oil fields. At the same time the Japanese, citing American approval as cover for their expansionist designs, returned in force to Vladivostok. On August 16 an American contingent of 7,500 landed there, and early in September a smaller U.S. force joined the British at Archangel.

The role of the United States, limited by Wilson's reservations, was never more than a token affair throughout the intervention. The troops in the Far East, under the cautious General William Graves, confined themselves to observing the vastly greater Japanese forces, and apart from a couple of minor skirmishes they avoided combat with the Russians. At Archangel, however, the Americans were immediately thrown into action under the command of the British; they suffered about 150 dead before they were withdrawn in July 1919. In neither case was their mission clear, either militarily or politically. General Graves wrote in his memoirs, "I was in command of the United States troops sent to Siberia and, I must admit, I do not know what the United States was trying to accomplish by military intervention." The same uncertainty was evidently felt at the highest levels, and in late September 1919 the U.S. government concluded, "The ideas and purposes of the Allies with respect to military operations in Siberia and on the 'Volga front' are ideas and purposes with which we have no sympathy." The Allies were informed that American troops would be restricted to guarding the ports, and that no more would be sent.

None of the Allied moves in 1918 had more than marginal influence on the civil strife in Russia, as the Soviet government in Moscow fought off attacks by anti-Bolshevik forces striking from the south and the east. But just as the tide turned decisively in favor of the Allies on the western front, ending the need for intervention in Russia, Soviet relations with the Entente reached their nadir. As a result of Allied occupation of the ports, acts of terror by the Communists, the temporary arrest of some British and French citizens, and the death of the British naval attaché in a scuffle, all contact between Moscow and the West came to an end. Even the military in Germany entertained thoughts of anti-Communist intervention, but the German government was mollified by further Soviet economic concessions. Soon afterward, in September, came the publication of the Sisson Documents—papers procured by the American propaganda chief in Russia, Edgar Sisson, purporting to prove that the Bolsheviks were German hirelings, after as well as before the October Revolution. Long afterward, George Kennan demonstrated that this material had been forged by anti-Communist Russians (unlike the later evidence from the German archives showing that subsidies had been paid to the Bolsheviks before the July Days); but at the time, Sisson's allegations confirmed the Allies in their belief that there could be no dealing with the Reds.

This mood did not abate when Germany, seeing that the war was lost on the western front and that its allies were succumbing one by one, sought armistice terms in October. If anything, the pending collapse of the Central Powers raised new concerns—well founded, as it turned out—that revolutionary influence might spread in the defeated enemy countries. Soviet overtures in early November for a resolution of the intervention were brushed aside.

The Armistice of November 11, 1918, ending hostilities between Germany and the Western powers, totally changed the circumstances and the rationale for Allied intervention in Russia. For those leaders who were antirevolutionary as much as they were anti-

German, intervention was all the more necessary to destroy the Communist threat—to "kill the snake in its own nest," as Winston Churchill, then First Lord of the Admiralty, urged. Now that Germany had been disposed of, Clemenceau's government became equally antirevolutionary. In mid-December, French troops were landed in Odessa to keep the Communists out of the Ukraine as the Germans evacuated it. This was the high point of direct intervention. Allied leaders on the liberal side, particularly Prime Minister David Lloyd George and President Wilson (together with many Congressional leaders), saw no justification for continuing the policy, and were reinforced in this view by Admiral Kolchak's right-wing coup in Siberia less than a week after the Armistice. (Kolchak's coup, along with the end of the war, terminated the involvement of Czech troops in the White cause, though the last of them were not evacuated from Siberia until mid-1920.) Allied policy after the end of 1918 was an inconsistent compromise: the Allies would not intervene directly in Russia except to maintain the troops already there; they would continue logistical support to their "loyal friends"; and, of special importance, they would back the governments of Poland and the three Baltic republics that had declared independence when Germany collapsed.

In January 1919 the heads of government of the "Allied and Associated Powers"—Wilson, Lloyd George, Clemenceau, Prime Minister Vittorio Orlando of Italy, and all the other leaders of the victorious coalition—gathered in Paris to write the terms of peace with Germany and the Central Powers. Their first decision was to exclude Soviet Russia from the conference, though they agreed to respond to Moscow's peace advances and support a negotiated end to the civil war and intervention. With Lloyd George's support, President Wilson called for a special Russian peace conference including the Reds, the Whites, and the Allies, to be held on the Turkish island of Prinkipo. The French and the Whites' representatives in Paris vetoed the idea. In March a special U.S. mission to Moscow headed by William Bullitt (later to become the first U.S. ambassador after Recognition in 1933) obtained Soviet agreement to peace terms that would leave the Whites in control of the border areas of Russia, but again the opportunity was rejected by the leaders in Paris. Nevertheless, the United States and Britain were able to dissuade the French from Marshal Foch's plan for massive Allied intervention in the White cause, and Clemenceau ordered an end to his Odessa venture, embarrassed as it was by Communist agitation and an incipient mutiny among the troops.

Subsequent vacillation and dissension among the Allied governments spelled the end of intervention. In May 1919 the Allies promised aid to Admiral Kolchak's regime in Siberia, in return for his recognition of Russia's international debts and a promise not to restore the monarchy. At the same time they agreed to continue the commercial blockade of Communist Russia despite the fact that the Versailles treaties had ended the state of war with the Central Powers. Nevertheless, Britain and the United States withdrew their forces from northern Russia in the summer and early fall of 1919, even though Lloyd George had to accede to Parliament's determination to continue funding Kolchak, Denikin, and Yudenich.

With the collapse of the major White armies, Lloyd George declared intervention at an end. In January 1920 the Allies lifted their blockade of Russia, and the British, French, and Italians agreed to resume trade relations. The United States followed suit, allowing American firms to do business with the Soviets "at their own risk." On April 1 the last Americans on Russian territory left Vladivostok. Following Allied advice, the Baltic states and Finland concluded treaties of peace and diplomatic recognition with Soviet Russia, opening the path to subsequent normalization of Moscow's relations with the outside world. The only remaining intervention consisted of the Japanese encampments around Vladivostok, until, partly as a result of American pressure, these forces withdrew in 1922.

Intervention, in the end, completely failed either to get Russia back into the war or to destroy the Russian Revolution on its own ground. The White armies, on whom the Allied governments had rested their hopes, collapsed one after the other in late 1919 and 1920. As in other episodes of antirevolutionary intervention around the world (one thinks of China and Vietnam), Allied intervention was sufficient to engage Russia in bitter hostility with the West but was inadequate to overthrow the Soviet government.

The Allies never made a unified effort. Their motives were mixed, they were divided in their interests, and they were internally split— along familiar right-left lines—between the advocates and opponents of intervention. The French were the most devoted to the antirevolutionary crusade, and Clemenceau at least succeeded in establishing a *cordon sanitaire* of new anti-Communist governments, to wall off revolutionary Russia from the West. Britain was probably the most divided, as the Labour Party assailed intervention and the cabinet vacillated. The United States could no longer justify the venture after the war with Germany ended. And the Japanese, seeking to dominate all of East Asia, were motivated by their own imperialistic aspirations.

Thanks ultimately to Allied indecisiveness and disunity, the Soviet government was able not only to subdue the Whites but to recover some of the non-Russian minority regions that had seceded from the Russian republic during the civil war. To the west, Poland and the three Baltic states, Estonia, Latvia, and Lithuania, which had been under German occupation until the Armistice, declared their independence and successfully maintained it with the blessing of the Allies. In the Ukraine, on the other hand, the Red Army overcame the Ukrainian nationalists and peasant anarchists and installed a nominally independent government of Communist-controlled soviets. To the northwest, in Belorussia, Moscow set up another nominal government when the German forces withdrew. To the southwest, Soviet forces were unable to prevent Rumania from occupying the border province of Bessarabia and holding it, unrecognized by Moscow, until 1940. But the Transcaucasian states of Azerbaijan, Armenia, and Georgia, abandoned by the Allies, were easily taken by the Red Army in 1920 and 1921, and placed under the jurisdiction of the local Communists.

The political and psychological implications of the intervention are ambiguous. Did it implant in the Soviet mind a jutified fear of the capitalist powers, and thereby account for the Soviets' subsequent hostility and defensiveness? Or was it a temporary phenomenon of the revolutionary epoch that did not necessarily dictate how either the Russians or outside powers would perceive their national interests in the future? To be sure, the memory of intervention has been regularly invoked by the Soviets to justify their suspicion of the Western Powers whenever their policy called for such a stance. But considering the vast changes in Soviet personnel, interests, and style that have occurred since the Revolution, particularly during Stalin's time, it is difficult to argue that the intervention could have had such an inexorable influence. For the West, it is equally difficult to formulate a simple conclusion. Certainly the war against Communism in 1918 and 1919 convinced many people that the Russians were a natural and enduring enemy. Many others, however, came to believe in the futility and even immorality of intervention. If the

Soviets' description of intervention as a concerted and single-minded conspiracy were true, nothing could have prevented its success.

▪ World Revolution

Governmental and business leaders in the West saw ample reason for intervening in revolutionary Russia. The Communist government was regarded as a mad aberration that could easily be swept away if the forces of order in Russia had a little help. The Communists had repudiated all the norms of traditional relations among states—obligations of an ally, confidentiality of diplomatic exchanges, respect for private property, and the obligations of foreign debt. They went so far as to call upon the people of other countries to overthrow their respective political and economic systems.

The Communists continued to anticipate world revolution even though they decided at Brest-Litovsk to make the security of the Soviet state their first priority. When the war ended in November 1918, amid revolutionary upheaval in Germany, Austria, and Hungary, it seemed to them that the dawn of the long-awaited day had come. The great hope was Germany, where a wave of radicalism following the kaiser's abdication and the creation of a provisional republic seemed to recapitulate the story of Russia's Provisional Government; but reverses soon came. An uprising by the pro-Soviet Spartacus League in Berlin in January 1919 was put down by the Social-Democratic government, and the left-wing leaders Karl Liebknecht and Rosa Luxemburg were murdered. A so-called soviet government proclaimed in Munich in April 1919 was easily overturned by central government troops. More substantial was the assumption of power in newly independent Hungary by a revolutionary government in which the radicals led by Bela Kun assumed the upper hand. This was the only case in those years when a foreign country was actually ruled for a time by pro-Soviet elements. The experiment was ended abruptly in mid-1919 by French and Rumanian military intervention at a time when Soviet Russia, fighting for its survival in the civil war, could not possibly come to the aid of the Hungarians.

Early in 1919, when revolution appeared to be brewing almost everywhere in Europe, Lenin took steps to realize his dream for a new international of truly revolutionary socialist parties. Convening a conference of foreign socialists—mostly people who just happened to be in Moscow, with no particular credentials from home—Lenin proclaimed the assemblage to be the first and founding congress of the Communist International (the "Comintern," or Third International, in opposition to the Second International of the moderate socialists). This ad hoc gesture had a dramatic effect on both the sympathizers and enemies of the Russian Revolution. "Our task," declared Trotsky in the manifesto he wrote for the occasion, "is to generalize the revolutionary experience of the working class, to cleanse the movement of the disintegrating admixtures of opportunism and social patriotism, to mobilize the forces of all genuinely revolutionary parties of the world proletariat, and thereby facilitate and hasten the victory of the Communist revolution throughout the world."

Encouraged by the message from Moscow, radical sympathizers with the Russian Revolution in socialist parties around the world systematically split away from their stodgy parent bodies to form new Communist parties, affiliated with the Third International. In some instances—notably in France and Italy, and the more leftist Independent Social Democratic Party in Germany—the Communists were able to capture half or more of the existing socialist organization. Elsewhere, including the United States, the Communists remained very small splinter groups.

All of the new Communist parties, large and small, were first brought together in a true international revolutionary forum at the Second Congress of the Communist International. This gathering, held in Moscow in July 1920, was the first real congress of the international movement, with genuine delegates representing their respective national parties. Lenin wasted no time in imposing his Russian-style politics on the often unruly or romantic foreign radicals, in the form of his "twenty-one conditions" of conspiratorial tactics and Moscow-oriented discipline, which all Communists were compelled to acknowledge. These steps molded the shape of the international Communist movement for the next forty years—doctrinaire, conspiratorial, monolithic, and Soviet-controlled according to the rationale of "proletarian internationalism."

The Communist belief in world revolution was not so much a commitment to forcible expansion as it was an expectation of favorable political developments in the outside world. However, the Soviet government never hesitated to intervene, either by political means or direct action, when it had the opportunity to promote the fortunes of its foreign sympathizers.

One of these instances was the brief war with independent Poland that broke out in the spring of 1920, when Poland tried to recover Russian territories that it had held before the partitions of the eighteenth century. The Red Army counterattacked successfully, and Moscow immediately saw an opportunity to establish a friendly revolutionary regime on Russia's western border. Only assistance from France and adroit generalship by Poland's Marshal Jozef Pilsudski enabled the Poles to drive the Soviets back and negotiate peace in early 1921. The Treaty of Riga was favorable to Poland, establishing the boundary that divided Poland and Russia until 1939 and left several million speakers of Ukrainian and Belorussian on the Polish side of the line.

The other, more improbable area of Communist expansion was Outer Mongolia. Russian influence had already penetrated there when the government of Nicholas II took advantage of China's disunity following the revolution of 1911 to promote an autonomous regime in the area. Mongolia was used as a base by both White Russian and Japanese forces during the Russian civil war, and in response Moscow cultivated a pro-Communist separatist movement among the Mongols. In July 1921 the Red Army marched in and set up the Mongolian People's Republic, under the Leninist-style rule of the Mongolian People's Party. Thus was created the first true Soviet satellite state, which hewed strictly to the Soviet line in foreign policy, though it was permitted more moderate internal policies.

These instances of the expansionary use of force were responses to specific situations that arose on Russia's borders. Elsewhere, until the Second World War, the international impact of the Russian Revolution was political rather than military. The Communist appeal found many followers, and not only among the industrial working class on which Marxism theoretically depended. Often the best-organized workers in the West remained with the socialists, while the Communists attracted the unemployed or the marginally employed—the "lumpenproletariat." For many frustrated intellectuals, the Soviet experiment was appealing as a demonstration that social transformation was possible. "I have been over to the future, and it works," announced the American writer and social critic Lincoln Steffens, after returning from Moscow with the Bullitt mission.

Equally significant was the reaction in the underdeveloped and colonial societies of the East, where, for intellectuals in particular, the Russian Revolution with its anti-imperialist flavor suggested a path of struggle for national independence or regeneration. These sentiments, though they did not fit the Marxist stereotype of proletarian revolution and often emanated from quite bourgeois circles, were welcomed by the Russian leadership. Shortly after the Second Comintern Congress, a "Congress of the Peoples of the East" was held in the Transcaucasian city of Baku to initiate an anti-imperialist movement with Soviet support. Said Lenin of this new strategy, "The road to Paris lies through Peking."

Despite the hopes of 1919 and 1920, the world revolution so ardently expected by the Communists failed to materialize. Communist insurrections were put down, Communist political advances were contained, and by 1921, just as the Soviets were consolidating their power within Russia, they had to concede the "stabilization of capitalism." This fact had deep implications for Soviet thinking, both practical and theoretical, about the relationship of the revolutionary government to the outside world. On the practical plane, it meant switching from a revolutionary foreign policy to a more or less conventional one in order to survive as a government. On the theoretical plane, the stabilization of capitalism meant that the Russians would have to rethink completely the relationship between their successful consolidation of power and the presumed need for a world revolution to sustain that power. This problem underlay Stalin's theory of "socialism in one country," a proposition of great importance in the subsequent development of Communism (see Chapter 7). But the Soviet leaders continued to view themselves as international pariahs, confronting a menacing "capitalist encirclement." At the same time, they had acquired a disciplined following abroad, which became an unconventional but effective instrument of Soviet foreign policy throughout the next three and a half decades.

The international effect of Communist revolutionary talk in the early years was primarily reactive. The Comintern failed to bring about Communist revolution anywhere outside Russia, but it did succeed in provoking serious antirevolutionary and even antidemocratic movements. Anti-Communism drew people to fascism when it first appeared in Italy in the early 1920s, to the right-wing dictatorships that followed in east-central Europe, and ultimately to the

Nazi Party in Germany, all of which suppressed the local Communists along with other opposition parties. Though democratic government stood much more firmly in Britain and France, the politics of both countries were polarized throughout the interwar period over confrontation or accommodation with Communist Russia.

In the United States, the intensity of the response to the Communist challenge had more to do with stresses and conflicts in American society than with the behavior of Soviet Russia, as repellent or threatening as that may have been. The Russian Revolution caught the United States at a time of deeply unsettling social change, intensified by U.S. involvement in the First World War. The social fabric was strained by the class struggle, the assimilation of millions of new immigrants, the women's rights movement, and the country's entry into the world power arena. Antiwar protests by groups such as the Socialist Party and the anarchist Industrial Workers of the World (IWW, the "Wobblies") had aroused public hostility against radicals even before the October Revolution. Then the appearance of Bolshevism, with its repudiation of every ideal cherished in America, brought on a national panic, far surpassing the reactions of the European powers that were much more directly confronted with Communism.

American radicals, like the socialists in Europe, had divided over the war, and the antiwar tendency was the main source of sympathy for the Bolsheviks. The Socialist Party, which under Eugene Debs had won 7 percent of the vote in the presidential election of 1912, was permanently crippled by dissension over the war, as well as by governmental repression. In 1918 Debs became the first and only defeated presidential candidate to be jailed for his opinions.

When the kaiser's vanquished militarism yielded its place in international concern to Lenin's world revolution, America's attention turned inward. There was, of course, no reason at the time for fearing the Soviet state, hemmed in as it was by the European powers; Americans were more concerned about the Communists' propaganda impact on life in the United States. By the same token, what slight sympathy there was for Communism was inspired more by issues and frustrations in American life than by any real understanding of what was going on in the land of the Soviets.

American Communism has never attracted a significant fraction of the industrial working class, or even of the largest and most exploited ethnic minority, the blacks. Moreover, the left, already divided by the war, was split even more deeply by the Russian Revolution. Moderates recoiled from the Soviet dictatorship and its use of terror, while radicals saw in Bolshevism the inspiration for their own revolutionary efforts. The American Communist Party, formed in September 1919 from the pro-Bolshevik wing of the Socialist Party, enlisted the immigrant east European workers of radical persuasion. The rival organization, set up at the same time, the Communist Labor Party, attracted native American intellectuals (John Reed was one of its founders) for whom the Russian Revolution seemed to promise a new social order. The two rival parties eventually merged, but only after an irreversible ebb tide was running in the fortunes of both.

The appearance within their midst of such sworn enemies of civilization horrified most Americans. So began that unique and traumatic period of national hysteria, the Great Red Scare, compounded of inherent social stress, radical excesses, and the panic of politicians scurrying to show their intransigence in the face of the Bolshevik menace. The tone was set early in 1919 when reports that the Bolsheviks had proclaimed the "nationalization of women" inflamed the minds of already anxious puritans. Senator Henry Myers of Montana read into the Congressional Record some rumored acts of this sort by a provincial soviet: "They have utterly destroyed marriage, the home, the fireside, the family, the cornerstones of all civilization, all society. They have undertaken to destroy what God created and ordained." This and other atrocity tales, both real and fictional, made a profound impression on the American public. Woodrow Wilson himself succumbed to the prevailing hysteria, warning, in one of his last speeches, against "the poison of disorder, the poison of revolt, the poison of chaos ... It is the negation of everything that is American." In the absence of a secure peace, "that poison will steadily spread, more and more rapidly until it may be that even this beloved land of ours will be distracted and distorted by it."

In the spring of 1919 a number of bombings by anonymous terrorists heightened public fears; the targets included the home of Attorney General A. Mitchell Palmer. In the fall, a series of alarming strikes including steel workers, coal miners, and the Boston police force made revolution seem like a real possibility. The strikes failed, amid charges that they were the work of Bolshevik plotters, and the union movement did not recover until the 1930s. The patriotic organizations that had been born during the war, together with right-wing extremists from the Ku Klux Klan, succeeded in making any form of liberalism or radicalism sound like treason. Vigilante justice was meted out to unionists and suspected radicals in towns across the country. Finally, in November, to drive home the new orthodoxy of "Americanism," Palmer's Justice Department began raiding leftist meetings, arresting radicals, and deporting accused "anarchists." Moscow's unofficial trade representative, the German-Russian engineer Ludwig Martens, had his New York office raided, and eventually was hounded out of the country. A key figure in all this work was the new head of the Justice Department's General Intelligence Division—a twenty-six-year-old zealot, fresh out of law school, by the name of John Edgar Hoover.

By the spring of 1920 the Red Scare was subsiding, and with it Palmer's presidential hopes (though the prize of the vice-presidency went to Massachusetts governor Calvin Coolidge for breaking the Boston police strike). The radicals had been subdued, and the nation was headed back to the comforts of isolationism and business as usual. But all the sensational first impressions about the Communist "monsters" persisted, while new and less spectacular changes in Soviet Russia failed to reach the public consciousness. Radicalism at home was taken simply as a projection of Communism abroad, guided by the insidious Marxist doctrine. Diplomatic recognition was out of the question, despite the fact that most other powers resumed ordinary relations with Russia in the early and mid-twenties. Nonrecognition, of course, did not prevent American business from pursuing profitable commercial ventures with the Soviets. The important thing, from the standpoint of domestic politics, was the appearance of unrelenting hostility.

7

Stalin and Politburo members at the Moscow Soviet, 1935
(Molotov fourth from right, Khrushchev at far right)

The Evolution of the Soviet Regime

First impressions die hard. So it was with the traumatic imprint of the Bolshevik Revolution upon the
world's perception of Soviet Russia. Later changes in
the Soviet system, no matter how substantial, were
often obscured by the initial revulsion or enthusiasm

that the Communists had aroused in their first few years.

These fixed perceptions have constantly impeded a realistic understanding of the Soviet system. What so many people, both enemies and supporters of the Soviets, fail to realize is that the most distinctive features of the system today are products not of the Revolution but of the two decades of wrenching change that followed it. From near-feudalism and the fanatical strife of civil war, Russia's path led through famine, purges, and foreign invasion to the disciplined industrialism that has enabled the Soviet Union to become one of the world's superpowers.

Even Soviet spokesmen have never been able to portray their system clearly, forced as they are to cast all historical explanations in terms of Marxist doctrine. According to the official view, the Soviet system is a deliberate implementation of the classless society predicted by Marx: the working class took power under the leadership of its Communist vanguard, beat back its enemies at home and abroad, and laid the basis for the ultimate society of communism while leading the international struggle against capitalist imperialism. Taking this image for granted, most outsiders have placed Soviet political philosophy on the extreme left and have endorsed or condemned it according to their own location on the political spectrum. The most impassioned anti-Communists do not dispute the Soviets' Marxist version of events; they simply denounce both theory and practice as the evil manifestations of a diabolical plot, first against the people of Russia and then against the world.

Critics and supporters alike tend to view the Soviet system in a historical vacuum, ignoring the fact that the ideological impetus of Marxism was only one of several powerful influences that shaped the postrevolutionary regime. Others, as we have seen, were the trauma of revolution and civil war, Russian habits of despotism, the costs of industrialization and national power in a half-modern country, the threats and opportunities posed by the international environment, and the role of fanatical dictators. Fusing and interacting during the two decades after the Revolution in a manner neither anticipated nor understood by Russia's Marxist leaders, these elements yielded the extraordinarily stable system that has been in place since the Second World War.

Historians generally agree on the main phases of Russia's postrevolutionary transformation. A period of revolutionary extremism, characterized by civil war, terror, and the utopian measures of War

Communism, began shortly after the Bolshevik coup and extended to 1921. Then came the Thermidorean reaction of the Russian Revolution, when the Communist regime was forced to retreat, ease up, and consolidate in the years of the New Economic Policy. Following the NEP came the Stalin Revolution of the late 1920s and early 1930s. This phase culminated in Stalin's Great Purge, and then yielded, in spirit if not in method, to an era of distinctly conservative consolidation, when Russia made its closest approach to a restoration of the prerevolutionary order. All these wrenching changes, however, were obscured by the continuity of Communist Party rule and Communist ideology.

■ Lenin's Dictatorship and War Communism

During its first few months, the Soviet government took a relatively moderate course. Following up the early decrees that had simply ratified what the workers, peasants, and national minorities had done for themselves in 1917, the Council of People's Commissars enacted a series of legal reforms comparable to what had been in force throughout liberal Europe for generations: titles of nobility were abolished; church and state were officially separated and education was secularized (assuring the enmity of the Orthodox Church); provisions were made for civil marriage and expeditious divorce; men and women of all classes were granted equality before the law. On February 14, 1918, the calendar was brought into line with the Western, Gregorian calendar, ending the thirteen-day lag. Four redundant letters were purged from the Russian alphabet.

Other early Soviet measures were more radical: the abolition of the courts and police, which were replaced by revolutionary tribunals and workers' militia (even today the regular uniformed police are known as *militsiya*); the municipalization of private housing; the abolition of the stock market and the suppression of dividend payments. Most business enterprise had not as yet been socialized, though workers' control had effectively superseded private management, and production had plummeted. A Supreme Economic Council was set up to bring some order into the chaos of industry.

Late in December 1917 came the first major act of nationalization: the entire banking system was taken over by the state, without compensation. In February 1918 the Soviet authorities repudiated all debts and bonds of previous Russian governments. Most serious of all, the new regime began to respond to the food supply crisis inherited from its predecessors by requisitioning foodstuffs, principally grain, from peasants who would not sell it for the depreciating currency. This threatened to set the Soviet government at odds with the vast majority of the population, who were just beginning to enjoy the fruits of the Revolution. But the most violent acts of these early months were the work of local soviets or workers, who meted out to the "bourgeois" their idea of revolutionary justice, ranging from confiscation of homes to summary executions.

The first internal crisis in the Soviet government occurred in February and March 1918. Protesting Lenin's decision to accept Germany's peace terms and give up the opportunity to promote world revolution, the antipeace idealists, led by Bukharin, almost split the party. At one point they even discussed with the Left Socialist Revolutionaries the idea of reshuffling the cabinet and easing Lenin out (a plan that the prosecution magnified into an alleged assassination plot when Bukharin was placed on trial for his life during the purges of the 1930s). When Lenin prevailed, Bukharin's group—the Left Communists, as they styled themselves—resigned all their party and government posts, while the Left Socialist Revolutionaries pulled their representatives out of the Council of People's Commissars and joined the beleaguered opposition of Mensheviks and Right Socialist Revolutionaries in the soviets. Shortly afterward the Left Communists took issue with Lenin on domestic issues as well as on foreign policy. They denounced his betrayal of workers' control in industry and his call for centralized administration of the economy.

The outbreak of civil war intensified the revolutionary struggle. In June the Right Socialist Revolutionaries and the Mensheviks were excluded from legal participation in the soviets—in effect, banned. In the following month, the Left Socialist Revolutionaries attempted to seize power in Moscow and provoke resumption of the war by assassinating the German ambassador. The Communist authorities easily put down the uprising, outlawed their former allies, and ended the last non-Communist political activity in soviet-held territories. Thus, the Communist Party achieved a political monopoly—a goal that it had never announced but readily legitimized after the fact by declaring a requirement of Marxism.

At the same time that it suppressed the non-Communist parties, the Soviet leadership plunged into an ultra-radical economic program. All large-scale businesses were nationalized and placed under the control of the Supreme Economic Council. In the following months smaller businesses were nationalized as well, until by the end of 1918 the entire urban sector of the economy had been socialized and placed under central or municipal administration. Lacking a blueprint in Marxist theory for running this system, the Communists turned for their model to Germany's World War I mobilization of industry, known as War Socialism. Meanwhile, grain requisitioning was stepped up to feed the army and save the cities from starvation, since inflation had disrupted normal urban-rural exchange. In the name of class war and Communist equalization, the fiscal situation was hailed as a virtue: the "withering-away of money" heralded the day when a natural economy based on barter and equal rations for all would supplant the commercial exchange of capitalism. These were the features of War Communism which guided the Soviet regime for the next two and a half years.

Just as terror and fanaticism were reaching a peak, the Soviet leaders proclaimed a constitution for what they called the Russian Soviet Federated Socialist Republic (RSFSR). No novelty was involved: the constitution merely codified the system of local soviets, congresses, Central Executive Committee, and Council of People's Commissars that had been operating since the October Revolution. Elections and representative procedures were still taken seriously, and so to bolster the workers' revolution the constitution gave urban areas an eight-to-one representational advantage over rural districts, more than offsetting the peasants' numbers. And, in a reversal of the prerevolutionary class bias, former "exploiters" and members of the clergy were denied the right to vote or to hold office. In reality the ban meant little, since the Communist Party monopoly had already nullified revolutionary principles of electoral participation. The 1918 Soviet constitution survived on paper until 1936, when Stalin recast it in a more conventional form.

One cannot stress too much the impact of the civil war on the fledgling Marxist regime. Threatened with political extinction, Lenin and his party grasped at every expedient to mobilize for war, crush dissent, and stay in power. They succeeded at a price: the profound and permanent militarization of the Communist system of rule.

To be sure, Lenin had pursued the military analogy when he formulated his notion of the Bolshevik Party. However, in 1917 the party grew rapidly beyond the hard core of professional revolutionaries, and behaved more democratically than it ever had, or ever would again. Debate and factional opposition continued at every level throughout the civil war; but in the course of that struggle for survival the leaders took a number of steps to restructure the party along military lines. Party discipline required members to implement orders wherever they were assigned to work in government, industry, or the army. The party thereby became a control network extending the power of its leaders through all public institutions. Thanks to the Communist monopoly on participation in the soviets and in their central and local executive bodies, political decision making shifted from the government to the party committees at each administrative level. Within both government and party, power was progressively concentrated at the center. At the same time, reinforcing the trend to centralism, power at each level began to shift from elected committees to individual executives—that is, to the party secretaries, nominally elected but in practice appointed by the higher leadership. The hierarchy of secretaries, with their paid staffs, constituted the "apparatus" of the party, and this network persists to the present day as the Soviet Union's real inner power structure, around which the civil government, the armed forces, and the other institutions of Soviet life operate within their defined scope.

The trend toward bureaucratic rule was given official sanction when, in March 1919, the Eighth Party Congress resolved to require "the strictest centralism" and "outright military discipline." To streamline the leadership, the congress created within the Central Committee of the party three new entitites: the Politburo, the Orgburo, and the Secretariat. The first and last have survived as the key executive and organizational bodies in the Soviet power structure; the Orgburo, designed to work with local party organizations, was eventually absorbed into the Secretariat.

These changes in the party's modus operandi did not go unchallenged. As the White counterrevolution abated with the defeat of Kolchak and Denikin, purists in the left wing of the Communist Party picked up the theme of the Left Communists of 1918 and began attacking bureaucratic centralism wherever they saw it—in the party, in the government, in the army, in the administration of industry. Most famous among the leaders of this effort was Alexandra Kollontai, a radical feminist, a proponent of free love and the only high-ranking woman in the party.

There were precedents for these ultra-left protests in the English and French revolutions, when idealist groups such as the Levellers and the Enragés railed at the betrayal of the poor by revolutionary dictatorships. In their suspicion of bureaucrats and experts and their belief that all intellectuals should periodically do manual work, the Russian ultras prefigured the antimanagerial bias of the West's "New Left" of the 1960s and even the Cultural Revolution in China.

Late in 1920 and early in 1921, it seemed that the Russian ultra-left, consisting of the "Group of Democratic Centralists" and the "Workers' Opposition," might be able to force upon the one-party regime a system of open factional competition such as the one that developed out of the Mexican Revolution at about this time. Ironically, it was at the Tenth Party Congress—the first after the end of the civil war—that Lenin successfully invoked the disciplinarian principles reinforced by that struggle, condemned the ultra-leftists as a "petty-bourgeois anarcho-syndicalist deviation," and secured an outright ban on factional competition. With this, the party took a giant step toward institutionalizing in its ranks the "culture of War Communism" (as Robert Tucker has termed it) and laid the foundations on which Stalin was later to build his personal dictatorship.

▪ Building Socialism and the New Economic Policy

It is often said that Russia was too backward to sustain the aspirations of socialism without dictatorship—in other words, that the Russian Revolution was premature. But Russia was neither extreme nor unusual in this respect. As a result of the gap between economic performance and political enthusiasm, all revolutions tend to outrun the current resources of society, and all are in that sense premature.

As the stages of a revolution unfold, one party after another finds that its theoretical premises fail as guides to policy decisions. Each social group is left to respond according to its crude emotional predispositions, be they legalistic, fanatical, or merely opportunistic. The Bolsheviks took power despite their Marxist belief (shared with the Mensheviks) that Russia was industrially underdeveloped and lacked an adequate working-class base to sustain socialism. Lenin convinced himself that the workers could smash the "bourgeois state," curb the capitalists, and form an alliance with the peasants until international revolution broke out, as he expected it would in a matter of months. Until the spring of 1918, however, Lenin's strategy was relatively cautious—"one foot in socialism," he called it. Then, in the face of the food supply crisis and the expansion of civil war, he abruptly adopted a program of coercive utopian socialism: he declared war on the peasants and on all forms of private enterprise, large and small, with his policies of grain requisitioning and total nationalization. Thus, in the sectors of the Russian economy where capitalist concentration had not yet squeezed out the small producers, as predicted by Marx in *Das Kapital,* Lenin acted according to old Russian biases against the petty trader and in favor of coercive authority, even though the effect was economically counterproductive and politically self-destructive. During the era of War Communism the Communist leaders, isolated and imperiled, forgot all their Marxist premises about the dependence of political possibilities on the progress of the economy, and reverted to the crudest Russian methods to ensure their survival.

The fact that the Soviet regime did survive, in a backward country isolated from political developments abroad, contradicted the philosophy on which the regime depended for its own sense of legitimacy. This theoretical quandary led, after Lenin's death, to the celebrated controversy between the Stalin and Trotsky camps over "socialism in one country"—a debate concerned less with foreign policy (as many observers took it to be) than with the metaphysical question of whether socialism could be considered complete and secure in Russia without world revolution. Trotsky's group claimed that it could not, and tried to use this reasoning to discredit the party leadership. Stalin's group countered by manipulating quotations from Lenin so as to suggest that Russia could build socialism on its own resources. The upshot of Stalin's victory was not a change in the Soviets' cautious foreign policy, but a trend-setting step toward the controlled interpretation of Marxist theory for political purposes.

The way in which Marxist-Leninist ideology is apprehended, interpreted, used, and enforced in the Soviet Union defies common sense. On the one hand, the Communist authorities have rigidly maintained the ideology and inculcated it through all available media. On the other hand, the Soviet regime has in practice contradicted some of the most fundamental assumptions of the Marxist-Leninist world view. The power of the state has intensified rather than withered; political power has overshadowed economic factors in steering the development of the system; the ideal of equalitarian-

ism has been abandoned and a new privileged ruling class of bureaucrats has arisen; internationalism has been enlisted in the service of Russian nationalism.

As a result of the tension between theory and expediency, ideology has lost its guiding, prescriptive character for the Soviet leadership. Hannah Arendt, in *The Origins of Totalitarianism,* noted the
"freedom from the content of their own ideologies which character-
izes the highest rank of the totalitarian hierarcy." In the hands of
strong leaders who could make ideology mean whatever was convenient for them without fear of contradiction, Marxism-Leninism became largely a system of self-justification and legitimation for the
Soviet regime, with incidental value as propaganda directed toward
the gullible at home and abroad. Ideology is still reflected in policy
only where it dovetails with the power-conscious concerns of the
leadership—mainly in the economic sphere, with the maintenance
of the collective farms and central economic planning despite the
cost in efficiency that these entail. In other areas, ideology is used
simply to maintain mental discipline and conformity among both
the hierarchy and the masses. Ideology functions in the Soviet system as a sort of nontheistic religion, couched in the language of science but demanding faith in its infallibility from all its loyal
communicants.

The discrepancy between Marxist-Leninist theory and Soviet
practice, coupled with the ruling party's commitment to uphold the
theory for reasons of legitimation and discipline, has had profound
consequences for the behavior of the Soviet political system. Here is
where the Soviets' concept of ideology differs most markedly from
"ideology" as it is understood elsewhere and was understood by
Marx—that is, as a system of belief more or less spontaneously generated by a party or a class to legitimize their interests. It is sometimes asked whether the United States, too, might have an ideology,
and whether the Supreme Court's reinterpretation of the Constitution might correspond to the reinterpretation of Marxism in the Soviet Union. In fact, there is no American comparison with the way
the Soviets enforce conformity to the official ideology, deny any discrepancy between theory and reality, and claim that the current interpretation of theory is the version that has always been valid.

Maintaining a belief system of the Soviet kind requires control
over every aspect of intellectual and cultural activity in the country.
This, in turn, severely inhibits the creativity of the nation in many

areas. The party feels compelled to manipulate its own history, to sustain its claims of infallibility despite the crimes or errors of particular leaders, who become historical scapegoats. Issues of the past as well as the present are denied and repressed, and Trotsky remains the devil incarnate.

The dogmatic imperatives of official thinking have made it impossible for the Soviets to allow the free flow of people and information across its borders. The regime exhorts its citizens to exercise "vigilance" against any infection by foreign ideas or "anti-Soviet ideology." This attitude has continually thwarted the popular American aim of "mutual understanding between peoples." There is nothing that the Soviet authorities, in their concern for their own political security, will oppose more than a genuine opportunity for understanding between their people and the outside world.

In 1921 the system of War Communism collapsed. World war, revolution, and civil war had devastated the Russian economy, and the attempted remedies of War Communism had only made matters worse. Measures of coercion and fiat brought privation and starvation to the entire country. Wildcat strikes, peasant uprisings, and factional dissent within the Communist Party testified to the limits of the nation's endurance. Most serious of all was a revolt by the soldiers and sailors at the naval base of Kronstadt (outside Petrograd), who called for a "third revolution of the toilers" against the "commissarocracy." Lenin realized what other revolutionaries, including Robespierre, had learned too late: a country cannot tolerate the strain of revolutionary fanaticism, strife, and sacrifice for more than a limited time. At the Tenth Party Congress in March 1921, he announced a "strategic retreat."

Lenin's key move in what soon came to be known as the New Economic Policy was to halt the requisitioning of food from the peasants and instead charge them a fixed tax (initially a "tax in kind," because the currency was worthless). The plan encouraged them to produce whatever surplus they could and sell it on the open market. In turn, this provision required the restoration of a stable currency (the gold standard was reinstated a couple of years later) and the tolerance of private trade. Small business was denationalized, leaving only the "commanding heights" of banking, public services, large-scale industry, and mining under the direct administration of the state. Even here (according to Lenin's new theory of "state capitalism"), decentralization, profit-and-loss accounting, and managerial responsibility became the rule. The last vestiges of workers' control in industry were eliminated, and the trade unions, under party control, were relegated to the role they had under capitalism: bargaining with management over wages and working conditions. (Strikes, though never legalized, occasionally took place.) Equality of wages was shelved as a goal in favor of incentive pay and differentials, to reward skill and responsibility and to attract qualified managerial personnel, whatever their social background. Trotsky described the overall system as "market socialism": the state owned the key enterprises and reaped the profits, but allowed supply and demand to determine prices, guide the decisions of economic units, and fuel the further development of the economy.

The NEP was an immediate success, particularly in comparison to the grim years that preceded it. When famine struck the southern part of the country in 1921–22, Moscow opened the frontiers to international relief efforts (spearheaded by the American Relief Administration under Herbert Hoover), and the crisis was weathered. By the mid-1920s food production was back to prewar levels and industrial output nearly so. Russians of all classes later looked back on these few years as a golden age of consumer satisfaction.

Although the NEP in many respects signaled an era of relaxation and normalcy, this was not so politically. The Communist Party held its monopoly all the more firmly; anti-Communists were put on trial and Communist dissidents were purged from the party. Faced with an exhausted and latently hostile population, the party leadership stressed the Leninist principles of party unity and discipline even more than in the dark days of the civil war. However, outright terror was abated when the Cheka was reorganized as the GPU— the "State Political Administration."

In the cultural realm, which was coming back to life after the disruptions of the civil war, the NEP allowed creative freedom as long as overt political opposition was avoided. Russian artists and writers of various contending schools rejoined the international modernist movement. Education for the rural population in literacy and the rudiments of technology became a major priority; the Communists talked of a "cultural revolution" to prepare the peasants for socialism.

One of the lasting creations of the NEP was the present federal structure of the USSR. This again was the product of expediency rather than theory, since Lenin's doctrine of self-determination had allowed the minorities only the choice between independence and citizenship in a centralized Russian state. Unwilling to let any part of the empire go, the Communists compromised by recognizing the minorities within a federal system and granting them rights of linguistic and cultural identity even though their politics were dictated by the party leadership in Moscow. On this basis the RSFSR and the five other nominally independent but Moscow-sponsored Soviet republics—the Ukraine, Belorussia, Georgia, Armenia, and Azerbaijan—joined together by treaty in 1922 to form the Union of Soviet Socialist Republics.

The NEP and the reforms associated with it seem in retrospect a reasonable compromise between revolutionary ideals and Russian reality, once the convulsion of the Revolution itself had subsided. Indeed, the NEP model—market socialism with substantial cultural and religious freedom, governed by Communist parties that confine themselves to "authoritarian" rather than "totalitarian" methods of rule—has become a recurring pattern since World War II in those Communist countries of Eastern Europe that have managed to preserve some measure of internal freedom of action independent of Soviet dictation: Yugoslavia since 1948, Poland between 1956 and 1981, Hungary since the early 1960s, and to a degree China since the death of Mao Tse-tung in 1976. But in Russia the NEP papered over some serious weaknesses. Agriculture was still backward, and the most productive units had been lost when the estates were divided in 1917. The peasants consumed more than before the Revolution, and the balance that they marketed was sufficient only for domestic needs; Russia's traditional grain exports were wiped out, and with them much of the foreign exchange needed for industrial imports. Industry, once restored to prewar levels, would be costly to expand, and the country had no ready source of capital because foreign investment was politically unacceptable. The Communists faced the same fundamental dilemma that had plagued them ever since they took power: Having overthrown capitalism before it had finished its task of industrial expansion and business concentration, how were they to complete the process of economic development? Russia had all the problems of an underdeveloped country that aims simultaneously at industrial prowess, national power, consumer affluence, and defiance of the international money market.

The economic quandary of the NEP led to an extended debate among party leaders and professional economists over ways to continue Russia's industrialization. The official view was represented by Bukharin, who had switched from the radical to the pragmatic wing of the party when he saw that the NEP was inevitable. Bukharin favored gradual and balanced industrial development through the mechanisms of market socialism, so that consumer demand would make light industry profitable and thereby indirectly stimulate the growth of heavy industry. The opposition, led by Trotsky and the economist Yevgeni Preobrazhensky, argued for direct development of heavy industry by planned governmental investments. These would be financed by higher taxes and the avowed exploitation of the peasants and small proprietors—in other words, by "primary socialist accumulation," paralleling the "primary capitalist accumulation" described by Marx in *Das Kapital.*

Through an odd political twist, the Trotskyist plan, based on forced savings and the command economy, became the basis of the economics of Stalinism. It was an effective route to industrial power, as the record of the 1930s and the Second World War proved, but terribly costly in human as well as economic terms. And it was not the only possible means of achieving rapid industrialization, as analysts of the Soviet system since Stalin's time tend to forget. One alternative was state-guided capitalism, as in Japan. Another was Bukharin's market socialism. Russia's choices—in 1917 to exclude capitalism, then in 1928 to exclude market socialism—were made not on economic but on political grounds.

▪ The Stalin Revolution

The comparative tranquillity of the NEP years was rudely interrupted in 1928–29 by a new period of violent transformation in Russian life, in some respects exceeding the Revolution in the depth and permanency of its impact. This was, for lack of a better term, the era of the Stalin Revolution, extending from the late twenties to the mid-thirties. Together with the October Revolution and the civil war, it was a decisive episode in fashioning the distinctive features of the present Soviet system. In the words of dissident physicist Andrei Sakharov, "The bases and structure of society that were formed in the Stalin era have been preserved to this day."

According to many commentators, both Communist and anti-

Communist, the Stalin Revolution merely returned to the socialist principles of 1917 after the temporary breathing spell of the NEP. Others contend that the Stalin Revolution was a new phenomenon, grounded in Russian problems and habits, perhaps, but not necessarily derived from the Bolshevism of 1917, and in some basic respects a repudiation of it. There is some truth to both viewpoints: the Stalin Revolution was neither a simple renewal of revolutionary extremism nor an aberration unrelated to it. It was the Russian manifestation of the usual sequel to revolution: the postrevolutionary dictatorship.

Although the details naturally differ from one country to another, the government in this phase is always built around an egocentric and opportunistic leader who takes advantage of a society's postrevolutionary fatigue and the weakening of both traditional and revolutionary convictions to impose a personal despotism. The postrevolutionary dictator restores the central authority and social discipline originally repudiated by the revolution, and through a combination of charisma and coercion mobilizes the flagging energies of the society for new struggles directed either outward (as with Napoleon and Hitler) or inward (as with Stalin). Distinctions between revolution and counterrevolution become hard to draw here: the postrevolutionary dictator is no longer either a revolutionary or a counterrevolutionary but a synthesizer of the new and the old, of the revolutionary and the traditional. Only a compromise of this kind can give stability to a society in chaos, and it is the peculiar genius of the postrevolutionary dictator that he can accommodate this need, even if he accentuates the worst in both the prerevolutionary heritage and the innovations of the revolution.

The Stalin Revolution is rooted in the Communist Party dictatorship as it emerged from the civil war—brutalized, militarized, centralized. Stalin himself rose from obscurity during the civil war to assume a key role in steering the party's organizational business; he was the only member in both the Politburo and the Orgburo, and was the power behind the Secretariat. In 1922 his position was officially recognized when Lenin, in one of his last initiatives, had Stalin appointed to the newly created post of General Secretary of the party.

Stalin's personality remains an enigma, perhaps the least understood element in the whole tangled history of Soviet Russia. He was not a Russian but a Georgian from Transcaucasia, the son of a village bootmaker. He always spoke Russian with a heavy Georgian accent. Educated briefly for the Orthodox priesthood, Stalin joined the revolutionary movement while still a teenager, like many other young people of his day. Lacking university education or experience as an émigré abroad (except for brief trips abroad to attend party meetings just before World War I), Stalin was the archetype of the professional revolutionary undergrounder. He sided with Lenin when the Marxists split, distinguished himself as an organizer of bank robberies to finance the party, and served repeated sentences in prison and in Siberia, where the February Revolution found him in 1917. Much has been made recently of the possibility that Stalin worked as a double agent for the imperial secret police (like the Bolsheviks' leader in the Duma, Roman Malinovsky). If there is substance to this charge, it probably reflects no more than the constant police effort to compromise and recruit revolutionary figures, and Stalin's opportunistic willingness to go along with the game. He appears to have been the kind of man who nursed resentments, quietly but deeply, particularly against the party intellectuals and above all against the flashy interloper Trotsky. His later record suggests that he was strongly anti-Semitic and profoundly suspicious of foreigners, whether or not they professed to be Communists.

Stalin's contribution to the Revolution has been clouded both by official hagiography and by the efforts of his enemies, including Trotsky, to discredit him. In fact, he directed Bolshevik organizational and propaganda efforts, but avoided initiatives and never openly disagreed with Lenin. His exact role in the October Revolution, apart from writing editorials for the party paper, is hard to document. A Central Committee resolution listed his name in a "military revolutionary center," and this was long cited in the official history as evidence of his leading position, but in fact that particular body never functioned. As a non-Russian, Stalin was considered the ideal man to represent the national minorities in the Council of People's Commissars. From there he went on to earn Lenin's esteem as a valuable organizational hatchet man.

As General Secretary, Stalin was strategically situated to manipulate the power that accrued to that office as the Communist Party became more hierarchical and centralized. This was a crucial advantage almost immediately, when in May 1922 Lenin suffered the first of a series of debilitating strokes, and the struggle commenced to determine who would succeed him. Technically the party's leadership was exercised collectively, though none disputed Lenin's preeminent personal authority; after he fell ill the leadership became collective in reality as well. It included, as Politburo members, Trotsky, Stalin, Zinoviev (chairman of the Comintern), Kamenev and Aleksei Rykov (deputy premiers), and Mikhail Tomsky (head of the trade unions), plus Bukharin as a candidate member and leading theoretician.

Stalin did not long go unrecognized as a threat. The bedridden Lenin was the first to sound the alarm, in a letter known as his "Testament" (published abroad but suppressed in the Soviet Union until 1956): "Comrade Stalin, having become General Secretary, has concentrated enormous power in his hands, and I am not sure that he always knows how to use that power with sufficient caution ... Stalin is too rude, and this fault, entirely supportable in relations among us Communists, becomes insupportable in the office of General Secretary. Therefore, I propose to the comrades to find a way to remove Stalin from that position."

But Trotsky, not Stalin, was the man the other members of the Politburo feared. They thought him a potential Bonaparte because he commanded the armed forces, and they maneuvered to isolate him politically. In the fall of 1923 Trotsky struck back and publicly charged his associates with violating intraparty democracy and denigrating the interests of the workers. His thrust was easily parried by the party organization, and in January 1924, just a week before Lenin died, Trotsky and his followers were condemned for "petty-bourgeois deviation" and violation of the rule against factionalism. There followed a violent propaganda campaign against the heresy of "Trotskyism" and the theory of permanent revolution, in place of which Stalin and Bukharin imposed the theory of socialism in one country. Trotsky continued the struggle for almost four years, but the effort was doomed after his initial defeat. It made little difference when Zinoviev and Kamenev switched to Trotsky's side after becoming alarmed about the growth of Stalin's power. One by one, Trotsky, Zinoviev, and Kamenev together with their supporters were stripped of their party and governmental titles, and in the fall of 1927 they were expelled from the party altogether. Just as in tsarist days, Trotsky and his more prominent followers were exiled to Siberia and Central Asia. In February 1929 Trotsky was deported from the country, and began the odyssey that ended with his murder in Mexico by an alleged Soviet agent in 1940.

In the course of Stalin's rise to power, the professional organization, or apparatus, of the Communist Party took on the form, functions, and authority that have characterized it ever since. Stalin began the practice of appointing the regional and local party secretaries according to the system of ranks known as "nomenklatura," and gave these secretaries de facto control of the pyramid of party committees. He staffed the party apparatus with his own men, and through them was able to control the makeup of the party congresses that elected the Politburo and the Central Committee. By the time of Lenin's death, Stalin had practically completed this process, and the party congresses ever since have been displays of orchestrated unanimity (except in 1925, when the Leningrad organization took orders from Zinoviev). Stalin was a master of machine politics; but the great distinction between his position and that of party bosses in the United States is that outside Stalin's realm there was no legal political life whatsoever anywhere in the country. Stalin had converted the dictatorship of the party into a dictatorship over the party. He had only to wait for an opportune issue in order to get rid of his rivals in the collective leadership, and pack the top party bodies with his own appointees.

The party controversies between 1923 and 1927 were only surface storms, never really threatening the basis of Stalin's power. In fact, Stalin used the opposition as a foil to build a spirit of unity and conformity within the party's ranks. His tactics appealed to the type of Old Bolshevik undergrounder who had little patience with theoretical hairsplitting and who looked to a firm authority to take the lead in practica¹ work. Typically the Stalinists were authoritarians, suspicious of intellectuals and happy to consider their party an infallible embodiment of the revolutionary mission of the proletariat. Nevertheless, most of those of the first generation would ultimately pay the supreme penalty for their support of Stalin's rule.

The demise of Trotsky's left opposition cleared the way for Stalin to settle with the right wing of the party, which was led by Bukharin, Rykov, and Tomsky. This battle, the culmination of Stalin's drive for power, was the setting for the sweeping decisions that shaped his revolution from above and determined the fates of millions of people. Until 1928 Stalin had supported the cautious implementation of the NEP, as advocated by Bukharin and the party's right wing. Then, evidently to force the latter into opposition so that he could discredit and destroy them, he abruptly adopted Trotsky's line of intensive industrial development supported by the rapid collectivization of the peasants. By 1929 the right had been ousted from the party leadership, just as the left had been two years earlier, and Russia was committed to solving its economic difficulties by way of a "Five-Year Plan" of industrialization and forced collectivization. The NEP was over and the Stalin Revolution had begun.

The decisive time under Stalin was the period of the First Five-Year Plan. Actually the plan ran for only three years and eight months. When it was adopted in the spring of 1929 it was backdated to the beginning of the fiscal year (October 1928), and it was declared "complete in four years" in December 1932. This juggling of the time frame illustrates the manipulative and propagandistic approach of Stalin's men toward planning after the leading economists had been purged for sharing Bukharin's caution. Industrial progress was nevertheless impressive: steel production rose from 4 million tons in 1928 (about the same as in 1913) to 6 million in 1932, and construction was begun of new mills sufficient to triple that output by 1937. Total industrial output grew approximately 75 percent during the plan period. During the Second Five-Year Plan of 1933–1937 it more than doubled again.

The secret of this success was simple: the command economy that allocated scarce resources without reference to consumer demand, and the generation of investment resources by forced savings. Industrial progress was financed through a combination of taxes (the turnover tax on retail sales was introduced at this time), inflation (prices were allowed to run far ahead of wages), and extraction of a surplus from the collectivized peasants (either as obligatory deliveries or as purchases at artificially low prices). Masses of new workers came out of the villages to work on the new projects, despite the desperate overcrowding of city housing—another condition that has never been fully cured. Thanks to collective-farm deliveries, the state was able to resume grain exports to pay for imported machinery and technological expertise. Numerous foreign firms, including the Ford Motor Company and other U.S. businesses, contracted to furnish engineering skills for a program of industrialization that had outrun Russia's educational base. When faced with inevitable shortages of materials and skilled labor, Stalin's men modified the plan de facto to give priority to heavy industry, and allow consumer living standards to deteriorate—part of the price for rapid growth in industrial plant.

The heaviest price was paid by the peasants, victims of the forced collectivization. Although the communal life had been favored by the Russian intelligentsia in the nineteenth century as well as by Marxism, the peasants themselves had shown little interest in such experiments. During the NEP, nearly all peasants worked for themselves, even though the village remained a residential entity. When Stalin suddenly started to collectivize them, it was not for ideological reasons but for reasons of economic urgency and political control: the collective farms gave him possession of the grain supply. His approach was decried by other Marxists; Bukharin termed it "military-feudal exploitation of the peasants."

Resistance to collectivization was naturally strongest among those who had the most to lose—the kulaks, nurtured by Stolypin's prerevolutionary reform, and the bulk of the peasants in the surplus-producing areas of the Ukraine, southern Russia, and western Siberia, where landlordism and the village commune had been much weaker. But the resisting classes and regions were precisely those on which Stalin wanted to impose collectivization most urgently. To accomplish his aim, Stalin uprooted kulak families (defined as anyone who resisted, and generally including the best rural labor) by the millions and deported them to Siberia or consigned them to near-certain death in the labor camps. Livestock raising suffered grievously, as peasants slaughtered and ate their animals—pigs, cows, horses, and all—rather than turn them over to the collectives.

Despite the cost and the resistance, Soviet agriculture was well over half collectivized by the end of the First Five-Year Plan (and would be totally so by the end of the second). Then, with farming badly disrupted, drought and famine struck for the second time in eleven years and again in the southern zone, where agriculture was most vulnerable to the weather. This time, however, the Soviet authorities denied the very fact of the famine, barred relief efforts, whether international or internal, and allowed starvation to decimate the rural population in those regions that had been most resistant to collectivization. The victims numbered in the millions, but the collective farm system was so effective by this time that the amount of grain delivered to the state for the cities and for export actually increased during the worst part of the famine. Stalin's only concession was to allow private plots and farmers' markets, which still provide a major share of the meat, dairy, and vegetable products for city and village dwellers alike.

Once Stalin had committed himself to rapid industrialization, he found reason for it in Soviet Russia's need to compete with the capitalist powers. In a famous speech of 1931 he explained:

To slacken the tempo would mean falling behind. And those who fall behind get beaten. But we do not want to be beaten. No, we refuse to be beaten! One feature of the history of old Russia was the continual beatings she suffered for falling behind, for her backwardness. She was beaten by the Mongol khans. She was beaten by the Turkish beys. She was beaten by the Swedish feudal lords. She was beaten by the Polish and Lithuanian gentry. She was beaten by the British and French capitalists. She was beaten by the Japanese barons. All beat her—for her backwardness: for military backwardness, for cultural backwardness, for agricultural backwardness.

Contrary to the old Marxist bias, nationalism was now acceptable to Stalin as justification for the industrial and military drive:

In the past we had no fatherland, nor could we have one. But now that we have overthrown capitalism and power is in the hands of the working class, we have a fatherland, and we will defend its independence. Do you want our socialist fatherland to be beaten and to lose its independence? If you do not want this, you must put an end to its backwardness in the shortest possible time and develop genuine Bolshevik tempo in building up its socialist system of economy. There is no other way.

Having inherited a party with a militarized system of rule, Stalin now began to militarize its goals, and applied his brand of socialism to the purpose of maximizing national power.

The years of the Stalin Revolution saw the establishment in Russia of a truly "totalitarian" system of rule. This term, bracketing the Soviet regime with the dictatorships of Hitler and Mussolini, is naturally rejected by Soviet spokesmen. It is also disputed by many Western authorities, who deny the likeness of left and right or find the Soviet system too complex to fit the totalitarian model.

The term "totalitarian" denotes an intensity and scope of coercive authority extending far beyond the autocratic political monopoly of a traditional monarchy or Latin-American-style dictatorship, or even Communism of the NEP style. The totalitarian system, which imposes its controls and demands on the entire citizenry and in all walks of life, is a twentieth-century phenomenon, relying on modern developments in communication, weaponry, and record keeping. It is a revolutionary phenomenon as well, breaking with tradition and the status quo and striving to remold society. Like the regimes of Mussolini and Hitler, who copied the party idea from the Communists, Soviet totalitarianism is based on the concentration of power in the hands of one individual or a small group, backed by secret police, censorship, purges, and concentration camps and promoting a single official version of ideological truth.

Beyond these similarities in political structure and method, the concept of totalitarianism does not have much general validity. The overt political values of the Communist regime are diametrically opposed to those of the fascist dictatorships, the former originating in a revolution with an attachment, however distorted, to internationalism and the rationalist intellectual tradition, and the latter based on counterrevolution, racist politics, and nationalistic megalomania. With respect to the degree of political control over society, the Soviet system became much more completely "totalitarian" than the fascist regimes, which apart from considerations of politics and racism were content to leave the social and economic structure of their respective nations more or less intact. Hannah Arendt's emphasis on the "isolating" effect of totalitarian rule on a society refers mainly to the political impact of Nazism on a complex society of special-interest groups. In the Soviet case, proceeding from a much more backward and mainly peasant society, the effect has been more integrating than isolating, welding people together in new groups and organizations, all tightly controlled by the Communist Party and putatively imbued with the proper collective consciousness.

Outside observers, though they may agree on the totalitarian character of the Soviet system, differ widely on its sources. Some attribute it to Marxist-Leninist ideology or to the experience of the Revolution. Others find its origins deep in the old political culture of Russia, or in the exigencies of economic and military progress in an underdeveloped and threatened country. But whatever its sources, the bias toward central control is so profound that Soviet citizens cannot understand how other parts of the world operate without it. Knowledgeable Soviets, according to a recent study by the U.S. Information Agency, actually believe that there must be a secret center coordinating all of the apparently chaotic movements of the American government and economy.

Economically, Stalin's most sweeping move toward totalitarianism was collectivization. At the same time, the small private enterprise in trade, services, and light consumer-goods production that had been allowed to spring back during the NEP was nationalized again, at great cost in efficiency and responsiveness to local consumer needs. A nation that was still far from attaining U.S. levels of mass-market production and chain services suddenly had nearly all of its village trades and handicrafts wiped out. In industry the trade unions lost the autonomy they had enjoyed during the NEP, retaining only the tasks of enforcing labor discipline, boosting productivity, and awarding pensions and vacations. Managers lost the freedom of action they had been allowed under market socialism, and were straitjacketed instead by quantitative output goals assigned from above. Failure was treated as sabotage.

Culturally, the Stalin Revolution brought an end to the uncensored opportunities and free-wheeling styles of the NEP in literature, the arts, education, even social science and legal theory. Stalin's new rule was "party spirit," demanding not merely political acquiescence but active promotion of the party's preferences in every field of thought and creativity. To implement party control, Stalin gave the nod to the most dogmatically Marxist schools in each area of cultural or academic endeavor to impose their own norms of "proletarian" thought and propagandistic service on all work in their respective fields. Holdouts were silenced or jailed as bourgeois class enemies.

Politically, Stalin's totalitarianism was an extension of the party machine that he had already built on Lenin's foundation. In policy and ideological matters there was only one line and one interpretation—Stalin's—subject to manipulation as he found expedient, but a matter of obligatory belief for the rank and file. The party member had no more freedom of expression than nonmembers, and in fact was expected to change his views by reflex whenever the "general line of the party" changed. Outside the official sphere there remained no political or social initiative whatsoever; every social, professional, cultural, and avocational organization was either broken up or placed under the control of party representatives.

For those who were suspected of nonconformity, or who got in the way of the Stalinist monolith, the answer was terror. The police (now transformed into the People's Commissariat of Internal Affairs, or NKVD) and the prison-camp system (the Main Administration for Corrective Labor Camps, or "Gulag") had been relatively restrained during the NEP. Stalin now gave them full reign to dispose of the peasants, intellectuals, recalcitrant bureaucrats, and hesitant party members who resisted his total control. Millions already populated the camps in remote timbering and mining regions by the mid-1930s, when the Great Purge began.

■ The Great Purge and Stalin's Counterrevolution

The Stalin Revolution, though brutal and painful, was at least describable and understandable in terms of its announced objectives. The same cannot be said for the succeeding era in Soviet history, clouded in secrecy, rumor, and calculated disinformation. Between 1934 and 1938, Stalin remolded Soviet society in his own image and exterminated a whole generation of Communist leadership, all the while presenting himself to the world as a champion of peace and progress.

The Great Purge was the most terrifying and at the same time most mystifying outcome of Stalinist totalitarianism. Numerous theories, ranging from rampant paranoia to the expediencies of foreign policy, have been put forth to explain it. The word in Russian (*chistka,* literally "cleansing") had been used to denote the sifting of misfits out of the party membership, and a "purge" in this sense was underway in 1933–34 when a startling event occurred. In December 1934 the Leningrad party secretary and Politburo member Sergei Kirov, reputed leader of a moderate faction among Stalin's lieutenants, was assassinated. Though later information (including hints by Khrushchev in his "secret speech" of 1956) implicated the secret police and perhaps Stalin himself in the crime, Stalin used it as a pretext to round up all his enemies of the 1920s and put them on trial for treason. Thus began the famous Moscow show trials, in which the accused—Zinoviev and Kamenev and their supporters in 1936, the leading Trotskyists in 1937, Bukharin and Rykov and the Right Opposition in 1938—all confessed to an increasingly bizarre series of accusations and were in most cases immediately shot. (One man, the former Trotskyist party secretary and deputy foreign commissar Nikolai Krestinsky, repudiated his confession, but he nevertheless suffered the same fate.) Some poetic justice was served in the third trial when the man who prepared the first one, ex-commissar Genrykh Yagoda of the NKVD, was convicted of arranging the murders of the writer Maxim Gorky and several high government officials.

There has been unending speculation as to why the accused confessed to such absurd charges as plotting with the German and Japanese governments to partition the Soviet Union and restore capitalism. Some innocent foreigners, including U.S. ambassador Joseph Davies, could not see through the sham of indictment and confession. Arthur Koestler in his novel *Darkness at Noon* probed more deeply, with a theory that the victims sacrificed themselves to the greater glory of the Soviet cause. In most cases, however, the explanation was probably more down-to-earth: torture, including deprivation of sleep, combined with false promises of clemency for the accused or for their families.

The Moscow trials were only one facet of the Great Purge, though they monopolized international attention at the time. Other trials were held secretly to dispose of national-minority leaders and the top marshals of the Red Army, including chief-of-staff Mikhail Tukhachevsky, who were charged with plotting to overthrow Stalin. (By this time there was good reason for them to try.) Simultaneously an extraordinary secret operation was launched by the NKVD to arrest suspected traitors still functioning in the government, party organization, and industrial administration. As each batch of victims was tortured into false confessions and the naming of names, new suspects were taken into the net. In all, perhaps two million people in responsible or skilled positions were arrested and shot or incarcerated in this colossal operation, the *yezhovshchina*, so called after NKVD chief Nikolai Yezhov (himself a victim of the purge at the end).

The focus of the purge, incredibly, was the system's own command structure: the higher the individual was placed in the party, the government, industry, or the army, the more likely he was to be purged. At the top, three members of the Politburo, five out of six candidate members of the Politburo, the bulk of the Central Committee (including nearly all the regional party secretaries), and a majority of the delegates to the most recent (1934) party congress were arrested and executed, secretly and summarily. These were mostly people who had risen with Stalin in the struggle against the opposition and had been advanced to their posts by him. Their fate was to become "unpersons" in Soviet history, until Khrushchev "rehabilitated" them posthumously. Age appears to have been a criterion: everyone of any note over the age of thirty-five (forty in the army), except for members of the Politburo and a handful of Stalin's other cronies, was purged.

The Great Purge eliminated virtually all the Old Bolsheviks of prerevolutionary days, with their links to the Westernized intelligentsia. The vacuum was promptly filled by new talent with none of the traditions of intellectual cosmopolitanism. These were the *vydvizhentsy* ("promotees") whom Stalin had recruited from factory and farm during the First Five-Year Plan and rushed through engineering institutes or other technical training programs.

In terms of the change in leadership, the Great Purge represented as much of a social revolution as the Revolution of 1917. Its beneficiaries, including such men as Brezhnev and Kosygin, Andropov and Chernenko, rose rapidly to the upper ranks, where, as a generation, they have grown old in office. As the Soviet Union entered the 1980s, the top leaders, in their seventies, were still the people trained, selected, and installed by Stalin. They were tough, pragmatic, anti-intellectual, and unschooled about the outside world, but devoted to the system that had made them what they were.

The analogy has often been drawn between Stalin's purges and the Terror in France under Robespierre: "The revolution devours its children," as the expression goes. The point is, however, misplaced. In Russia the purges came much later in the revolutionary process and were directed against revolutionaries-turned-bureaucrats who had been in office for as long as two decades; in this sense, the purges were a repudiation of the revolution rather than an extension of it. Stalin killed more Communists than have all the world's right-wing dictators combined. If Marxist labels are disregarded and the real meaning of the era is measured, the Great Purge was indeed Russia's counterrevolution.

Stalin's counterrevolution has not been widely recognized for what it was because he so skillfully camouflaged it with revolutionary language. This applies both to his annihilation of the Communist old guard, and to the new social policies and cultural values that he imposed on his realm. During the years when the world was preoccupied by World War II and the Cold War, there were few outsiders who troubled to inquire into these fundamental changes. (A ground-breaking exception was Nicholas Timasheff, whose book *The Great Retreat,* written in 1946, inspired later researchers.) In fact, in the guise of extirpating anti-Leninist ideas, Stalin repudiated virtually everything in the revolutionary tradition save its aversion to private business and religion. Instead, he embraced the heritage of the prerevolutionary past in the political camouflage of Marxist vocabulary, thereby effecting the postrevolutionary synthesis of new and old.

In his social and cultural reorientation of Russia during the mid-1930s, Stalin worked step by step, avoiding general pronouncements that might make his direction clear to the world. As policy controversies came to his attention, he invoked the authority of the party to set things right according to his own values. Without acknowledging any deviation from the Marxist-Leninist line, Stalin responded to each situation by insisting that the specialists in that particular field conform to an essentially conservative, nineteenth-century standard of conduct and judgment. But he maintained that what he was demanding had always been party orthodoxy, and that the views, styles, and policies he condemned had always been counterrevolutionary deviations from that standard—this despite the fact that the ideas he rejected had been taken for granted as the revolutionary line ever since 1917.

In economic policy Stalin made a virtue of necessity, and endorsed as a permanent feature of the socialist system the monetary inequality and incentives that the NEP had accepted as a temporary concession to bourgeois habits. He asserted in 1934, "Every Leninist knows (that is, if he is a real Leninist) that equalization in the sphere of requirements and individual life is a piece of reactionary petty-bourgeois absurdity worthy of a primitive sect of ascetics, but not of a socialist society organized on Marxist lines." In other words, to each according to his needs, but even in the classless society different people have different needs. Stalin's hero was the miner Aleksei Stakhanov, whose exploits in digging coal inspired the "Stakhanovite" policy of incentives and exhortation to boost productivity. Proclaiming the abolition of classes and the attainment of socialism in 1936, Stalin nonetheless acknowledged the continued existence of the different "strata"—workers, collective farmers, and "toiling intelligentsia." Here is the programmatic basis for the permanent stratification of Soviet society in terms of income, prestige, and perquisites, even though "classes" in the Marxist sense are not supposed to exist, and a lingering embarrassment about conspicuous consumption encourages the Soviet elite to enjoy their material privileges in secret.

Along with the hierarchy of economic rewards, Stalin had to justify the all-powerful state, in the face of the Marxist prediction that the state would wither away once classes had been officially abolished. On the contrary, he told the Central Committee at the height of the Great Purge, "We must smash and throw out the rotten theory that with each forward movement we make, the class struggle will die down more and more." The defeated exploiters, led by the Trotskyists, were turning to sabotage and treason, and must be ruthlessly suppressed. In a 1939 speech, Stalin catalogued the functions of the state: defend the country, catch spies, build the economy, and "protect socialist property from thieves and pilferers of the property of the people." The state would not wither away even after the transition from socialism to communism, unless the "capitalist encirclement" was replaced by a "socialist encirclement." Marxist legal theorists who spoke of the withering away of law under communism were purged for emitting "putrid vapor"; Andrei Vyshinsky, prosecutor at the Moscow trials, emerged as Stalin's chief legal theorist to rehabilitate the concept of "socialist law" as a permanent feature of the "superstructure" of the system.

At the same time, the regime sought legal respectability in the eyes of the world when in 1936 it adopted the Stalin Constitution, to alter the form of the Soviet electoral charade. The new structure eliminated everything that was unique about the soviets—representation on the basis of class and workplace and the decentralization of sovereignty, which back at the time of the Revolution were supposed to be their great virtues. Instead it provided for direct elections and universal voting by geographical districts, a system that still holds for the soviets at each administrative level. Although it assured all the usual democratic rights (just at the time of the purges), the new constitution made the Communists the only legal party.

Capping the new system was the Supreme Soviet, a two-chamber body which by all appearances was modeled on the United States Congress (except that the two houses were to be of equal size—currently 750 members each). One chamber, the Soviet of the Union, consists of deputies from districts of equal population, just as in the U.S. House of Representatives. The other, corresponding to the U.S.

Senate, is the Soviet of Nationalities, which represents the units of
the Soviet federal system, though here the rules are more complex
owing to the multitude of national minorities and the different administrative levels on which they are recognized. Each of the fifteen
"union republics" has thirty-two deputies in the Soviet of the
Union, regardless of population differences. "Autonomous republics" have eleven deputies of their own, separate from the representation of the union republic to which they belong. "Autonomous
regions" have five deputies, and "autonomous areas" one each.
Elected for a five-year term, the Supreme Soviet convenes twice a
year for only three or four days each time, and delegates interim legislative power to its Presidium of thirty-nine members. It is the
chairman of this body who serves as the constitutional chief of state.
Executive authority under the Stalin Constitution continued to be
vested in the Council of People's Commissars, responsible for ad-
ministering all the diverse departments of government and economy
and nominally responsible to the Supreme Soviet, like the cabinet in
a European parliamentary system.

Later, at the close of World War II, Stalin abandoned another
revolutionary tradition by changing "commissars" to "ministers"
and the "Council of People's Commissars" to the "Council of Ministers." Civil servants ranging from diplomats to railroad workers
were put into uniform. The Red Army, whose top officers were
changed from "commanders" to "generals" and "marshals" just before the war, became the "Soviet Army," and the "Internationale"
was replaced as the national anthem by the "Hymn of the Soviet
Union," specially commissioned by Stalin. (Because of a line referring to "our great Stalin," the words could not be sung with the anthem from 1956 to 1977, when a correction was authorized.)

In addition to more conventional political theory and terminology, Stalin embraced the political force of nationalism. Once accused by Lenin of exhibiting "the Great-Russian chauvinism of
Russified non-Russians," Stalin identified himself with the Russians
just as the Austrian Hitler did with the Germans and the Corsican
Bonaparte with the French. He did not, as often supposed, wait until
the dark days of World War II to begin exploiting this deep potential for loyalty, but as early as 1934 incorporated the nationalist line
in propaganda and educational policy. His constant theme during
the purges was the menace of foreign conspiracy and espionage, and

in addition to the Old Bolsheviks he liquidated most of the foreign Communists who had taken refuge in Moscow.

Stalin's rediscovery of nationalism dovetailed with other amendments to the revolutionary tradition, particularly in the treatment of non-Russian minorities and in the depiction of Russia's past by historians. A total purge of Communist leaders in the union republics allowed Stalin to install a new cadre of compliant young Russian-speakers (with Russian second secretaries alongside them functioning like military commissars) who would impose not only firm party control but the new line of russified culture. The pattern continues to this day: Russia, present and past, even tsarist, must be acknowledged as the model for the cultural life of the minorities. Emphasis by local intellectuals on their distinctive historical or cultural traditions, let alone political separatism, has been systematically suppressed as "bourgeois nationalism."

The new line included the revival of Russian history as a saga of national glory and pride. During the First Five-Year Plan, the party line on history still stressed anti-imperialism and ultra-Marxist economic determinism. The leading Communist historian Mikhail Pokrovsky had caused "bourgeois" historians to be harassed and jailed. But in 1934 the Central Committee complained, "The textbooks and oral instruction are of an abstract schematic character. Instead of being taught civic history in a animated and entertaining form with an exposition of the most important events and facts in their chronological sequence and with sketches of historical personages, the pupils are given abstract definitions of social and economic formations, which thus replace the consecutive exposition of civic history by abstract sociological schemes." Finnish ex-Communist Arvo Tuominen, a frequent visitor in the Kremlin before he left the movement, tells how Stalin one evening was helping his daughter Svetlana with her homework and quizzed her about Catherine the Great. "Catherine the Great was a product of society," said the girl, parroting the official text.

That was enough. Pokrovsky, who had died in 1932, had the dubious distinction of being posthumously purged for "vulgar economic materialism," and his antinationalist line went with him. Tsarist imperialism, castigated by classical Marxist historians of the Pokrovsky school, was now recast as a minor evil or even a positive good, since it had brought the benefits of Russian culture and protection to lesser nationalities. The new line was dramatically exemplified by Sergei Eisenstein's 1938 film *Alexander Nevsky,* which celebrated the victory of the Russians over the Teutonic Knights on the ice of Lake Peipus in 1242. Marxism was translated into a vehicle of Russian national superiority: "On the face of the globe there is but one socialist state," began the revised high-school history text of 1938; "this is our motherland." A practical offshoot of the rehabilitation of the Russian past was the program to restore historic churches and palaces, especially after the devastation wrought in World War II, in order to preserve the symbols of national tradition.

Stalin's authoritarian and traditionalist political outlook was mirrored in the way he tightened the Soviet educational system. Experimental notions of progressive education, influenced in the 1920s by John Dewey and other American innovators, were condemned in 1931 as "the anti-Leninist theory of the withering-away of the school." Perhaps liberation of its children was a luxury that Russia could not yet afford, since it was only then implementing universal compulsory primary schooling. Again necessity became a virtue, as Stalin swung around to the disciplined classical model of academic education that imperial Russia had imported from western Europe. This is the system still in force, complete with exams, grades, uniforms, and standing at attention when the teacher enters the classroom.

In its behavioral norms no less than in its institutional structure, Stalin enjoined upon Soviet society a new traditionalism. The nuclear family, expected by some early Communist theorists to "wither away" like the state, was resuscitated as a permanent norm of socialism. Abortion, unrestricted since shortly after the Revolution, was outlawed in 1936 and remained so until the 1950s. The "postcard divorce" of the 1920s gave way to a stiff judicial procedure. (This, too, was eased up in the 1950s, and the Soviet divorce rate now equals the American.) Censorship of the media and of public entertainment became puritanical as well as political. This persists still: except to fans of opera and ballet, Moscow is the world's dullest capital at night—though the private lives of the young and the powerful leave nothing to fantasy.

Stalin's family policy reflected his implicitly traditionalist social philosophy. He and his appointees condemned all the liberationist attitudes of the 1920s in matters of sex, education, and artistic taste, and demanded instead a disciplined commitment to serve the state.

The deterministic social science that blamed deviant, criminal, and insane behavior on the social environment was unacceptable now that the environment was the Communist Party's responsibility: henceforth the individual was to be held strictly accountable for his acts. Punishment, not treatment, was the answer to lawbreakers. Research in criminology was simply abolished; sociology dissolved in Marxist sermonizing; and psychology was confined to Pavlov's behaviorism, while Freud's theory of the unconscious was condemned as "bourgeois idealism." Stalin found that he could now suspend the social laws of Marxism: "There can be no justification for references to so-called objective conditions," he told the Party Congress in 1934. Hinting at his reasons for the purges, he continued: "From now on, nine tenths of the responsibility for the failures and defects in our work rest not on 'objective conditions' but on ourselves, and on ourselves alone."

Party control was even extended to research in the natural sciences. Einstein's Theory of Relativity, like Freudianism, was condemned as "bourgeois idealism," though this did not go so far as to stop the research in nuclear physics that produced Russia's first atomic bomb in 1949. Matters were much worse in the field of biology, where the quack plant breeder Trofim Lysenko won Stalin's ear with his theory of the inheritance of acquired characteristics, and caused eminent researchers in Mendelian genetics to be sent to their death in the labor camps. Lysenko's baneful influence on agricultural practice as well as on scientific theory was not entirely eliminated until Brezhnev took over the Soviet leadership in 1964.

Stalin's conservative line was imposed in literature and the arts under the banner of "socialist realism." The term itself was coined by Maxim Gorky, the radical writer of prerevolutionary renown who returned to Russia to serve Stalin and died under circumstances that are still unexplained. Socialist realism became the generic formula for the styles imposed by the party upon all the arts in the mid-thirties, once it became clear that the futuristic forms of propaganda art attempted during the First Five-Year Plan were satisfying no one.

The shift began in literature, when the party-sanctioned writers' organization, the Russian Association of Proletarian Writers (RAPP), was condemned, like all other ultra-Marxist groups, for anti-Leninist tendencies; the present Union of Soviet Writers, embodying the doctrine of socialist realism, replaced it in 1934. In practice, "socialist realism" meant highly conventional premodernist forms and a banal, propagandistic content, avoiding any critical treatment of actuality (as in Western "realist" literature) and instead depicting what Soviet life was supposed to be or would someday be. The nineteenth-century classics, like the nation's historic exploits, were revived as cultural models.

Similar criteria were soon extended to the other arts. In painting, sculpture, architecture, drama, ballet, and even music, modernism was banned as "bourgeois formalism," and the abstract, experimental, and contemplative yielded to the classically heroic. Visitors to Moscow can see the residue of these policy shifts in public architecture, whose past deviations Stalin did not undertake to purge. One has only to compare the clean, functional lines of the Council of Ministers building (now the Gosplan) or the Pravda editorial office, built in the 1920s, with the wedding-cake style of Moscow University and the Florentine battlements of Gorky Street, legacies of the 1940s. Some intellectuals—the composer Dmitri Shostakovich, for instance—learned how to conform after their knuckles were rapped. Many others—the stage director Vsevolod Meyerhold, the writers Isaac Babel and Osip Mandelshtam, to name a few—perished in the purges.

Stalin's social and cultural counterrevolution was the final stage in his postrevolutionary synthesis of new and old, rather to the disadvantage of the new. To a degree, perhaps, the shift was a concession to public opinion—not, of course, the opinion of the Westernized intellectuals who were being killed off in the purges, but the opinion of newly educated or still uneducated men of the masses. In American terms, Stalin's new value system might be described as populist conservatism. It was no doubt reassuring to those arrivistes of an authoritarian bent for whom the cultural and theoretical dimensions of the Revolution had always been a strange contrivance. Stalin had found a formula to satisfy not only himself but the ruling class that he had created by purge and promotion. These people were the ultimate beneficiaries of the proletarian revolution, and the Stalinist value system was their natural ideology.

This last point helps explain the rigid doctrinal controls and Marxist literalism that have been maintained ever since the purges. The pose of orthodoxy gave the new leaders an assurance of legitimacy and a sense of self-satisfaction, and it reinforced the system of power that kept them in office. Smothering criticism, sustaining discipline, and gulling impressionable foreigners, the ideological façade of Marxism was finally turned into the state religion of the Soviet system.

■ From Stalin to Brezhnev

Since the Stalin Revolution of the 1930s, the Soviet Union as a political and social structure has changed less than any other major nation. This is so despite the cataclysmic impact of the Second World War and all the challenges and opportunities that the postwar world has offered. In the strictest sense of the word, the Soviet Union has become the most conservative country on earth.

The fact that Stalin's regime even survived the Second World War, let alone with its basic institutions unchanged, is something of a historical miracle. When Germany invaded the Soviet Union—just a few years after the purges, the collectivization, and the famine—disaffection was so widespread that peasants and minorities welcomed the enemy with open arms and soldiers of the Red Army surrendered by the hundreds of thousands. Between 1939 and 1941, to be sure, Stalin had profited from his relations with Hitler to advance the borders of the Soviet Union westward and repossess some of the territory lost in World War I. The Baltic states and Bessarabia were incorporated into the USSR as union republics, and eastern Poland was divided between Belorussia and the Ukraine. (The slice of Finland taken in 1940, together with the sparsely populated area of Karelia to the east, was recognized as a union republic until 1956.) But subjected as they immediately were to the telescoped impact of Communist revolution, collectivization, and the purges, these areas were seething with anti-Soviet hatred by the time the Germans struck.

Stalin's survival in 1941 owed more to Hitler's racial madness and political blindness than to the inherent strength of his own system. The Germans' atrocities and exploitive aims—they even kept the collective farms to control the peasants—quickly made Stalin appear the lesser evil, and officially encouraged nationalism evoked massive self-sacrifice among Russians in the "Great Patriotic War." Multitudes defected to the Axis side in the early months of the war, and an anti-Stalin army of Soviet prisoners was eventually organized under General Andrei Vlasov, who had himself been captured during an attempt to break the German siege of Leningrad. However, no anti-Communist Russian government was allowed to form, since the Germans were convinced that the Slavs were destined to be their colonial subjects. It is conceivable that if Nazi Germany had been as adept in political warfare as imperial Germany, Stalin could have been overthrown. The result (presumably some form of pro-German military rule) would have brought postrevolutionary Russia in form as well as in substance closer to the restoration of the Old Regime.

World War II was Russia's fifth and worst demographic disaster in a third of a century, following the heavy military losses of World War I; the losses to terror, famine, and emigration during the civil war and its aftermath; the millions of deaths due to the deportations during collectivization and the famine that followed; and finally the purges. Soviet military casualties in World War II exceeded ten million, and nearly as many civilians died from privation and enemy action, including a million Jews caught by the Germans in the western part of the Soviet Union and shot down on the spot (contrary to legend, few were evacuated). Counting the birth deficit during the war and in the immediate postwar years, the total shortfall in population growth as a result of the disasters of the thirties and forties could have been as much as fifty million.

During the war Stalin relaxed Communist ideological rigor in favor of more nationalistic themes. In 1943 the Communist International was officially dissolved, and the present limited accommodation with the Orthodox Church was reached the same year when the office of Patriarch was restored. But hopes at home and abroad for a permanent liberalization of the regime had no basis in Stalin's intentions. He made this clear in 1946 when he opened a new campaign for doctrinal purity and ideological vigilance against contaminating influences from the West.

Throughout the war Stalin allowed no change in the fundamentals of his system, including the party apparatus and its ideological monopoly, the police and the camps, the bureaucratic structure of society, traditionalist norms in social and cultural policy, and the russification of the minorities. There was no party congress between 1939 and 1952, and the Central Committee rarely met; the "cult of personality" reigned supreme. Stalin had to be acknowledged the ultimate genius in every field, from agriculture to military science, and his praises were sung in every artistic medium. Meanwhile police terror remained endemic, and the labor camps were crowded with Axis war prisoners, rearrested Soviet prisoners, other displaced persons forcibly repatriated by the Allies, members of national minorities in the "liberated" regions, and anyone whose loyalty left any grounds for suspicion. The population of the camps reached totals that can only be guessed at: probably somewhere between ten and twenty million in the late 1940s. (Alexander Solzhenitsyn, then a young Red Army officer, was arrested for expressing some indiscretions in a personal letter that the censor happened to read.) Factional infighting among Stalin's entourage continued after the war, with occasional purges resulting, but it is difficult to identify the contending individuals. The purges took an overtly anti-Jewish direction in 1949, with the liquidation of Yiddish-speaking intellectuals and the condemnation of Zionism and "rootless cosmopolitans."

The overriding imperative of the postwar regime, along with tight political security, was to rebuild the country's industrial plant. Stalin's new cadre of leaders, hardened by the purges and the war, were totally dedicated to heavy industry and military power. They had no intention of negotiating with the West from a position of weakness, and wanted to take full advantage of the command economy to catch up militarily with the United States. To this end, the five-year plans were resumed in 1946 with the same commitment to central planning and consumer belt-tightening as in the 1930s. Thanks to these priorities, Soviet industry had exceeded prewar output by the time of Stalin's death, even though agriculture languished and consumer living standards had not attained prerevolutionary levels.

Like nearly all dictators, Stalin showed no readiness to hand over the reins during his lifetime. However, he did designate as his heir a relative newcomer to the top echelon, Georgi Malenkov, the party secretary in charge of personnel. This step was followed by revelation of the sensational "Doctors' Plot": a number of prominent physicians, mostly Jewish, were accused of having conspired with the U.S. Central Intelligence Agency and international Zionism in the alleged murder of several Soviet officials. The air was filled with rumors of a new purge, when Stalin died of a stroke in March 1953.

Within a matter of days, Stalin's succession arrangements were undone. Malenkov's associates, led by foreign minister Vyacheslav Molotov and police chief Lavrenti Beria, forced him to accept a collective leadership and to give up command of the party organization, though he would retain the post of prime minister. The main beneficiary of this arrangement was Nikita Khrushchev.

Khrushchev came from a family of peasants and miners in Kursk province (adjacent to the Ukraine). He joined the Communist Party and fought in the Red Army during the civil war, and then worked his way up in the party apparatus. As party chief of the Moscow province and then of the Ukraine, he was one of the few men of his rank and age to survive the Great Purge. His direct implication in that bloodbath can only be guessed at, but he was seated on the Politburo immediately afterward. In 1953, still relatively unknown and presumably nonthreatening to his colleagues, Khrushchev took over command of the entire party apparatus with the title of First Secretary. In fact, this post placed him in a position identical with Stalin's in 1922.

The contest for the succession to Stalin recapitulated step by step the struggle that followed Lenin's death. Almost immediately the collective leadership united against the man whom they saw as most threatening—namely, Beria. He was arrested in June 1953, charged with a list of treasonous crimes recalling those of the show trials of the thirties, and shot. This, as it turned out, was the last time a Soviet leader was ever executed after falling from power. (In England, by comparison, this level of political maturity was reached after the Restoration of 1660.) Khrushchev then began to restore individual control over the party by using his power to make appointments, much as Stalin had in the 1920s. Less than two years after Stalin died, he was able to force Malenkov out of the prime ministership and replace him with his own man, Nikolai Bulganin, another career functionary who had run the State Bank and the Defense Ministry. Khrushchev consolidated his position at the Twentieth Party Congress in February 1956, installing his new appointees in the Central Committee and astounding the world with his "secret speech" (actually read aloud in meetings all over the Soviet Union and soon published abroad) denouncing Stalin's crimes of the purge era.

Khrushchev's secret speech signaled the era of "de-Stalinization." Arbitrary police terror was curbed, a large part of the labor camp population was granted amnesty, and Stalin's victims of the thirties (except for those who had been publicly tried) were rehabilitated. A few of the latter actually turned up alive. Curbs on artists, writers, and scientists were gingerly relaxed, and Russia's borders, after being closed for twenty years, were finally opened to foreign tourists and professionals. The Stalinist restraints on divorce and abortion were repealed. In economic policy more attention was paid to the needs of farmers and consumers, and the first gestures toward equalitarianism in a quarter-century were made by raising pensions and minimum wages. But none of Khrushchev's reforms entailed a fundamental alteration in the institutions or the powers of the Stalinist system. The party apparatus continued to monopolize political life; propaganda and censorship sustained the ideological line of the moment; the command economy dictated the allocation of the nation's resources; and the police, now reincarnated as the Committee for State Security (KGB), retained the power to harass and arrest anyone who questioned the legitimacy of the regime. In his retrospective condemnation of Stalin's record, Khrushchev stopped at the year 1934. He did not question Stalin's campaign against the left and right oppositions (though they had each warned against the menace of Stalin), or question the methods of the five-year plans and the forced collectivization of the peasants. De-Stalinization was a highly restricted policy of ridding the regime of its most counterproductive excesses and the taint of terror; it involved little reconsideration of the fundamentals of the Communist system.

Khrushchev's reforms, limited though they were, posed a clear threat to his old Stalinist associates. Malenkov, Molotov, and Lazar Kaganovich conspired to stop Khrushchev: in June 1957, taking advantage of his absence abroad, they secured a vote in the Party Presidium (as the Politburo was designated between 1952 and 1966) to remove him from his post as First Secretary. Khrushchev hurried home and, with the support of defense minister Georgi Zhukov (the great hero of World War II) and his air force planes, convened the 133-member Central Committee to overrule the Presidium. Such an appeal was unprecedented—the Central Committee had been a rubber stamp since the 1920s—but the tactic worked. Khrushchev was sustained in office, and his enemies were condemned as an "Anti-Party Group" and stripped of all their posts. This was as far as the punishment went: there were no trials, no executions, no expulsions from the party. Nevertheless, Khrushchev appeared to have completely restored the personal dictatorship. This impression seemed confirmed during the next few months, when he dismissed Zhukov and made himself chief of the government (prime minister), just as Stalin had done after the purges.

Yet appearances were deceiving. Compelled to select his lieutenants from the Communist leaders, Khrushchev was never able to rid himself of a potent neo-Stalinist opposition behind the scenes. His heyday lasted no more than two or three years, during which he decentralized industrial administration, launched the "Virgin Lands" project to increase food production, tried to turn the educational system back to vocationalism, pursued détente with the West, and broke with Communist China. All these dramatic steps were later to come back to haunt him as "hare-brained schemes."

By 1960 Khrushchev appeared to have lost control of the appointment process to a cabal of neo-Stalinists headed by the Leningrad secretary, Frol Kozlov. At the Central Committee plenum convened in May, five Khrushchev supporters on the ten-member Party Secretariat were abruptly removed, and only one individual was installed in their place—Kozlov himself. A potential rivalry for the succession between Kozlov and Secretariat member Leonid Brezhnev appeared to be resolved shortly afterward, when Brezhnev was elevated to the post of titular chief of state. Apparently responding to increased pressure from his opponents, Khrushchev launched into a series of impulsive policy initiatives at home and abroad, but was able only to stave off the day of reckoning.

At the Twenty-Second Party Congress in October 1961, Khrushchev apparently recovered. He pressed de-Stalinization again (this was when Stalin's remains were removed from the Lenin tomb) and secured the adoption of a new program for the Communist Party— the first and only rewrite since 1919, incorporating promises of equality and abundance after the transition to true Communism. However, the election of the new Central Committee reflected the neo-Stalinists' gains in the party apparatus. Of the 133 members elected to the Central Committee at the de-Stalinization Congress in 1956, no less than 64 were missing in 1961, and 3 more were demoted to candidate status. Only 66—a shade under 50 percent of the old group—were reelected to the new Central Committee of 175 members. Such a turnover was exceeded only by that of the purge era between 1934 and 1939. Moreover, it is clear that the changes of 1961 were wrought by the opposition to Khrushchev, because the bulk of the 1961 Central Committee (79 percent) was reconfirmed in office at the first congress under Brezhnev in 1966.

Khrushchev won a respite early in 1963, when Kozlov suffered a heart attack (he died soon after). This gave Khrushchev the chance to resume his policy of accommodation with the United States. Nevertheless, the anti-Khrushchev people rallied, this time around Brezhnev. Brezhnev reclaimed his seat on the Secretariat and, with the cooperation of elder statesman and veteran ideologist Mikhail Suslov, laid his plans for a legal overturn in the country's leadership. In October 1964, when Khrushchev was vacationing in the Crimea, they struck just like the opposition of 1957. This time the Central Committee sustained the removal of the leader, in strict accordance with the party rules. Khrushchev had no recourse, and power passed to the leaders of the opposition, Brezhnev as First Secretary ("General Secretary" since 1966) and Alexei Kosygin as prime minister. The era of corrective adjustments in the Stalinist course had come to an end, leaving all the fundamental features of the system—political, economic, ideological—still intact.

Foreign commissar Maxim Litvinov and embassy
counselor Boris Skvirsky after U.S. recognition

Isolation and Alliance

While Soviet Russia was going through the diverse
phases of its postrevolutionary transformation—the
NEP, the Stalin Revolution, and the Stalin counterrevolution—in international affairs its practice conformed more and more to the usual behavior of great

powers. Revolutionary Marxism had not overwhelmed the capitalist world; in fact, it had had greater effect in provoking right-wing fascist counterrevolutions than in promoting the fortunes of the working class. Russian power was insufficient to back world revolution, due to the strength of the other major European powers and to Russia's own exhaustion from defeat, revolution, and civil war between 1914 and 1921. In order to survive in a hostile world, the Communists had to address Russia's old problems and fall back on traditional approaches to foreign policy.

The result of these constraints was a distinct dualism in the international behavior of the Soviet regime, reflected in wide oscillations between revolutionary and traditional strategies. Each swing to the left or the right corresponded closely with one of the main phases in Soviet internal politics. From their accession to power until the end of the civil war, the Communists took a bold revolutionary stance toward both the outside world and their internal enemies. During the pragmatic period of the New Economic Policy, the government aimed at the normalization of foreign relations. A "Third Period," extending from 1928 to 1934, accompanied the Stalin Revolution in domestic affairs with confrontationist rhetoric abroad. Then came the era of "collective security" and the Popular Front, when Stalin pursued antifascist alliances abroad while purging his enemies at home. Two more startling turnabouts occurred when the Soviets changed their alliance partners—first, when the Hitler-Stalin Pact was signed in 1939, and, second, when the Grand Alliance was formed after Germany attacked in 1941.

To many observers, all these twists and turns in Russia's foreign relations seemed devious and unpredictable. Yet each sudden shift was rooted in the mix of national and revolutionary traditions, as well as in threatening international realities that Russia could not control. Between the end of one war and the end of another, the Soviets learned how to deal with the capitalist world when they could, and to resist it when they had to.

▪ The NEP in Foreign Policy

In 1921 Soviet Russia's relations with the world changed as abruptly as did its domestic policy. Even as it implemented the NEP, the regime appeared throughout the 1920s to be reestablishing conventional international relations. Normalization was the theme:

despairing of world revolution for the time being, the Soviet government sought diplomatic recognition, resumed trade with capitalist countries, and formed alliances with other governments regardless of their attitude toward revolution.

The principal architect of this remarkable shift was the Soviet commissar of foreign affairs, Georgi Chicherin, who had assumed the office after Trotsky resigned to protest Brest-Litovsk. An upper-class revolutionary intellectual in the old Russian tradition, Chicherin was uniquely qualified for his role by virtue of his experience in the tsar's diplomatic service. Under his leadership the Foreign Commissariat recruited a remarkable cadre of cosmopolitan intellectuals, ready to staff the new Soviet embassies as they were opened in foreign capitals. The talent pool was deepened in the course of the twenties, as other men of intellectual background lost their political battles within the Communist Party and were consigned—for the time being—to diplomatic exile abroad.

Moscow's earliest steps toward normalization came just as the civil war and intervention were winding down. In late 1920 treaties were concluded with the three Baltic states and with Finland, initiating diplomatic relations and registering Soviet acknowledgment of their independence. A similar agreement with Poland early in 1921 formally ended the hostilities of the previous year. Almost simultaneously, Moscow offered to cooperate with three neighboring governments in the Middle East—Turkey, Persia, and Afghanistan, all resentful of the pressure of the Western powers and hoping to find a counterbalance in Soviet Russia. This set a pattern for future Soviet diplomatic successes based on anti-imperialism without proletarian revolution. More immediately, the security of the Middle Eastern frontier proved valuable to the Soviet government during the next couple of years, as it moved to put down the Basmachi guerrilla rebellion of Pan-Turkic nationalists in Central Asia.

Normalization of relations with the governments of the Baltic and the Middle East presaged the new Soviet international strategy, but the great breakthrough was the conclusion of the Anglo-Soviet Trade Agreement in March 1921. This was the first formal opening of regular contact between Moscow and one of the major powers since the Bolshevik Revolution (except for the relations of duress maintained with the Central Powers between Brest-Litovsk and the Armistice). Moscow abjured hostile propaganda, and Britain extended de facto recognition; a Soviet mission was established in

London to facilitate commercial exchanges. Almost every other European country followed suit within the year, but when the same arrangement was proposed to the new Harding administration in the United States, Secretary of State Hughes and Secretary of Commerce Hoover dismissed the possibility of meaningful trade unless the Russians were to "abandon their present economic system." Evidently Washington did not yet appreciate the extent of economic normalization represented by the NEP and Lenin's decision to grant concessions for foreign enterprise to operate on Soviet territory, though the U.S. government no longer attempted to bar ventures by American businesses that were prepared to take the risk. The first American industrial concession (to mine asbestos) was obtained late in 1921 by Armand Hammer, launching his extraordinary series of business deals with Communist Russia.

Moscow's return to the community of nations took another great step in 1922, when the Soviets were invited to their first international meeting, the Genoa Conference on world economic problems. During the conference the representatives of the two pariah powers, Russia and Germany, stole away to the nearby resort of Rapallo and there signed a treaty of formal recognition and secret military cooperation. From then until the rise of Hitler, Germany provided the Soviet Army with staff training and arms manufacturing know-how, while the Soviets gave the Germans facilities to train pilots and tank crews (forbidden under the Treaty of Versailles). Soviet Russia thus secured an old-fashioned alliance, based on mutual self-interest rather than ideology, even while the German Communists were preparing their last uprising against the Weimar Republic.

In the years that followed, Moscow pursued the Rapallo model of recognition and alliances with considerable success. In 1924 the first British Labour government of prime minister Ramsay MacDonald extended de jure recognition to the Soviet Union. As before, the other major powers followed Britain's lead, again with the signal exception of the United States.

Washington's refusal to recognize the Soviets was as controversial at the time as it has been in retrospect. It set a distinctive pattern for American responses to revolutionary movements in other countries: in China after the Communist takeover in 1949, in Cuba after Castro's rise to power, and in Communist Vietnam. The reason for this consistent refusal to accept formal relations with ideologically unacceptable governments is to be found more in internal American politics and values than in any calculations of the national interest. In the Soviet case, it was the fear of radicalism engendered by the Red Scare that barred recognition—this, ironically, during the Soviet government's most moderate phase, both externally and internally. One tangible link that both the Soviet Union and the United States did accept, despite their ideological reservations, was the great famine relief effort conducted by the American Relief Administration in 1921 and 1922, a boon to the Soviet regime in one of its most desperate moments.

Throughout the twenties the Soviet government continued to form expedient alliances with any available partner, however improbable. Downplaying talk of proletarian revolution, it sought through the Communist International and its member parties abroad to develop a "United Front" with the non-Communist left, to dissuade foreign governments from dangerously anti-Soviet policies. At the same time, still nervous about the "capitalist encirclement" allegedly masterminded in London and Paris, the Soviets supported nationalist movements in Asia, presaging their third-world strategy of the post-Stalin era. Their great hope was the Chinese Nationalist Party led by Sun Yat-sen and Chiang Kai-shek, who welcomed Soviet aid and advisors and concluded an alliance with the newborn Chinese Communist Party. But Sun died, and the arrangement came to an abrupt end when Chiang Kai-shek, having clinched his military victory over the feeble Peking government, turned against his Communist allies in 1927 and destroyed their mainly urban movement. Communism survived in China thanks only to Mao Tse-tung's unorthodox strategy of organizing the peasantry for revolution through guerrilla warfare.

Russia's foreign policy in the 1920s caused much soul-searching and controversy among the leaders in Moscow, who were still genuine Marxists. Trotsky, after he fell from grace in 1923, attacked the overcautious attitude toward foreign revolution in an effort to advance his argument that the post-Lenin leadership was fainthearted about pursuing socialist goals. It was in reply to this needling that Stalin fashioned the theory of socialism in one country, and castigated Trotsky's theory of permanent revolution for betraying "lack of faith" in Russia's own revolutionary potential. The debate marked Stalin in the eyes of the world as a pragmatic nationalist, whereas Trotsky was seen as a firebrand of world revolution, though there was little practical difference between the two. Trotsky was prepared to integrate Russia's incomplete socialism into the world economy much more fully than Stalin. By the same token, Stalin's pragmatism did not extend to the abandonment of the Communist International.

During the early 1920s the Comintern—Russian-controlled from the start, under Zinoviev's chairmanship—was frequently at odds with the Foreign Office under Chicherin. As late as 1923, when it sponsored an abortive Communist uprising in Germany, the Comintern was still geared to the idea of imminent world-wide proletarian revolution, and it was this prospect which attracted foreign radicals to the Soviet banner. But new patterns were emerging both in Moscow's perception of the world and in the lines of control within the international Communist movement. Acknowledging the postwar stabilization of capitalism, the Soviet leadership redefined the mission of foreign Communists: to build influence by peaceful means according to the United Front strategy, and to resist any action by their respective governments threatening the security of the Soviet Union, the "citadel" of the world revolution. Such threats were considered quite real by Moscow, if not by the Western capitals. In 1927, following the collapse of United Front overtures to the British Labour Party and the rupture of relations by the Conservative government of Stanley Baldwin, the Soviet leadership was seized by a genuine panic over the prospect of war with Britain.

Meanwhile, at Soviet insistence, first-generation Communist leaders abroad who could not shift their style from defiance on the barricades to the slow penetration of rival organizations were removed from command of their own parties. This process of "Bolshevizing the Comintern" was facilitated by the factional struggles in Russia, as first the left-leaning Trotskyist Communists were ousted from the movement, and then the right-leaning Communists sympathizing with Bukharin. By 1930 virtually every Communist party outside the Soviet Union had bowed to Stalin's influence, replacing leaders of independence and principle with pliable tools of Moscow. Only one party went its own way in disregard of Soviet orders: this was the Chinese Communist Party of Mao Tse-tung.

In the United States the Communist Party, suffering from police repression at home and Stalinist control from outside, declined from an alleged peak of ninety thousand members in 1919 to a mere seven thousand a decade later, sustained mainly by their quasi-religious devotion to Soviet promises of a new way for the world. Splits corresponding to the factional struggles within the Soviet leadership and extending throughout the world Communist movement further weakened the American party. Trotsky's followers under James Cannon were expelled in 1928, eventually to create the Socialist Workers Party as a shadowy challenge to the Communists from the left; Bukharin's sympathizers, led by Jay Lovestone, were ousted in 1929 and abandoned radical politics.

Stalin's rise to power in the 1920s and the changes in world Communism that he brought about set the character of the movement for the next thirty years. From an association of youthful revolutionaries spontaneously identifying with the Soviet cause, it became a disciplined and unthinking instrument of Soviet foreign policy. No matter how the party line might zig and zag to justify new directions and new alliances in Soviet foreign policy, good Communists were expected to follow without question. It is remarkable that the movement endured at all; indeed, its survival is attributable to events that suddenly altered the world scene for the worse.

▪ The Third Period

In the 1930s the threats as well as the opportunities that the Soviet leadership professed to see in the outside world took on new reality. The Great Depression of 1929, with its financial panics and massive unemployment, shook the capitalist system and offered Communist parties in most industrial countries the possibility of rapid political gains. Shortly afterward the Soviet Union found itself confronted by newly belligerent governments—first militarist Japan and then Nazi Germany—pledged to destroy Communism and to partition the Soviet realm. Meanwhile the Soviet Union had isolated itself and its Comintern allies with a line of renewed revolutionary propaganda against democratic elements abroad. Coming after the revolutionary time of the civil war and the normalization of the NEP, the new hard line of the First Five-Year Plan era was known to Communists themselves as the "Third Period."

The radical stance of the Third Period, though it would seem a logical response to the Depression, had in fact been adopted by Stalin the year before, in 1928, when no one had had cause to doubt the stability of capitalism. The reason lay in Soviet domestic politics: Stalin needed to consolidate his political control and eliminate

Bukharin sympathizers both at home and abroad. Along with his industrialization and collectivization drives that forced the Bukharin-
ists into ill-fated opposition at home, Stalin abruptly ended the
United Front line and ordered foreign Communists to fight democratic socialists, whom he villified as "social fascists." This "left
turn" was accomplished in the summer of 1928 at the Sixth World
Congress of the Comintern, which cited "intensification of the class
struggle between the bourgeoisie and the proletariat in the capitalist
countries" and called for "exposure of the predatory striving of various imperialist groups in all countries." The new line succeeded in
flushing out the old Communist leaders whom Stalin wanted to get
rid of. By happenstance it also gave the Communists a new radical
appeal, after the Depression set in a year later. Communists immediately scored electoral gains wherever they were allowed to present
candidates, and they became a significant political force in France
and Germany.

On a much more modest scale the same effect occurred in the
United States, where the Depression gave new impetus to the Stalinist wing of the Communist Party under William Z. Foster. Foster
received a hundred thousand votes when he ran for president in
1932—still a trifle compared with the million cast for Socialist candidate Norman Thomas, or the substantial vote Eugene Debs had
polled before World War One, or the 10–15 percent of the total electorate that voted for the Communists in France and Germany. With
capitalism in trouble, anti-Communist publicity made it natural for
dissidents to embrace Communism as an alternative, since it was
known largely by whatever the Establishment called "communistic."

Despite momentary successes stemming from the world economic
crisis, there was grave risk to the Soviet Union itself in Stalin's Third
Period line, as events in Germany were soon to show. Parliamentary
government throughout central Europe was threatened by Depression conditions and the growth of the left; it was also undercut
by the panicky flight toward the extreme right by the middle class,
whose fear of the left was given new substance by Moscow's revolutionary rhetoric. Reformist movements ranging from the Social
Democrats in Germany to the New Deal in the United States, striving to resolve the economic crisis by democratic means, were denounced by the Communists as a mere front for fascism. When
parliamentary government in Germany was challenged by the

Nazis, the Communists (holding 10 percent of the Reichstag seats) voted consistently to deny any moderate coalition a working majority, on the theory that a Nazi overthrow of the Weimar Republic would make it easier for the Communists to follow up with a revolutionary coup of their own. The result in 1933, of course, was Hitler's dictatorship, proscription of the Communists along with all other opposition parties, and the mobilization of Germany to effectuate the plans of *Mein Kampf* for conquest in the east.

While Stalin, for his own purposes, succeeded in isolating the Soviet Union and the Communist movement politically, he continued to cultivate economic relations with the capitalist world. In this era of the five-year plans, the Soviet industrialization program depended heavily on foreign-made machinery and foreign technical skills. Although Washington had not yet recognized the Soviet regime, U.S. firms, beset by the Depression, competed for the Soviet market, and in 1930 the United States became for a time the leading supplier of Soviet imports. American engineers hired under contract guided many construction projects of the First Five-Year Plan. All this the Soviets paid for mainly by resuming the grain exports for which Russia had been famous before the Revolution—grain now extracted from sometimes starving peasants through the collective farms, and shipped abroad at Depression prices to earn vital foreign exchange.

Trade was one of the factors responsible for the dramatic turnabout in U.S.-Soviet relations in 1933. Others were the rise of Japanese militarism following the Manchurian crisis of 1931, the election of Franklin Roosevelt to the presidency in 1932, and the advent of Hitler in Germany. The new Democratic administration was more pragmatic than its predecessor about international economics and the balance of power, and on the occasion of the World Economic Conference in London in the summer of 1933, the American representatives made overtures to the Soviet Union's new foreign commissar, Maxim Litvinov. Formal negotiations commenced in the fall, and the treaty of recognition was signed in November. The Soviets agreed to refrain from propagandizing in the United States and to guarantee the rights of U.S. citizens in Russia, though they evaded the matter of the country's prerevolutionary debts. The first Soviet ambassador to Washington was Alexander Troyanovsky, a one-time Menshevik and a star in Chicherin's diplomatic corps. (His son Oleg became chief Soviet delegate to the United Nations in the

1970s.) To represent the United States in Moscow, Roosevelt picked William Bullitt, head of the abortive peace mission to Russia in 1919 (and ex-husband of John Reed's widow, Louise Bryant), who was soon to be disabused of his hopeful sympathy and turn into an embittered anti-Communist. So ended sixteen years of American efforts to wish away the Communist Revolution.

▪ From Collective Security to the Hitler-Stalin Pact

The U.S.-Soviet recognition negotiations were a harbinger of another drastic change of line in Russia's relations with the outside world. Just as Stalin was initiating his cruelest purges, he reversed his foreign policy, abandoned his Third Period attitude of revolutionary defiance, and once again pursued allies wherever he could find them. His immediate motivation was the rise of militant right-wing dictatorships (in part provoked by Soviet-sponsored revolutionary agitation), which promised to rid the world of Communism. Anti-Communism was specifically the rallying point when Germany and Japan concluded their anti-Comintern pact in 1936 (joined by Italy in 1937).

In relations with foreign governments Stalin's new approach, as formulated by Litvinov, was "collective security": the Soviet Union would band together with any other peace-loving states to restrain potential aggressors. Litvinov was well equipped for the role. He was an Old Bolshevik intellectual who had spent years in exile in the West, particularly England (his wife was English), spoke several languages, and combined conviction with pragmatism. In pursuit of collective security, the Soviets sought membership in the League of Nations (which they had previously denounced as a club of capitalist bandits) and gained admission in 1934, just as Nazi Germany was quitting the organization. Litvinov became the league's most articulate spokesman for disarmament and international peace-keeping efforts. Soon afterward, Stalin secured the more tangible support of the French, just as his imperial predecessors had done. In 1935 Moscow and Paris concluded an old-style defensive military alliance, including joint guarantees to Czechoslovakia. The oldest principle of diplomacy had prevailed again: the enemy of my enemy is my friend.

Paralleling the shift from revolutionary isolation to collective security, the Communist International abandoned its talk of proletarian revolution and instead promoted alliances between Communists and socialist, democratic, or otherwise antifascist parties throughout the world. This was the Popular Front strategy, formulated at the Seventh and last World Congress of the Communist International in 1935 under the leadership of the Bulgarian stalwart Georgi Dimitrov. The first non-Russian head of the organization, Dimitrov served as its chairman from 1934 until its dissolution during World War II.

The Popular Front policy scored some early successes, notably in France, where the Communists supported the cabinet of socialists and radicals headed by Leon Blum for a year and a half. In the United States, the Communist Party stopped calling Roosevelt a fascist, and replaced William Z. Foster with Earl Browder. Browder proposed the doctrine of "American exceptionalism": no revolution was required to promote social justice in the democratic United States. Everywhere, Communists were instructed to give up the language of class struggle and couch their appeals in terms of antifascist unity, democratic reform, and liberation for oppressed minorities. With this candy coating, Communism became more palatable in the United States and England as the radical chic alternative, and for a few years the movement had some influence among intellectuals (more the artistic than the politically sophisticated and never great in number). "Front organizations" were set up to bring every conceivable social cause under surreptitious Communist leadership, and the sympathy of "fellow travelers"—nonrevolutionaries persuaded of the justice of the Soviet cause and the sincerity of Soviet opposition to fascism—was carefully cultivated. (Some, like the British socialist scholars Sidney and Beatrice Webb, projected such millennial hopes on the Soviet experiment that they called it "a new civilization.") Just as Hitler professed to be the world's greatest anti-Communist, so Stalin presented himself as the staunchest antifascist.

During the years of the Popular Front, Communism's influence around the world reached an extent that it had never approached when the party line was stridently revolutionary. Ironically, this appeal was based on outdated notions about the Soviet system, since Stalin had by now abandoned the spirit of social revolution and was spreading terror with his purges. As a result of Stalin's actions and the Comintern's style of discipline, turnover in the American Communist Party was high; the typical member, according to Morris

Ernst's *Report on the American Communist,* spent no more than two or three years in the party before becoming disillusioned. The party reached its peak (50,000 members) for the least revolutionary reasons during the Grand Alliance of 1941–1945, when the stigma of the Moscow Trials and the Stalin-Hitler Pact had been glossed over by the image of heroic female snipers and stalwart Red Army artillerymen. Although there are no definite figures, hundreds of thousands of Americans were to some degree involved with the Communist Party or its front organizations, and thus liable both to disillusionment with the left and vilification by the right.

Meanwhile, the great test for Stalin's new policies—collective security among nations and the Popular Front among parties—came in Spain, during its years of revolution and civil war between 1936 and 1939. Communism had never figured prominently in Spain, where the extreme left was the province of the Anarchists, but when the republic (born in 1931) was beset by right-wing insurgency in 1936, the Spanish Communists were taken into the government and the Soviet Union became its only foreign source of support. The International Brigade, composed largely of Communist volunteers (including the Abraham Lincoln battalion from the United States), fought heroically to stem the early rightist offensives, while Hitler and Mussolini poured aid in for Franco, and the democratic powers, including the United States, dithered over neutrality and nonintervention. The upshot was that the Spanish republican regime became virtually a Soviet captive, albeit a nonrevolutionary one; the true revolutionaries, the Anarchists and Trotskyists, were put down by the Madrid government with Communist help. Ultimately Moscow decided that the Spanish effort was an exercise in futility, and allowed the republic to be overwhelmed in 1939, but by then Stalin's entire strategy of alliances was a shambles.

Soviet diplomacy, like every other facet of Soviet life, was rudely disrupted by Stalin's purges in the late 1930s. One after another, seasoned Soviet diplomats were called home to be shot or otherwise disposed of. Jews and cosmopolitan intellectuals were conspicuously absent from the post-purge diplomatic service, which was dominated by young xenophobic bureaucrats. Typical of these was peasant-born Andrei Gromyko, who became ambassador to Washington in 1943 at the age of 34.

The facility with which Stalin was able to switch both his policies and his allies invites some reflection on the nature of his leadership. At the time he first gained international prominence in the 1920s, most foreigners thought him a pragmatist, in contrast to Trotsky, whom they saw as the apostle of world revolution. When Stalin adopted the revolutionary line of the Third Period, it was out of political expediency; and no ideological compunctions prevented his rapprochement with the democratic powers and his espousal of Russian nationalism in the mid-thirties. His record in diplomacy as in domestic affairs shows a man of intense suspicions and extreme ruthlessness, who was nevertheless able to bide his time and then strike with full force when the opportunity presented itself. Marxism and the Communist movement, to such a man, were only instruments to assure his own power and self-glorification. George Kennan argued persuasively in *Russia and the West* that Stalin feared foreign Communists, whom he might not be able to control: "His fundamental motive was the protection of his own personal position . . . Unless other states were very small, and contiguous to Russia's borders, so that there were good prospects for controlling them by the same concealed police methods he employed in Russia, Stalin did not want other states to be communist."

Stalin carried the divorce of ideology and foreign policy a step further in 1939 by a move that astounded the entire world, though it represented no great change in principle. He was evidently persuaded by his experience in Spain and by the Munich Pact (when Britain and France turned Czechoslovakia over to Hitler's mercies without consulting France's nominal ally, Russia) that collective security against the fascist powers was dead. Accordingly, he made overtures to the government that threatened him most directly—namely, Germany. He replaced Litvinov (who was of Jewish ancestry) with Molotov, and put out feelers for a rapprochement. (Kennan suggests that one of Stalin's reasons for the general purge of the Old Bolsheviks was to clear the ground for such a move.) Hitler, no less cynical than Stalin, responded eagerly in order to upstage the British and French, who, alarmed by Germany's occupation of Prague in March 1939, were negotiating with the Russians to restore the pre-Munich alliance. The upshot was the Molotov-Ribbentrop Nonaggression pact of August 1939, which gave Hitler the green light to invade Poland and start World War II.

Stalin's volte-face in 1939 was the Soviet government's most shocking diplomatic move since the Revolution—shocking especially to foreign Communists, who were suddenly ordered to drop their antifascist line and oppose the war against Nazi Germany as an imperialist venture. But Stalin's temporary accommodation with Hitler represented less a fundamental change of strategy than a pragmatic change of partners within the traditional framework of realpolitik. It was in justification of the pact that Molotov first articulated a now-familiar refrain: "In our foreign policy toward non-Soviet countries, we have always been guided by Lenin's well-known principle of the peaceful coexistence of the Soviet state and capitalist countries."

The pact with Hitler offered considerable short-term advantage to the Soviets. Having given up on the Western alliance and bought off the immediate German threat, Stalin was able to act without the worry about the reactions of other powers that had inhibited Soviet expansion since the end of intervention. Russia scored its first territorial gains of the twentieth century and recovered much of the land it had lost under the Treaty of Brest-Litovsk in 1918.

Stalin's first move came barely two weeks after Hitler's attack on Poland when, pursuant to a secret clause in the Nonaggression Pact, he sent the Red Army across Poland's eastern frontier (the 1921 line) and took possession of the mainly Belorussian and Ukrainian-speaking areas of Poland that Hitler had promised to the Soviet Union. The pact also gave the Russians a free hand in the Baltic area, and they immediately compelled Estonia, Latvia, and Lithuania to grant military bases on their territory.

When Finland rejected similar demands, Moscow launched the so-called Winter War of 1939–40. This was the first broad combat experience for the Red Army since 1920, and at first the Finns threw the Russians back ignominiously. The British and French, unable to punish Hitler during the "phony war" of 1939–40 and enraged by Stalin's recent behavior, contemplated military aid to the Finns; only Scandinavian neutralism blocked the scheme, which would have forced Russia into the general war on Germany's side. The Finns were overpowered in March 1940, and had to surrender to the Soviet Union the Karelian Isthmus north of Leningrad and a base at Hangö near Helsinki. But Finland's government remained intact and hoped for revenge; when Germany invaded the Soviet Union the following year, Finland joined in, the only nondictatorship on Hitler's side. Meanwhile, in the summer of 1940, while Hitler was celebrating his victory over the French and his dominance of western Europe, Stalin annexed the three Baltic states and declared them union republics, after mass arrests and staged plebiscites.

In the Balkans, German-Soviet competition proved more difficult to reconcile. Hitler did allow Stalin to repossess the Rumanian province of Bessarabia (which became the Moldavian Republic) and offered him the prospect of expanding into the Indian Ocean area when Germany, Italy, Japan and the Soviet Union eventually divided up the world. But, like the British and French in the nineteenth century, he was reluctant to see Russian power extend further into the Balkans and threaten the Turkish straits. Full of confidence after the fall of France, Hitler lost patience when the Soviets presented such demands late in 1940. He made up his mind—just as Napoleon had—that before conquering England he must first destroy Russia.

▪ The Grand Alliance

On June 22, 1941, Germany and its Axis allies launched Operation Barbarossa, as 190 divisions crossed the Soviet frontier. Fighting for survival, Stalin found himself allied with the same government in London that had refused to cooperate with him at the time of Munich. The imperialist war immediately became the Great Patriotic War, while Communist parties everywhere reversed their line once again, to champion all anti-German governments.

Prime Minister Winston Churchill, the arch-enemy of Bolshevism since its inception, welcomed his unexpected new ally with old-fashioned realism: "No one has been a more consistent opponent of Communism than I have for the last twenty-five years. I will unsay no word that I have spoken about it. But all this fades away before the spectacle which is now unfolding ... Any man or state who fights on against Nazidom will have our aid." Some in the United States, though sympathetic to the British cause, were not so sure of the new political bedfellow. Said Senator Harry Truman of Missouri, as the panzers were churning ahead into Belorussia and the Ukraine, "If we see that Germany is winning we should help Russia and if Russia is winning we ought to help Germany and that way let them kill as many as possible, although I don't want to see Hitler victorious under any circumstances." But America's equally involuntary entry into the war in December 1941 eliminated most qualms about cooperating with Stalin's government, and gave post-purge

Russia a novel air of repectability. The aims of collective security and the Popular Front—symbolized by the rehabilitation of Litvinov and his appointment as ambassador to Washington shortly after Pearl Harbor—were finally achieved under the direst of circumstances.

Stalin and his generals, anxious to give Hitler no excuse for turning against them, were taken completely by surprise when the Germans attacked, despite warnings by the British and by Soviet spy Richard Sorge in Japan. The Red Army, badly positioned for a defense in depth, was quickly cut up by German armored thrusts, and whole divisions, once encircled, surrendered en masse. Some two million Soviet prisoners were taken by the Germans in the first six months of the campaign; most of them were starved to death the following winter.

As the German drive reached the suburbs of Leningrad and Moscow, Stalin panicked, for once in his life, and disappeared from public view for days, while the Soviet government moved its offices to Kuibyshev on the Volga. Then the Russian winter closed in, and Red Army reserves mounted the first effective counterattacks. The Soviet regime was saved.

Hitler's military success in the early months of the campaign was offset by his political blunders, inherent in the Nazi racial ideology. Where he could have won grateful allies by granting the Soviet minorities autonomy and by offering the Russians an anti-Communist government, he chose instead to enslave the *Untermenschen.* Germany was still able to recruit substantial military and auxiliary police forces from Soviet prisoners and defectors, who were used widely in Hitler's empire as garrison troops or as aides in exterminating Jews. But it was relatively late in the day when anti-Stalin Russians were allowed to form the army corps commanded by General Vlasov. Vlasov's troops were never trusted in action, and in May 1945, in the last days of the Third Reich, they joined the Czech resistance to help liberate Prague. This did not spare them from swift retribution once they fell into Soviet hands.

To Stalin's regime, shaken by the traumas of five-year plans, collectivization, and purges, the war proved to be a political boon once the initial crisis of 1941 had passed. Stalin intensified the nationalistic propaganda that he had initiated in the mid-1930s, and, for the benefit of his subjects and his allies, he muted his Marxist-Leninist line. This pose, along with his dissolution of the Communist International and his rapprochement with the church, raised great hopes both in Russia and abroad that the Soviet Union was prepared to join the democratic powers in preserving a peaceful status quo. This was the sanguine frame of mind in which Britain and the United States joined Russia in the great crusade to turn back the Germans and destroy fascism.

The road to victory was not easy, despite the power of the Allies. The United States was at first preoccupied with the war in the Pacific, and Washington and London resisted Stalin's entreaties to establish immediately a second front in western Europe to take pressure off the Red Army. In 1942 the Germans thrust to Stalingrad and the Caucasus, planning ultimately to link up with the Japanese in India, isolate Russia, and win the war. The tenacious Soviet resistance at Stalingrad, denying to the Germans the Volga crossing, showed how fully patriotism and defensive ardor had repaired the prewar damage to Russia's morale. Stalingrad was Hitler's high-water mark; the tide turned when the Soviets struck back and surrounded the army of Marshal Friedrich von Paulus, just when British and American forces opened their offensive in North Africa. Hitler's demise was only a matter of time and diplomacy.

The unity of the Allies began to crack as soon as they realized that they could not be defeated. As was so often the case during World War II, the Cold War, and the New Cold War in the 1980s, the trouble spot was Poland. When the Nazis invaded, Poland's conservative government had fled to Paris and then to London, where it continued to be recognized by the United States and Britain as the legitimate government-in-exile. As part of the comradely spirit of alliance, Stalin had recognized the London Poles, while yielding no claims on the Polish territory he had held from 1939 to 1941. But in April 1943 the Germans announced that they had discovered in the Katyn Forest near Smolensk, in German-occupied territory, the mass graves of Polish officers whom the Russians had captured in 1939 and then allegedly executed. The Russians immediately rejected the charge, though the preponderance of the evidence points to Soviet culpability. When the London Poles insisted on an accounting, Moscow broke diplomatic relations.

Soon afterward, in July 1943, the Red Army began its great counterdrive with the classic tank battle at Kursk, and did not stop until it finally reached Berlin. By the end of 1943, the Germans had been driven almost completely out of pre-1939 Soviet territory.

During the winter of 1944 the Soviets broke the siege of Leningrad and pushed into the Baltic states, and in the spring of 1944 for the first time they crossed their 1941 boundary into ethnic Poland and northern Rumania. It became apparent, much to Churchill's dismay, that all of eastern and southeastern Europe was to be liberated from the Nazis by the Soviets. The ultimate fate of this region was the main subject of debate at the summit conferences held by the Allied leaders during the last two years of the war.

Bargaining among the Allies began in Moscow in October 1943, with the first meeting of the respective foreign ministers, Molotov, Anthony Eden, and Cordell Hull. The Americans and British promised to invade France the following year; the Russians agreed to attend a summit conference in Tehran; and all three endorsed the concept of a United Nations organization to secure postwar order. At Tehran in November, in return for Stalin's assurances that he would cooperate in the destruction of Nazism, the defeat of Japan, and the establishment of the UN, the Americans and the British agreed to Russia's 1941 frontier with Poland and accepted his offer of German territory east of the Oder to compensate the Poles. The Americans, in their concern to crush Hitler and put an end to traditional balance-of-power diplomacy, appeared to stand closer to the Russians than to the British, a point that only encouraged Stalin in his determination to dominate eastern Europe.

The potential for East-West friction grew during 1944, as the Red Army advanced and the D-Day invasion tempered Stalin's fears that the Americans and British might leave him to fight Hitler alone. Having occupied that portion of ethnic Poland west of the river Bug and east of the Vistula, the Soviets in July established a provisional Polish government in the city of Lublin. This was the Communist-dominated Committee of National Liberation, including only token representation from the prewar government-in-exile. Stalin knew that only such a Soviet-dominated regime would readily accede to the 1941 boundary that he was determined to hold.

The issue of postwar boundaries was thus compounded by the prospect that Communist regimes would be imposed on Soviet-liberated countries. This was understood clearly by the Polish underground loyal to the prewar government, when it rose up in Warsaw in August 1944 in the expectation of greeting the Russians with an autonomous government. Stalin's response was to hold the Red Army inactive on the opposite bank of the Vistula and (save for some futile sorties by the Polish units operating with the Russians) allow the Germans to crush the non-Communist Polish resistance.

A parallel struggle between revolutionaries and traditionalists had already erupted in Yugoslavia and Greece, where Communist and royalist resistance movements were competing for ultimate control and on occasion fighting each other as much as the German occupiers. Again, it was the advance of the Red Army that determined the fate of one country after another. When the Russians pressed down through Rumania late in the summer of 1944, Rumania and Bulgaria deserted the Axis cause and concluded armistice agreements with Moscow. These developments compelled a general German withdrawal from the Balkans, including Greece and southern Yugoslavia. Churchill, convinced that the Americans would not support a drive from Italy into the Balkans and sensing that eastern Europe would inevitably be divided into spheres of influence, struck his famous percentage deal with Stalin in October. The Western Allies would accord the Soviets 90 percent influence in Rumania and 75 percent in Bulgaria and Hungary; Greece would be 90 percent British; and Yugoslavia would be fifty-fifty. It is by no means accidental that to this day the spheres of the North Atlantic Treaty Organization and the Warsaw Pact, as well as Yugoslav neutrality, follow just these lines in southeastern Europe, for Churchill's proposal reflected and delimited the actual zone of domination by Soviet military forces.

The partition of the Balkans entailed the first direct application of Western force in what was shortly to be recognized as the Cold War division of Europe. Churchill, though he had supported Tito as the most effective enemy of the Germans in Yugoslavia, had no intention of letting the Communists control Greece. Within days of the agreement with Stalin, British forces landed in Athens with the Greek government-in-exile; when the Communist guerrillas resisted efforts to disband them, fighting broke out. This was the beginning of the Greek civil war that lasted, with interludes, for four years.

Postwar cooperation among the superpowers was already under a cloud when the three Allied chiefs of state met for the second time, in February 1945, at Yalta in the Crimea. Stalin held most of the cards. Roosevelt urgently wanted the Russians to join the war against Japan and to participate in the UN, while Churchill tried to hedge against Soviet domination of eastern Europe. The future of Germany was central for all three, but they agreed on little, save that the country should be divided into military occupation zones—Soviet, British, American, and French—and that it should make reparations. Poland, now largely liberated and administered by the Soviet-sponsored provisional government, was the focus of contention, not so much over its new boundaries as over its political future. Stalin was determined to keep the country under a "friendly government," which, considering the recent past, was inconceivable except under Soviet occupation or a Communist dictatorship. Roosevelt wanted a democratic Poland but had to settle for Soviet promises of free elections—promises that proved to be worthless. He did succeed in persuading the Soviets to participate in the UN and to help finish the war in the Pacific, though their natural interests hardly required the concessions that were offered to secure these commitments.

From the American standpoint the Yalta Conference was a critical event, both in its immediate effect in world politics and in its long term impact on American foreign-policy debates. Yalta was the turning point from war to cold war. It was the culmination of the Grand Alliance, and at the same time it set the stage for the subsequent East-West confrontations in Europe and the Far East. Yalta was for just this reason the focal point of domestic controversy in the United States for the next decade and a half.

For many Americans, Yalta was a capitulation to Communism; for some, the beginning of a quixotic provocation; for others, the most reasonable division of great-power influence that could be achieved under the circumstances. Underlying these differences was a profound tension between American hopes and international realities, between the American vision of world justice and democracy and the Soviet (and British) expectation of a world divided, as in the past, into great-power spheres of influence. At Yalta, the United States wanted above all to assure the defeat and punishment of the Axis powers and the formation of the United Nations. Stalin's priority was to establish as wide a sphere as he could manage, whether by persuasion or coercion. But the United States could never approve of his combination of imperialism and Communist dictatorship, and inevitably came to assume the role of world policeman against the Marxists.

In the remaining months of the war, the Allies' once-cordial relations rapidly deteriorated. Germany's collapse came quickly in March and April 1945, amid Soviet charges that the British and Americans were conspiring with the German command to occupy the country and keep the Russians out. But stiff German resistance in the east could not prevent the Red Army from taking Berlin on May 2, the day after Hitler committed suicide. Hitler's designated successor, Admiral Karl Dönitz, endeavored to surrender all his forces to the Americans and British, and even though an unconditional surrender had been signed at Rheims in France (effective May 8), Stalin demanded a separate act of surrender in Berlin on May 9. V-E Day is still commemorated on different dates in the West and the East.

The end of the war in Europe registered an epochal turn in Russia's fortunes. Not only were the Soviets able to liberate their prewar territories and to repossess their gains of 1939–40, thus reversing most of the losses of Brest-Litovsk; Germany's collapse removed the last barrier to Russia's domination of the whole of eastern Europe, which had been dreamed of by the Pan-Slavists but thwarted by the German, Austrian, and Ottoman empires. Stalin had no intention of relinquishing such extraordinary strategic gains, and all the diplomatic efforts of Britain and the United States were unable to alter the outcome.

The last Allied summit meeting—now with Harry Truman in place of Roosevelt—was the Potsdam Conference in Soviet-occupied eastern Germany in July 1945. Areas of friction were already multiplying: the Russians' promotion of Communist governments in Poland and Rumania, Soviet suspicions that the Allies had schemed to accept the surrender of the Germans unilaterally, near-hostilities between the Yugoslav Communists and Allied forces in Italy over Trieste, and the abrupt American termination of lend-lease aid to the Soviet Union (made more provocative by the decision of foreign economic administrator Leo Crowley, afterward countermanded by President Truman, even to stop ships en route). By this time, Russia's control of eastern Europe was irreversible; it was enough that the Western powers could rebuff Stalin's demands for concessions by Turkey. Potsdam did confirm that the Soviets would enter the war against Japan, although the successful test of the first American atomic bomb made the need for this costly aid questionable. Preparations were begun for peace treaties with Germany's lesser allies. But the main issue was the future of Germany itself. It was agreed that the country would remain occupied in four zones, without its own government, until Nazi influence had been uprooted and a peace treaty prepared. Stalin's greatest interest was in reparations, in the form of German assets in eastern Europe and the physical transfer of German industrial facilities. The Western leaders acquiesced but did not specify precise limits, so that Stalin proceeded to extract all he possibly could from the Soviet occupation zone. The ultimate partitioning of Germany was already implicit.

The last act of the Grand Alliance soon followed. Japan's fighting spirit evaporated under the blast of the Hiroshima bomb. Two days later, brushing aside Japanese appeals to act as a liaison in peace negotiations, the Russians invaded Manchuria and overwhelmed the Japanese forces there. After the destruction of Nagasaki, the Japanese quickly accepted Allied conditions for "unconditional" surrender, yielded to the Russians in the field, and finally, on September 1, signed the surrender agreement on the battleship Missouri in Tokyo Bay. The circumstances dictating Russia's last real venture in alliance politics had come to an end.

9

Checkpoint Charlie, Berlin

Cold War and Coexistence

With the end of the Second World War, the subject of Russia and its relations with the United States grows almost unmanageably complicated and controversial. The two countries had emerged as the world's superpowers, and each automatically became the central concern of the other's foreign policy. Their hostility affected events all over the world, which in turn intensified the contest between them.

According to Bernard Baruch, it was Herbert Bayard Swope of the *New York Herald Tribune* who coined the phrase "Cold War"; but it was Walter Lippmann who made it common currency in every language. The Cold War had no precedent in modern history: two victorious allies, between them dominating international affairs after a world war, immediately squared off in a pattern of mutual denunciations and military brinkmanship. One face-off followed another, through changes of leadership and alternations in tactics on both sides. Gradually, the very bad relations under Stalin modulated to the occasionally good relations under Khrushchev, though no dramatic event signaled the change, and some would say today that the Cold War never ended.

Nevertheless, Soviet-American relations eventually entered a distinctly new era. By the time Khrushchev's reign gave way to Brezhnev's, world politics had moved beyond simple U.S.-Soviet bipolarity. International Communism had splintered into hostile segments ranging from Chinese radicalism to Eurocommunist revisionism; American political life had become preoccupied with domestic turmoil and the Vietnam War; nonaligned nations of the third world were growing in influence; and the specter of nuclear destruction hovered over everyone. The clear alignments and simple answers that had characterized the Cold War had become things of the past. These were the circumstances that made possible the politics of détente in the 1960s and 1970s.

■ The Big Two

The overriding novelty of the postwar era was the superpower confrontation of the United States and the USSR, in a world where every other major country had slipped from the ranks of the independent great powers. World War II had brought the fall of France, the collapse of Italy, the destruction of Hitler's Germany, and the surrender and demilitarization of Japan. Although liberated France and China were occasionally taken into the confidence of the superpowers, their influence was limited, and even the British, drained by the war and outclassed economically and demographically, found that they had neither the means nor the will to play a leading role independent of the Americans. Only the United States and Russia remained as independent centers of power capable of determining their own destiny.

This redistribution of power, coupled with the vast historical and philosophical differences between the two countries, made distrust inevitable and conflict likely, regardless of the aims of any individual leaders. History's new twist was to define Russia as America's main problem and to define America in the same way for the Soviets.

For the Soviet Union, the war was an unprecedented opportunity to address age-old anxieties and ambitions. Despite the toll it had paid in blood and treasure, the USSR had emerged with its political and economic systems intact and with the military might to decide the fate of half of Europe. All those powers—Germany, France, Britain, Japan—who had stood in the way of Russian expansion during the past two centuries were defeated or exhausted. Not only had the Soviets been able to repossess the territories they had once lost in Europe and the Far East, but by V-E Day the Red Army had occupied the entire eastern European power vacuum between Russia and Germany. If Stalin could maintain his influence over these small countries, he would realize the wildest dreams of the Pan-Slavists and the imperial court. Russia would gain a security zone in the west such as it had never enjoyed before. No power was left on the European continent—or in the Eastern Hemisphere, for that matter—that could seriously threaten the Soviet Union or challenge its hegemony within its newly won sphere.

Yet postwar Russia was still driven by a mania for security that no assurances from the United States could assuage. The "Yalta Axioms" (to use Daniel Yergin's term)—that is, the Roosevelt administration's optimistic assumptions that Stalin could be cajoled with understanding words and tangible concessions into helping to keep the peace—were simply wrong. Stalin, after all, was the man who thought that class struggle intensified the nearer his purges came to extirpating the last remnants of "bourgeois" opposition within the Soviet Union. His assumptions about the outside world followed a similar logic: after the demise of Hitler, the capitalist encirclement became even more dangerous under U.S. leadership. The Grand Alliance was finished, and the Soviet Union could look only to its own resources, guile, and tenacity to assure its survival.

Contrary to the almost universal belief among Americans during the Cold War, this reasoning did not mean that Russia was still driven by a Marxist commitment to export the Communist faith. Postwar Russia was no longer a revolutionary society in any meaningful sense, but only a dictatorial amalgam of conservative policies and revolutionary rhetoric. The country had fallen into the hands of a paranoid and vindictive despot who used Marxism to rationalize his obsessions and who made his terroristic methods an integral part of the nation's politics. With the exception of a handful of Stalin's sycophants who had survived the purges, the Soviet leaders were new men, crudely educated bureaucrats who knew little of the outside world and cared nothing for the original Marxist values of equality and internationalism, let alone democracy and world understanding. Though they knew something of the history of European power politics, men like Stalin, Molotov, and Andrei Zhdanov could not understand the naiveté, idealism, and self-righteousness of the Americans, or their belief in good-faith bargaining, or their need to placate the electorate. Any statements to this effect they took as veiled threats or devious deceptions, and refused to believe that the United States wanted little more than cooperation and understanding. To the Soviets, all independent countries and all independent political movements were by definition their adversaries.

Stalin's real goals were system maintenance and national power, as they had been since the 1930s. Socialist economic planning, military force, and police coercion were the means to these ends. Marxist-Leninist ideology had become wholly instrumental, legitimizing the bureaucracy and defining the foreign threat that justified the discipline and sacrifices of the Stalinist system. As a source of political guidance and inspiration, ideology had been dead for years, certainly since the purges. In foreign policy it had been moribund since 1921. Ideology was perhaps most useful in rallying foreigners— whether party members, well-meaning liberals, alienated workers, or frustrated nationalists—to support Soviet influence or Soviet interests in the belief that they were contributing to the brave new world.

In 1945 the United States was just coming out of its traditional isolationism—untouched by invasion, economically healthy, enormously powerful. Though inept at peacetime power politics and uncomfortable with the new superpower bipolarity, the country found itself simultaneously challenged by the Soviets and responsible for the security of all of its democratic friends, with no option of withdrawal. The problems of the postwar world were much more foreign to the American tradition than to the Russian.

American reactions to the new confrontation with the Soviets were spread, as befit an open society, all across the political spectrum, left, right, and center, each relying on different assumptions about Soviet motives. Most arguments were marked by great ignorance about the Soviet Union and all were influenced by the controversies that the United States had gone through in the thirties over domestic as well as foreign policy.

Liberals on the left, hoping to continue New Deal reforms and the One World ideal of the Grand Alliance, saw the Cold War as a threat to both. People of this mind, including former vice-president Henry Wallace and former ambassador Davies, supposing that things would have gone differently had Roosevelt lived, believed that the Soviets' security concerns were valid and blamed the Truman administration for provoking Moscow's Cold War stance. Subsequent Soviet actions undercut the credibility of this reasoning, though revisionist historians revived it in the 1960s.

Political moderates found the Soviet Union a threatening power, whatever its motives. The Truman administration, fearful that Americans would relapse into isolationism, quickly adopted this attitude and called upon the country to accept its role as the leader of the "free world." As time passed, Truman's formulation of Soviet motives became more and more simplistic and ideological even though this ultimately strengthened the hand of alarmists on the right.

Conservative American thinking about the Soviets had two different sources—on the one hand, the isolationist and anti-European tradition of Middle America, and, on the other, the legacy of the first Red Scare, which perpetuated the view of Communism as a virulent ideological poison. Irrational fear of Communism peaked after the Communist victory in China, an area where isolationist axioms never applied, and then it focused above all on alleged subversion and betrayal within the United States.

The revolutionary interpretation of Soviet policy was highly plausible in the Cold War years. It corresponded to what the Russians were saying (or, more precisely, to what they were believed to have said) and it appeared to be validated by Russia's actions in

Eastern Europe and in Asia. U.S. government agencies published voluminous collections of quotations from Marx, Lenin, and Stalin, and high officials were reported to take these materials to bed with them in order to extract hints as to what the Soviet Union would do next. But interpretations based on this documentation fell short in two major respects: they misread the teachings of Marxism on world revolution, and they failed to appreciate the changes in the relation between theory and practice under the Soviet regime. The Marxist theory of world revolution is a socioeconomic prediction, not a military prescription. Some confusion stemmed from Marxist talk of the inevitability of war, but this was war among the imperialistic capitalists, as described in Lenin's *Imperialism*. Whatever their secret staff plans for opportune contingencies, the Soviets have never believed that they are required to attack in order to advance the proletarian revolution. Furthermore, with the emergence of Stalin's dictatorship and his practice of manipulating Marxism-Leninism to justify his policies, ideology lost all power either to compel or restrain Soviet actions, whether foreign or domestic. If the Soviet leadership has at any time considered war as a means of expansion, it is in spite of Marxism, not because of it.

▪ The Expansion of Communism

From a strictly national point of view, the two years following the end of the Second World War were the most successful period in Russia's international relations since the reign of Alexander I. Impervious to Western outrage, Stalin imposed Communist rule on all of eastern Europe, and bequeathed to his successors a determination never to relinquish any lands won with "Soviet blood." From this commitment has stemmed the whole series of crises in Europe between the Soviet Union and the democratic West.

The confrontation over Moscow's influence in eastern Europe and Germany has obscured the fact that Soviet expansion beyond the zone of wartime occupation was easily restrained, at least in Europe. All the areas communized in eastern Europe had been occupied by the Soviets during the war or by wartime agreement; in Yugoslavia and Albania, Communist guerrillas took power when the Soviets forced the Germans to retreat from the Balkans in late 1944 and early 1945. Subsequent East-West controversy concerned not Russian expansion but only Communist political consolidation behind

Map legend:

Boundaries of 1938 — ·—·—·—

Soviet Boundary in 1941 — •••••••••

Farthest Axis advance, 1941-42 — ◊◊◊◊◊

Boundaries of 1947 — ------

Boundaries of Union Republics — ··········

Soviet Gains 1939-1945 ▓

Satellite States ▤

Nonaligned Communist States ▨

World War II and the Soviet Sphere in Europe

the limit of the Red Army's farthest advance—a line that was shortly to become immortalized as the Iron Curtain. West of the Iron Curtain, to be sure, the Soviets faced a more serious American commitment as well as governments that were far stronger than the regimes in the Soviet-occupied East. But it is questionable whether Stalin seriously intended to press the fortunes of Communism beyond the region of traditional Russian interest and feasible Russian control, into major industrial countries.

According to Milovan Djilas, the former Yugoslav leader who went to Moscow on missions for Tito, "Stalin felt instinctively that the creation of revolutionary centers outside Moscow could endanger its supremacy in world Communism ... He was always ready to leave them in the lurch whenever they slipped out of his grasp." He ordered French Communists who had fought in the Resistance to surrender their weapons to De Gaulle's government, and to refrain from any attempted uprising that might provoke a new war. He made no effort to challenge Anglo-American influence in Italy or U.S. control of Japan, except to cite these situations as justification for his own dominance in the Balkans. Some of Stalin's lieutenants in Zhdanov's camp may have contemplated a more revolutionary strategy built on the support of the Communist parties of France and Italy as well as on a political appeal for an undivided Germany; but the Soviets' Cold War effort, especially after Zhdanov's death in 1948, was mainly directed at preserving their postwar gains rather than extending them.

Poland remained the prime source of East-West tension during the incubation of the Cold War in 1945–46. Since the Polish underground had been crushed in the 1944 uprising, the Soviets easily installed the Lublin Communist regime in Warsaw after finally pushing the Germans out early in 1945. They made only the barest gestures toward the coalition promised at Yalta. Averell Harriman, American ambassador to Moscow at the time, confided to Secretary of the Navy James Forrestal, "We might well have to face an ideological warfare just as vigorous and dangerous as fascism or Nazism." He advised President Truman, a mere ten days after Roosevelt's death on April 12 elevated him to the White House, to get tough with the Russians lest the United States be faced with "a barbarian invasion of Europe." The same day Truman met Molotov, on his way to the UN founding conference in San Francisco, and berated him for Russia's manipulations in Poland. Said Molotov, "I have never been talked to like that in my life"—a strong comment for a graduate of the Stalin school of politics. Stalin responded with an angry cable to Truman: "You evidently do not agree that the Soviet Union is entitled to seek in Poland a government that would be friendly to it, that the Soviet government cannot agree to the existence in Poland of a government hostile to it. This is rendered imperative, among other things, by the blood that the Soviet people freely shed on the fields of Poland for the liberation of that country . . . To put it plainly, you want me to renounce the interests of the security of the Soviet Union."

Discounting Western outrage, Stalin continued to gather power for the local Communists in Poland and also in Rumania and Bulgaria. In the fall of 1944 both of these two Balkan satellites of Nazi Germany had signed armistice agreements with the Allies (like Finland at the same time and Hungary a few months later) that gave ultimate authority to the Soviet military. Though the Americans and British sat on the Allied Control Commissions in each country, they had as little influence as the Soviets had in Italy and Japan. In Bulgaria the local Communists, organized as the "Fatherland Front," staged an uprising and greeted the arriving Russians with a new Communist-dominated government. In Rumania, where King Michael ousted the pro-Axis government in a palace coup, the Soviets were content to work more gradually through the established regime; in December 1944 they put local Communists in charge of the police ministries, and the following February installed the pro-Communist Petru Groza, leader of the "Ploughman's Front," as prime minister. Andrei Vyshinsky, of Moscow Trial fame, now deputy foreign commissar, went to Bucharest to preside over this last operation. Only some months later, however, did the tightening grip of the Communists in the two countries draw the West's attention.

Warnings from the American Embassy in Moscow in the fall of 1945 prompted the Truman administration to dispatch to Rumania and Bulgaria an investigating team headed by Kentucky publisher Mark Ethridge. The Ethridge Report, submitted in December, found the Russians guilty of "constant and vigorous intrusion into the internal affairs of these countries." Nevertheless, the Moscow Foreign Ministers Conference a few days later arrived at a compromise: the Soviets would allow free elections and coalition governments, in the spirit of the Popular Front, in return for Western recognition. On this basis, peace treaties with all of Hitler's former satellites were drawn up and signed in the summer of 1946. But nothing prevented the Soviets and the local Communists from gaining power through "salami tactics"—that is, gradually slicing up the opposition by arrests and rigged elections. By 1947 the "People's Democracies"—Rumania, Bulgaria, Hungary, and Poland—had to all intents and purposes been converted into one-party Communist dictatorships closely controlled by the Soviet military and police.

There were three distinct exceptions to this pattern. One was Finland, where parliamentary government had remained essentially intact through the war and continued to function despite the country's capitulation to the Russians and the presence of a large Communist Party. Another exception, temporarily, was Czechoslovakia, where the Soviets permitted the restoration of the prewar government-in-exile, since they were assured of powerful Communist participation and the sympathy of the only pro-Russian public in eastern Europe. A third case was Yugoslavia, where an indigenous guerrilla revolution had put Tito and the Communist Party in power immediately after the Germans retreated from Belgrade in October 1944. The same path was taken by Yugoslavia's satellite Communists in Albania, and would doubtless have been followed in Greece had it not been for British intervention.

Greece illustrates the limits of Stalin's shifting tactics during the onset of the Cold War. Honoring his sphere-of-interest deal with Churchill, Stalin offered no objection to the return of the prewar Greek government from Cairo and allowed the British-backed royalists to put down the Communist resistance army, ELAS. This did not dispose of the local Communists, who resumed their struggle a year and a half later when the Cold War battle lines had been drawn; but for the moment Greece was left to the West.

Confrontations over Stalin's sphere-building spread rapidly from eastern Europe to other areas. At issue were portions of two Asian countries—northern Iran and China's Manchurian provinces—occupied by the Soviets in the course of the war. Both areas had been zones of tsarist influence and ambition. Stalin's aims were immediate and restorationist: in Iran he wanted to secure oil concessions and to make the northwest, Turkic-speaking part of the country a Soviet satellite; in Manchuria he strove to prolong his occupation and exploit the region by claiming Japanese assets there as reparations. A treaty concluded with Chiang Kai-shek's government in August 1945 satisfied the Yalta arrangements and restored Russia's pre-1904 privileges in Manchuria. But Chiang's government and, by extension, the United States were quickly angered when Stalin stripped Manchuria of its industrial equipment and permitted Chinese Communst forces to make the region a base for their brewing civil war with the Nationalists. The case of Iran, meanwhile, became the first order of business for the newly formed United Nations. Convening in London in January 1946, the UN Security Council heard Iran's complaints about the Soviets' prolonged occupation and their support of separatists in the northern part of the country. In the face of strong American protests, but with the promise of oil concessions (soon to be repudiated), the Soviets pulled out of Iran. Here, as in its ill-considered efforts to pressure Turkey into sharing control of the Dardanelles, Moscow's sphere-of-influence policy was a failure, and the USSR still faces hostile states on its Middle Eastern borders.

As East-West tensions grew, Anglo-American perceptions of Soviet motives changed abruptly, and this in turn affected Soviet perceptions of the West. The triggering event was a speech by Stalin on February 9, 1946, in the course of the "campaign" for election of a new Supreme Soviet. His remarks seem unexceptional in retrospect, but at the time, they were thought to signal an end to Allied cooperation and an unabashed return to the ideological politics of Communist revolution. Stalin did indeed revive the Marxist theory of war as "the inevitable result of the development of world economic and political forces on the basis of modern monopoly capitalism"; and he made clear his conviction that the recent victory of Soviet arms confirmed the virtue of party control, planned industrialization, and collectivized agriculture. He did not appreciate, however, how this return to orthodoxy could be misread by nervous Western leaders as a pronouncement of the inevitability of war *between* the Soviet state and the capitalists, not just *among* the capitalists, and hence as a threat to export revolution on the tips of Soviet bayonets. No less a liberal than Supreme Court Justice William O. Douglas thought that Stalin's speech was "the declaration of World War III."

The Soviets' new rhetoric prompted the so-called Long Telegram dispatched to the State Department on February 22 by George Kennan, then chargé in the American Embassy in Moscow. Kennan had served previously in Moscow, from the reestablishment of diplomatic relations until the height of the purges in 1937. Returning in

1944, he was dismayed to find that the old spirit still prevailed. "There is serious evidence," he reported, "for the hypothesis that there are influences in the Kremlin which place the preservation of a rigid police regime in Russia far ahead of the happy development of Russia's foreign relations." Unsurprised by the Soviets' designs on eastern Europe, Kennan was nonetheless shocked by the electoral charade of 1946—the first since he had observed the initial installation of the Supreme Soviet under the Stalin Constitution in 1937. It confirmed that the system had not changed. Kennan therefore took it upon himself to argue against the assumption, carried over by most Americans from the wartime alliance, that conciliatory gestures and agreements on specific sore spots could mollify the Soviets and preserve the peace. The problem, as he analyzed it in his cable, was compounded by Marxist suspicions of capitalist intervention and old Russian fears of the outside world, a "neurotic view of world affairs" providing "justification for that increase of military and police power of Russian state, for that isolation of Russian population from outside world, and for that fluid and constant pressure to extend limits of Russian police power which are together the natural and instinctive urges of Russian rulers." He predicted that overt and covert political action by foreign Communist parties would be revived to help promote Soviet security by undermining America's strength at home and influence abroad. Nevertheless, he maintained (along the lines of the containment theory he published a year later) that the West could restrain the Soviets with superior force and self-confidence while Russia's internal problems gradually moderated the system.

Kennan's assessment, disseminated throughout the U.S. government, had a landmark effect. Everyone now expected the worst, and each successive Soviet action confirmed the expectation. Meanwhile, for the general public in the West the great sensation was the speech delivered on March 5, 1946, at Westminster College in Missouri by former prime minister Churchill, who was visiting the United States as a guest of President Truman: "From Stettin on the Baltic to Trieste on the Adriatic, an iron curtain has descended across the Continent." Though Truman did not immediately endorse Churchill's plea for the Anglo-Saxon powers to cooperate in the defense of freedom, Stalin gave *Pravda* an interview in which he denounced the Americans and British for conspiring against the Soviet Union's right to exist. Attributing to Churchill a Hitlerite racial theory of Anglo-Saxon superiority, he recalled the intervention of 1918 and charged the British leader with "a call to war with the Soviet Union." As the German invasion had shown, eastern Europe was essential for Russia's defense: "Why should one be surprised by the fact that the Soviet Union, desiring to ensure its security for the future, wants these countries to have governments that are loyal in relation to the Soviet Union?" Stalin's reaction to Churchill's speech suggests that he had been abruptly disabused of the prospect of a three-power world in which war between capitalist states was still conceivable. Now he saw the likelihood of a united enemy, underscoring his fear of capitalist encirclement. This meant to Stalin that he might as well abandon diplomatic restraint in expanding and consolidating Russia's security zone.

With the battle lines clearly drawn in Stalin's mind, the locus of East-West confrontation shifted to Germany, where the Allies were endeavoring to agree on the country's future. The immediate issue was reparations, agreed on in principle at Yalta and Potsdam but never in specific amounts. More broadly, with great import for the future of Europe, the question was whether Germany would be pulled West, fall under Soviet domination, maintain a neutral balance, or suffer partition. Stalin's lieutenants apparently argued over the options and their implications for the Soviet zone of occupation; presumably the ideologist Zhdanov hoped to use it as a base for expanding Communist influence, whereas the pragmatist Georgi Malenkov preferred to keep it a Soviet outpost while exploiting it economically. Malenkov eventually prevailed, with the result that the Americans and British, who were supporting the entire German economy, found themselves subsidizing reparations to the USSR.

Convinced that Germany was the key to restraining Soviet expansion, Britain and the United States took steps by mid-1946 to halt the drain of reparations from the western zones and prepare for the eventual creation of a viable West German state. Secretary of State James Byrnes, in his famous Stuttgart speech of September 1946, sketched a positive future for the Germans: "Germany is a part of Europe, and recovery in Europe, and particularly in the states adjoining Germany, will be slow indeed if Germany with her great resources of iron and coal is turned into a poorhouse ... The American people hope to see peaceful, democratic Germans become and remain free and independent." But as a practical matter, "If complete unification cannot be secured, we shall do everything in our power to secure maximum possible unification"—that is, without the Soviet zone. Short-range Soviet behavior and the Western response it had provoked thus dictated the outcome of the German question: the country would be partitioned into a Soviet-dominated eastern zone (given up for lost by the Western powers, however much they talked about German unity) and a far more powerful West German state committed to the anti-Soviet alliance. Once he recognized this frightening prospect, Stalin softened his stand on German unification, but it was too late. General George Marshall, newly installed as secretary of state, returned from discussions with Stalin in April 1947 convinced that Western economic recovery was essential to stop the Russians: he had not taken advantage of the opportunity to bargain for a united, neutralized Germany.

Marshall's reaction reflected Washington's new view of Soviet policy. In September 1946, presidential aide Clark Clifford had prepared a top secret report summarizing U.S. diplomatic and military opinion about Soviet actions and motives. This crucial report articulated the assumptions of Soviet aggressiveness that underlay U.S. policy throughout the Cold War era, and anticipated all of the major policy initiatives that followed: the containment policy, the Truman Doctrine to aid nations threatened by Communism, the Marshall Plan to restore economic stability in Europe, the revival of Germany as a Western partner, the North Atlantic Treaty Organization, the domestic Loyalty Program and the prosecution of the American Communist leaders, and the pursuit of national security based on U.S. superiority in nuclear weaponry. "Soviet leaders appear to be conducting their nation on a course of aggrandizement designed to lead to eventual world domination by the USSR," Clifford wrote. Such was his extreme conclusion, drawn from Stalin's election-speech comment that World War II had been the inevitable result of capitalism. Clifford presumed without any textual foundation that "Soviet leaders adhere to the Marxian theory of ultimate destruction of capitalist states by communist states," while claiming that "they strive to postpone the inevitable conflict in order to strengthen and prepare the Soviet Union for its clash with the western democracies." The report prescribed all the vigorous anti-Soviet steps that the American government in fact took in the next three years. However, it also reflected Kennan's belief that U.S. military strength and firm actions could eventually moderate the Soviets' behavior and persuade them that "peaceful coexistence of capitalistic and communistic states is possible."

Stalin's response to the worsening of relations mirrored Washington's new worries about international Communist revolution. Intensifying his anti-Western propaganda, he charged that the United States had undertaken a fascist program of world domination. At the same time, Zhdanov began a domestic campaign for ideological tightening against the "putrid and baneful" influence of "bourgeois culture." Politically, culturally, and economically, Stalin's Russia elected to seal itself off from the entire world outside the sphere of its direct control.

Meanwhile, Maxim Litvinov, soon to retire from his post as deputy foreign minister, confirmed the West's worst fears. He held a series of secret talks with U.S. diplomats and journalists in Moscow, culminating in a sensational interview with CBS correspondent Richard C. Hottelet (passed on to the American Embassy but not published until after Litvinov's death several years later). "If the West acceded to the current Soviet demands," he warned, "it would be faced, after a more or less short time, with the next series of demands." Lamenting Stalin's rejection of coexistence with the West, Litvinov reflected on the aggressive acts that a totalitarian ruler could commit in the name of security—and the example he cited was Hitler.

It was in this unpromising atmosphere that the first modest efforts at nuclear arms control and atomic energy regulation through the UN came to grief. Notwithstanding the arguments of revisionist historians, there was little sign, initially, that America's possession of nuclear weapons caused much hardening of attitudes in Washington or softening in Moscow. Stalin put his own atomic weapons program into high gear, while continuing to espouse a conventional military doctrine relying on mass ground armies. By the time the Americans were ready to propose international supervision of the A-bomb (the so-called Baruch Plan), they had in fact come to regard their nuclear advantage as a major deterrent to alleged Soviet expansionism. Hence, Washington proposed the Baruch Plan in June 1946 with secret hopes that the Russians would reject it and leave the United States with the propaganda advantage. When the plan came up for formal UN consideration in September, this is exactly what the Russians did, on the obvious grounds that the inspection and verification required by the plan constituted an unacceptable breach of Soviet security. Stalin found it far easier to accept an arms race with a power he saw as his implacable enemy than to expose his police state to foreign scrutiny.

▪ Containment

By the beginning of 1947 Stalin's prophecy of Western hostility had come true. As a result of Soviet actions in eastern Europe, the dispute over Germany, the Iranian crisis, tension over Manchuria, and the breakdown of cooperation with the Soviets in occupied Korea, the U.S. government had come to the conclusion set out in the Clifford Report: that the Soviet Union was an expansive threat which would have to be vigorously countered. Stalin had actually been reasonably circumspect about areas he understood to lie in the Anglo-American sphere, but this did not prevent the Western powers from perceiving a grand design to push further.

Ironically, the situation that actually triggered America's psychological mobilization against the Soviet Union was one which Stalin apparently did not initiate and could not control. In the summer of 1946, fighting again broke out in Greece between the restored royalist government and the Communist Resistance. No doubt the Greek Communists took their cue from the signs of growing East-West tension, and they received direct support from Tito, as part of his scheme for a Balkan federation dominated by Belgrade. Guerrilla pressure on the Athens government was transmitted to its British backers, and the latter, withdrawing rapidly from the costly game of power politics, turned the problem over to the United States. The result was a series of reactions in Washington that roused the American giant to full force in its confrontation with the Soviets. Led by President Truman, Secretary of State Marshall, and Under-Secretary Dean Acheson, the United States finally began to consolidate an anti-Soviet sphere of influence that in its power and extent far overshadowed the realm of Soviet dominance. Stalin's expectation of Western enmity was now amply fulfilled by the opposing coalition that his own insensitive moves and his impetuous allies had provoked.

Within days of Britain's plea for help in Greece in March 1947, Truman called upon Congress to underwrite a program of economic and military aid not only for Greece but for Turkey as well. Without naming the Soviet Union, Truman presented an early version of the domino theory, and declared, "I believe that it must be the policy of the United States to support free peoples who are resisting attempted subjugation by armed minorities or by outside pressures." Dubbed the Truman Doctrine (by analogy with the Monroe Doctrine, also directed against Russia), the new policy implied that the United States would assist any government anywhere in the world threatened directly or indirectly by Soviet influence. Work then commenced on the ambitious plan, put forth publicly by Marshall in June 1947 and tagged with his name, to provide financial aid to the governments of Western Europe to save them from economic collapse and Communist subversion. In May the two most potent Western Communist parties, the French and the Italian, which had shared power in their respective governments since the end of the war, were forced into opposition.

As the West closed ranks, Stalin tightened all the bolts in his own security system. The last remnants of opposition in Poland, Rumania, and Bulgaria were liquidated (often physically) and the coalition government in Hungary was finally replaced by a Communist-controlled regime. When the British and French invited the Russians to the conference assembling in Paris at the end of June 1947 to consider the Marshall Plan, they sent an impressive delegation headed by Molotov. Whether Stalin had intended to participate and divert the effort or only to disrupt it is unclear, but three days after the opening of the conference the Russians walked out, declaring that it was only a scheme to subject European national sovereignty to American domination. A few days later the Poles and Czechs made clear the constraints on their own sovereignty by following Molotov's example. All this merely played into the hands of the framers of the Marshall Plan, who could not, for political reasons, start out by excluding the Soviets, but who knew that both the efficacy of the idea and its salability to Congress depended on Soviet nonparticipation.

Stalin's next provocative step was to establish a new international Communist organization to replace the defunct Comintern. This "Communist Information Bureau," or Cominform, was evidently the brainchild of Zhdanov and the ideological militants. Its task, Zhdanov declared at the founding conference held in Poland in September 1947, was to counter "America's aspirations to world supremacy" and to defend "the principle of national sovereignty against the schemes of imperialist domination represented by the Marshall Plan and World Government." The new organization linked the Communist Party of the Soviet Union with the parties in all of its new satellites—including Czechoslovakia, where the Communists were still part of a coalition government. Outside the Soviet sphere it gave membership status only to the Communist parties of France and Italy. With its headquarters in Belgrade, until then the most revolutionary of the satellite capitals, the Cominform did little but confirm the solidity of the Soviet sphere and further arouse Western opinion with this apparent proof of Russia's revolutionary intentions. After less than a year, Tito had to be expelled from the Cominform because of his resistance to Soviet domination, and the organization moved its offices and its newspaper to Bucharest. Thereafter it was mainly limited to producing anti-Tito propaganda, until in 1956, to appease the Yugoslavs, Khrushchev abolished it. Coordinating the foreign Communist parties then became the function of two departments of the Secretariat of the Communist Party of the Soviet Union: one for relations with nonruling parties, and one—headed from 1957 to 1967 by Yuri Andropov—for relations with the "Communist and Workers' Parties of Socialist Countries."

Credit for the theory underlying U.S. resistance to Soviet expansion has traditionally gone to George Kennan and his idea of containment. Having returned to Washington late in 1946 as head of the State Department Policy Planning Staff, Kennan updated his assessment of Soviet motives in a long memorandum solicited by Navy Secretary Forrestal, the leading "hawk" in the Truman cabinet. This document, after it was cleared for publication, became the celebrated "Mr. X" article printed in *Foreign Affairs* in July 1947 under the title "The Sources of Soviet Conduct."

The impact of the "X" article was doubly ironic. The concept of containment was only a derivative of Kennan's main argument, which was a pioneering explanation of the instrumental nature of Soviet ideology under Stalin. There was no Marxist timetable for world conquest, Kennan maintained; instead, he stressed the interplay between Russian xenophobia and the revolutionary state, and the Soviets' need "to justify the retention of the dictatorship by stressing the menace of capitalism abroad." The Soviets would therefore persist in their hostility and duplicity, but this did not mean "a do-or-die program to overthrow our society by a given date." Ideology was dogmatic but manipulable: "The leadership is at liberty to put forward for tactical purposes any particular thesis which it finds useful to the cause at any particular moment . . . This means that truth is not a constant but is actually created, for all intents and purposes, by the Soviet leaders themselves." From this Kennan concluded that the Soviet Union would respect outside power: "Soviet pressure against the free institutions of the western world is something that can be contained by the adroit and vigilant application of counter-force at a series of constantly shifting geographical and political points, corresponding to the shifts and manoeuvers of Soviet policy." Kennan argued, then, not so much for the *necessity* of containment as for the *possibility* of containment, meaning that the Soviet ideological drive was not so inexorable as to rule out successful resistance short of war: "The United States has it in its power to force upon the Kremlin a far greater degree of moderation and circumspection than it has had to observe in recent years, and in this way to promote tendencies [such as popular fatigue and the succession problem] which must eventually find their outlet in either the break-up or the gradual mellowing of Soviet power."

Kennan's rationale for containment was only one contribution—though the most famous, the most enduring, and possibly the most accurate—to the sweeping American reconsideration of Soviet motives that took place during these months. Most opinion leaders went far beyond Kennan's judgment and embraced the conviction that the Russians were bent on world domination to accomplish their revolutionary mission. By 1948 even the dispatches from the American Embassy in Moscow were couched in these terms. The enemy was not a government or a country, but a political force, ill-defined and dimly understood: World Communism.

The second Great Red Scare in the United States was not understood by the Soviets any more than the first; they could only blame the capitalist ruling circles for duping their subjects with alarmist fictions. In reality, America's Cold War reaction to Stalin's Russia, like the original Red Scare, was a complex psychological process compounded of many deep-rooted political and emotional factors. "To a remarkable degree," wrote John Gaddis in *Strategies of Containment,* "containment has been the product not so much of what the Russians have done, or of what has happened elsewhere in the world, but of internal forces operating within the United States."

Many commentators have noted how the country was strained by its new superpower obligations without the chance to pull back into its isolationist shell. For anxious leaders, placed in the global spotlight but unsophisticated about revolutionary ideologies, it was easy to read Marxism as aggression and see Stalin in the role of Hitler— much as Stalin and Zhdanov, likewise ill at ease as superpower leaders, read capitalism as aggression and saw Harry Truman in the role of Hitler. Among the American public, distressed by the erosion of small-town values and other social changes accelerated by the Depression, the New Deal years, and two world wars, there was a widespread tendency to equate the advocacy of any controversial novelty—progressive education, modern art, racial equality, sexual freedom, medical insurance, industrial unionism, the Tennessee Valley Authority—with Communism. Particularly important was the religious factor: Roman Catholics and conservative Protestants, especially, saw Soviet atheism as the fountainhead of a worldwide assault on traditional values and beliefs. In the more strictly political realm, associations of liberalism with "creeping socialism" and of socialism with Communism were avidly exploited by the Republican opposition. Given all these misplaced connections of domestic issues and value conflicts with the Soviet threat, it was not altogether illogical for many Americans to see subversion everywhere.

In March 1947 Truman promulgated his Loyalty Order, designed to remove suspected Communists and sympathizers (on the basis of the "Attorney General's List" of alleged subversive organizations) from the roster of federal employees. Periodic cases of espionage gave credibility to the Truman loyalty program and in many minds raised doubts about the vigilance of the administration itself. The issue was epitomized in the memorable case of Alger Hiss, accused of espionage for the Soviets when he worked in the State Department in the 1930s but nevertheless defended by New Deal and administration figures from Truman and Acheson on down, until his ultimate conviction (for perjury) in 1950. So strong were the public's fear of Communism and the political forces bent on exploiting it, that the Red Scare did not soon subside as it had in 1919–20; instead, it escalated for the next half-dozen years, to climax in the national hysteria of McCarthyism.

Communist revolutionary sentiment in the United States was in fact negligible. Relying on Popular Front tactics, the American Communists concentrated on opposing the government's postwar commitment in Europe. They joined the third-party presidential campaign launched by Henry Wallace after his break with the Truman administration, but did the effort more harm than good by exposing the movement to charges of Communist control. In November 1948 Wallace won only about a million votes—not enough, even with the Dixiecrat defection on the Democratic right wing, to deny Truman his come-from-behind victory over Thomas Dewey. From that point on, patriotism, the domestic witch-hunting mood, and a wider awareness of the nature of Stalinism rapidly eroded both the membership of the Communist Party and the public's desire for accommodation with the Soviets. The trade union influence won by Communists in certain industrial unions during the thirties was largely repudiated by the rank and file. Meanwhile, election jitters in 1948 prompted the Truman administration to take the unprecedented step of indicting and convicting the entire Communist Party leadership for conspiring to overthrow the government, on the evidence mainly of Lenin's and Stalin's early writings. The Korean War and the Hungarian Revolution delivered the coup de grace to the orthodox Marxist left, reducing it to a skeleton organization of nostalgic old-timers. When new fields for revolutionary activity were opened up in the 1960s by the Black Revolution and the Youth Revolution, the Communist Party was unable to make use of the opportunity and yielded the ground to the peculiar collection of un-ideological protesters and utopian schismatics known as the New Left.

Nowhere else in the democratic world, save perhaps in West Germany, was postwar Communism so ineffectual. This may, ironically, explain Americans' irrational fear of internal Communism: living in a tension-filled society, they found it easy to make a vague and unseen enemy the scapegoat for their various anxieties. Throughout continental Europe, by contrast, Communists had become respectable through their energetic role in the anti-German resistance movements. In the early postwar elections, they won 10 to 30 percent of the vote, not as revolutionaries but as anti-Nazis and champions of social justice. Their appeal rapidly faded in northern Europe, but in France and Italy they remained entrenched opposition forces, solidly based in the trade unions and adhering to the Soviet line until Muscovite discipline over the movement began to break down in the late 1950s.

Outside Europe and the Far East, Soviet influence was negligible in the forties and early fifties. Stalin's government saw little or no advantage in cultivating ties with newly independent, non-Communist governments such as India and the Arab states, which it regarded as creatures of Western imperialism. In 1948, following the Zhdanov line of encouraging revolutionary adventures, the Russians (so the pattern suggests) inspired and coordinated a series of uprisings by local Communists in Southeast Asia and southern India. In India and Indonesia the rebels were easily put down; in Burma, Malaya, and the Philippines they set in motion guerrilla actions that the local authorities (or, in the case of Malaya, the British) took years to suppress. The Vietnamese Communists, already in revolt against the French, began to receive Soviet and Chinese aid once Mao's forces reached their border at the end of 1949. But the Soviet Union made no broad attempt (as it had in the 1920s and 1930s) to seek new friends solely on the basis of anti-imperialist sentiment. The world that Stalin aimed to create was hermetically sealed: he granted no autonomy within the bloc, and placed no credence in political opportunities outside it, unless Soviet puppets were in charge.

The American policy of containment, sustained by growing popular support for any measure that promised to stop Communism, was an immediate success. Although—or because—it seemed to validate the presumption of imperialist hostility, it compelled the Soviets to step more cautiously. In Europe they allowed their various probes to be checked or deterred almost before the containment policy went into effect. Beyond the Soviet sphere, there was serious Communist pressure in four European countries: in Greece, through renewed guerrilla warfare; in France and Italy, through election campaigns and strikes aimed at disrupting participation in the Marshall Plan; and in Germany, in the effort to extract reparations and increase Soviet influence. All these efforts were frustrated by the Western powers: the guerrillas in Greece were beaten back with American advice and aid; the center-right coalition governments of France and Italy withstood attack by the Communist-controlled unions; and the Soviet bid for influence in Germany was rebuffed as the United States, Britain, and France gave up the idea of four-power administration and combined their three zones into the eventual Federal Republic of West Germany.

Again Stalin responded by hardening his own position. In February 1948 the Czechoslovakian Communists, holding the premiership and 40 percent of the seats in Parliament, took advantage of a cabinet crisis (with Soviet guidance—deputy foreign minister Valerian Zorin was in Prague for the occasion) to exclude anti-Communists from the government and impose one-party rule. A similar fate might have been in store for Finland had not the Finnish military intervened, forcing Stalin to settle for guaranteed neutrality on the part of his northern neighbor.

To the U.S. government, the coup in Prague immediately confirmed the world-domination theory of Soviet policy, even though Czechoslovakia—like Afghanistan in 1978–79—was only the victim of Soviet tightening within an established sphere of influence. Truman commented privately, "We are faced with exactly the same situation with which Britain and France were faced in 1938–39 with Hitler." A genuine war scare gripped the American government, as the president went before a joint session of Congress to denounce Russia's "ruthless course of action and the clear design to extend it to the remaining free nations of Europe." A new policy analysis by the National Security Council (NSC-7, dated March 30, 1948) abandoned Kennan's thesis of eventual moderation and set forth the premises that governed American policy for the next decade: "The ultimate objective of Soviet-directed World Communism is the domination of the world ... In its relations with other nations the USSR is guided by the communist dogma that the peaceful coexistence of communist and capitalist states is in the long run impossible ... The USSR is attempting to gain world domination by subversion," with time on its side, "but might ultimately resort to war if necessary to gain its ends." It was in this state of alarm that Congress finally passed the appropriations bill for the Marshall Plan, and the concept of the North Atlantic Treaty Organization—a permanent alliance binding the United States to the defense of Western Europe—was born.

These responses did not deter Stalin from one last confrontation, this time in Berlin. Pursuant to wartime agreements, West Berlin remained an enclave of Western military rule in the midst of the Soviet occupation zone, even after the Russians had terminated four-power administration. Challenged by Western steps to unite their zones of Germany and introduce a new currency, the Soviet leadership resolved to eliminate the irritating presence of the Western powers in Berlin by cutting off the access routes across Soviet-occupied territory and starving them out. So began the Berlin

Blockade in June 1948, countered, to the Soviets' great surprise, by the successful Western airlift of food and fuel to the beleaguered city all through the winter of 1948–49. As tension mounted, Washington became convinced that the anticipated Soviet attack on Western Europe was imminent. Stalin had overplayed his hand so far that by the spring of 1949 Truman ordered the deployment of nuclear-armed bombers in Europe. Faced with this threat, Stalin backed down and ordered the blockade lifted. The theory of containment was signally validated: resistance at the point of pressure made the Soviets yield. More than that: against the backdrop of the Berlin crisis the three Western allies had consummated the division of Germany by granting sovereign independence to the new Federal Republic in the West, leaving Stalin to follow suit by recognizing the Communists in the Soviet zone as the German Democratic Republic.

In the meantime, during the Berlin Blockade a new permanent mechanism of containment was put in place, over the lingering protests of American isolationists. The NATO treaty was signed in April 1949 by England, France, and the United States, plus Norway, Denmark, the Netherlands, Belgium, Luxembourg, Italy, Canada, Iceland, and the Portuguese dictatorship of Antonio Salazar (valued by the United States for its Atlantic island bases). Any conceivable Soviet attack in Europe would now be deterred by a ring of American-backed states (extended to Greece and Turkey in 1952), in most of which U.S. troops and weapons were stationed.

Despite the Western alarm that prompted these steps, there is no evidence in any published Soviet source or in any accessible intelligence that the Soviets contemplated an assault on Western Europe either during the Berlin crisis or at any time since. This is not to say that the potential for such an attack never existed. But it is puzzling that U.S. policymakers, on the basis of their shallow understanding of old Soviet doctrinal pronouncements, should have felt so certain of Russia's offensive intentions ever since 1948.

Events in Eastern Europe during the Berlin crisis validated the containment theory in another respect: they pointed to the potential disintegration of Communist power. The more Stalin endeavored to tighten his hold on the region, the more he assured the eventual opening of fissures in his bloc. The weak point was Yugoslavia, the most enthusiastic of his satellites but also the most independent, where the native Communists had won power largely on their own, frequently ignoring Soviet advice to restrain their revolution and avoid antagonizing the West. Tito found himself threatened by Soviet efforts to infiltrate his military and police systems and to control the Yugoslav economy through binational corporations. His resistance infuriated Stalin, who tried to bring down his government with external pressure and internal subversion. Said Stalin, according to Khrushchev's secret speech of 1956, "I will shake my little finger and there will be no more Tito." The shake was a startling resolution announced by the Cominform in June 1948, expelling the Yugoslav Communists from the organization on grounds of "anti-Party and anti-Soviet views, which are incompatible with Marxism-Leninism" and which allegedly caused them to take "the road of nationalism." Tito, of course, did not fall, in part because he was quickly assured of Western backing in the event of Soviet intervention. Balanced between the superpowers, he succeeded in pursuing a line of neutralism in foreign policy while instituting domestically a modified Communism resembling the Soviet NEP. Thus, Stalin's overconfidence resulted in the first rollback in the USSR's sphere of influence. It also demonstrated—though few Americans realized this at the time—that the essence of the Cold War problem was not Marxism but Soviet power, which might well find itself opposed by foreign Marxists. The seriousness of this problem was underscored later on by the falling out between Russia and China.

For the areas of Eastern Europe more firmly under his control, Stalin applied the lesson of Tito's defection with a vengeance. Flexing the sinews of Soviet control through the party and police organizations of each country, he caused charges of "rightist-nationalist deviation" to be brought against the best-known Communist leaders of Poland, Hungary, Rumania, and Bulgaria—installed in power only recently by Soviet leverage. In Poland the Communist General Secretary, Wladyslaw Gomulka, was ousted and later jailed, before making a political comeback in 1956. In Hungary and Bulgaria the action was more severe: show trials, resembling these in Moscow in the 1930s, were conducted to demonstrate that the "national-Communist" heretics had conspired with the Titoist renegades and Western intelligence services. Albania purged its pro-Yugoslav faction and allied itself with the Soviet Union to prevent being absorbed by Belgrade. Particularly inflaming to American opinion was the 1948 attacks on the Catholic Church in Poland, Czechoslovakia, and Hungary, culminating in the trial and incarceration of leading prelates.

Tito's defection and the crackdown in the other Communist states of Eastern Europe had fatal consequences for the Communist insurrection in Greece. A serious threat in 1947, it had been turned back in 1948 with the American aid supplied under the Truman Doctrine. Stalin concluded, as Djilas reports in *Conversations with Stalin,* that the uprising should be terminated so as not to provoke the Americans and British further. Then, after his split with Moscow, Tito cut off aid to the guerrillas; the Greek Communists dissolved into factionalism; and the Athens government successfully liquidated the insurgency by the end of 1949.

The USSR's shifting fortunes in the Cold War, marked by Tito's defection, the abandonment of guerrilla war in Greece, and the failure of the Berlin Blockade, had their counterpart in the country's internal politics. Zhdanov died in August 1948, and his entourage was purged during the following months, to the presumed benefit of the Malenkov faction and the policy of retrenchment. Whatever the connection between this shakeup and Soviet foreign policy, Stalin quickly adjusted to containment by Western power in Europe and the Middle East.

In the Far East, the political situation remained much more volatile, with a number of opportunities for the extension of Soviet influence. Crucial to the whole region was the civil war in China between Chiang Kai-shek's Nationalists and Mao Tse-tung's Communists. Though Stalin had never been enamored of Mao, the only leader of a foreign Communist Party who did not owe his position to Stalin's favor, he did provide aid, above all by allowing Mao's forces to establish a base of operations in Manchuria and help themselves to captured Japanese arms. The United States, in contrast, after initially favoring Chiang's cause and antagonizing the Communists, gave up on the Nationalists' corruption and terminated all aid in 1948. This was an acknowledgment that in the absence of an effective and popular government in an area threatened by Communism, containment would not work, certainly not without direct American military intervention. When Mao's forces overwhelmed the Nationalists in 1949 and took control of the entire country except for Chiang's island refuge of Taiwan, Stalin was well positioned to incorporate China into his security system. In February 1950, after two months of hard bargaining in Moscow, Mao announced that he was "leaning to one side" in the global confrontation, and the two Communist powers concluded a treaty of friendship and alliance.

This alliance with the world's most populous country was Soviet Russia's greatest breakthrough against the "capitalist encirclement." But China was not Soviet-controlled like Eastern Europe, and posed the threat of a separate center of authority in the Communist movement. This was one of Stalin's unspoken worries, and rightly so. Tito's defection had underscored the distinction between Communism as a political movement and the interests of Soviet power, and this divergence became potentially much more serious with the establishment of the new regime in Peking.

The new Moscow-Peking axis encouraged the Soviets to make their most daring—and most puzzling—move of the entire Cold War era. This was the Soviet-sponsored invasion of South Korea in June 1950 by the North Korean satellite government. In 1945 Korea had been divided into Soviet and American occupation zones, pending the formation of a joint provisional government, but negotiations had been broken off by the Soviets after the rupture over the Marshall Plan in mid-1947. Drawing on cadres from the Korean minorities in Siberia and Manchuria, the Russians quickly organized their zone as the Korean People's Democratic Republic, similar to East Germany; but going further, they recognized it in May 1948 as the government for all of Korea, and armed it generously. Perhaps Stalin was annoyed by the Americans' success in implanting a pro-Western regime in Japan; perhaps he was lured by remarks aired in Washington to the effect that the U.S. security zone did not extend to the Asian mainland. In any case, he evidently calculated that the new government which had been set up in South Korea under the American occupation, and then left unprotected by American troops, would not be defended by the Western powers. Little is known of the actual decision to attack South Korea, apart from the account in Khrushchev's basically authentic memoirs. Khrushchev says that North Korean chief Kim Il-Sung pleaded with Stalin for permission to unify Korea forcibly, in the expectation of an uprising in the south against the dictatorship of Syngman Rhee. Stalin, so the story goes, obtained the approval of Mao Tse-tung during his visit to Moscow and gave the go-ahead to the North Koreans, but at the same time he pulled out all Soviet advisors lest he be compromised in the venture. On June 25, 1950, Kim's

Soviet-trained and Soviet-equipped forces lunged across the thirty-eighth parallel.

The North Korean invasion was the only across-the-border military attack against a non-Communist government ever initiated by the Soviet Union or its satellites, apart from the occupation of Eastern Poland in 1939 and the Winter War against Finland in 1939–40. (China was acting on its own when it attacked India in 1962 and Communist Vietnam in 1979.) But after initial successes against the South Koreans, armed expansion in Korea threatened to backfire when General Douglas MacArthur's counteroffensive destroyed the North Korean army. Ignoring hasty Soviet peace feelers, the United States, with UN sanction, pushed on across the thirty-eighth parallel to overthrow the helpless North Korean government and unite Korea on American terms. The Communist bloc was faced with its second instance, even more humiliating than Yugoslavia, of "rollback" and "liberation." This was a serious test of Stalin's will, with grave implications not merely for his interests in the Far East but also for his security zone in Eastern Europe. The new Chinese government, too, was threatened, since a potentially interventionist army was heading toward its northeastern border. Mao (according to Khrushchev) sent Chou En-lai to Moscow to obtain Stalin's assent to Chinese intervention, while warning the West via India's ambassador to Peking that China would be compelled to step in if non-Korean troops approached the Yalu River border. The United States ignored the threat, whereupon masses of Chinese "volunteers" crossed the Yalu, drove the U.S. and South Korean forces back, resuscitated the Communist government of North Korea, and eventually stabilized the campaign roughly along the thirty-eighth parallel.

The Korean experience proved that any action on the part of Russia or its satellites would provoke an equal and opposite Western reaction designed to preserve the international equilibrium. Politically, however, the war intensified Americans' anti-Communist fears, which had already been magnified by Mao's victory in China. The United States immediately renewed its support to the Chinese Nationalists on Taiwan and offered assistance to the French battling the Vietminh nationalists in Indochina. At the same time, it used the Korean War to isolate the Russians in the United Nations and won UN endorsement of its anti-Communist military action. The UN remained a preserve of the anti-Soviet coalition until the wave of

decolonization in the 1960s gave it a majority of third-world governments and made it susceptible to Soviet influence.

The impact of the Korean War extended all the way to Europe,
appearing as it did to confirm the Soviets' plan for a massive assault
to conquer the continent. It now seemed imperative to bring West
Germany into the Western orbit not only politically and economically, but militarily as well. Within weeks after the outbreak of war
in Korea the Americans, British, and French had decided to include
West Germany in the new North Atlantic Treaty Organization. This
entailed German rearmament, presumably (but, as it turned out, not
necessarily) under the aegis of a multinational military force, the
abortive European Defense Community. Stalin's worst fears were
realized: he had failed to control Germany, except for the Soviet
zone; he had failed to keep Germany neutral; he had failed to take
over West Berlin; and now, as a result of his Korean provocation, he
had failed to prevent Germany's rearmament. For the feverish
minds in the Kremlin, the nightmare of a revanchist assault on Russia was becoming a real possibility.

■ From Freeze to Thaw

Containment worked. It kept the Soviet Union out of Western Europe, the Mediterranean, and the Middle East. It steered all three
major Axis countries (except a quarter of Germany) toward democracy, preserved their capitalist economies (all too successfully, in the
long run), and allied them with the United States. In Korea it
showed that Communist military expansion could be stopped with
action limited to the original point of aggression. Containment
made most of the world safe for American business, even though
this was not explicitly the Truman administration's objective. It left
the Soviet Union dominant in the area of its wartime occupation,
but stabilized the two hostile blocs. The United States had failed to
prevent the division of the world into spheres of influence, and had
to accept the existence of an array of repressive Soviet-sponsored
regimes; any possibility that the West might have made concessions
to Stalin and thus softened his policies died with the political fortunes of Henry Wallace.

Confronted with the determination of the United States and its
allies to hold fast in Europe and to counter force with force in the
Far East, Stalin surrendered the political initiative. As Marshall

Shulman argues in *Stalin's Foreign Policy Reappraised*, he devised his own version of containment to keep his newly won sphere intact while avoiding general war with the imperialists. The shift coincided with the death of Zhdanov and the purge of his entourage, followed by the apparent ascendancy of the more pragmatic Malenkov. Symbolically, just before the Berlin Blockade was called off in the spring of 1949, ten-year veteran Molotov was relieved as foreign minister by Vyshinsky and consigned to the amorphous post of deputy prime minister.

The Kremlin perhaps gained some confidence in East-West equilibrium when it successfully tested its own atomic bomb in September 1949, though in fact this contributed further to the rising anti-Communist anxiety in the United States. Equilibrium did not dissuade the Soviet Union and its satellites from intensifying political repression, with a new round of purges and trials focusing on the theme of Zionist plots in league with the U.S. Central Intelligence Agency. Commercial and personal contacts between the Soviet bloc and non-Communist countries were reduced to a minimum.

At the same time, Stalin attempted to discredit American talk of "counteroffensives" and "liberation" by appearing to be a champion of peace. Early in 1950 he promoted the so-called Stockholm Peace Appeal and a worldwide petition effort. The cause of peace (in other words, opposition to Western unity and rearmament) supplanted revolution as the mission of the foreign Communist parties and their innumerable front organizations. Stalin backed this line in his last doctrinal statement (*Economic Problems of Socialism*, 1952): "The aim of this movement is not to overthrow capitalism and establish socialism—it confines itself to the democratic aim of preserving peace." Although war might still be inevitable among capitalist countries, the Soviet Union could avoid war with the capitalists by persuading them of both the risks to themselves and its own peaceful intentions.

A more tangible step was the Soviet initiative in June 1951 that led to the beginning of armistice negotiations in Korea. In 1952 the Soviets tried to appeal to German nationalism by suggesting reunification without demilitarization. But what in 1946 or 1947 might have secured a neutral Germany was by this time impossible, and Stalin probably made his offer only for propaganda purposes, certain that it would be rejected.

Despite the sort of confidence expressed by Malenkov in his anniversary speech of November 1949 ("Never before in all its history has our country been surrounded with neighboring countries so friendly to our own state"), Stalin's Russia had only one voluntary ally remaining: Mao's China. Moreover, as later developments would show, the Chinese Communists' friendship for the Soviet Union, though ideologically plausible, was historically and geopolitically unnatural. A contributing factor behind Peking's temporary alignment with Moscow was the belated but very successful—even overly successful—American application of the containment doctrine in the Far East. As the U.S. public became more anti-Communist in response to Mao's victory in China and the Korean War, the Truman administration reversed its nonintervention decision of 1948. Thanks to American support of anti-Communist governments, China's power was contained close to its borders, and in consequence not one but three Far Eastern countries remained partitioned—Korea, Vietnam, and China itself (with respect to Taiwan). China enjoyed no such security buffer as the Soviets established in Eastern Europe, but confronted American power directly. For the next twenty years, China loomed larger in the American consciousness than the Soviet Union as a revolutionary evil. The policy of nonrecognition was maintained by Washington even more rigorously than against Russia after the Revolution, even to the prohibition of all trade contacts. For ten of those years the United States, in turn, served as the devil around which Mao's regime forged a sense of national militancy and righteousness, until a nearer and greater devil appeared on China's political horizon.

The advent of the Communists in China raised Americans' fear of world Communism to a new pitch, beyond any concerns shared by U.S. allies. Rather than subsiding into the political unconscious like the Red Scare of 1919–20, the new anti-Communist panic took on dimensions that appeared to some Americans and many foreigners—including the Soviets—to portend a crisis of democratic government such as those precipitated by right-wing anti-Communists in Central Europe between the wars. As the hunt for "subversives" shifted from the Executive branch to Congressional committees, as scientists and diplomats were pilloried (among them Robert Oppenheimer and the State Department's Old China Hands), and as loyalty purges spread from government to the private sector, education, and even the film industry, the United States experienced a distant analogue of the political and cultural climate of Russia under Zhdanov and Malenkov. America's Zhdanov, if the comparison may be extended, was the junior senator from Wisconsin, Joseph McCarthy, who catapulted himself to fame in 1950 by broadcasting the claim that he had a list of two hundred (never identified) Communists in the State Department. To him and to others whose anti-Communism was a displacement of less articulated national and personal concerns, the main enemy was within, not without: "The reason why we find ourselves in a position of impotency is not because our only powerful potential enemy has sent men to invade our shores, but rather because of the traitorous actions of those who have been treated so well by this nation."

With such accusations proliferating, it was inevitable that the conduct of the Cold War should become a partisan issue. The low point came in the 1952 presidential campaign, when Republicans assailed the Democrats for being soft on Communism and selling out to the Russians at Yalta. In the rhetoric epitomized by the soon-to-be secretary of state, John Foster Dulles, containment was repudiated as the craven acceptance of ill-gotten Communist gains in Eastern Europe and Asia. "It is only by keeping alive the hope of liberation," declared Dulles at his confirmation hearing in January 1953, "that we will end this terrible peril which dominates the world." Adlai Stevenson, according to vice-presidential candidate Richard Nixon, had disqualified himself for the presidency by taking a degree from "Dean Acheson's College of Cowardly Communist Containment."

With even the administration that took up the postwar Russian challenge subjected to such assault, it became politically impossible for any American statesman to respond to Stalin's retrenchment or to question any measure taken in the name of anti-Communism. Though "liberation" remained at the rhetorical level except for General MacArthur's venture into North Korea, the practice of containment now entailed—contrary to Kennan's original intention—an equal and opposite reaction, usually military, to any perceived Communist threat anywhere in the world. Even before the Korean War, Truman began to aid the French fighting the Communist insurgency in Vietnam, which was given new life when the Chinese Communists reached the border and both Peking and Moscow extended diplomatic recognition to Ho Chi Minh. At about the same time, convinced that America's security rested on its lead in nuclear weapons, Truman gave the fateful order to develop the hydrogen bomb. Dulles took office with a grand design—not for "rollback," which he left to "moral pressures," but for a super containment system consisting of NATO-style alliances ringing the Soviet Union. The Southeast Asian Treaty Organization (SEATO) went into effect in 1954, and the Baghdad Pact (among Britain, Turkey, Iraq, Iran, and Pakistan, backed up with American aid) in 1955. Neither proved of great significance except as a rationale for American or British bases and as evidence of inflexible posturing in disregard of major changes by then taking place in the Soviet Union.

The ultimate American theory of the Communist menace was formalized in the now famous National Security Council memorandum NSC-68 of April 1950, authorized principally by Paul Nitze, Kennan's successor as head of the State Department Policy Planning Council and eventually President Reagan's chief arms control negotiator. Though the document has been touted—and damned—as the blueprint of American confrontation with the Soviets ever since, NSC-68 actually did little more than elaborate the assumptions guiding U.S. policy since the Prague and Berlin crises in 1948. It declared that the Soviet Union was "animated by a new fanatic faith, antithetical to our own," aiming "to impose its absolute authority over the rest of the world," and "implacable in its purpose to destroy us." First on the timetable was "the domination of the Eurasian land mass," but if Cold War tactics did not work, the Soviets would put "a premium on a surprise attack against us" (that is, with atomic bombs). The answer was neither "preventive war," as some American hard-liners had been suggesting, nor negotiations, which could do no more than mollify public opinion until there was "such a radical change in Soviet policies as to constitute a change in the Soviet system." What the report called for was a general mobilization of U.S. military and economic resources, plus "dynamic steps to reduce the power and influence of the Kremlin inside the Soviet Union and others under its control" by "fomenting and supporting unrest and revolt in selected strategic satellite countries." Failing to recognize that Stalin was retreating to his own containment strategy, the report frankly borrowed from Soviet tactics of the first Cold War phase: "It would be the current Soviet Cold War technique used against the Soviet Union." Stalin, certainly aware of these American notions and perceiving that the balance of forces had shifted against him, must have realized the urgency of his peace campaign and the need to reformulate the Marxist theory of war.

The naive belief in a Soviet ideological crusade expressed by NSC-68 was protested by the State Department's Soviet experts, including Kennan and Charles Bohlen. In fact, both Acheson and Nitze knew better, as the former conceded in his memoirs, but they thought they had to "bludgeon" the administration and Congress (Acheson) with the "persuasive impact" (Nitze) of the world domination theory. To a public already convinced of Communist expansionism Acheson did not want to appear to be waffling as he "went about the country preaching this premise of NSC-68." Yes, he admitted, "we made our points clearer than the truth"—none of which spared him vilification at the hands of his Republican opponents, who really believed in the world domination theory.

Was the question of the preeminence of ideology in Soviet foreign policy only a "sterile argument," as Acheson contends? It became the basic assumption of the American public and American policymakers as well, and never disappeared entirely. It led to the definition of any anti-Westernism as Communism, to the warping of relations with China, and to the failure to understand Communism as nationalism in countries like Vietnam and Cuba. It impeded efforts to limit the arms race and to find openings in the Communist front. It was historically wrong and diplomatically counterproductive.

Stalin's death on March 5, 1953, came just six weeks after the installation in Washington of an administration elected on the promise of liberation from Communism. His passing left Russia without the fearsome dictator who had brought the country intact through war and Cold War, defying first the Nazis and then the entire capitalist world. But only days later, his successors showed that they recognized the impasse to which Stalin's tactics had brought Soviet diplomacy. The change of leadership altered the whole tone of Soviet foreign relations, and created possibilities both for new forms of coexistence and for new lines of Soviet influence in the outside world. Within two years Moscow was settling problems, finding non-Communist friends, and even resuming top-level conferences with the Western powers. Malenkov, assuming as prime minister a leading role in foreign policy even though Molotov had regained the

Foreign Ministry, bore out his reputation for caution by calling for a broad East-West effort to negotiate differences. He followed this up with such symbolic gestures as easing restrictions on foreign journalists and permitting the emigration of Soviet wives of foreigners.

These overtures were not enough to reverse the political momentum that had carried Dwight Eisenhower into the White House and had given the Republicans control of Congress. Unlike Churchill (prime minister again since 1951), who recognized the opportunity for a conference of governmental chiefs to address specific East-West problems, Eisenhower and Dulles voiced suspicions and demanded a series of Soviet concessions as the price for better relations. Meanwhile they continued to implement the grand design for containment by increasing the troop commitment to NATO, bargaining with Franco for Spanish bases, preparing for German rearmament, and working on the paper chain of anti-Soviet treaties in the Middle East and Southeast Asia. Nevertheless they stayed their hand when "liberation" had its first spectacular chance. Bearing out the theory that the Soviet bloc would eventually deteriorate, a workers' uprising broke out in East Berlin in June 1953. The West did nothing, and Soviet troops restored order. The implication was clear: the spheres of influence in Europe had become established fact, and neither side would seriously attempt to alter them.

While the Eisenhower administration thus fell quickly back from liberation to containment as its real strategy, the challenge to containment was extended to unexpected areas. Stalin's successors initiated a major shift in diplomatic strategy when they took to wooing neutral governments and nationalist movements in the third world. This meant that containment might have to be applied not only to protect other countries from Communism but to deny them the choice of a pro-Soviet foreign policy. The CIA began covert counterrevolutionary operations, starting in Iran, where the nationalist premier Mossadegh was toppled in August 1953 in favor of the pro-American shah. The method succeeded again in 1954 against the mildly revolutionary president of Guatemala, Jacobo Arbenz, who had expropriated the United Fruit Company and accepted arms from the Communist bloc. U.S. aid was extended to various European colonial powers, especially the French in Vietnam and the Portuguese in Africa, as well as to incumbent authoritarians in Latin

America and the Middle East, to maintain the status quo by force. World Communism, thrown on the defensive, was outdone at its own game by American practitioners of the cloak-and-dagger arts. But the long-run consequences of such antirevolutionary intervention were not so favorable to the Western powers. Third-world nationalism, particularly among educated young people, identified imperialism and neocolonialism as its sworn enemies and turned to the Soviet Union as its natural friend and protector. Moscow was soon able to exploit this tendency effectively in many parts of the world.

U.S. hostility did not sway the new Soviet leadership from its determination to moderate some of the outstanding East-West differences and undo some of the damage caused by Stalin's confrontationist tactics. Most significant was the conclusion of an armistice in Korea in July 1953, evidently pursuant to Soviet advice to the Chinese and North Koreans. Teaming up with the British, the Russians cohosted the Geneva parley of 1954, which arrived at a truce in Vietnam between the French and the Vietminh and temporarily partitioned the country. Turning to the old sore spot of Germany, the Russians once again called for a conference on reunification; when this was rebuffed, they settled for a two-Germanies policy to normalize relations with West Germany. They recognized Konrad Adenauer's government in Bonn in January 1955, shortly after granting nominal sovereignty to the German Democratic Republic in the east. Austria was offered a "state treaty" (not a "peace treaty," because Austria had had no government during the war), pursuant to which the Soviet Union voluntarily withdrew from its occupation zone around Vienna and recognized Austria as the unified, neutral country that Germany might have become. The nagging problem of Yugoslavia was addressed head-on by Khrushchev shortly after he displaced Malenkov as number one in the Soviet hierarchy: he went personally to Belgrade in the spring of 1955, to apologize for Stalin's excommunication of the Yugoslavs and to approve their doctrine of "separate roads to socialism." A year later he abolished the now functionless Cominform.

The initiatives taken by Malenkov and Khrushchev, remarkable as they might seem when measured against the inflexibility of the Stalin era, evoked only a gradual and grudging response from Washington. Surprised by Soviet concessions when he least expected them, Dulles warned, "The new set of dangers comes from the fact that the wolf has put on a new set of sheep's clothing, and while it is better to have a sheep's clothing on than a bear's clothing on, because sheep don't have claws, I think the policy remains the same." The United States had institutionalized its belief in the Soviets' design for revolution by blitzkrieg, and dismissed conciliatory gestures as tricks and deceptions. Containment had not only succeeded in holding the line against the Russians but had actually caused them to mellow, just as Kennan foresaw. Yet the Eisenhower administration was so wedded to its hard line that it could not moderate either its suspicion of the Soviets or its rancor over Communist rule in Eastern Europe and China. Policies that had been originated to stop Stalin and Mao continued to be implemented. West Germany was officially taken into the NATO alliance late in 1954, which in turn provoked the formation of an eastern counterpart: the Warsaw Pact. In the Far East, Washington made itself the patron of the South Vietnamese government originally set up by the French, to curb the expansion of Communism allegedly invited by the Geneva truce. Mirroring Stalinist Russia, the United States had made its military preeminence and the security of its sphere ends in themselves.

This stiff anti-Communist position loosened first among the West Europeans, who had never been entirely persuaded of the eternal Marxist motive in Soviet behavior and were ready to respond pragmatically to the new dawn in Moscow. The French, as nervous about Germany as they were about Russia, broke ranks in 1954 when they killed the idea of a European army with West German contingents. Churchill pressed for a general conference, and the result, with Eisenhower's concurrence and quick Soviet acceptance, was the Geneva Summit Conference of July 1955.

The Geneva Summit was one of those diplomatic events that are much more important for what they symbolize than for what they accomplish. Bringing together First Secretary Khrushchev and prime minister Bulganin for the Soviet Union, premier Edgar Faure of France, prime minister Anthony Eden (who had just replaced the ailing Churchill), and Eisenhower and Dulles, Geneva was the first—and last—conclave of the world's top leaders since Potsdam. Though it deadlocked on the stale question of German unification and accomplished little else, the Geneva Summit represented a return to more communicative relations among the great powers and serves as well as any other point to mark the end of the Cold War.

■ From Coexistence to Polycentrism

A new era in the history of Communism began in February 1956, when First Secretary Khrushchev delivered his sensational attack on Stalin at a closed session of the Twentieth Party Congress. Less noted but equally important was his public address to the congress in which he affirmed the principles of peaceful coexistence and separate roads to socialism. These two statements signaled a willingness both to purge the worst sins of Stalinism and to tolerate a world of political variety. Relations with the West quickly improved, despite occasional shocks. Relations with the Communist world were thrown into disarray, and Muscovite discipline faded wherever Soviet armed forces did not have the last word. All this meant that world politics were returning from bipolar confrontation to more traditional rules of multipower diplomacy and accommodation.

The ideological basis of Western (and especially American) anxiety about Russia had evidently been made clear to Khrushchev and his advisors, and the First Secretary determined to deal with it: "The Leninist principle of peaceful coexistence of states with different social systems has always been and remains the general line of our country's foreign policy." Thus did a new set of tactics become eternal truth. Brushing aside as capitalist slander the notion that "the Soviet Union is out to overthrow capitalism in other countries by 'exporting' revolution," Khrushchev reiterated the traditional Marxist propositions about the superiority of the socialist (that is, Communist) economic system and the eventual overthrow of capitalism by the workers. This, of course, is all he meant by his unfortunate remark "We will bury you," made during his 1959 visit to the United States and interpreted by editorialists for years afterward as a threat to launch his missiles.

The initial response to Khrushchev's new face was not auspicious. There was internal opposition from the unregenerate Stalinists, and Molotov had to be relieved of the Foreign Ministry. (He was replaced by party secretary Dmitri Shepilov, who yielded to the indestructible Andrei Gromyko the following year.) In the East European satellites, those who had hoped for reform after Stalin's death—even Communists—were encouraged to rebel by the new mood in Moscow. Action in Poland was triggered by a workers' riot in Poznan in June 1956, followed by the rehabilitation of the jailed National-Communist leader Gomulka and his installation as party chief in October. Overruling Molotov and the hard-liners, Khrushchev accepted Gomulka's demand for internal independence and reform in return for international solidarity with the Soviet Union.

In Hungary the news from Poland precipitated a crisis that was far more serious and violent, though ultimately similar in its outcome. In this case the combination of reform promises and police provocations triggered a genuine popular uprising against the Communist regime and a general collapse of its authority. Again, a discredited National-Communist leader, Imre Nagy, was recalled to take command and try to regain popular confidence through reform—in this case, by proclaiming an end to one-party rule and forming a coalition government. Unfortunately for Nagy, he took the further, unforgivable step of disassociating Hungary from the Warsaw Pact. Now Soviet security was directly threatened, and Khrushchev felt compelled to send the Soviet army into action. Ambassador Yuri Andropov arranged an appeal for Soviet aid by the turncoat Hungarian Communist Janos Kadar; the Russians assaulted Budapest, deposed Nagy, and installed Kadar to assure Hungary's allegiance to the bloc. The pattern was closely followed when the Soviets had to deal with other troubled satellites: Czechoslovakia in 1968 and Afghanistan in 1979. As in the case of East Berlin, the Western powers kept their response to the Hungarian crisis strictly on the rhetorical plane, and refrained from the risks of liberation.

With the upheaval in Eastern Europe came the first fruit of the Soviets' post-Stalin approach to the third world, stemming from their new alliance with the revolutionary government of Gamal Abdel Nasser in Egypt. Rebuffed in his quest for aid by an American administration that still thought of neutrals as enemies, Nasser nationalized the Suez Canal and provoked the last gasp of Western imperialism: the Anglo-French-Israeli invasion of Egypt. Khrushchev seized the opportunity to pose as the guardian of small countries' liberties by threatening London and Paris with his rockets, and incidentally managed to distract international attention from his own intervention in Hungary. He won in both arenas.

In an earlier period, a manifold crisis like that of November 1956 would have been devastating to East-West relations. Yet such was the changing climate of assumptions in the great-power capitals that within months all were on the road to détente again. Arms control negotiations were pursued more intensively than ever before, spurred by controversy over fallout from nuclear testing. After beating down the Stalinists of the "Anti-Party Group" in the summer of 1957 and removing the popular Marshal Zhukov, Khrushchev proceeded with his announced reduction in the Soviet armed forces. This move was made less risky as the Russians exploded their own hydrogen bomb and narrowed the nuclear advantage of the United States. Khrushchev felt confident enough to take the propaganda initiative in the spring of 1958 by unilaterally suspending nuclear tests.

Meanwhile, in the fall of 1957 the Soviet Union seized the technological lead by getting the first artificial satellite—the memorable sputnik—into orbit around the earth, and thereby shattering America's complacency about its scientific and industrial advantage. Nervous Western strategists deduced that the Soviets had usable intercontinental missiles—a reason, they thought, for Khrushchev's renewal of the German issue when, in November, he threatened to turn over control of the West Berlin access routes to the East German authorities. The Middle East also continued to generate tension: the Soviets brought Syria into their alliance system at the cost of a crisis with Turkey, and a Nasser-style revolution in Iraq in 1958 prompted the United States to send marines to Lebanon. Washington announced the "Eisenhower Doctrine," which promised American support to any Middle East country threatened by Communism.

Despite all these frictions, the mutual sense of ideological enmity continued to subside (abetted by the retirement and death of Dulles), and the stage was set for the extraordinary exchange of official visits that took place in 1959. Soviet elder statesman Anastas Mikoyan went to Washington early in the year, Vice-President Nixon visited Moscow in July (the occasion of his "kitchen debate" with Khrushchev at the American trade fair), and Khrushchev himself toured the United States in September. This trip generated the top-level cordiality expressed as the "Spirit of Camp David," and Khrushchev's grand plea to the UN General Assembly for "universal and complete disarmament."

It is a tribute both to American political flexibility and to Khrushchev's persistence in search of accommodation, that an administration commencing in the panicky days of McCarthyism could reach this point of relative amity toward the Soviets. Part of the explanation lies in the fact that, ever since the Korean War, American animosity had been directed more toward the Communists in China, a tendency refreshed by continual clashes between Communist and Nationalist forces in the Formosa Straits. But U.S. policymakers were oddly impervious for some time to the indications of trouble between the Russians and Chinese—trouble that made détente with the United States particularly desirable for Khrushchev. During his 1959 visit, Khrushchev ventured to bring up his concerns about China; Eisenhower refused to discuss the subject.

The roots of the Sino-Soviet schism go deep in the history of Russian imperialism and Soviet attempts in the 1920s and 1930s to manipulate the Chinese Communists. The rift was a compelling demonstration of the way in which national differences can transcend a common ideology, and recalls the schisms in the Christian Church between Rome and Constantinople in the Middle Ages or between Catholics and Protestants in more recent centuries. From the time Stalin died, Mao evidently aspired to be the leading voice in the Communist movement. At first he took the lead in formulating a more open foreign policy, embracing the principle of peaceful coexistence (in his accord with India in 1954) and courting the neutralists of the third world (at the Bandung Conference of Asian and African states in 1955). Then, miffed because Khrushchev had denounced Stalinism without consulting him, Mao shifted to a harder line, played up tensions with the United States over Taiwan, and upbraided the Soviets for fearing to fight the imperialists. In 1958 he condemned the Yugoslavs for "revisionism" just as Khrushchev was trying to conciliate them, and proclaimed a new drive toward the Marxist utopia with his "Great Leap Forward," which called for swift industrial development and instituted rural communes. Khrushchev found himself compelled to declare ideological independence from Mao; after wavering briefly, he rejected the Chinese attack on Tito, dismissed the commune movement as an adventurist error, and withdrew Soviet aid from the Chinese nuclear weapons program. The schism had begun.

By the time the Sino-Soviet split was generally recognized in 1960, the division of authority between the rival centers was making it difficult for Moscow to counter the loss of faith caused by de-Stalinization. Both the ruling and nonruling Communist parties found new leeway to assert their particular interests. As early as 1956, Italian Communist chief Palmiro Togliatti declared, "The whole system becomes polycentric, and even in the Communist movement itself we cannot speak of a single guide but rather of a progress which is achieved by following paths which are often different." Among the Communist governments, Rumania and North Korea asserted their neutrality in the Moscow-Peking rivalry, and won the right to make their own foreign policy. Numerous Communist parties split into old-guard Muscovite factions and hot-headed Maoists sympathetic to the youth agitation of the sixties. In democratic countries, the relative conservatism of the Muscovites led most of them to accept democratic politics and ultimately democratic theory as well. Thus was born Eurocommunism. By the time of Khrushchev's fall, little was left of orthodox, disciplined, Moscow-oriented Communism other than the eroded band of satellites subject to Soviet military domination.

Khrushchev's troubles with China, as well as his overoptimistic pursuit of détente and his precipitous reduction of the Soviet armed forces, no doubt contributed to the political difficulties of his later years. In 1960 he abruptly switched to a much more adventurist and confrontational foreign policy. Circumstantial evidence suggests that he did so either as a concession to the neo-Stalinist faction or as a diversion to throw them off balance. At any rate, Soviet-American relations entered a dangerous new period—virtually a second Cold War—until the illness of the neo-Stalinist leader Frol Kozlov gave Khrushchev a reprieve.

A turn for the worse came on May Day 1960, when a high-flying American U-2 reconnaissance plane was brought down by a Soviet missile in the middle of the USSR. Embarrassed by this penetration of Soviet airspace and challenged by Eisenhower's refusal to disavow responsibility, Khrushchev began a violent anti-American propaganda campaign. Two weeks after the incident he broke up the second Big Four Summit meeting just as it was convening in Paris. He canceled his planned military cuts, jousted with the United States for influence in the newly independent Congo, pursued an entente with Cuban revolutionary Fidel Castro, increased the pressure on Berlin, and came to New York in September as an uninvited guest at the UN General Assembly to bang his shoe for the world's attention.

Along with all of these moves in defiance of the West—and this supports the theory of his internal political motives—Khrushchev stepped up his dispute with the Chinese, especially over their willingness to risk nuclear war with the imperialists. He locked horns with them publicly while attending the Rumanian Communist Congress in Bucharest in June 1960, and then ordered the termination of all Soviet economic aid to China. A series of indirect polemics ensued: the Chinese attacked the "revisionism" and "opportunism" of Yugoslavia (read: the Soviet Union), and the Russians denounced the "dogmatism" and "adventurism" of tiny Albania (which had turned to the Chinese for protection against Yugoslavia). Whether by coincidence or direct encouragement, it was at this point (late 1960) that the National Liberation Front was set up in South Vietnam to unify the country by guerrilla warfare.

By 1961 Khrushchev's Cold War had generated a new war scare. The powder keg (as in 1948) was Germany, and the fuse was Berlin. Rebuffed by the Western powers in every attempt to curb German rearmament and end Allied rights in West Berlin, Khrushchev shocked the entire Western world in August 1961 by sealing off all movement between East and West Berlin (which had allowed millions of working-age East Germans to flee to the West) and constructing the infamous Berlin Wall. He followed this act of defiance with another: he ended Russia's self-imposed nuclear test moratorium by exploding the world's first hundred-megaton hydrogen bomb.

The American reaction was predictable, and, if anticipated by Khrushchev, was obviously the price he was willing to pay. All of the Cold War reflexes came into play, and the old fears of Communist revolution and Soviet blitzkrieg came back to life, to the refrain of Khrushchev's careless boast, "We will bury you." This was the heyday of fallout shelters and the John Birch Society. The new Kennedy administration, chastened by its defeat in Cuba at the Bay of Pigs in April 1961, prepared for confrontation at every level, and planned a "flexible response" through the deployment of tactical nuclear weapons. The ultimate confrontation was the Cuban missile crisis of October 1962.

Khrushchev's Cuban policy represented a major new gambit in the Soviet quest for overseas influence in the third world. Here the Soviets actually captured a nationalist revolutionary for the Communist faith. The Castro alignment, creating the first Communist regime established outside the post–World War II power vacuum, was an unexpected windfall for Khrushchev, provoked as it was by Washington's coolness toward the new Cuban regime and by Cuba's expropriation of American property. Until the U-2 affair, Khrushchev moved cautiously in Cuba. Castro had been in power over a year when Mikoyan arrived to negotiate. Then, as part of his post-U-2 hard line, Khrushchev cemented his alliance with Castro by offering diplomatic recognition, military aid, and guaranteed sugar purchases, all topped off by the famous embrace of the two leaders at the Cuban UN mission in September 1960. The Bay of Pigs episode in 1961 confirmed for Havana and Moscow the dependence of the one on the other, and in December of that year, Castro proclaimed that he had always been a Marxist. He absorbed the Cuban Communists into his revolutionary party, while weeding out their old Moscow-dependent leaders.

Why Khrushchev risked placing nuclear-armed missiles in Cuba in the fall of 1962 is still a matter of conjecture. In his memoirs he claimed that Soviet prestige was at stake and that he believed the missiles might deter another American attempt at intervention in Cuba as well as correct the global strategic imbalance. But the very boldness of the move, and its ready retraction when the U.S. blockaded Cuba and threatened to attack, suggest that the emplacement of missiles was intended to serve as a political demonstration, or probe, or bargaining ploy rather than to achieve permanent strategic gains. In agreeing to withdraw the missiles, Khrushchev did secure Washington's promise to remove missiles from Turkey and to desist from intervention in Cuba. Beyond this, what is known of internal political pressures on Khrushchev and his subsequent enthusiastic return to détente suggest that the venture was intended to test the U.S. reaction: to profit from it if it was weak; but if it was firm, to demonstrate this fact to the Kremlin hawks. The strong American response confirmed, to Khrushchev's apparent satisfaction, the wisdom of a cautious line. At the same time, U.S. policymaking had progressed sufficiently from the obsessions of the Cold War to recognize Khrushchev's retreat to reasonableness, and to take advantage of it.

Khrushchev's Cold War ended in the summer of 1963, as abruptly as it had started. Washington at last took an initiative that was acceptable to the Russians (facilitated by the temporary eclipse of the neo-Stalinists), when President Kennedy, in his celebrated speech of June 1963 at the American University in Washington, proposed a resumption of negotiations in the cause of peace. Just then involved in a last effort to talk out his differences with the Chinese, Khrushchev was in the enviable position of Stalin in 1939 when both the Allies and the Axis were seeking an accommodation with the Soviet Union. Khrushchev's choice spared Washington the threat of a double enemy, and assured another decade of world stability: he opted for an accord with the United States. The immediate outcome was the acrimonious collapse of Sino-Soviet talks in Moscow and the conclusion in August 1963 of the long-sought treaty among the United States, Britain, and the Soviet Union to ban the testing of nuclear weapons in the atmosphere. With this step, the long era of détente had truly begun.

As a statesman, Khrushchev was everything Stalin was not—a flamboyant gambler, willing both to make concessions and to take risks, in retrospect the most open Soviet leader the West has ever had to deal with. He represented just the sort of change in Russia that containment anticipated but that the United States was reluctant to recognize when it finally occurred. In part, Khrushchev was himself responsible for this failure: impulsive and inconsistent, he failed to appreciate the alarm that his tactics generated abroad. He bequeathed to his successors tasks that seemed mutually exclusive—mollify the West, contain China, build Soviet strength—but he also introduced Russians to the idea that major powers could reconcile their differences despite ideological incompatibility. Given the chance, he might have dispensed with the notion of a necessary foreign enemy; forced to choose one, he preferred it to be China rather than the United States.

10

May Day parade with portraits of Lenin and the Politburo,
Leningrad, 1976

The Contemporary System

The Stalinist form of government and society, hardened during the Great Purge and World War II, survived the leadership changes and factional rivalries of
the next two decades and remains today the basis of
the Soviet system. On this foundation, since the fall of

Khrushchev in 1964, the Soviet Union has enjoyed a period of unprecedented stability in its institutions, policies, and leadership. Since 1964 there have been no dramatic leadership initiatives. Change has been incremental, beneath the surface of institutions and policies, and more difficult to observe and measure. Not even the novelty of two leadership changes in fifteen months, as Leonid Brezhnev was succeeded by Yuri Andropov and then by Konstantin Chernenko, affected the Soviet Union's political and economic structure. It remained to be seen whether the advent of a younger, post-Stalinist generation of leaders would open the country to genuine change.

Up to a point, the political tranquillity after Khrushchev benefited the country: growth continued, though at a declining rate; parity with the United States in military power was attained; the Russian people became more urbanized and better educated, and their skills and interests became more diverse. The problems of the Soviet system in recent years are those not of backwardness but of progress and the expectations it engenders. A degree of sophistication and modernity has been achieved in many of the specialized areas of Soviet life, and these advances call into question both official formulas and outsiders' generalizations. Tension is growing between the system that realized the goals of modernization and national power, and the requirements and wishes of the modern nation that it created. The Soviet political system has outlived its usefulness and has become, particularly since the late Brezhnev years, concerned above all with preserving itself in defiance of the march of history. Continuity of leadership has meant an aging leadership, bound to give way eventually to new blood and new attitudes. A novel dialectic has been at work: the advanced technological society built by the Communist regime finds its maker not only dispensable but, as Karl Marx said of capitalism, a "fetter" that is inhibiting the nation's development.

▪ The Politics of Leadership

The coup that overthrew Khrushchev in October 1964 had contradictory implications. On its face it was a rebuff to reform and de-Stalinization. It installed in power representatives of the post-purge generation who personified bureaucratic conservatism; political liberalization and reexamination of the historical record came to a dead halt. Cultural activity was rudely frozen again, and many members of the intelligentsia went underground to become the movement of unofficial and often illegal dissent. Alexander Solzhenitsyn, for instance, had published his novel of labor-camp conditions, *One Day in the Life of Ivan Denisovich,* with Khrushchev's imprimatur; the rest of his work, until he was expelled from the Soviet Union, had to be smuggled abroad.

Despite these signs of retrogression, Khrushchev's fall indicated a new stage in the evolution of the Soviet power structure. For the first time in the entire history of Russia the established leader was removed by legal means rather than death or revolution. This meant that Khrushchev had not, after all, been able to recreate the kind of power that Stalin enjoyed, but that he was in fact removable by the top party leadership with the support of the Central Committee.

Nothing has happened under Brezhnev and his successors to alter the dependence of the party leader on the constituency immediately beneath him in the Politburo and the Central Committee. There is now a relationship of mutual vulnerability—not unlike that in bureaucratic, corporate, and educational organizations in the West: the top leader can remove any individual subordinate, but the subordinates in concert can cause the removal of the top leader. Brezhnev could not be described as a personal dictator, nor did he act like one until his last few years. Merely first among equals, with a slow and cautious style of leadership, he made himself the advocate of the post-purge generation of Communist bureaucrats. His only structural change was to repair the awkward division Khrushchev had introduced in the provincial party organizations between the urban-industrial and rural-agricultural sectors. The party and the government enjoyed unprecedented continuity as officials aged in office, with only rare instances of intervention and removal by the central leadership. Andropov attempted something more, but did not live to carry his plan through. Chernenko, judging by everything in his record, was a reincarnation of Brezhnev.

In all probability the ultimate repository of authority in the Soviet system is a small oligarchy, including the members of the Politburo and the Secretariat and a few others in key apparatus positions, with residual influence extending to the members of the Central Committee when they are called upon to ratify a major move, such as the ouster of Khrushchev. Both the Politburo and the Central Committee are made up of representatives of all the key institutions and territorial entities in the Soviet social structure. In their decisions they can presumably reflect the concerns of these constituent parts of the system at the same time that they are obligated to carry back to their constituencies, according to the principle of democratic centralism, the policies adopted by their oligarchic group.

The Party Presidium (after 1966, again called the Politburo) constituted in 1964 of eleven men, all bearing other specific responsibilities. From the central party apparatus there were four: Brezhnev, the First Secretary (after 1966, again General Secretary); Nikolai Podgorny, the number two generalist in the Secretariat; Mikhail Suslov, the Secretariat's ideological specialist and *éminence grise* since the early fifties; and Alexander Shelepin, head of the Party-State Control Commission and former chief of the KGB. Also included were Andrei Kirilenko, head of party affairs for the Russian Republic, and Pyotr Shelest, First Secretary of the Ukraine. Representing the government were prime minister Kosygin, chief of state Mikoyan, and deputy prime minister Dmitri Poliansky, along with Gennadi Voronov, prime minister of the Russian Republic. Nikolai Shvernik, former chief of state under Stalin, held membership as an honored retiree. The top eleven were followed by six candidate members: the member of the Secretariat for culture; the deputy party chief for the Russian Republic; the party secretaries for Belorussia, Georgia, and Uzbekistan; and the head of the trade unions. The Party Secretariat, which continued through its staff departments to exercise power over local organizations and appointments as well as over the government and the economy, comprised, in addition to the four Politburo members and one candidate, five other members with specific supervisory responsibilities (including Andropov, in charge of relations with other Communist countries). Together, the men in the Politburo and the Secretariat constituted, as they still do, the power elite of the Soviet political system.

At the next, much broader level is the Central Committee, which is likewise composed of representatives from the various geographical and functional areas, all elected by the Party Congress on a prearranged slate. The membership of the Central Committee has been steadily expanded at each congress, reaching at the Twenty-sixth Congress in 1981 a total of 319 members, together with 151 candidate members and 75 members of the so-called Central Auditing Commission. (Membership in this body is a sort of honorable-mention for officials whose status falls just short of candidate member.) The total of 545 seats at the three ranks in this institutionalized elite group was, as of 1981, distributed among the functional areas as follows: central party apparatus, 63; party organizations in the Russian Republic, 80 (including the First Secretary of every province and autonomous republic); central and provincial party officials of the other union republics, 68 (apportioned according to their relative demographic and economic importance); central government, 123 (including all cabinet ministers and state committee chairmen); government leaders of the Russian Republic, 21; governmental chiefs of the union republics, 35 (including at least two from each); military leaders, 40 (tying in with military rank and including all marshals and full generals); the police agencies, 6; ambassadors abroad, 21 (mostly former party officials stationed in Communist capitals); trade union leaders, 11; cultural and scientific leaders, 22; miscellaneous organization heads, 4. Finally there is a group of 51 individuals drawn from everyday walks of life, ranging from factory directors to dairy maids, to serve as token representatives of the masses.

Although Central Committee members are nominally elected by the Party Congress, it is clear from the assignment of rank and representation that the lists are always carefully made up beforehand. They have been made up, moreover, according to certain unwritten but highly consistent rules of status—recalling the hierarchy of prerevolutionary officialdom—governing the bureaucratic and territorial entities whose leading functionaries are accorded seats. The party apparatus always accounts for the largest single component, and the civil government for a slightly smaller one. Then come the military, the diplomats, the scientific and cultural sector, and the trade unions. In the party component the Russian Republic ranks a bit ahead of the total for the minority republics. Representation of the latter is finely graduated according to the status imputed to each individual republic. In any given administrative unit, the party leader will be given a seat that ranks equal to or higher than that of the governmental chief.

These rules can be illustrated by constructing a status matrix for the Central Committee members representing the union republics (see page 264). The matrix shows the almost perfect correlation among Central Committee rank, the importance of the republic, and the status of particular jobs.

The system of rank and representation embodied in the Central

Status matrix: Central Committee representation of union republics (1981).

Republic	First Secretary	Second Secretary	Prime Minister	Chairman, Presidium	First Deputy Prime Minister	Third Secretary	Other Ministers	Provincial Secretaries
RSFSR	—	—	Cand. PB	CC (Deputy chairman, Cand.)	CC (2)	—	CC (4) Cand. (5) CAC (3)	CC (66) Cand. (13) CAC
Ukraine	PB	CC	CC	CC	CC Cand.	CC (2) Cand. (2)	CAC (2)	CC (12) Cand. (4) CAC (2)
Kazakhstan	PB	CC	CC	CC	CAC	CAC		CC (6) Cand. (5)
Uzbekistan	Cand. PB	CC	CC	CC	CAC			CC Cand. CAC
Belorussia	Cand. PB	CC	CC	CC	CAC			CC Cand.
Georgia	Cand. PB	CC	Cand.	CAC				
Azerbaijan	Cand. PB	Cand.	Cand.	CAC				
Latvia	CC	Cand.	Cand.	CAC				
Kirghizia	CC	Cand.	Cand.	CAC				
Moldavia	CC	Cand.	CAC	Cand.				
Lithuania	CC	Cand.	CAC	Cand.				
Tadzhikistan	CC	Cand.	CAC	Cand.				
Armenia	CC	Cand.	CAC	Cand.				
Turkmenia	CC	Cand.	CAC	Cand.				
Estonia	CC	Cand.	Cand.	CC				

Note: PB = Politburo member; Cand. PB = Candidate member of the Politburo; CC = Central Committee member; Cand. = Central Committee candidate member; CAC = member of the Central Auditing Commission. The numbers in parentheses indicate more than one official at a given rank. There are no central party officials for the RSFSR, the USSR party bodies having served this purpose directly since 1966.

Committee has a long history, going back to Stalin's rise to power in the 1920s and the appointments he made to staff the party apparatus with his own people. Between Lenin's illness in 1922 and Stalin's emergence in the number one spot in 1927, the Central Committee had changed from a small group of political luminaries to a much larger group of more or less faceless functionaries whose membership derived from the party and government offices they represented. This principle of composition has held true ever since, despite great expansion of the body and the almost complete replacement of its membership in the wake of the Great Purge, with only one revealing change: the military have replaced the trade unions as the third-largest component.

The members of the Central Committee, as well as the two lesser ranks of candidate members and Central Auditing Commission members, enjoy power only on the basis of their particular bureaucratic functions, which depend on appointment or approval by the party Secretariat. Their Central Committee seats derive only from their bureaucratic status, and membership will be withdrawn no later than the next party congress if an incumbent is removed from the job that entitles him to the seat. Meeting as it usually does for a few days at a time, two or three times a year, the Central Committee probably exercises little direct power except during succession crises, though its members are consulted regularly by phone and correspondence and can drag their feet if they are not convinced of the merit of a particular policy initiative. Individually, members of the Central Committee are vulnerable to the General Secretary, who can cause their removal; collectively, as in the case of Khrushchev in 1957 and in 1964, they have the final voice in sustaining or removing the leader.

To conceive of such an institutionalized elite in comparable American terms, one would have to imagine an exclusive policymaking body about the size of Congress but made up of the following: the president, the vice-president, senior White House advisors, all cabinet secretaries and agency heads of equivalent rank, the directors of the CIA and the FBI, all five-star and four-star generals and admirals, the ambassadors to major powers, congressional leaders such as committee chairmen, all the governors, the heads of the largest corporations and banks, major industrial association leaders, a few union chiefs, heads of a few major universities, foundations, and religious organizations, the baseball commissioner and the president of the League of Women Voters, a few eminent but non-controversial scientists, artists, and writers, and finally a few dozen ordinary citizens representing major occupational and ethnic groups. Further, one would have to assume that all these people held their positions by appointment or recommendation of the White House, but that on occasion they could act in concert to remove the incumbent who appointed them. This, of course, is fantasy; in the United States, the only badge of institutionalized civic status comparable to Central Committee membership is a low-number license plate.

The top Soviet leaders are a distinctive group. To begin with, nearly all of them have been men; only one woman has ever reached the level of the Politburo—Yekaterina Furtseva, for four years during Khrushchev's heyday. Only 34 women appeared in the 1981 elite list of 545, all but six of them Great Russian. Twenty-two of the 34 were merely mass representatives, with no power-wielding jobs of their own. (Among elite members with significant jobs the percentage of women was 2.4, distinctly below the percentage of women in the U.S. Congress (4.3 percent in the Ninety-eighth Congress.) Women with leading jobs in the Soviet hierarchy have been clustered in the stereotyped cultural and welfare sectors. Only two women in the 1981 elite group served as First Secretary of a party organization, and they did so only at the district level; since these were the only cases where the district job has carried Central Committee rank, their inclusion appears to have been pure tokenism.

Apart from a few old Stalinists—including Khrushchev—who survived the purges of the thirties, all of the men who have run the country since Stalin's death were born after 1902—too young to have participated in the Revolution. They share a common social and career background: they are sons of workers and peasants, have been party members since the 1920s or 1930s, were educated in special technical and political programs, and are practically devoid of international experience. Emerging from the masses and just young enough to escape the purges, they advanced rapidly into the vacuum of higher office left by the liquidation of their seniors. For example, Kosygin, born in 1904, was a textile mill foreman in 1937; by 1940, at the age of thirty-six, he was one of the deputy prime ministers of the Soviet Union. Brezhnev, born in 1906, was a local agricultural official and then a technical school principal in the Ukraine until 1937; by 1939 he had become second secretary of the party in the

Dnepropetrovsk province, and he then moved up through the military-political administration during World War II and into the party hierarchy. As a group, the post-purge generation took over the entire government and party structure and held power for decades; any replacements tended to come from nearly the same age cohort.

This demographic fact explains why such continuity was possible during the Brezhnev era—the leadership generation was not old enough to die off rapidly until the 1970s. Between 1961 and 1981, the median age of the Central Committee increased from fifty-three to sixty-two, and the aging of the Politburo was even more striking: from a median of fifty-eight in 1961 to a median of seventy-two in 1981. At the Central Committee or candidate level some individuals have had extremely long tenure in the same position, particularly in the central government and in the minority republics. B. P. Beshchev, for example, was minister of railways from 1948 until his retirement in 1977 at the age of seventy-three, and A. A. Ishkov headed the fishing industry through various ministerial reorganizations from World War II until 1978. A. Y. Snechkus was First Secretary of the party in Lithuania from the time of the Soviet takeover in 1940 until he died in office in 1974 at the age of seventy. To some extent this gerontocracy was offset in the Central Committee by the inclusion of younger men (mostly new provincial party chiefs), but new appointees have had to spend ever-longer apprenticeships in technical training and party organization work.

During the Brezhnev era, the Politburo was as stable in its membership as were the ruling policies and institutions. Whereas there had been repeated shuffles within the Party Presidium between Stalin's death and Khrushchev's fall, Brezhnev had a solid corps of leaders around him almost until he died, eighteen years after assuming the leadership. Between 1966 and 1977 there was no change whatsoever in the top five positions—General Secretary (Brezhnev), prime minister (Kosygin), chief of state (Podgorny), chief ideologist (Suslov), and party second-in-command (Kirilenko). This was an extraordinary record for the Soviets, testifying to the extent to which they had developed a cohesive bureaucratic team. Below the highest level of the Politburo, to be sure, there was gradual turnover, and eventually age and ambition took their toll among the top group. The greatest political tension surrounded Alexander Shelepin, the former KGB chief who became a party secretary and chairman of the Party-State Control Commission when the neo-Stalinists were rallying against Khrushchev and was rewarded in 1964 with a Politburo seat. Shelepin was suddenly shunted aside in 1967 to head the trade unions, though he retained his Politburo seat for a few years more.

In the mid-seventies, presumably when Brezhnev and his entourage felt their power more secure, there came a series of replacements in the junior half of the Politburo. In 1973 Ukrainian party chief Shelest was dropped, reportedly for leniency toward Ukrainian nationalism, and RSFSR prime minister Voronov fell also, while the heads of three key governmental functions—defense minister Marshal Grechko, foreign minister Gromyko, and KGB chief Andropov, were elevated to full Politburo status. The most visible change came in 1977: chief of state Podgorny, by then in his seventies, fell into disgrace, and Brezhnev took the titles of Marshal of the Soviet Union and chief of state for himself, amid a rising chorus of glorification in the media. Needless to say, these steps were not accompanied by any great policy initiatives or leadership rejuvenation; new members of the Politburo tended to be almost as old as the men they replaced.

By the late seventies the biological laws of limited longevity were catching up with the Soviet leadership, claiming not only the elderly like Grechko (who died in 1976 at the age of seventy-two) and Kosygin (who died in 1980 at the age of seventy-six) but also the overstressed middle-aged (first deputy prime minister Kirill Mazurov, a Politburo member since 1965, retired in 1978 at the age of sixty-four, and party agriculture secretary Fyodor Kulakov, a member since 1971, died the same year at the age of sixty). Podgorny's ouster and Kosygin's death spelled the breakup of the tight group that had ruled ever since 1964, at a time when the Soviet Union's steady economic progress was slackening as it approached the limits to growth.

One might question why Brezhnev, in deteriorating health, did not see fit to retire, as rumor often predicted from the mid-seventies on. But the Soviet Union still does not know the concept of honorable retirement for the top leader: he has only the options of holding out until death or of succumbing to demotion and disgrace. Brezhnev clung even tighter to his position as his old team disintegrated and the scramble for succession began among the newer (though not much younger) Politburo members.

The stability secured by perpetuating an aging cadre of leaders cannot, for obvious reasons, last indefinitely. Its ultimate fragility was underscored by the dual succession to Brezhnev, when the elderly collectivity of powerbrokers had to replace their first choice, Andropov, in a mere fifteen months and, betraying their fear of passing the torch to younger and less familiar candidates, installed the even older Chernenko.

The succession process was set in motion in January 1982 by the death of Suslov at the age of seventy-nine. Chernenko, then seventy, was the heir apparent. He had followed in Brezhnev's footsteps ever since the early fifties, and had elbowed aside the more experienced but ailing Kirilenko. But a dark horse candidate suddenly emerged: KGB chief Andropov, only sixty-seven. At the Central Committee plenum in May 1982, Andropov relinquished his secret police post and positioned himself for the post-Brezhnev struggle by securing Suslov's vacant seat in the party secretariat. Most likely with support in the Politburo from the military (represented by defense minister Dmitri Ustinov), the non-Russian cadres (represented by Vladimir Shcherbitsky of the Ukraine and Dinmukhamed Kunaev of Kazakhstan), and younger party apparatus men (represented by Grigori Romanov and Mikhail Gorbachev), Andropov won the day.

Andropov's takeover after Brezhnev suddenly died on November 10, 1982, was almost anticlimactic. Relying on the same coalition that had supported him in May, he lined up a majority against Chernenko in the Politburo and at an unofficial gathering of Central Committee members held the day after Brezhnev's death. Andropov had himself designated chairman of the Brezhnev funeral committee, so that when the full Central Committee convened on November 12 the outcome was already clear. Chernenko, the loser, was prevailed upon to nominate Andropov to replace Brezhnev as General Secretary, and the Central Committee ratified the proposal unanimously.

Yuri Vladimirovich Andropov was the subject of great speculation abroad; some viewed him as a potential reformer and some as a new Stalin, though there was little in his background to suggest the former. He was born in 1914, the son of a railroad worker in the North Caucasus, and he devoted his entire adult life to party work. He served as a functionary in the Komsomol in the 1930s and during the war, as a party official during the late Stalin period in what was at the time the Karelo-Finnish union republic, and then as a department head in the central Secretariat. Appointed ambassador to Hungary in 1954, he became notorious in 1956 for his role in deceiving the Hungarian revolutionary government about Soviet plans to intervene. Subsequently he took over the department of the Secretariat that handled relations with other Communist countries, and held the post during the difficult time of polycentric discord and the break with China. He commanded the confidence of the Brezhnev team to the extent that in 1967, when Shelepin was being eased out, they chose him as the man to assert party authority over the secret police and replace Shelepin's protégé Vladimir Semichastny in that capacity.

As head of the KGB, Andropov distinguished himself by crushing the dissident movement that had begun during Khrushchev's thaw. He had no known role in formulating new approaches to the country's problems; his job was to stabilize and shield from criticism a leadership that avoided such approaches. But once in the top office himself, Andropov sounded a new spirit of reform, discipline, and efficiency. He purged the Ministry of Internal Affairs and the militia (ousting Brezhnev's protégés, including his son-in-law), and ordered a dramatic campaign against absenteeism and malingering throughout the economic system. The popular response to these old police tactics was mostly favorable, as hopes were raised that the impasse of corruption and bureaucratic stagnation under Brezhnev would be broken.

Within the party apparatus Andropov set the circular flow of power in motion again. Soon after his selection as party leader, he took for himself the titles of chief of state (chairman of the Presidium of the Supreme Soviet) and commander-in-chief (chairman of the National Defense Council), which Brezhnev had assumed only toward the end of his reign. Otherwise Andropov moved carefully at the top level, disturbing none of the Politburo incumbents and initially adding only one man—the Azerbaijan party chief and former police official Geidar Aliev, who headed the efficiency campaign as first deputy prime minister. Leningard party chief and Politburo member Grigori Romanov got himself elevated to the Secretariat in Moscow, thereby positioning himself for the next succession crisis. Police representation in the Politburo was maintained by the designation of Andropov's KGB successor, Viktor Chebrikov, as a candidate member. At lower levels there was more activity, as younger men were moved into cabinet ministries, departments of the Central Committee staff, and provincial secretaryships. Altogether about 20 percent of the party and government positions of Central Committee rank changed hands during Andropov's brief tenure.

Though heralding a transition from an old and stagnant generation to a younger and more dynamic one, Andropov's leadership itself fell victim to the hazards of advanced age. Already sixty-eight when he became General Secretary (Brezhnev was fifty-eight when Khrushchev fell, as was Khrushchev when Stalin died), Andropov became terminally ill within less than a year. After his death on February 9, 1984, events moved exactly as they had after Brezhnev. The news was withheld for almost twenty-four hours while the Politburo made its arrangements. The successor was made known by announcing the chairman of the funeral committee—it was Chernenko. Then there was a delay of three days until the Central Committee could be brought together to formalize the selection of the new General Secretary. All that was surprising was the identity of the successor—not a younger man, as might finally have been expected, but one even older, and the loser in the 1982 contest. He was the Politburo member most closely identified with the Brezhnev regime and least with the sort of reforms Andropov had set in motion.

The choice might be explained by the role of Gorbachev, at fifty-two the youngest member of the Politburo and, with Romanov, one of the two people besides Chernenko who held membership in both the Politburo and the Secretariat and were in practice eligible to become General Secretary. Judging by the prominence he assumed following Chernenko's takeover, Gorbachev may well have induced the younger party officials to back Chernenko as an interim leader in order to head off the sixty-year-old Romanov, whose success might have precluded a future takeover by Gorbachev himself.

Konstantin Chernenko, like his immediate predecessors, was a member of the generation of Stalin's "promotees." He was born in Siberia in 1911 to peasant parents who were, judging by the family surname, Ukrainian migrants, though Chernenko listed himself as Russian by nationality (and was reputed to have some native Siberian ancestors among the Turkic-speaking Khakass). He joined the party in 1931 after serving with the border guards, and became a professional in the party apparatus. By the age of thirty, in the wake of the purges, he had risen to become a member of the party Secretariat for his home province of Krasnoyarsk. Although he never distinguished himself as a speaker or a thinker, he trained as a propagandist during the war, and this won him the job of agitprop chief for the Moldavian Republic, where he began his association with Brezhnev before the end of the Stalin era. Shortly after Brezhnev displaced Khrushchev as First Secretary, he made Chernenko head of the "General Department" of the Central Committee staff, which was responsible for handling all the paperwork for the top party organs. In this capacity Chernenko achieved membership in the Central Committee in 1971, in the Secretariat in 1976, and in the Politburo in 1978. He was often a chief of staff, never a chief, until his surprise elevation to the office of General Secretary and his investiture a few weeks later with the leadership of the National Defense Council and the ceremonial function of chief of state.

The sure-footed transfer of power from Brezhnev to Andropov and from Andropov to Chernenko suggests that the Soviet system has more or less solved the old problem of leadership succession, which proved so disruptive after Lenin and, to a lesser extent, after Stalin. The head man is selected by the leaders of the party oligarchy embodied in the Politburo, with the backing and assent of the Central Committee—a method not unlike that used by a West European political party when it chooses a leader. The succession has become smoother because the power of the leader has been progressively more constricted, and the stakes are correspondingly lower. The members of the oligarchy seem willing to live with whichever chief is chosen, and he with them, without the bloodletting that accompanied such transitions in the past.

The choosing of elderly leaders, in order to delay the complete shift of power to a new generation, has further limited the opportunity for the head man to become a threat to his associates. Both Andropov and Chernenko, even more than Brezhnev, were constrained by time and the political environment to act as the representative of the party bureaucracy rather than its master, even though their opportunities to restaff high positions made vacant by death or retirement had, as a result of the aging of the post-purge generation, become much broader than when Brezhnev had taken over. By the time of Brezhnev's death, a distinct bifurcation had appeared between the post-retirement survivors and the newer, working-age people, and the prospects of a rapid renovation of the leadership were rising. Andropov was dead before he had fairly begun, and Chernenko's record gave little indication that he would fundamentally change either the system or the policies that had guided the

Soviet Union under Brezhnev. The rehabilitation of the ninety-four-year-old Molotov in July 1984, after decades of political oblivion, underscored the old guard's link with Stalinism. What a younger and more modern leader might be able to accomplish in a different direction remains the central question of Soviet politics.

■ The Political Structure

The governmental system of the Soviet Union has changed little since Stalin's time, despite the fact that a superficially revised constitution was adopted in 1977 with Brezhnev's imprimatur. However, significant developments have taken place, and may still, in the way the system actually functions. Not only have the personalities in command changed, but their role has evolved as well. Throughout the political structure there have been gradual modifications in the relationships that gear all citizens into the system.

Soviet politics remain, of course, a one-party monopoly, and the party as an institution continues to control nearly everything that goes on in the society. Party functions are still embodied in the apparatus—the hierarchy of full-time party secretaries at every level of administration from the Kremlin down to each factory and village. The apparatus is distinct from the party membership, which consists of about eighteen million people in all walks of life who pursue their careers under the watchful eye of the organization.

In support of its political functions, the Communist Party maintains a pyramid of committees that provide a democratic façade paralleling the soviets in the government. The lowest unit, the Primary Party Organization, consisting of the party members in a factory, office, or collective farm, sends its delegates to a district or city committee, which elects the party secretary for that level. Similarly the district elects delegates to a provincial conference, which has its corresponding committee and secretary, and the same holds for each union republic (except for the huge Russian Republic, which has no central party institutions distinct from the all-union leadership). At the top level, party policy is set by the All-Union Party Congress—about five thousand delegates who meet once every five years. The congress ratifies the slate of Central Committee members prepared by the leadership, and the Central Committee in turn elects the Politburo, the Secretariat, and the General Secretary, who is a member of both of these bodies. Over the years, the party leaders have reinforced their prestige by assuming a governmental title—in the case of Stalin and Khrushchev that of prime minister, and in the case of Brezhnev, Andropov, and Chernenko the less functional office of chairman of the Presidium of the Supreme Soviet.

The dictatorial character of the Soviet political structure, implicit in the one-party system and the exclusion of organized alternatives, is confirmed by the role of the party apparatus and the coercive and regulatory agencies of government under the direction of ranking party members. Furthermore, the party apparatus is itself run on dictatorial or at least bureaucratic lines, from the top down. A secretary in the party apparatus (as far as recorded evidence indicates) is de facto appointed from above—that is, "recommended" by higher secretaries and the Secretariat—and his "election" by the local committee only rubber-stamps the choice. In turn, the secretarial hierarchy manages the party's committees at each level and produces the electoral choices intended by higher authority, all the way up to the designation of delegates to the Party Congress and the selection of members of the Central Committee. These links perpetuate the circular flow of power set in motion by Stalin. Real power is exerted downward through the apparatus and upward through formal channels, so that the leader can manipulate the entire process that confirms him in office.

Developments since Stalin's time have qualified the circular flow and somewhat enlarged the political role that middle and high officials can play. Khrushchev endeavored to use Stalin's methods to consolidate his own power, and succeeded up to a point, only to fall victim to the same system after the neo-Stalinists took over the power of appointment through the Secretariat. Brezhnev made little rapid or obvious use of the circular flow, preferring (or being compelled) to rely on the men who had taken office during the period of anti-Khrushchev maneuvering. Andropov tried to step up the pace of change, but ran out of time. By and large, from the 1960s to the 1980s party and governmental officials at all levels enjoyed more security in office than they had ever known before. In turn, they have had the opportunity to strengthen their bailiwicks by making power plays and currying constituents' favor—tactics that characterize machine politics everywhere. By using the party committee structure and advisory contacts, governmental and economic officials and experts of every sort have been able to debate policy details and influence decisions, provided they did not challenge the premises of the regime or the positions of those in charge. The Soviets have made much of the principle of "mass participation in administration," which hold true, at least in form, for the local soviets and control commissions. More effective, however, is participation by the hierarchy—the ruling class, so to speak. The Soviet system is not a participatory democracy but a participatory bureaucracy.

Whatever the possibilities for high bureaucrats to share in the policymaking process, the Communist Party maintains a monopoly on political activity and expression. All citizens, whether or not they are party members, are constrained by the apparatus to observe discipline and carry out orders. The oft-quoted statistic that eighteen million party members (7 percent of the population) dictate to the majority is misleading in two ways. First, the party member is no freer than any other citizen to express and assert his will. Second, party membership approaches 50 percent where it is concentrated in the population of educated, urban, working-age men. This means that a very large population of the people performing jobs involving responsibility and technical knowledge have, usually for career reasons, submitted to the extra discipline and surveillance imposed on party members. Lower down the age pyramid the party assures its future through a sequence of youth organizations—the Little Octobrists (aged seven to nine), the Young Pioneers (aged ten to fifteen), and the Komsomol ("Communist Union of Youth," aged sixteen to twenty-six)—from which new party apparatus personnel are usually recruited.

The civil government of the Soviet Union, the "state" as opposed to the party, has always been overshadowed by the latter in the decision-making process and in the rank of its personnel. Traditionally the party makes policy and the government carries it out, under party control. Bureaucrats may shift back and forth between government and party positions, but to go from government to party at the same administrative level is always a career advancement, often registered by promotion in rank within the Central Committee.

At each level of the Soviet administrative structure—village, city, district, province, republic, and the union, as well as the various minority entities—undivided power is theoretically vested in an elected council, the soviet. Though they have been chosen on a territorial rather than occupational basis since 1936, the soviets are still officially regarded as uniquely democratic bodies that represent the toiling citizens of a classless society. As the legislative branch of government at each level, they are considered the supreme authority and merely delegate executive and judicial powers, somewhat like European parliaments.

In theory, nationwide legislative power continues to be exercised by the Supreme Soviet. This body, which meets briefly and infrequently, has long been deprecated by most foreign observers as a mere rubber stamp for the decisions of the Communist Party leadership. Party control of nominations, elections, and debates and the invariable habit of unanimous voting make any challenge to the government through the legislative channel inconceivable.

Nevertheless the Supreme Soviet is not insignificant. It reflects, like the party organs, the Soviets' long-standing obsession with carefully scaling institutional and geographical representation according to the imputed importance of the given function or region. Forty percent of its members are leading government or party officials—the country's ruling elite, who are automatically nominated to the body when they achieve high political rank. Members need not reside in the district they represent, and it has become the practice to recognize prestigious leaders by nominating them to the Supreme Soviet in several different districts at once; the favored candidate then resigns all but one of the seats and yields them to a replacement in a by-election.

The award of multiple nominations illustrates the Soviet leaders' fine sense of status, as well as their ability to arrange the prescribed number of nominations in different districts for a given individual. To take the most recently available compilation, that of 1970 (the scores are not published and must be culled from press reports of individual nominations), Brezhnev naturally led the field with 138 nominations to the Supreme Soviet. Prime minister Aleksei Kosygin followed with 80, and then chief of state Nikolai Podgorny with 77. After them came the remaining members of the Politburo in a descending logarithmic distribution, with no member receiving less than 13 nominations. The nine men who held candidate membership in the Politburo received from seven to three nominations. No one else received more than an individual nod. Partial tabulations for the 1984 elections, based on nominations made while Andropov was still alive, showed him in first place, naturally, with Chernenko and prime minister Nikolai Tikhonov tied for second.

Potentially significant is the Supreme Soviet's recent elaboration of its committee system. On the committees of approximately thirty members (and in the smaller "preparatory groups" within each committee), which meet more often than the parent body, individual members of the elite have an opportunity to meet with their counterparts in other bureaucratic hierarchies representing the same policy area, be it foreign affairs, economic planning, education, or whatever. Thus, a certain deliberative if not representative process appears to take place within the framework of the Supreme Soviet, though as Jerry Hough has pointed out in *How the Soviet Union Is Governed,* "Incredibly, the regime has revealed exceedingly little information on that aspect of Supreme Soviet activity which almost surely has the greatest claim to 'democratic' discussion and exercise of influence."

The executive side of the Soviet government operates like a European cabinet under a prime minister. It includes a panoply of economic ministries covering everything from ferrous metallurgy to fruit and vegetable growing. There is also an array of "state committees" to administer a variety of specialized fields ranging from cinematography to scientific research. Groups of ministries are presumably coordinated by the deputy prime ministers, who currently number about a dozen. The chairman of the State Planning Commission (Gosplan) also holds the rank of deputy prime minister.

With appropriate variations, the ministerial structure is replicated at the union republic level and lower, handling such matters as health, education, housing, and local industry. Each union republic has a prime minister and cabinet; provinces, cities, and lesser entities are headed by the chairmen of the executive committees of their local soviets, who are the nearest equivalent to American governors, mayors, and county executives. Thus, V. F. Promyslov, called "mayor" of Moscow in the Western press, is officially chairman of the Executive Committee of the Moscow City Soviet. In the case of certain ministries, termed "Union-Republican Ministries," the ministry at the republic level serves as a branch of the federal ministry. This is the pattern in finance, agriculture, the police, most social service and light industrial areas, and, oddly enough, foreign affairs. (This curious arrangement dates from 1945, when Stalin set up foreign offices in all of the union republics so that he could demand United Nations seats for each one of them. Eventually, he settled for separate representation for the Ukraine and Belorussia, along with

the seat for the USSR as a whole.) Constitutionally there is no analogue of the Union-Republican Ministry in the U.S. system, though
in practice it is approximated where departments of state government (welfare and unemployment security, for example) have been
coopted by federal law and matching funds to serve as Washington's
local agents.

One practical limit on Soviet federalism is the lack of taxing
power at any level but the highest. All lesser jurisdictions, even the
union republics, are dependent on appropriations from the central
budget. There is a modest income tax with a ceiling of 13 percent
(except for confiscatory rates on successful self-employment and authors' royalties from abroad), and levies on enterprise profits. But
most revenues come from the turnover tax, which is actually a vari-
able-rate sales tax reflecting the margin between the state's cost of
production of any particular commodity and the price that can be
charged at retail to dispose of the available volume.

The judicial branch of the Soviet government differs substantially
from the U.S. judiciary in both its form, which is more decentralized, and its substance, which is more centralized and less independent. Not counting the quasi-legal "comradely courts" that deal
with such matters as neighborhood brawls and labor discipline, the
lowest judicial entity is the People's Court, a tribunal of one professional judge and two elected laymen who dispose of everyday civil
and criminal matters without benefit of jury. Above this level, both
for appellate functions and for original jurisdiction in more serious
cases, rises a pyramid of district, provincial, and republic courts,
culminating in the Supreme Court of the USSR. All kinds of cases
go through the single system: there is no separate hierarchy of federal courts distinct from republic courts. The Supreme Court maintains a special Military Collegium, which not only heads the system
of justice for the armed forces but also exercises direct jurisdiction
over high crimes of political opposition, espionage, and treason.
There is no concept of judicial review of the constitutionality of legislative and executive acts. In this respect the Supreme Soviet and
the representatives of its authority in the Council of Ministers are,
even in theory, beyond challenge. As for constitutional amendments, such as the relatively minor changes made in 1977, the Supreme Soviet simply votes in its proposals by a two-thirds majority
(in practice, unanimously), after what passes for a public discussion.

The democratic appearances of the Soviet constitutional structure are belied by the privileged role of the party, whose political monopoly is explicitly affirmed by the constitution. Although every citizen eighteen or over has the right, and in practice the duty, to vote, there is never more than a single ticket offering candidates preselected by the party. Almost invariably voters register a yes vote by dropping their printed ballot directly in the ballot box rather than attract attention by using the curtained booth to cross out the name of the official candidate. Not surprisingly, the percentages both of voter turnout (carefully checked as an index of conformity) and of regime victories are in the very high nineties. "Needless to say, comrades," declared Brezhnev at the time of the 1977 constitutional changes, "the draft constitution proceeds from the premise that the rights and liberties of citizens cannot and must not be used against our social system or to the detriment of the Soviet people's interest."

Although the Soviet system of rule would hardly qualify as a democracy in the Western sense, it has come a long way from Stalin's terroristic methods. Officials who fall into disfavor are no longer secretly executed; people are not capriciously arrested when they have expressed no opposition to the regime; scientists and experts are not dictated to in the Stalinist manner; some foreign travel in and out is permitted. Nevertheless, the machinery of totalitarian control is still in place, and those who transgress the permissible limits—by intellectual dissent, engaging in illegal enterprise, or only expressing the desire to leave—quickly feel the grip of the police state.

The Soviet regime sustains itself and runs the country by means of a vast interlocking system of controls. The party apparatus is the heart of this system, supervising all the mechanisms of government that apply sanctions to the populace. Within the party, the Commission of Party Control is responsible for discipline over its individual members; the Main Political Administration maintains political control over the armed forces. Within the governmental and economic structure, fiscal and performance controls are exercised by the Ministry of Finance and the State Planning Commission. Efficiency and honesty of individual functionaries are monitored by the People's Control Commission. But of all the agencies of control, the harshest, the best known, and the most crucial to the preservation of the one-party system is the police.

Since the fall of Beria in 1953, police functions have been divided between the Ministry of Internal Affairs (MVD) and the Committee of State Security (KGB). Both are organized on the union-republican principle, with the chain of command running from Moscow straight down to the lowest precinct. The MVD directs the conventional uniformed police (*militsiya*), maintains registries and vital statistics, provides fire protection, administers prisons and prison camps, and commands the internal security troops numbering about 400,000. The KGB is the secret police and the major foreign intelligence service, resembling a combination of the FBI and the CIA but subject to far fewer legal and political restrictions. (It also directs the border guards, another military-style force of 200,000 or more.) As in Stalin's time, the KGB penetrates all Soviet institutions (including the military) with its informers. The party, in turn, rides herd on the KGB and other law enforcement agencies through the Secretariat's "Administrative Organs" Department.

The Soviet system of police surveillance and repression now works more selectively than in Stalin's time, without resorting to mass disappearances and executions. Thanks to the amnesties and rehabilitations of the immediate post-Stalin period, the population of the prisons and camps was substantially reduced. Estimates for the 1970s, including persons released from prison to do compulsory labor, range between two and three million or about 1 percent of the population. These were mainly common criminals, along with people guilty of activities—"parasitism" and economic crimes—that in other societies would not be punishable offenses. (In the United States, prison inmates total about 600,000, plus several hundred thousand more on probation or parole; some states, mostly in the South, have prison rates that approach one-half of the Soviet figure.) True "political" prisoners in the Soviet Union have been estimated in recent years to number only about 10,000, though they draw more world attention today than they did when their numbers were much greater. The reduction does not mean that political control has been relaxed; rather, it indicates the degree of outward political docility that has been induced in the Soviet population as a whole.

Can the contemporary Soviet political system still be fruitfully analyzed in terms of the monolithic, "totalitarian" model? Some Western scholars claim that it cannot, suggesting instead a "conflict model" or "interest group model" that reflects the functional segments and power centers of the Soviet bureaucracy—the military, the police, the industrial chiefs, the scientists and academics, the regional organizations of the party, and so forth. It is indeed important to recognize that such centers, all with distinctive interests, do exist in the Soviet system and that they no doubt lobby for their points of view within the councils of the party. Interest group politics may be particularly important during a succession phase, when the direction of the top leadership is unclear. On the other hand, it would be highly misleading to equate Soviet interest group politics with the free-wheeling interplay of economic, ethnic, professional, and geographical interests in the U.S. system of representative government. All of the competing interests in the Soviet system are parts of one vast bureaucratic structure, subject to the dictates of the Communist Party leadership.

The Soviets still have no concept of constitutional and legal restraints on those who rule. The limitations they observe are only self-imposed and pragmatic: terror of the Stalin style is counterproductive in a modern society. The individual citizen may be "free" in the nonpolitical sense to pursue his or her career and family life, but has no rights against the state or the party. No public expression of opinion in any channel or on any subject, no organized activity for any purpose whatsoever, can take place without the sanction and even the initiative of the authorities. Defiance of these requirements constitutes "anti-Soviet activity," punishable under the criminal code, as the organizers of even such an innocuous activity as the unofficial Soviet peace movement found to their dismay in the early 1980s. "Information is power," say those in control, and they guard access to it jealously. Secrecy shrouds the decision-making process and even conceals the private lives of the leaders. Anything that might expose Soviet citizens to unchecked ideas—foreign books, foreign travel, foreign broadcasts, the presence of foreigners—is carefully restricted. In terms of citizens' rights, as in the workings of the power structure, there has been little evolution in principle away from the totalitarian model of Stalinism.

▪ Ideology

Neither the maturation of the Soviet system nor the vicissitudes of its leadership have softened one of its salient features—namely, its insistence on Marxism-Leninism as the official philosophy of the country. Marxism-Leninism still provides the conceptual framework and vocabulary to describe and justify all aspects of the system and exclude any competing form of belief. It is inculcated through all channels of the media and education as received truth, to which all citizens must conform in their public pronouncements on pain of prosecution for anti-Soviet activity.

Soviet ideology asserts that the course of history is foreordained and that the USSR is leading humanity along the path to the communist utopia. Americans, with little or no concept of objective forces in history, read such statements not as predictions but as intentions. As U.S. policy documents of the Cold War illustrate, they presume that a government wedded to the formulas of Marxism must be committed to making them come true by whatever means are necessary.

In reality, Soviet ideology is neither a valid interpretation of history nor a reliable guide to the evolution of Soviet society. The forces of history, compounded of the imperatives of industrialism, the dynamics of revolution, the authoritarianism of the Russian political culture, and many other elements, have changed the Soviet regime in ways totally unanticipated by its founders. As a result of the Soviets' political interpretation of ideology, their annihilation of criticism, and their rejection of empirical validation, ideology is left with no fixed meaning that could steer actual policy. In the long run, ideology has not determined Soviet reality; rather, reality has reshaped the meaning given to ideology. The Communists, as Alain Besançon has observed, have failed to remodel things, so "they remodel the representation of things."

Why then, does the Soviet regime insist on an ideology that no longer conforms to historical fact? The answer lies in Russia's unique revolutionary experience. Unlike revolutionaries of earlier times, the extremist party in Russia managed to keep in power by adapting to postrevolutionary circumstances. Instead of changing ideologies during this process, as the French did so often in the wake of their revolution, the Communists kept devising new interpretations of the original ideology, each of which was presented as the correct Marxist doctrine. Ideology was thus made to serve the changing political needs of the regime, though at each stage it was turned further away from original revolutionary beliefs by the need to make it square with the country's postrevolutionary development. Under post-purge Stalinism, Marxism came to legitimize a functionally conservative dictatorship and a bureaucratic social structure. In the Soviet Union today, ideology operates in the special sense Marx gave the term; it has become the legitimizing "false consciousness" of the new social order that emanated from the Revolution.

Because the historical outcome is at odds with the original prescriptions of the ideology—transcendence of nationality, abolition of classes, withering away of the state, liberation of the individual from coercive institutions—it is impossible to make ideology play its legitimizing role without dictating both the content and the form of public discourse. The resulting control system must then be justified by even greater ideological rigor.

The price paid for this vicious circle of control is heavy. It severely limits freedom of thought and smothers creativity and initiative in nearly every field of endeavor. It burdens the discussion of public issues with dull and irrelevant abstractions, whose only practical function is to serve as a vehicle for what some observers term "esoteric communication," as insiders play on the nuances of theoretical terminology to suggest reforms or warn of dangers. It posits a "Marxist-Leninist Method" in thought and inquiry which is never spelled out except to justify political interference in intellectual life and condemn people who are too independent.

During the era of détente, much was written in the West about the presumed "erosion" of ideology in the Soviet Union. Indeed, even official sources have acknowledged the increasing cynicism and corruption among Soviet citizens. As a real political motivation, the original ideology lost its force decades ago. Yet to the extent that it serves to exact professions of loyalty and to stifle alternative lines of thought, ideology continues to be imposed as firmly as ever.

The Soviet authorities have the effrontery to complain about the barrenness of their "ideological work" while they use the same dull language to berate their underlings. Proclaimed Chernenko in a major address on ideology in 1983, "The party devotes unremitting attention to instilling in Communists a need for theory and an interest in and taste for it . . . The more completely and decisively we rid ourselves of formalism, dogmatism, inertia, and obsolete and ineffective forms of instruction . . . , the better that system will perform its role. We must consistently and persistently reorganize our work in this regard." This hopeless appeal sixty-six years after the Revolution is nearly on the same plane with the Stalinist practice of shooting factory managers for underfulfilling the plan after their material allocations were cut. The requirements of ideology have distorted the language of politics and philosophy beyond any dependable meaning. The system cannot look at itself and its problems in any objective terms. No matter what the subject, published Soviet thinking long ago ceased to be a genuine intellectual article, much to the confusion of foreigners who have tried to take it seriously. At the conceptual level in any political, cultural, or philosophical discussion, the Soviets can only offer politically commanded manipulation.

The official Soviet mind has something in common with the Scholasticism of the Middle Ages. Both systems of thought proceed from certain high truths that cannot be questioned, and from these they try to deduce explanations of terrestrial phenomena that must conform with the core dogma. In official Soviet thinking, ideas are not derived from or tested by experience; instead, experience is catalogued into the preconceived verbal pigeonholes provided by ideology.

The Soviet authorities still view their history as the tangible realization of the future projected by Marx: the proletarian revolution, the expropriation of the bourgeoisie, the abolition of classes, the achievement of what Marx called the first phase of communism and Lenin called socialism, and more recently preparation for the transition to the final phase of communism. Since phase one communism, or "socialism," calls for the continuation of individual reward according to "work" rather than the presumably more equalitarian principle of reward according to "need," it is more or less compatible with the hierarchical society of bureaucratic industrialism which the Communists actually fashioned. But genuine steps toward equalitarianism or the withering away of the state have steadfastly been avoided. In the early seventies some workers were charged with anti-Soviet activity because they ventured to circulate the official Party program of 1961 containing all of Khrushchev's embarrassing promises.

With the passage of time, the Soviet leadership has invented new historical stages to fill the gap between reality and utopia—"laying the foundations of socialism," "building socialism," "completing the building of socialism," and "beginning the transition to communism." Near the end of the Brezhnev era, the Soviet regime found itself in a new, previously undiscovered stage, "developed socialism," during which the "repatterning of social relations" was to be completed, and the prerequisites for the transition to communism would supposedly be prepared. Said Brezhnev in 1977, explaining the indefinite duration of this new stage: "The development, the perfecting of socialism is a task no less complex . . . than the laying of its foundations." But these distinctions among stages are purely verbal contrivances bearing no relation to sharp policy changes; the pragmatic Brezhnev had to admit, "No one could tell in advance what these stages would be concretely." One cannot tell in retrospect either, except by measuring the expansion of industry. The Soviets' theory of their society's own development is just another example of the scholastic pigeonholing of events in the effort to explain away the perpetuation of a system that has practically nothing in common with the outcome hallowed by doctrine. "Why is the transition to communism like the horizon?" goes one joke. Answer: "It is an imaginary line that recedes as you approach it."

The more abstract elements of Marxism have been less affected by official reinterpretation than its programmatic features, though the quasi-religious aura they have today might not have rested well with the founders of the movement. Insisting that the materialist philosophy is unassailable truth, the Soviet authorities continue to ban all non-Marxist and "idealist" philosophies and to condemn religion. In its place they prescribe a belief in science, so simplistically and dogmatically as to make it a substitute faith. The "scientific-technical revolution" is supposed to guarantee the superiority of the Soviet system and its progress toward the communist future.

Soviet Russia still adheres verbally to the Marxist theory of history as the expression of the forces of production and the class struggle. The view that history is a series of class systems—feudalism, capitalism, and the classless society of communism, each resulting from changes in the mode of production—is imposed on all Soviet historical and political writing, to the point of absurdity. Contending with the fact that revolutions calling themselves Communist have come to pass not in mature industrial countries but in countries of varying degrees of "feudal" backwardness, Soviet theory relies heavily on Lenin's notion of imperialism as an international class struggle between capitalist governments and the colonial and semicolonial peoples whom the imperialists aim to exploit. Accordingly it has been alleged, ever since Stalin's theory of socialism in one country, that the Soviet Union and countries following its example could, with the correct political leadership, leap over part or all of the capitalist stage of their history and pursue a "noncapitalist path" toward socialism.

Even though—or perhaps because—this proposition contradicts the major premise of historical materialism (namely, that political results cannot be obtained without the economic prerequisites), it fits the situation of third-world elites confronted with the challenge of modernizing but embittered over actual or felt humiliation by the capitalist powers. For this reason the theory of imperialism and the noncapitalist path has, since World War II, had wide influence among third-world nationalists, both those whom it drew toward the Communist fold and those who remained non-Communist but anti-Western neutralists. The Marxist condemnation of capitalism and the theoretical expectation of Communist revolution in the industrial countries are still trumpeted when it is politically expedient to bait the West. But ideology has been able neither to overcome nor to explain the tensions between the Soviet Union and other Marxist governments that have escaped its military reach. In no case have the Soviets been capable of seriously analyzing situations where the Marxist prognosis has gone awry.

Andropov picked up the themes of protracted development and unequal reward in a major statement shortly after he assumed the leadership: "Marx was a determined opponent of leveling . . . The character of distribution is, in essence, one of the most important indicators of the degree of social equality that is possible under socialism. Any attempt arbitrarily to exceed this possible degree, to run ahead to the communist form of distribution without an exact accounting of the labor contribution of each person in the creation of material and spiritual goods, can and does generate undesirable phenomena." The state, needless to say, still shows no signs of "withering away"; the "dictatorship of the proletariat" has been changed by a mysterious process of verbal transsubstantiation into "the state of all the people," which looks as if it will exercise its functions indefinitely. The simple if not always apparent fact is that, since Stalin's First Five-Year Plan over fifty years ago, with the exception of some superficial gestures by Khrushchev the Soviet leadership has had no interest in changing the real structure of their state and society. "Building socialism" and "building communism" have been reduced to slogans of industrial development.

In the course of the Soviet experience, particularly in the 1930s, new policies that were neither required nor specifically envisaged by

Marxism were embedded in the ideology and then made obligatory reference points. These policies included the collectivization of the peasants, the formation of the central planning system, and the suppression of all individual economic enterprise—innovations that became more rigidly locked into the policy framework than any of the sketchy predictions inherited from Marx. They also extended to the repudiation of artistic modernism in favor of the conventional-propagandist norms of socialist realism, and the rejection of the behaviorist-reductionist view of human nature embodied in much of modern social science (including Marxism) in favor of a philosophy of absolute rules and personal responsibility.

Along with these ideological revisions in economic and social matters came Stalin's encouragement of Russian nationalism. This has remained a core element in the regime's internal propaganda, and one of its genuine sources of emotional support. It has entailed a major revision in the Marxist theory of history: the rise and expansion of the Russian state and its international struggles are glorified, and the cultural traditions of the non-Russian minorities are straitjacketed lest they encourage "bourgeois nationalism."

What is presumed to be Communist morality, based on a few early remarks by Lenin, has always caused much offense in the West. Supposedly, the good and the true are that which advance the interests of a particular class, and professions of absolute right and wrong are bourgeois hypocrisy. This was the revolutionary rhetoric expressing the Marxist theory that all values reflected class interests. With or without this rationale, the Soviet regime found itself free of moral scruple as early as the onset of the civil war and the Red Terror, expediency and self-preservation serving as the only restraints on its behavior thereafter. But on the rhetorical plane a major reorientation took place as part of the sweeping ideological revision of the purge period. In place of the quasi-sociological moral relativism of the revolutionary epoch, Stalin's regime asserted a new set of higher criteria for the public and private conduct of Soviet citizens. The "New Soviet Man" sounded like a radical figure of social engineering, but in detail he was a paragon of the bourgeois virtues of diligence, discipline, puritanism, and patriotism—hardly distinguishable from the ideal Boy Scout.

The New Soviet Man and his version of the Protestant Ethic have distinguished Soviet propaganda ever since the thirties. Ponderous themes of patriotism and productivity dominate not only May Day speeches but the whole tenor of public life and cultural creations. Frivolity, introspection, and above all pessimism are taboo. Every visitor to the Soviet Union is immediately taken aback by the ubiquitous placards—"Glory to the Communist Party," "Forward to the Victory of Communism," "Fulfill the Plan to Raise the Efficiency of Production."

The ideological facet of the Soviet system is replete with paradoxes: the regime insists on an ideology that bears little relation to reality; it succeeds in imposing this image on public discourse within the Soviet Union; the outside world still tends to see the Soviet system in these ideological terms. One of the most curious by-products of this ideological success is the fact that conservatives in the West have hated and feared the Soviet Union for its ostensible values, even though their own thinking is closer to its operative values than is the thinking of liberals who would like to make allowances for the Soviets. One of the significant differences between fascist totalitarianism and Stalinist Communism is that fascism could bluntly proclaim its authoritarian beliefs, whereas Communism must mask its identity in phrases of democracy and classlessness that are belied by the reality.

The Brezhnev regime preserved the entire ideological legacy of its predecessors, with perhaps an even more ritualistic use of stereotyped verbal formulas. Neither Andropov nor Chernenko gave any sign of change in this respect. On every conceivable occasion ideology is made the vehicle of absolute self-righteousness and childish self-glorification. The Lenin cult still holds sway with unyielding solemnity. There is no humor, no recognition of tragedy, and no sense of irony—certainly not of the colossal irony represented by the history of the Soviet system. The regime identifies itself with everything it considers good: science and democracy from the Western tradition, socialism from the Marxist movement, patriotism from the Russian past. Evil no longer arises from the human condition: it is the work of malevolent conspirators and moral defectives.

The Soviets' system of politically enforced thought has existed in essentially its present form for approximately half a century. The longer they maintain the dogma, the more difficult it becomes to dispense with its services of legitimation and control. A generational factor has also been at work: the most dogmatic and ideologically rigid behavior has been associated with the post-purge leadership generation, perhaps because, unlike their predecessors, they were unprepared to defend themselves in genuine argument. Khrushchev was an exception to this pattern, showing the latitude permitted the man at the top, but this was assuredly one reason for the bureaucracy's hostility toward him. Whether the demise of the post-purge leaders will relax the regime's dependence on dogma or whether their designated successors will perpetuate this dependence remains to be seen. However, the chances for any dramatic change seem remote in this era of collective politics, when each leader fears to expose himself in matters of theory. The only true critics are the now virtually silenced dissidents.

▪ The Socialist Economy

Ever since Communist power was consolidated during the Russian civil war, the economy has been the centerpiece of Soviet thought and effort. The socialist economic structure that was perfected in the 1930s has been the regime's most fundamental claim to virtue, and the success of central planning has been touted as the decisive test of the Communist system. Implicitly, socialism and communism have been equated with industrial progress, and this has been the central point in the self-justification offered by the Soviet regime not only to its own people but to other nations who might be persuaded to emulate the Soviet brand of politics and development.

It is common in the West to consider the Soviet economic system a failure, but this is a relative judgment. Certainly, by comparison with North American and West European standards, the Soviet economic record leaves much to be desired. In recent years it has become more and more difficult in all sectors of the economy for the Soviets to achieve growth and narrow the performance gap between themselves and the West. Nevertheless, by certain material criteria the Soviet economy has been a remarkable success, not least in the industrial base of military power. A country that outproduces the United States in steel, coal, oil, even wheat, can hardly be called a failure, even if the quality and quantity of meat, housing, automobiles, and footwear persistently fall short of consumer demand. The Soviet economic system is not so much a failure as it is a paradox of industrial plenty in the midst of consumer poverty.

As noted earlier, the economic principle of socialism is one of the main residual elements of revolutionary ideology still operative in the Soviet Union. Obviously, the Soviet economy falls within the broad definition of socialism as a system based on public ownership. Beyond this, as early Soviet experience as well as that of other Communist countries illustrates, there are many forms of "socialist" economic organization and policy, ranging from the centralized command economy of the Stalinist model to the decentralized market socialism with private farming and family enterprise that is practiced in Yugoslavia, and the mixed economies and welfare states of Western Europe. Soviet-style socialism stands near one extreme of this continuum, where nearly all resources are owned or controlled by the state and disposed of through central planning and bureaucratic administration.

The description of the Soviet system as "socialist" has been contested by some left-wing thinkers who believe that Moscow's totalitarian politics rule out genuine socialism. Critics on the right maintain that socialism, as shown by the Soviet experience, must necessarily be totalitarian. In fact, most of the specific features of the Soviet economic system do not necessarily follow from a generic definition of socialism, but represent particular choices that arose out of the history of the Soviet regime and were then codified as ideological imperatives.

The most distinctive of these commitments is the centrally planned command economy. This means that economic priorities and allocations are determined not by buyer demand in a free market but by the government authorities. Since 1929 the State Planning Commission and the five-year plans have guided the development of the Soviet economy in minute detail, down to the enterprise level. Monetary exchange and accounting were revived at an early date, after the brief experiment of War Communism, and the ruble has long been pegged to gold (though not convertible to foreign currencies). Nevertheless, profitability and cost-effectiveness have been assigned less importance than the gross quantity of output. In accordance with Marxist anticapitalism, the rate of interest is rejected as a basis for economic planning, although credit allocations to various enterprises by the State Bank are an important tool for channeling capital. The consequence of this ideological stricture is that the costs of long-term construction projects are regularly underestimated. But notwithstanding ideology, interest is paid on personal savings accounts.

Another striking characteristic of Soviet socialism is its totality, contrasting even with the Communist countries of Eastern Europe.

No private trade or enterprise of any scale is allowed, except for small cooperatives and family service establishments working directly for their customers. Private employment of help is banned as "exploitation," and even casual purchase and resale of goods is outlawed as "speculation." Real estate is all legally the property of the state, though it can be obtained for indefinite use as housing sites or personal farm plots. Likewise, all foreign trade transactions must flow through one official channel, the Ministry of Foreign Trade. Trade in the Soviet Union is an instrument of national policy, and considerations of individual benefit or enterprise profitability are not allowed to intrude.

Popular thinking about the Soviet Union often exaggerates or imagines features of the system following presumed definitions or early historical impressions. Soviet socialism, though it professes to have created a classless society by eliminating private owners, has not by any means abolished differences of income and status. Recent awareness of Soviet use of wage incentives and income differentials has prompted the suggestion that the Russians are "going capitalist"; in fact, they have pursued such practices almost since the Revolution, demonstrating that inequality is not ruled out by a socialist system of ownership.

Some have termed the Soviet economic structure a system of "state capitalism"—that is, state-owned and state-controlled, but capitalist in the patterns of organization and operation below that level. Each major industry is directed by a government ministry, and lesser entities, variously known as trusts or "production associations," supervise groups of enterprises on a regional or specialty basis. Manufacturing, construction, mining, and other enterprises are operated in essentially the same manner as branch plants of a great corporation, with a managerial hierarchy bearing responsibility for fulfilling the assigned plan. Trade unions, by contrast, are allowed none of the rights to collective bargaining and strikes that distinguish them in politically free capitalist countries. Wage levels are set by the state, and the role of trade unions (under firm Communist Party control) is to inculcate habits of productivity and efficiency in the work force and to administer social security and fringe benefits (including the important incentives of housing and vacation resort allocations). Sporadic worker protests have been reported in recent years, together with one or two pathetic attempts to organize free trade unions—all quickly suppressed.

It is in the agricultural sector that the Soviet system differs most from the West. Nearly all agriculture, including even nomadic animal husbandry in Central Asia and the Far North, is collectivized, in one of two forms. In the *sovkhoz,* or state farm, used mainly for specialty crops such as cotton or sugar beets and, in the "Virgin Lands" of North Kazakhstan, for grain, the peasants work for wages in the same manner as industrial workers or the employees of a capitalist agribusiness. More prevalent is the *kolkhoz,* or collective farm, comprising anywhere from a hundred to a thousand peasant families who live in their old villages and work in what is legally a cooperative. They receive payment partly in money and partly in kind, derived from the collective output after contractual deliveries at set prices have been made to the state. Each family has, in addition, a private plot of an acre or two with a few animals, the produce of which they may consume themselves or sell in the kolkhoz markets in the towns. The kolkhoz system has been advantageous in the past because the state could arrange prices and deliveries to fulfill its needs, leaving the collective farmers (*kolkhozniki*) to absorb the shortfall in poor crop years.

The Soviet economic system is geared neither to private profit nor to distributive justice. Soviet priorities are directed toward developing the material base of national power, through the continuation, in a socialist framework of state ownership and planning, of the industrialization process left half-finished when the Revolution put an end to capitalism. As a model of noncapitalist development, the Soviet path involves the formation of a managerial elite to function as a corps of business executives without the taint of private or foreign ownership. It relies on the coercive power of the state (exerted by taxation, pricing, and allocation) to accumulate the investment capital required for industrial growth by imposing forced savings on the public, rather than by using the capitalist mechanisms of private savings and credit or foreign investment funds. Finally, it allocates its investments not according to market demand but according to the plan, formulated and implemented by a leadership free from the constraints of public opinion.

The Soviets have always claimed that the plan proves the superior rationality of their system; yet they have never been able to spell out the methodology that actually guides their planning. Political considerations and unspoken priorities have always overridden the science of planning, both in formulation and execution. V. A.

Medvedev, director of science and education in the Party Secretariat, made the incredible statement in *Pravda* (August 5, 1983), "A great deal must still be done to drastically turn economic theory toward the problems of the economy of mature socialism. We still do not possess a comprehensive, detailed conception of its economic system." He went on to quote what Andropov had said in June: "We have not properly studied the society in which we live and work and have not fully discovered its inherent laws, especially its economic laws. Therefore, we sometimes are compelled to act empirically, so to speak, using the highly irrational trial-and-error method."

In pursuing socialist industrialization, the Soviet leadership has consistently given priority to heavy industry ever since Stalin's time. Such areas as energy, iron and steel production, machine tool construction, and heavy transportation equipment have been regularly favored in the allocation of investment funds and materials, at the expense of consumer goods industries and agriculture. As a result, the Soviets have created an industrial foundation for modern military power, but have allowed general living standards to lag far behind those of Western Europe and North America.

Bootstrap industrialization administered in a socialist framework by a totalitarian state is undeniably effective in its early-to-middle stages, when the priority is on the rapid completion of massive construction projects, raw material exploitation, and the development of basic industries such as steel. Total Soviet industrial output, as measured by Western statisticians, increased at least fourfold during the five-year plans of the thirties, and more than tenfold from the Revolution to the present. In the course of the Tenth Five-Year Plan (1976–1980), the USSR's gross national product reached 60 percent of that of the recession-plagued United States, and its net investment in absolute terms was actually greater than U.S. investment.

Although it has been effective by quantitative standards, the Soviet method of industrialization is not the only way to accomplish such results. In fact, the recent Soviet record has not been any more impressive than that of the capitalist United States in the second half of the nineteenth century or that of Japan in the twentieth. Moreover, Soviet industrialization has been more costly in human terms, and less efficient in the use of resources. With a work force made up of transplanted peasants, standards of quality and maintenance have been notoriously deficient in the lower-priority, nonmilitary areas of consumer goods and construction.

Having built a massive industrial plant and infrastructure, the Soviets now face the problem of a falling rate of growth. The troubles of economic maturity emerged during the Ninth Five-Year Plan (1971–1975) and became more apparent during the Tenth, when Soviet progress fell short of planned targets in almost every area. Steel output hit a peak of 151 million metric tons in 1978, and then, in the face of depleted iron ore resources and a shortage of scrap metal, declined. (Recovery came only under Andropov's stricter administration.) The overall annual rate of economic growth, which had been about 6 percent in the 1950s and 5 percent or better in the 1960s, sagged to 3.7 percent in 1971–1975, and slid further to only 2.7 percent in 1976–1980. This sluggishness continued into the early eighties, when the USSR was replaced by Japan as the nation with the second-largest total industrial output.

One reason for this leveling off is inherent in any mature economy: capital investment meets with diminishing returns as the cost of advanced technology increases faster than the value of the product, as natural resources become scarcer or more expensive to exploit, and as it becomes more difficult to squeeze higher productivity out of the labor force. The most modern stage of industrialization involves a high degree of technological complexity, particularly in the development and application of computers, in the nuclear power industry, and in weapons development. At this level some of the distinctive features of the Soviet system—its highly centralized planning, the narrow discretion it allows its operating managers, the lack of incentives for innovation (and the climate of conformity and self-protection that discourages it)—have become liabilities in the pursuit of productivity growth and technological advancement.

In preparing the Tenth Five-Year Plan in 1975, Soviet leaders apparently decided to reverse their usual priorities: they would reduce the rate of increase in capital investments and give consumers a better break, while continuing a high level of military spending—both politically popular moves. It was evidently their hope that they could make up for the leveling off of investment by stressing technological upgrading and more efficient use of existing plant, a theme that Brezhnev confidently touted at the Twenty-fifth Party Congress in 1976. This alternative proved inadequate, and the economic growth rate sank to its lowest figure since the Stalin Revolution. The Eleventh Five-Year Plan (1981–1985) projected a mere 2 percent annual increase in investment, and hinged its hopes on labor incentives and increased productivity.

Relative stagnation has beset the USSR's economy at a time when its per capita performance is still much below that of the United States and Western Europe. The Soviets continually face a fundamental difficulty: How can they adapt the system of central planning to the complexity of modern industry and the rising expectations of consumers? A particularly serious symptom is technological lag. Except for certain military applications, high technology in the Soviet Union is ten to twenty years behind developments in the West, making it urgent for Moscow to maximize trade and scientific contacts in order to keep learning from the capitalists. Yet even the accomplishments of Soviet research are not readily applied by production enterprises.

The problems of economic overcentralization and departmentalism have long been recognized by Soviet experts, who have from time to time proposed reforms to give more discretion to enterprise managers and freer play to the market forces of supply, demand, and price. Such modifications of the planned economy in the direction of "market socialism" have been quite successful in some of the East European Communist countries, particularly Yugoslavia and Hungary; but the Soviets' penchant for centralized authority has been too strong to allow reform of this sort. The economist Yevsei Liberman attracted much attention when he proposed such a model in the last years of Khrushchev, and at least a gesture in this direction was made by Kosygin after he became prime minister. The "Kosygin Reforms" of 1965 gave enterprise directors a slightly longer leash and shifted the criterion of plan fulfillment from physical output to sales and profits. But so powerful were the central bureaucratic interests that by the time the reforms were in place in the early seventies, the planners were supervising individual enterprises even more closely than before. Top party organs have had to intervene in such questions as the supply of laundry detergent and the quality of schoolgirls' uniforms. Economic successes in the Soviet Union still depend on political directives to concentrate human and material resources on narrowly defined objectives, which in practice lie in the sector of military-related industry. For some years the Russians led the world in the race to develop space rocketry and missiles—but they could not produce a good contraceptive.

In 1983 an extraordinary document, stating what Soviet economists have long known about their own system, was leaked to the
Western press. This was the "Novosibirsk Paper," an in-house report on "problems of improving socialist production relations and
the tasks of economic sociology," presented by academician Tatyana Zaslavskaya at a seminar of the Institute of the Economics
and Organization of Industrial Production in the Siberian branch of
the Academy of Sciences. Zaslavskaya's report attacked the whole
planning system as outdated: "The social mechanism of economic
development at present operating in the USSR does not ensure sat-
isfactory results." She cited doctrinaire resistance to change in the
economic ministries and implicitly called for decentralized market
socialism. Some of this philosophy, no doubt encouraged by Andropov's brief period of activism, was incorporated in a decree of
July 1983 which provided for experiments in true enterprise autonomy in selected lines of industry and regions of the country.

Soviet methods and priorities have failed most consistently and
seriously in agriculture. To be sure, Soviet agriculture suffers from
extremes of climate and until recently from overpopulation in some
rural areas. The proportion of the population still living on farms in
the USSR—about 25 percent—far exceeds the proportion in most
Western industrial countries. (In the United States it is down to
about 3 percent.) The peasants must feed their own surplus numbers
as well as the urban population on an arable acreage no greater than
that of the United States and with yields per acre that have—due to
disadvantages of climate, soil, skill, and investment—traditionally
been much lower than in the United States.

Soviet agriculture suffers, moreover, from the fact that centralized
economic control is unsuited to farming. Unlike industrial workers,
the peasant family (probably hostile to collectivization in the first
place) is not offered rewards that would spur it to maximum effort in
the collective work. Peasants typically devote all the time they can to
working on their private plots, which yield an extraordinary share of
the country's animal, dairy, and vegetable produce despite the fact
that they comprise a very modest part of the total cropland. The
collective farms suffer from overcentralization in their own operations and from the rigid production directives that are imposed by
the central authorities. Much of the potential harvest is lost because
work is not coordinated with the weather, or because machinery
cannot be repaired, or because sufficient labor cannot be mobilized

at critical moments. As a result of all these difficulties, Soviet agriculture is virtually stagnant.

The Soviet authorities do not seem inclined to relax the collective system and tolerate individual peasant farming, as Yugoslavia and Poland have done. Still, the Brezhnev regime did recognize that it could not build a strong agricultural base without adequate incentives and investments. In the early 1970s large investments were made in farm machinery, fertilizer, and land reclamation projects. The kolkhoz "brigades" (work groups) were offered credits, guaranteed minimum wages, and overfulfillment bonuses, and procurement prices were increased to the point of becoming subsidies. Farms of the sovkhoz type, accounting for one third of the units, were put on a more autonomous profit-making basis, in a move that paralleled the abortive reforms in industry. The difference between the kolkhoz and sovkhoz systems has become one more of law than of substance, as both are geared into agricultural supply and marketing entities termed "agro-industrial complexes."

Overall, agriculture uses one fourth of the USSR's labor force, draws one fifth of all current investment, and yields one sixth of the gross national product. From the early sixties to the late seventies output rose by 50 percent or more, but costs outran the gain. The future was further clouded by an unexpected labor shortage, as adult males left the farms for better employment and the authorities tried to figure out how to move surplus Central Asian peasants northward. In the late seventies and early eighties severe winters and summer droughts contributed to a series of substandard harvests, reducing the livestock feed supply, threatening the already minimal supplies of meat and dairy products, and forcing the government to use foreign exchange resources to import grain. Shortly before Brezhnev's death the Politburo promulgated a grandiose "food program" to stimulate production, cut losses due to handling and shipment, and make rural life a little more attractive—but the method was the characteristic decree from the top, leaving implementation still in doubt.

The limitations of Soviet agriculture bear major responsibility for the plight of the Soviet consumer, who must pay high prices for food products that are scarce and often of poor quality. Although wages have risen steadily since World War II, citizens are still limited in what they can spend their rubles on; consumer goods manufacturing, meat and dairy production, and service industries have failed to keep pace with the public's buying power. Housing, especially, has been in short supply because construction has lagged behind the pace of urbanization. Only recently has the government come even close to making a private apartment (eight or nine square meters of living space per person) available to every family, now often in huge suburban blocks. Priority in securing housing depends heavily on political status and employer needs. Such amenities as are available are often very unevenly distributed between urban and rural areas or between the major metropolitan centers and the provinces. Cities that are centers for the bureaucracy or that are likely to be frequented by foreigners (Moscow and Leningrad in particular) are consistently better supplied at the expense of less visible places. Though the system offers monetary incentives to workers and functionaries, its heavy-industry bias does not allow for sufficient consumer goods, services, and facilities to make those incentives more meaningful. Resource allocation thus poses a basic dilemma for the military-oriented planned economy.

Economic deficiencies are undoubtedly a major reason for the Soviets' desire to keep Russia a closed society—much more so than even the Communist countries of Eastern Europe—and to constrain both natives and foreigners to travel only with official permission. Russia has been sensitive for centuries about its inferiority with respect to the West, and the Soviets are unwilling to reveal the human cost of their policies. The legitimacy of a revolution and its heirs is at stake.

Beneath the official surface a very different economic life has developed, as Soviet citizens try to cope with shortages and red tape by unauthorized or illegal means. The result is a "second economy" of moonlighting, bribery, favor-swapping, black-marketeering, and outright thievery. Such practices exist even at the highest levels; in 1961 the entire government and Communist Party leadership of a union republic (Tadzhikistan) had to be removed on grounds of corruption, and shakeups almost as complete occurred in Georgia and Armenia in the mid-1970s. Farther down, prosecutions for economic crimes are commonplace, as individuals' pursuit of gain or comfort collides with the imperatives of state control.

Despite Russia's long-standing aspirations for self-sufficiency—which are not unrealistic, considering the country's tremendous resources—the maturing Soviet economy has become steadily more dependent on its trade relations with the rest of the world. Russia was traditionally a raw materials exporter, and financed the industrial drive of the thirties partly on this basis. From World War II to the 1960s, the emphasis was on forging economic integration of the USSR and its satellites through the Council of Economic Mutual Assistance (Comecon), which enabled the Soviets to export energy and heavy industrial equipment and to import a range of specialty products and consumer goods. But the stringencies of food supply and technological innovation forced the Soviets to turn more and more to trade with the capitalists, and this was a major consideration underlying the push for détente in the 1970s. Trade with non-Communist countries rose from 27 percent of the USSR's total in 1960 to 46 percent in 1980. The Soviets have proved to be shrewd bargainers: in 1972–73 they scored a coup with their massive purchase of American grain, and they overcame the post-Afghanistan diplomatic freeze to continue grain purchases and technology acquisition. Imports are still mainly financed by the sale of raw materials and energy (dramatized by the vast project to supply natural gas to Western Europe in return for technology and investments). The Soviet Union is in the enviable position of being the world's second-largest exporter of both oil and gold, though much-publicized CIA estimates suggest that the Soviets will be importing oil before 1990.

The ultimate limitations on the Soviet economy are political. Whether one blames ideology or political obsessions or conservative rigidity, the regime is still wedded to centralism and bureaucratic administration, alleviated only superficially by gestures toward local initiative and incentives. The weakest areas—agriculture and consumer services—are precisely those in which political zeal overcame Marxist analysis and led the Stalin regime to impose socialism on the precapitalist economy of the peasants and petty proprietors without waiting for economic forces to bring about efficient concentration. Large-scale enterprise has always been more amenable to socialist principles, but the potential benefit has been compromised by the economy's military bias. Russia lives in a garrison state economy, where steel is almost deified and the amenities of personal living never attract the necessary commitment of the planners.

The difficulties that stem from these traditions are now recognized by Soviet experts and even by the leadership. Lack of labor discipline, inefficiency, and the lag in applying available technology became major concerns in the late 1970s, when the Brezhnev regime shifted its emphasis from raw production to upgrading and fine-tuning. They figured again among the targets that Andropov attacked, with brief success. But outside observers must remain skeptical: Will the Soviet regime really change its economic ways, or will it continue to address its problems with the same methods of centralized coercion that created those problems in the first place?

Holiday crowd, Leningrad

Soviet Life and Culture

The Soviet Union is still a land of paradoxes and contradictions. The first-time visitor, expecting to find a society utterly new or bizarrely Asiatic, is more likely to be surprised by what seems normal and Western. Everyday Soviet life, in the family, on the job, at leisure, is not altogether different from that in the West, taking into account the disparity in living standards. Russia has become more or less modernized and Westernized, although these achievements are often uneven and puzzling in their inconsistency. Russia also suffers from the contradictions and claims of a theoretically new social system which, in many of its achievements, is merely commonplace or even deficient. In these circumstances, mutual understanding between Russia and the West would be difficult at best, even without the political anxieties of the Soviet authorities.

■ The Social Structure

Though official doctrine holds that the Soviet Union has achieved a classless society, Soviet theoreticians commonly speak of three social "strata": workers, collective farmers, and "toiling intelligentsia." The last term has been expanded to embrace everyone in white-collar employ, from the lowliest office clerk to the top political leaders, as well as those in the scientific and cultural professions.

Within Soviet society, there are vast differences of income and, perhaps more important, of access to scarce amenities and perquisites. Salaries, just as in any Western bureaucracy or corporation, depend on the training, responsibility, and loyalty expected in a given position. Wages of manual workers reflect skill and effort; although inequality was tempered during the Khrushchev years by substantial increases in the minimum, wages range from 60 rubles per month for women street-sweepers to 1,000 rubles per month for the most productive miners (the ruble is now valued at about $1.30). Enterprise managers may earn up to ten times as much as a rank-and-file worker. (In U.S. industry managers' pretax income may be twenty to fifty times that of workers, with pay at all levels at least double the Soviet counterpart.) The salaries of eminent scientists, artists, and performers match those of managers, though there is nothing comparable to the incomes of film and sport celebrities in the United States. There are no opportunities for personal enrichment through individual business operations or investment (apart from the often lucrative but dangerous black-market activities). Generally speaking, the pyramid of income distribution in the Soviet Union lacks the very high peak of that in the United States and shows its big bulge at a much more modest level than the American working class. But in the Soviet upper brackets, monetary income is not as significant as the free or subsidized amenities which are made available to those in the top political and professional echelons, including such benefits as the use of official automobiles, availability of good apartments and weekend country houses (*dachas*), access to special stores with lower prices and goods otherwise unavailable, vacation and foreign travel priority, and even special medical services. Much of this favored treatment is played down or unacknowledged, to minimize conflict with the ideology of classlessness. Some of it is secured through corruption and abuse of power.

Except in cases of political malfeasance, the Soviet population enjoys a good deal of economic security, albeit at a minimal level. Health care is completely free (though personal attention is enhanced by bribery or private payment to moonlighting professionals), and social insurance provides modest pensions for the elderly and the disabled. Unemployment is officially nonexistent—in fact, there is a chronic labor shortage. Workers have substantial job security and the freedom to shop around for higher pay (particularly if they are willing to move to a hardship area such as the Far North or Siberia). Failure to hold down a job makes one liable to the criminal charge of "parasitism," even if one's unemployed status has been the involuntary consequence of political dissidence. No special welfare program, aside from modest child-support allowances, is available for female-headed families. The great majority of women, with or without husbands, are employed full time, leaving small children in day-care programs where available (perhaps half the time in the cities) or with grandmothers and other relatives (typical in rural areas). Women's pay and the scales for professions dominated by women (including teaching and medicine) are distinctly on the low side. A few women have achieved eminence in science and in administration, but, as noted earlier, women have reached the upper levels of the political structure only on a token basis.

Soviet Russia is a classless society in much the same way that the United States is a classless society. Both countries profess to believe in equality of individual rights, and both deny the existence of any formal class divisions; both are uncomfortable in the face of the social stratification that actually exists, and prefer to describe it with various euphemisms—"strata" in the Soviet Union and "socioeconomic levels" in the United States—rather than with the naked word "class." As Soviet ideological manipulations of the last half-century show, the USSR has developed a new kind of noncapitalist system of class stratification, based on function and reward. This system is accepted and justified by the authorities as a reflection of the individual effort and responsibility that will always be necessary, even in a perfect communist society.

Both Marxist and non-Marxist thinkers outside the Soviet Union have had to reconsider the nature of the Soviet social system and to recognize that, despite Soviet claims of a "dictatorship of the proletariat," the Soviet Union has actually developed a new ruling class or stratum. Trotsky, in *The Revolution Betrayed* (1936), was one of the first to describe this outcome of the "bureaucratic degeneration" of the workers' state, and his American follower James Burnham generalized the notion in *The Managerial Revolution* (1940), arguing that the rise of a class of bureaucratic officials lay behind the diverse phenomena of Stalinism, Nazism, and Roosevelt's New Deal. Writing after he was dropped as vice-president of Yugoslavia, Milovan Djilas revived and popularized the concept in *The New Class* (1958), and it has figured prominently since then in New Left and Euro-communist critiques of the Soviet system.

Despite the crystallization of a new class structure independent of private property, social mobility in the sense of movement from the lower strata to the upper was wide open in Russia from the time of the Revolution until the end of the Stalin era. Opportunities to rise from the ranks were created by the elimination of the old ruling classes, the industrial expansion of the five-year plans, the millions of offices made vacant by the purges, the casualties of World War II, and the resumption of industrial expansion after the war's end. However, by the 1950s and 1960s, just as the expansion of opportunity was slowing down, the new ruling stratum drawn from the workers and peasants under Stalin began to turn into a hereditary elite, striving through contacts and schooling to place their children on the ladder to positions of comfort and prestige like their parents'. The problem since then has been to keep people functioning as workers and peasants despite their aspirations to rise, which have been encouraged by their education. In sum, the USSR is suffering from a serious contraction in the opportunities for social mobility, with all that this portends for public morale and social cohesion.

Among the various strata in Soviet society, substantial cultural and life-style differences survive or have been revived. Foreign observers have noted of late the growing disparity between the Soviet intelligentsia and the working class—brought out, for instance, in conflicts between their children at school. Since higher education is now the primary route to elite status and income, the younger members of the upper class, including the Communist Party, are naturally distinguished by a certain sophistication in their perspectives and life style. Even more striking is the persisting isolation of the peasantry from the cultural mainstream, while the country as a whole becomes more heavily urbanized. The old Russian problem of a cultural cleavage between the masses and the educated and Westernized elite appears to have emerged again, despite all the changes of the Revolution. At the same time, literary and artistic expressions of rural nostalgia are surfacing among the intelligentsia and lending support to the Russian New Right, in a manner not unlike that of the Slavophile movement of the nineteenth century.

■ **Education and Science**

Education is one aspect of life where Soviet and American views nearly coincide. In both the Soviet Union and the United States, education is a pillar of national belief and a key determinant in the social structure. Its functions and expectations are similar in both cases, stressing not only the training of the young for the specialized demands of a modern economy but also equal opportunity for everyone. It is education, more than any other feature, that enables each country to think of itself as a classless society in which there are no barriers or inequalities among those who acquire socially valuable skills. It is education that underlies the development in both societies of a new hierarchical system of meritocracy. Although the two societies have evolved from the opposite extremes of collectivism and egalitarian individualism, both now determine status above all by one's academic degree and the prestige of the school that bestowed it.

In both the USSR and the United States, education is intended to inculcate the values and attitudes that make a "responsible" citizen. American students are supposedly educated for democracy; Russian pupils are indoctrinated in the premises of Soviet patriotism and Marxist-Leninist ideology. Soviet schools are entrusted with the shaping of the New Soviet Man, with all his virtues of social responsibility, and self-sacrificing service. More pressing in the USSR is the need for cultural transformation of the masses to complement the country's rapid modernization and industrialization. (This is also apparent in the United States in the education of racial minorities.) At the time of the Revolution, nearly half of Russia's population was still illiterate and largely ignorant of the mechanical basics of industrial civilization. The Soviet government had not only to teach specific technical skills but also to overcome centuries of lag behind the West in what John Nef in his *Cultural Foundations of Industrial Civilization* has termed "habits of quantitative precision." These educational hurdles help explain why the Soviet economic performance in many sectors leaves so much to be desired with respect to quality, efficiency, and timeliness.

Soviet education has not been easily adapted to its role in modernization. In the days of the Revolution, it had aimed to liberate individual creativity and self-fulfillment from bourgeois restraints. This outlook led Marxists to predict the "withering away of the school" along with anticipation of similar atrophy of the state and all other coercive institutions. Under Stalin, Soviet education was compelled to switch to the more practical "polytechnic" approach, and then to the traditional European model. Despite abortive reform schemes under Khrushchev, the latter pattern still prevails, emphasizing scientific knowledge and technological competence, along with political orthodoxy.

The Soviet school system provides universal, free, compulsory education in an eight-year primary-school program (starting at age seven until the Chernenko reform lowered it to six). Instruction is normally in the students' native language—Russian or one of the nearly one hundred minority languages. In minority schools, Russian is taught as a second language beginning in the second grade, since it is the nationwide lingua franca. In the major cities there are special schools (preferred by the elite) where English, French, or other foreign languages are taught from the second grade on. By contrast, little or no effort is made to teach Russians any of the languages of the Soviet minorities.

Secondary education, in the three-year "middle school" (high school) or the parallel technicum (vocational school), is optional but standard in the cities; in some remote rural areas it is still not available at all. The curriculum at this level becomes exceptionally demanding, especially in mathematics and the physical sciences. The school week lasts five and a half days and homework assignments are heavy, leading some Soviet educators to protest the physical and emotional burden placed on students. Apart from the distinction between secondary schools and technicums, different ability groups are not separately tracked, and intelligence testing is not allowed. Officially, the difference between high- and low-performing students is attributed to their diligence. A five-point grading system is used, and examinations are usually oral.

Since personal success and affluence in the Soviet Union depend mainly on educational achievement, along with political loyalty, there is intense competition for admission to prestige institutions of higher education. Though tuition is free, admission is based on competitive examinations. The old preference for children of workers and peasants has long disappeared; today, extra weight might be given to high-level political connections or exemplary extracurricular activities—factors that can also influence admission decisions at U.S. universities. However, the extracurricular record that counts most in Soviet education is dutiful work in the Communist Youth Organization.

The preferred institutions in Russia are the universities, much fewer in number and narrower in scope than those in the United States. Each is like a liberal arts college plus a graduate school of arts and sciences, and is organized into faculties corresponding to departments or groups of departments. From the outset, the universities channel students into highly structured and specialized curricula, leading to the bachelor's degree in three years and the degree of "candidate" in four more years. A candidate, corresponding to an American Ph.D. with a scaled-down dissertation, goes into academic or industrial employment and becomes eligible for the doctor's degree only after years of distinguished professional accomplishment (as in some West European countries).

Professional training for such fields as medicine, engineering, pedagogy, and agronomy is offered not in the universities but in special professional institutes, which form the second level of prestige among the institutions of higher education. Each combines the equivalent of an American undergraduate preprofessional program with advanced professional training, for a total of five or six years. Less exalted technical training institutions produce a variety of industrial specialists and subprofessionals in programs lasting one or two years after secondary school. Needless to say, curricula, appointments and course content at all institutions of higher education are firmly controlled by the Ministry of Higher Education and its branches in each republic, under close party supervision.

In the earlier decades of the Soviet experiment, education was an important channel for social mobility, allowing ambitious sons and daughters from worker and peasant families to reach high-level positions via night school and technical institutes. In recent years, as noted earlier, status lines have hardened, as members of the elite and the white-collar class use education to pass their status on to their offspring. Khrushchev tried to break these educational ties to status by requiring all students to do manual work during their high school years and to attend classes in their spare time, but a foot-dragging bureaucracy foiled implementation of the idea. The same concern may have lain behind Chernenko's stress on vocational-technical training. Soviet citizens from educated families strive to avoid manual work, even though most deskbound employees are no better paid. People vie for the privilege of living in Moscow or Leningrad, since assignment to the provinces or rural areas is often considered intellectual oblivion (much as Frenchmen feel about life outside Paris or New Englanders about the territories west of the Hudson). To offset this bias, professional graduates are obligated for a specified term of years to serve wherever in the country they are needed, those with the better grades receiving the preferred locations. As in the United States, though less openly, the educational system is strained between the criterion of social need and the goal of personal advancement.

The stress on science in Soviet education is more than a utilitarian choice to serve industry and the military. Science is the public faith in the Soviet Union. Even more than Americans, the Soviets believe that science holds the answer to every human problem. Marxism-Leninism, with its philosophical materialism and its espousal of "scientific" socialism, supports this attitude and draws sustenance from it.

Soviet science has not, any more than other areas of life and thought, been immune from political interference, but it still offers more freedom than most fields, as well as greater prestige and material rewards. Since science consequently attracts the best and most independent minds, it is not surprising that political dissenters such as Andrei Sakharov have emerged from the scientific community. Moreover, because of the importance of keeping up with developments abroad, Soviet scientists have had better than average opportunities for international travel and communication.

Science, like all other important activities in the USSR, is highly centralized and bureaucratized. Most research work takes place not in the universities, which are primarily teaching institutions, but in the research institutes of the Academy of Sciences and the various industrial ministries. Founded by Peter the Great, the Academy of Sciences was revived by the Soviet regime to administer pure research in all disciplines ("science" in Russian, *nauka*, extends to all learned subjects, including the social sciences and humanities). The Academy is one of the most prestigious institutions in the country; its president is a full member of the Central Committee, and several institute directors serve as full or candidate members. The national scientific effort is coordinated and supported at the governmental level by the State Committee on Science and Technology, which is equivalent to a ministry.

The contributions of Soviet science, in the judgment of Western authorities, have been uneven. True to the Russian tradition, the Soviets' theoretical and mathematical work continues to be the equal of any in the world. The physical sciences have done better at keeping up with the West than the biological, partly for political reasons. Applied technology varies greatly; the best (for example, military applications and the space program) depends on heavy and costly concentrations of governmental effort. As one moves from the center to the provinces, from the leading experts to the rank and file, and from professionals to support personnel, scientific quality falls off much more abruptly than in the United States and other advanced Western countries. Nevertheless, Soviet science and technology manifest much creative vitality, dampened though it may be by political interference, naïveté, and parochialism.

▪ Intellectual Life and Dissent

In Russia, as in Western Europe, intellectual life has held a prominent place in the national scheme of things for centuries. Compared with the United States, intellectuals in Russia command more respect among the populace and cause more concern among the authorities. The special tradition of the Russian intelligentsia, placing devotion to ideas and cultural creation above politics, nation, or even personal material interest, still survives in that segment of the Soviet white-collar class which, through education or family tradition, has absorbed these priorities. Certain traditional habits of mind within the intelligentsia survive as well, notably a penchant for

broad theorizing and philosophical debate, and habitual careless-
ness in matters of practical organization and accomplishment. Lenin
lamented these traits as the "circle spirit," when he was trying to
lead the intellectuals out of their discussion circles into a more practical revolutionary movement.

Russian intellectual life bears a peculiar relation to the national
tradition: since the time of Peter the Great, it has essentially been an
importation from the West. Educated Russians have been quite at
home in Western civilization for two centuries. For the majority,
however, European culture has been an unnatural transplant, and
this fact has provided a basis for periodic appeals, both before and
after the Revolution, to xenophobic nativism. (Likewise, in the
United States there used to be much populist disdain for European-
derived "highbrow" tastes.) Soviet cultural propagandists, mixing
Marxist and nativist themes, have for decades harped on the superiority of the Russian "socialist" culture over its "decadent" and
"bourgeois" Western counterparts.

Intellectual life in its public manifestations is especially subject to
political direction by the Communist Party. The old Russian tradition of censorship lives on more vigorously than ever: no book or
pamphlet can appear without the imprimatur of Glavlit, the "Main
Administration for Literature." Periodical publications, from the
party organ *Pravda* ("Truth") and the government daily *Izvestia*
("News") on down, all function under the direction of party-con-
trolled boards and automatically police themselves. (According to
an irreverent Soviet saying, "There is no news in the *Truth* and no
truth in the *News.*") The State Committee for Broadcasting maintains equally firm control of radio and television programming.

Control of communication in the Soviet Union takes a more positive form than mere censorship of overt opposition or ideological
deviance. The party still clings to Stalinist standards in cultural and
intellectual work, and by controlling what will be rewarded and
published, it secures the ideas and styles that conform. No work is
allowed to question the basic premises of Marxist-Leninist doctrine
as currently interpreted. Writers on almost any subject, from ancient
archeology to problems of urban life, feel compelled to preface and
conclude their work with references to the infallible Marx, Engels,
and Lenin (but no longer Stalin). Generally, the more remote a
piece of writing or research is from politics and from the present, the

more objectivity is possible in its substance. On matters affecting current public issues, comment must always be carefully couched in the correct ideological terms, leaving room on occasion for the author to convey subtle messages in the way he emphasizes or criticizes certain matters.

Socialist realism has been the official Soviet norm in the arts for five decades. Although it is defined as a style that is "national in form, socialist in content," in practice the literary and artistic creations that pass muster, especially for wide audiences, still follow traditional (that is, nineteenth century) forms, and their content is expected to be optimistic and hortatory. Pessimism, introspection, and serious social criticism—not to mention religious subjects and political dissent—are firmly repressed. Under these circumstances, it is surprising that the official Soviet artistic world has produced as much talent as it has: writers such as Konstantin Simonov, Ilya Ehrenburg, and Yevgeni Yevtushenko; composers such as Dmitri Shostakovich and Sergei Prokofiev; stage and film directors on the order of Konstantin Stanislavsky and Sergei Eisenstein. But frequently the most gifted people have run afoul of the party and have had to trim their work to fit its conservative orthodoxy. Almost all modernistic experimentation continues to be condemned as "bourgeois formalism." Architecture is the exception, embracing modernism in the 1960s and perpetrating such atrocities as the new Palace of Congress, which intrudes among the historic structures of the Kremlin. Classical nineteenth-century literature, music, and stage productions—Russian and Western alike—are widely published and performed, and found more interesting by a culture-hungry public than current work that has complied with the antiseptic requirements of the authorities.

In the late 1950s and early 1960s, during the "thaw," it appeared that the stringency of these controls in Soviet cultural life might be permanently relaxed. Brezhnev and Kosygin quickly disappointed such hopes and reasserted the control mentality, signaled by the 1966 trial of the writers Andrei Sinyavsky (pen name Abram Tertz) and Yuli Daniel (pen name Nikolai Arzhak) on charges of slandering the Soviet state and social system. As the regime thus turned against the intelligentsia, cultural activists became underground dissidents.

"Dissent" in the Soviet Union is whatever opinion the authorities wish to muzzle. "Anti-Soviet activity" is a crime, punishable by long sentences in the labor camps. The term is applied to almost any public manifestation of opposition, be it organizing demonstrations, circulating clandestine literature, or smuggling writings abroad. For first offenders there may be less severe sanctions—warnings by the police or loss of a job. More intransigent dissidents have been committed to the worst of the labor camps or tortured in what are supposed to be psychiatric hospitals. The regime actually maintains that one has to be crazy to oppose it.

Active dissent is confined to very small circles of intellectuals, except in cases where it has spread to ethnic minorities and non-Orthodox religious groups. Much more common (although their real numbers are unknown) are the closet dissenters, who keep their jobs by keeping quiet. Perhaps 10 percent of all adults are sympathetic listeners to Radio Liberty, the quasi-official American broadcasting service (corresponding to Radio Free Europe for the satellites) which systematically supports the dissent movement. Writings by dissident authors, both political and literary, are circulated unofficially (less in the eighties than in the late sixties and early seventies) by means of *samizdat*—meaning "self-publishing," the typing and retyping of multiple carbon copies of manuscripts. Not even a duplicator or a photocopier is free of surveillance by the police and the censors.

It is not strictly accurate to speak of *a* dissent movement in the Soviet Union, because there are many diverse and often conflicting currents of opinion among the government's critics. They can be roughly classified into three schools: left, right, and center. The left, led by historian Roy Medvedev, is made up of Marxist reformers more or less in the spirit of Eurocommunism or the Prague Spring of 1968, who hope to work for incremental change within the system. The right, typified by the exiled Solzhenitsyn, harks back to prerevolutionary Russia with a religious philosophy and a nationalist suspicion of the West. The center, represented by Andrei Sakharov, is animated by the spirit of Western liberalism and its stress on personal freedom. There is no evidence that any of these groups has much influence among the public—communication is simply too difficult; but speculation persists that some dissenters of the left and right have protectors in the upper echelons of the leadership and the police. Certainly if restraints on the dissidents' activity were relaxed, there would be a renaissance of inquiry into the great unanswered questions of past and present in Soviet public life.

▪ Religion

The one area in which the Communist regime has unflaggingly adhered to its revolutionary ideology is religion, in line with the biases of the prerevolutionary intelligentsia and the tenets of Marxist rationalism. During the civil war and the period of collectivization, this meant severe persecution of all faiths. Since World War II a substantial if grudging toleration has been accorded the Russian Orthodox Church, which has been recognized as a potential force for loyalty and patriotism.

The Orthodox Church was a privileged state religion in Russia for centuries. Like Catholicism in present-day Poland, it was closely bound up with the identity and survival of the Russian nation. In more recent times it became a symbol of oppression, conformity, and reaction, and as such it was targeted by the revolutionaries for oblivion. But persecution could not root out religious feeling, and, starting as a war measure, the Communists have tried to enlist the nationalistic impetus of the church despite their repugnance for religion in general.

Orthodox Christianity shares the same ancient tradition as Roman Catholicism, but differs in certain visible respects going back to the schism between the Eastern and Western churches in the eleventh century. The Orthodox have always used the vernacular language, which for the Slavs is the Balkan dialect originally employed by Cyril and Methodius to translate the Bible and known today as Church Slavonic (related to Russian more or less as Latin is to Italian). The Orthodox service dispenses with musical instruments and enjoys instead a remarkable tradition of unaccompanied vocal music. Sculpture in the round, proscribed because of the biblical strictures against graven images, is replaced by icon painting, which has flourished for a thousand years. The Orthodox Church not only permits but expects its parish clergy (the "black" clergy) to marry, and the office of village priest has often been passed on from father to son. However, the monastic or "white" clergy, from whom the bishops, metropolitans, and patriarchs are drawn, are celibate. Theologically, the Orthodox Church has been less given to deductive rationalism than the Catholic, and more inclined to mysticism. In its organization, it is run on the national level, not internationally. This has fostered a tradition, dating back to Constantinople, of subservience to the secular authorities, even if they were non-Christian conquerors. Thus, it has been possible for the Orthodox Church to accept whatever modest niche it can find in the Soviet scheme of things.

Since the office of Patriarch was restored in 1943, the church has functioned more or less undisturbed in a very restricted sphere tightened further by Khrushchev. It is watched by the police and the government's Council on Religious Affairs (a curious agency for a country in which state and church are presumably separate). Ritual and theology remain very conservative. Orthodox services are open and normally unobstructed, but the training of priests, the dissemination of religious literature, and the opening of churches in new industrial areas are made very difficult by the authorities, and young people are sometimes kept out of church by the police. Religious instruction of children outside the family is forbidden, and career advancement may be barred to people who declare religious affiliations. It is no wonder that services are attended mainly by women and the elderly, though they are packed with people of all ages and sexes at holiday time. Sometimes even Communist Party members have to be censured for allowing their children to be baptized. The overall extent of religious belief is difficult to gauge, but Soviet sources concede that up to 20 percent of the adult population are churchgoers and another 10 percent "still under the influence of religion, to one degree or another." Allowing for "waverers" and a much higher incidence of religious involvement among the non-Slavic minorities, William Fletcher in *Soviet Believers* has calculated the religious fraction of the Soviet population at around 45 percent. Despite the hostility of the authorities, religious sentiment probably remains stronger and more widespread in the USSR than in the more urbanized and affluent societies of Western Europe.

Conditions are much more difficult for non-Orthodox faiths, which remain suspect because of their links with international movements, their encouragement of minority separatism, or their withdrawal from the mainstream of society. The last tendency has been represented since the seventeenth and eighteen centuries by the Old Believers and other Orthodox sectarians, by certain Protestant denominations (mainly Baptists), and more recently by Pentacostalists, Seventh-Day Adventists, and Jehovah's Witnesses. These groups have been hounded unmercifully by the Soviet authorities. The plight of the Jews is a familiar story, but it is in some respects shared by the Lithuanian Catholics. The Uniate Church, centered in the western Ukraine, was forcibly merged with the Orthodox Church after World War II. The Moslems, who are large in numbers and linked with the politically sensitive Middle East, have been treated more carefully by the authorities in recent decades, although they were forced to end the seclusion of women and to make other concessions to modernization.

The most notorious case of religious mistreatment under the Brezhnev regime has been that of the Jews, labeled as a separate nationality but persecuted for their attempts to preserve their religious and linguistic traditions. Nevertheless, Brezhnev, unlike his predecessors, did allow Jews to emigrate, though he was soon embarrassed by the great number of those who applied. When he responded by establishing "emigration taxes" and persecuting "refuseniks," he probably created more international embarrassment for the Soviet Union than if he had never permitted emigration at all.

Despite quasi-official anti-Semitism and educational and career quota limitations, Soviet Jews—generally Russian-speaking and assimilated in all but the legal respect—have played a disproportionately large role in Soviet scientific and intellectual life. This may help explain why the emigration issue has been so sensitive for the Soviet authorities: they risk losing a great deal of captive talent. However, the constraints of recent years and a sense of discouragement about the future have impelled growing numbers of Soviet Jews to risk all manner of harassment and deprivation in order to emigrate to Israel and the West. This movement and the prominence of Jews in dissident activities has fueled the old anti-Semitic attitudes, but the response has not been entirely negative: a recent Jewish emigrant to Israel tells of his Ukrainian neighbor back in the Soviet Union, who lamented enviously that he had no independent homeland for which to leave!

■ The Nationalities

Owing to the concentration of the major national minorities in their traditional areas, modernization and urbanization have done little to overcome nationality distinctions and sensitivities in the Soviet Union. Furthermore, demographic trends are at the point of making the Russians a minority within their own empire. The nationality problem has become the soft underbelly of the Soviet Union.

The multinational character of the Soviet Union is altogether different from that of the United States. Ethnic differences and tensions are major problems in each country, but on the Soviet side they seem more intractable and in the long run much more threatening to the strength and stability of the state. Claims by the regime that it has "completely solved" the nationality problem are among the least convincing of its propaganda positions. In fact, national and religious minorities contribute most of whatever broad popular support accrues to the dissident movement.

The problems of minority nationalism are well recognized by the Soviet leadership, which has tried a series of sharply different policies over the years. Lenin's theoretical position at the time of the Revolution was the same as Woodrow Wilson's: he favored self-determination, the right for any nationality to choose independence. In practice, because this entailed the possible loss of economically and strategically important provinces, the new Soviet leadership rejected self-determination by the "bourgeoisie" and argued that true proletarians would share their fate with the Russians. Accordingly, Moscow shifted to a policy of political centralism tempered by cultural autonomy and equality; this was the line institutionalized in 1924 in the Union of Soviet Socialist Republics, with its complex subdivisions for the minorities. A third phase accompanied Stalin's purges of the 1930s, when the government took to heavy-handed russification and repressed interest in local history and culture as evidence of "bourgeois nationalism." Russification continues, and, if anything, has been intensified since the 1970s: the Soviets have tried to force linguistic assimilation by establishing Russian as the universal second language of the minorities, and are striving for an eventual "merger" of nationalities after all economic and cultural differences among them have disappeared. History is being rewritten for the minorities to prove that they all "voluntarily" joined the beneficent Russian Empire long before the Revolution—a story that approaches truth only for the hard-pressed Georgians and Armenians.

It may well be said that, just as the American "black" problem is really a "white" problem, the Soviet minority problem is really a

Russian problem. Nationality unrest is the result of a long history of discrimination and pressures for russification on the part of the Great-Russian–dominated central government, both before and after the Revolution. Russia, it may well be said, is the last colonial power, continuing to rule the subject nationalities that it conquered when the West European powers were engaged in overseas expansion and colonization. Russia merely extended its imperialism into contiguous territory, so that it appears on the map as a single state, legitimized by the Marxist-Leninist doctrine of "proletarian internationalism."

Although the Soviets proudly advertise their "enlightened" minority policy, the United States has probably gone further in recognizing the cultural rights of minorities and the historical sins of the majority. America's nationality policies since the 1960s are more like those of the Soviets in the 1920s. As a result of retrogression under Stalin, Soviet attitudes are dominated by a complacent sense of Russian superiority; they resemble the outlook of American WASPs prior to the Civil Rights movement of the 1950s and 1960s.

The nationality issue is the USSR's most serious internal problem. The European minorities, confident of their cultural superiority over the Russians, resent the fact that the latter still dominate the political structure (the Politburo is disproportionately Russian, and in 1984 all but one of the members of the Party Secretariat were Russian.) The Asiatic minorities, faced with the pressures and temptations of modernization and the example of nativistic reaction in the Middle East, are potentially an explosive force by virtue of their large numbers. Social stratification is assuming a racial aspect, as Central Asians are recruited for the lower ranks in industry and the army. Given all these centrifugal tensions, political liberalization might allow minority separatism to disrupt the Soviet state, as it already threatens to do in Yugoslavia. This possibility could well inhibit any possible reformist inclinations on the part of future Soviet leaders.

▪ The Soviet Way of Life

Soviet propaganda boasts of the creation of the New Soviet Man, with his collectivist discipline, his devotion to self-improvement and upright conduct, his dedication to the common good. Needless to say, outsiders who meet Soviet citizens rarely find such puritanical

Pollyannas (though they do occur on occasion, more often among women). In his manner of thinking, feeling, and acting, the real Soviet man (and woman; the Russian word *chelovek*, like the German *Mensch*, means a human of either sex) is in most situations not very different from his counterpart in the West. Soviet society contains the same range of personality types—from the jovial to the morose, from the idealistic to the opportunistic, from the public-spirited to the criminal and sadistic. Russians have traditionally been thought of as impulsive extremists, and they are still intense in their commitments; they are not known for moderation or compromise. However, the "Slavic soul" of fatalistic self-abnegation is a romantic myth.

Much of the congruence between Soviet and Western forms of life stems from their common experience of industrialism and urbanization. Typically the Soviet city-dweller is a member of a nuclear family with one or two children. As in the West, the divorce rate has risen and the birth rate has dropped. Most women, married and unmarried, are employed, out of economic necessity; however, few husbands help with housekeeping and childrearing, despite the lack of domestic conveniences and the inordinate amount of standing in line that is required to do the family shopping. The lot of most Soviet women is not an easy one.

In some ways the Revolution has brought Russian lifestyles more into line with those in the West and particularly in the United States, though signal differences persist because of the political system. Russia has been socially democratized, so that differences of manners and taste have been evened out considerably, except for the gap remaining between the cities and the villages. The Russian Revolution, like the American, put an end to a society of deference in which ordinary people acknowledged the natural superiority of the elite. Psychologically, Americans often find that they have much in common with Russians—personal openness, informality, simplicity of manner, and lack of ceremony, in contrast to the greater polish and protocol that embellish life in Western Europe.

Like Americans, Russians tend to be materialistic and quantitative in both their public and private standards of judgment. Both give consumerism and careerism high priority, though there is a vast discrepancy between the two societies in the actual availability of creature comforts—housing, automobiles, consumer goods, personal services. To be sure, Soviet citizens have certain forms of security—pensions, free health care, and job security. But benefits, like wages, generally are meager by Western standards, and the quality of health care has been deteriorating. Recent data indicate lowered life expectancy and higher infant mortality—a reversal of the usual trends in an industrialized country. There have been many recent accounts (often in officially published complaints) of corruption, bribery, moonlighting, absenteeism, alcoholism, and below-maintenance birth rates, suggesting a crisis of morale in Soviet society. Taught to think like modern people with modern expectations, Soviet citizens are losing the hope that life might someday become comfortable, as the regime has constantly promised.

Some of the more distinctive characteristics of Soviet life can be attributed to the totalitarian state. The media and all forms of entertainment, restrained as they are by the official puritanism and didacticism, are unbelievably dull except to those who enjoy the classics of high culture. The tremendous pressure for conformity seems to turn Russians into schizophrenics—dour and pettifogging on the job, spilling out their emotions with family and friends. The great tension they live under—political control, job discipline, close quarters in housing, lack of recreational excitement—leads directly to the nation's greatest social problem: alcoholism. Sharing the tradition of most northern countries, Russians drink to get drunk, not merely to accompany a meal or a social occasion. Vodka, a state monopoly like every other commodity, poses a major dilemma for the authorities: it is an important source of revenue and an obvious safety valve, but it is also responsible for great social cost in terms of lost worktime and broken lives.

Other forms of social pathology—crime, broken families, mental illness—are characteristic of any industrialized country. Philosophies of treatment differ; the Soviets favor direct repression or exhortation rather than a therapy that tries to reach the causes of antisocial behavior. One extensive form of deviance is inherent in the Soviet system—namely economic crime, covering theft, blackmarketeering, and illegal private enterprise.

Recognizing the growing similarity between lifestyles in the USSR and the West, many observers have endorsed the idea of "convergence." This theory maintains that under the impact of industrialism, urban living, and a highly technological mode of life and work, the Soviet and Western social systems are growing more and more alike: Soviet society is becoming more complex, stratified,

and consumer-oriented; Western society is becoming more bureaucratic and controlled. This is basically true. One cannot, however,
leap to the conclusion, based on a new sort of economic determinism, that the antithetical political systems of the two societies will
also converge and inaugurate a new era of harmony between East
and West.

Soviet earth satellite

The Soviet Union and the World

Russia's relations with the outside world, like its domestic leadership and institutions, have remained more consistent since the mid-1960s than at any time since the nineteenth century. Since the fall of Khrushchev the Soviet Union has taken no sudden or spectacular initiatives (except in reaction to perceived threats); it has exhibited no deep change of heart such as Americans have often demanded; and it has made no great shifts in its alignments with other powers, despite ups and downs of tone. The détente years, from the nuclear test ban treaty of 1963 to the signing of the SALT II treaty in 1979, were the longest period of amicable relations between Russia and the Western democracies since the Revolution. Even with the greater tensions since the late seventies, there have been no sudden and precarious crises like those of the late forties and early sixties.

Underlying the stability of the last third of the twentieth century has been Russia's attainment of rough equality with the United States in military power. U.S. pursuit of strategic superiority in nuclear weapons was eventually offset by Moscow's concentration of national resources in the military and technological realms, to the point where many Americans feared a permanent Soviet advantage. This, coupled with the conservative swing of the American political pendulum during the seventies and the success of Soviet political probes in the third world, sufficed to undermine the spirit of détente on the U.S. side almost as soon as it was firmly established. The Soviets' quest for worldwide influence, transforming the USSR from a continental to a global power, proved incompatible with American expectations of amity and understanding.

▪ The Road to Détente

The development of a relaxed and relatively normal relationship between the United States and the USSR in the 1960s defied all probability. The two powers had just weathered a new period of crisis in 1960–1962, when they repeatedly appeared to be on the verge of war. Moscow had a new leadership that had presumably been taking the hard line against Khrushchev. Washington was preoccupied by the Communist insurgency in South Vietnam, a country considered vital to the containment of the Sino-Soviet bloc in the Far East. Yet the U.S. and Soviet governments entered into a long, cautious, low-profile search for practical accommodations, culminating in a series of mutual visits by the respective heads of state, and a treaty—the Helsinki Act of 1975—that appeared to reverse the whole history of superpower enmity.

This halcyon epoch of détente was made possible by certain tran-

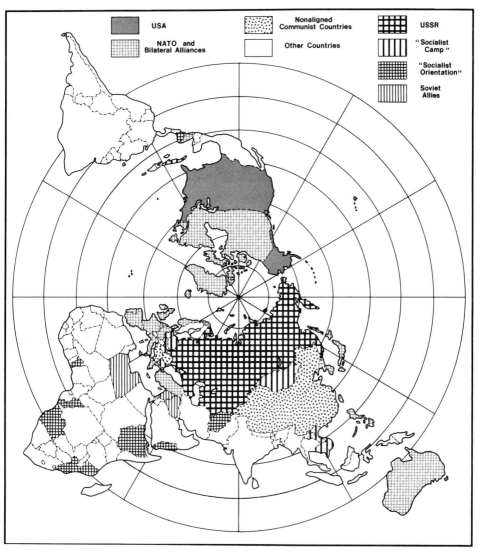

The Global Confrontation

sitory circumstances in the domestic affairs of the two superpowers, as well as by new developments in the rest of the world. Moving out of its ideological mood of the 1950s, the United States had learned from the crises of the early sixties to look at the world more realistically. Then in the mid and late sixties it had been preoccupied by President Johnson's Great Society, Vietnam, the Civil Rights movement, and the New Left. The USSR settled down under stable bureaucratic leadership and addressed the need to catch up with the United States economically and technologically, with all that this implied for trade and investment decisions. Faced by the unpredictable consequences of the Sino-Soviet schism, the splintering of international Communism, and ferment in the third world, Moscow had to reconsider its whole international outlook. It was a time of incremental building of strength, relationships, and influence—military and nuclear strength, détente with the United States and Western Europe, and influence among the developing countries.

There were bumps on the road to détente. Vietnam was one: the Soviets supported North Vietnam politically and logistically to avoid being upstaged by China, even though at times they favored a negotiated settlement. They sought ties with the Arab world and supported the 1967 war against Israel, highlighting the chronic instability of the Middle East. And in 1968 they occupied Czechoslovakia and put an end to the reforms of the Prague Spring, demonstrating the tactics of force and deceit they were prepared to use to maintain their sphere in Eastern Europe. But, as in the early sixties, the two superpowers were able to transcend these episodes and find ground for pursuing their common interests.

Détente offered several advantages to the Soviets. It helped them deal with China and the new multipolar world, since it required a return to the sort of balance-of-power politics that had not been practiced since World War II. It enabled them to secure Russia's European borders: West Germany accepted the status quo in East Germany ("Ostpolitik"), the Berlin problem was stabilized, and the Helsinki Treaty on European Security and Human Rights was signed—a grand symbolic gesture. Perhaps most important, the Soviets had the opportunity to expand trade with the West, exemplified by their unprecedented purchase of American grain in 1972.

The USSR began to exploit détente in earnest in the early seventies, stimulated perhaps by the first signs of a thaw in American relations with China. Despite Nixon's previous rhetoric, Henry

Kissinger (then chief national security advisor) was able to turn the administration from moralistic confrontation to realpolitik. Late in 1969 the United States and the USSR began negotiations on the most serious of all the questions that divided them: the strategic arms limitation talks (SALT). Simultaneously, the Americans opened the unofficial contacts with China that eventually led to normal relations. In 1972 Nixon went to Moscow to sign the SALT treaties limiting strategic missiles and antiballistic missile systems; but by that time he had already been to China. A series of technical agreements followed in a matter of months: the grain sale, a major U.S.–Soviet trade agreement, the final treaty normalizing relations between West and East Germany, the Paris Accords (in which the Soviets helped the United States achieve a truce in Vietnam), and the commencement of the Helsinki European security negotiations.

Détente was consummated in June 1973, when Brezhnev visited the United States and the two governments agreed that neither would unilaterally seek a military advantage over the other. This agreement, in which the Americans openly acknowledged Soviet parity, is referred to by Soviet spokesmen as the true beginning of détente (thus crediting it to Brezhnev rather than to Khrushchev).

Seen in historical perspective, Soviet behavior during the era of détente was consistently cautious. This did not prevent the country from building its economic and military power and extending its political and diplomatic influence as occasion permitted. Under the direction of a remarkably stable core of political, diplomatic, and military leaders, the Soviet Union looked to its own resources of power and influence while minimizing conflict with the United States and its allies. The industrial establishment was steadily expanded, still emphasizing heavy industry and military-oriented technology, though constraints on economic growth and the technology race became serious by the late seventies. Détente was exploited as far as possible to ease these strains, through trade and technology acquisition. At the same time, conventional military and naval forces as well as nuclear weaponry were rapidly upgraded, alarming the West and threatening the economic advantages of détente.

U.S. judgments of détente were never undivided. To some Americans, détente meant approaching the old goal of accommodation based on mutual understanding. To others, it was the era when the West allowed itself to be lulled by Moscow's blandishments while the Soviets quietly maneuvered for the strategic upper hand. Still others, recognizing the constancy of the closed Soviet society and its militaristic bent, perceived détente as a tacit pact: each side acknowledged the power of the other and their common need to keep the peace and restrain the nuclear arms race.

The premises of détente began to unravel along with Nixon's presidency, after the Watergate scandal that eventually led to his resignation in August 1974. Meanwhile, Soviet aid to the Arabs in the Yom Kippur War against Israel in October 1973 had caused many Americans to lose faith in the possibility of U.S.–Soviet peacekeeping efforts. Other troublesome issues included the Soviets' treatment of dissidents (the expulsion of Alexander Solzhenitsyn, for example) and barriers to Jewish emigration, especially the infamous emigration tax of 1972. In the fall of 1974 Congress passed the Jackson-Vanik Amendment to the Trade Reform Act, granting the Soviets most-favored-nation tariff privileges on the condition that they allow more Jews to emigrate. Predictably, the Soviets denounced this act of pressure as interference in their internal affairs, curtailed Jewish emigration, and repudiated the trade agreement. Nevertheless, the momentum of arms control continued until November 1974, when Brezhnev and President Gerald Ford, at a meeting in Vladivostok, tightened the SALT limit on missile launchers and extended it to multiple-warhead missiles. The high point of détente came in 1975: in the first joint U.S.–Soviet space exercise, crews of the two nations docked together in orbit and fraternized while they circled the globe.

With the successes of Soviet-American accommodation in the seventies, détente was exalted, like modern marriage, to a mystical institution that would solve all problems between the partners and that would be treasured as an end in itself. In actuality the relationship was fragile and transitory, the expression of interests that happened to coincide rather than of true respect and confidence. Détente was quickly undermined. On the one hand, it falsely encouraged Americans to expect human-rights concessions and sphere-of-interest restraint from the Soviets; on the other, it provided cover for the Soviets' behind-the-scenes maneuvers including the development of new missiles and the accumulation of influence in the third world.

Détente was both encouraged and undermined by the China question. The rupture with China was a major reason for Khrushchev's efforts at accommodation with the United States. The ongoing confrontation with China compelled his successors to continue the same course, in the belief that they could achieve equality with the United States while enlisting its aid against a common enemy. Then China, entering into the pragmatism of the seventies and discovering a receptive ear in President Nixon, undercut détente by creating the prospect of a Washington-Peking axis. Brezhnev's reversion to the line of aggressive sphere-building paralleled Stalin's response to Churchill's Iron Curtain speech and the specter of an Anglo-American alliance.

This was the setting for the invasion of Afghanistan and the suppression of the Solidarity movement in Poland, actions that dealt the death blow to détente. The rightward shift in the American political climate meant that Washington would maximize such issues rather than minimize them. Just as the first Cold War was a reaction to the domestic revolution of the thirties, the New Cold War marked a period of recuperation after the turmoil of the sixties. In both eras, a resurgent conservatism led Americans to perceive the Soviet Union as a revolutionary and expansive evil, with which there could be no trusting coexistence or lasting accommodation.

▪ The Bloc and the Triangle

To the Soviets, détente was a product not of good will but of the realities of power—realities that put the USSR at a greater disadvantage than at any time since the beginning of the Cold War. While the United States was still well ahead in economic power and nuclear weapons and enjoyed the support of all the industrial democracies, Russia's countervailing system of international influence and alliances was coming apart. As a result of de-Stalinization, Moscow-oriented discipline in the international Communist movement was evaporating almost everywhere beyond the reach of Soviet military power. One satellite government after another endeavored to extend its autonomy. Above all, the alliance with China that had made the international Communist challenge seem so formidable in the 1950s had come to an unexpected and rancorous end.

The diplomatic impact of Peking's independent course was dramatized by the undeclared border war between China and India in 1962. With Soviet aid flowing to New Delhi and China reaching an accommodation with India's enemy (and America's ally) Pakistan, the international political system abruptly became much more complex. In the bipolar world of American-Soviet competition, each knew who the adversary was, and the only question was how the lesser countries would line up as allies. In the tripolar world where China had become an unpredictable entity for both the USSR and the United States, none of the three powers could be sure which of the other two would be its enemy and which its ally. Thus, the opportunity for traditional diplomacy was reborn. The prime concern of each of the three powers became—or should logically have become—the prevention of an alliance between the other two, and each had to overcome its ideological repugnance in order to engage in practical diplomacy.

Initially the United States government refused to consider the Sino-Soviet schism as anything more than a tactical disagreement or a ruse to get Americans to let down their guard. Far from exploiting the schism, the Kennedy and Johnson administrations pressed the war in Vietnam, the one area where Moscow and Peking cooperated. Once the schism was recognized, in the mid-sixties, Washington went counter to Machiavelli's advice: rather than encourage the weaker party, the United States began to focus its generalized anti-Communist hostility on China, while gradually responding to Soviet overtures for détente. Vice-President Hubert Humphrey, pressed in 1968 to clarify his position on coexistence and the Communist threat, defined "Asian Communism" as the proper target for U.S. containment tactics. The devil-hating reflex was not called into question but only deflected onto a newly defined enemy, somewhat the way anti-Hitler passion was redirected against Stalin after 1945.

Although a revolution in America's China policy was logically called for, changes were delayed by escalation of the Vietnam War in 1965 and by the onset of the Cultural Revolution in China in 1966. This bizarre and mysterious era in Chinese history—with its mob violence by youthful Red Guards, purges of intellectuals, and apparent power struggles between the Communist Party and the army—virtually closed the country to all outsiders. The Chinese hardened both their anti-Soviet and anti-American lines, engaging in armed clashes on the Siberian border and increasing their aid to Vietnam. The ideological battle between the Chinese and the Russians intensified as the Chinese attempted to purify their own revolution and condemned the bureaucracy of the Soviet Union as a degenerate bourgeois perversion of Marxism-Leninism. Like the Americans, the Chinese were in effect doing everything they could to drive their two main adversaries together.

When the turmoil of the Cultural Revolution began to subside in 1969, China faced an embittered Soviet Union but a very different America, where public opinion had been revolutionized as a result of Vietnam. In its magnitude, direction, and rapidity, such a shift in national sentiment was altogether unprecedented. It amounted to a massive rejection of the policy of containment.

It took an arch-conservative to recognize what the American public really wanted and to give it to them in rhetorically acceptable terms that would not be exploited by the opposition party. Just as the conservative nationalist De Gaulle managed to extricate the French from their colonial war in Algeria, the Republican Richard Nixon suspended the U.S. military commitment in Vietnam and opened the way to an accommodation with China. Overtures were made at the intermittent Warsaw talks between the U.S. and Chinese ambassadors, and the Chinese signaled their readiness for a rapprochement by suggesting an exchange of ping-pong teams. Pursuing the opportunity hinted at by this "ping-pong diplomacy," Nixon put an end to twenty-two years of estrangement in June 1971 by announcing plans to visit China and clearing the way for Peking's UN membership.

This diplomatic revolution might have been considered a master stroke, had it not occurred long after the need for it had become obvious. Finally the United States was cultivating an alliance of convenience with the weaker of the two powers facing it, and the effectiveness of this move was attested to by immediate professions of alarm from Moscow. Within the United States it was welcomed by all except the far right. The Nixon China policy seemed to have disposed of the international Communist bogeyman and temporarily defused the anti-Communist passion that had played such a prominent role in U.S. politics ever since World War II.

While the Soviets became more hostile to China and the Americans tried to understand Peking, Russian influence over international Communism steadily deteriorated. De-Stalinization and the Sino-Soviet rupture broke the exclusive association of Communist orthodoxy and Russian guidance, leaving Communist parties every-

where (save in the presence of Soviet troops) to choose between
Muscovite conservatism and Chinese militant utopianism. Youthful
factions, in tune with the New Left currents of the sixties, formed
within most Communist parties to support Peking. In a few organizations, mainly in Asia, they commanded a majority; other parties, notably in India, openly split; most of those in Europe and
Latin America had to contend with obstreperous Maoist minorities
who threatened the official policy of electoral respectability and
détente with the Soviet Union. In the United States the so-called
Progressive Labor Party split from the American Communist Party
and denounced the Soviets and their supporters for capitulating to
the imperialism of the U.S. government.

In most non-Communist countries the Maoist tendency proved as
ephemeral as the broader rebellion of the New Left. Meanwhile,
many anti-Peking Communists, charged with "revisionism" by the
ultra-left, became revisionists in fact: they advocated a nonviolent
path to power, the nonrevolutionary implementation of socialism,
and the abandonment of the Marxist formula of the "dictatorship of
the proletariat." Here was the basis of Eurocommunism, which was
centered in Italy but soon spread to most of the Communist parties
of the West and to the previously Maoist Communist Party of
Japan. The test was the Soviet intervention in Czechoslovakia in
1968, which for the first time provoked criticism from nearly all
Communist parties, even the orthodox French (though not from the
hapless Muscovite remnant of the American Communist Party).

Established Communist governments were affected almost as
much by the new latitude within the movement. One—Stalinist Albania—sided with Peking, seeking support against absorption by
the "revisionists" of Yugoslavia at a time when Moscow seemed an
uncertain patron. Two governments—those of Rumania and North
Korea, originally abject creations of the Russians and still Stalinist
internally—took advantage of the schism to assert their independence from both of the major Communist powers, and the Rumanians minimized their cooperation with the Warsaw Pact (much as
the French had with NATO). The Communists of Vietnam benefited from the competition between Moscow and Peking to aid
them, though the Chinese Cultural Revolution made them more
sympathetic to the Soviets. Only in Cuba were the Russians able to
secure the total cooperation of a Communist regime far from their

borders. In the mid-sixties, under the influence of the guerrilla theoriest Che Guevara, Cuba had leaned toward Chinese ultra-radicalism, but Castro's endorsement of Soviet intervention in Czechoslovakia (condemned by Peking) showed the effectiveness of Soviet military and economic support in pulling him back into Moscow's orbit. Thenceforth, until the Nicaraguan insurrection of 1979, the Soviets accepted the status quo in Latin America.

In Eastern Europe the fissures of polycentrism were restrained, but not without repeated crises. Rumania asserted diplomatic independence while maintaining Stalinist controls internally, a combination that the Soviets tolerated. Hungary, still under Janos Kadar, took the opposite tack, gradually reforming internal controls and economic policy in the direction of the Yugoslav model, to the benefit of intellectuals and consumers, while remaining loyal to the Warsaw Pact diplomatically. East Germany and Bulgaria conformed both internally and externally to Moscow's dictates, the former under the influence of half a million Soviet troops, the latter on the foundation of its pro-Russian and Orthodox tradition. But Czechoslovakia and Poland proved to be great embarrassments for the Soviets.

Czechoslovakia, with its modern industry and large working class, had appeared to be the most orthodox and compliant of all Soviet satellites. But in 1967 a reform movement directed against president and party chief Antonin Novotny began to gather steam in party and intellectual circles. In a manner reminiscent of the political upheaval in Poland in 1956, the Communist reformers succeeded in removing Novotny in January 1968 and replacing him with Alexander Dubček. Then commenced the Prague Spring—the most extraordinary development ever witnessed within a ruling Communist party: the new Czechoslovak leadership opened the way for liberalization and democratization, suspended censorship, and allowed the nation to begin to rethink its principles and its destiny. Although there was no overt challenge to the Warsaw Pact, the implications were too much for the Soviets, particularly because the Czech reforms paralleled the demands of the growing dissident movement in Russia and because it offered a formula of change from within that could have spelled grave insecurity for the Soviet leadership. Accordingly, in August 1968, the Soviets sent in masses of troops without warning, occupied the whole of Czechoslovakia without a shot, arrested the reformers, and found turncoats to do their bidding. Despite outrage not only on the part of the Western powers but of other Communist governments and parties, the Russians demonstrated their readiness to use any means to preserve their security zone and the inability or unwillingness of any outside forces to stop them. They justified their action by what the West called the "Brezhnev Doctrine"—the Soviet Union was obliged to protect its socialist friends from counterrevolutionary attempts to restore capitalism. Czechoslovakia, having tasted freedom, has since then lived more unhappily in the Soviet shadow than any other country in the Soviet sphere.

The other source of disturbance within the bloc, Poland, has had a much more checkered history. After the restoration of Gomulka to the leadership in 1956, Poland appeared to be swinging toward the Yugoslav model, with more lenient policing, abandonment of collectivization, and full freedom for the church, while it reassured the Soviets in foreign policy and avoided the fate of Hungary. With time, however, Gomulka stiffened his rule, returned to Soviet-style economics, placed tighter curbs on intellectuals, and conducted an anti-Zionist purge. In December 1970 workers rioted to protest food prices, and Gomulka was forced to yield the leadership to Edward Gierek. However, overrapid industrialization and consumer shortages brought on renewed riots in 1976, and in 1980 the Solidarity union movement was born. Again the Soviets were confronted in the satellite zone with an intolerable example of reform applicable to Russia itself. Evidently after threatening to invade, they induced Polish prime minister General Woiciech Jaruzelski to declare martial law and drive Solidarity underground. As an immediate measure to restore Soviet control, this response was almost as effective as direct intervention in Czechoslovakia, but with détente already crumbling, it dealt a much more serious blow to East-West relations.

As polycentrism loosened the ties of Marxist loyalty to Moscow, the Russians fought a vain rearguard action in one international conference after another to try to salvage some semblance of Communist unity. By the end of the 1970s there was no one within the Communist movement whose loyalty the Russians could count on; there were only countries subservient to Soviet military power or, like Cuba and Vietnam, dependent on Soviet economic aid and military protection. For more dynamic support in the global contest, the Russians had to look in a less traditional direction.

▪ Third-World Competition

The era of détente and polycentrism was accompanied by a major shift in the USSR's global political strategy. Like the tsarist regime when it pressed outward in a new direction after being blocked in the old one, the Soviets bore their frustration in Europe and their setbacks in the Far East and directed their pursuit of influence at the newly independent developing countries in Asia and Africa.

Soviet political success in the third world was a function of conditions that the Soviet Union itself had created. By counterbalancing the power of the United States and the former colonial powers in Western Europe, the Soviets hastened the process of decolonization and created a broad zone for political maneuvering by new Asian and African governments. Western responses were limited or deterred by potential Soviet counteraction and the danger of driving third-worlders even more solidly into the Soviet camp. Vietnam demonstrated that it was impossible to enforce colonialism if the Soviet bloc supported the nationalists, and the Suez Crisis of 1956 demonstrated that it was impossible to overawe independent third-world governments if they could count on the Soviet Union for backing. Ever since the fifties the scope of independent third-world political action, shielded by the Soviet-American standoff, has steadily broadened. Neither the Organization of Petroleum-Exporting Countries (OPEC) nor Iran's revolutionary defiance of the West would have been conceivable in earlier circumstances.

Moscow scored major ideological gains in the third-world power vacuum by invoking the theory of imperialism. Despite their own imperialist legacy in Central Asia and other border regions, the Soviets successfully identified the capitalist West with colonial oppression and presented themselves as the natural champions of "national liberation movements" and "revolutionary democracies." Manifold opportunities opened for them to encourage neutralism, win allies, or even establish Communist governments in far-flung parts of the world.

From the Russian Revolution until the Khrushchev years, Marxist-Leninist theory gave an ambivalent reading of the potential of the third world. According to the classical Marxist analysis, under-developed colonial and "semicolonial" countries were too immature for real proletarian socialist revolution (even Russia's status is historically dubious). All that could be expected in the immediate future were "bourgeois-democratic" or "bourgeois-nationalist" revolutions. Nevertheless, Lenin reasoned that Soviet Russia could develop a commonality of interest with movements of this sort, alienated as they were from the Western bourgeois powers by imperialism and exploitation. Accordingly, in the 1920s and 1930s the Communist International directed a great deal of attention to the third world. Where possible, it helped create local Communist parties, relying on students with some Western education, even though there was often no working-class base. The Communists were then used to prod the larger nationalist movements into cooperation and alliance with the Soviet Union. This was the strategy employed in China, unsuccessfully, until Mao began his own revolution based on the peasants. The prototype of broader application was the Communist movement in India, which by the time of independence was the second-largest party (after the Congress Party of Nehru and Gandhi) but which held to a nonrevolutionary role as the new government of India adopted a policy of nonalignment with the Soviet Union. A case of special signficance was Soviet sponsorship of the Communist Party of Indochina founded by Ho Chi Minh.

When widespread decolonization followed World War II, the Soviet Union was well positioned to attract nationalist leaders. Yet in the early Cold War period, Stalin showed little interest in wooing them; he was more intent on consolidating spheres of interest immediately around his borders, and he distrusted any movement beyond the reach of Soviet military power or Communist Party discipline. The new postwar governments in the Middle East and in South and Southeast Asia he scorned as tools of the imperialists, and in fact he appears to have sanctioned the abortive wave of Communist uprisings *against* them in 1948. Latin America was entirely beyond his reach.

One of the most dramatic reversals of the Malenkov-Khrushchev era was Moscow's opening to the third world and its return to the strategy of anti-imperialist alliances with nationalist movements and governments. The Soviets looked with favor on the nonaligned movement launched at the Bandung Conference of Asian and African states in 1955 (unlike the Americans, who believed with Secretary Dulles that "anyone who is not with us is against us"). Russia won a firm place in the affections of India, which it maintains to this day, thanks to the U.S. alignment with India's enemy Pakistan.

The most remarkable alliance struck up by the Soviet Union, one that was to serve as the model for this kind of diplomacy, was concluded with the revolutionary government of Egypt. Backing Egypt in the Suez crisis of 1956, Khrushchev successfully identified Russia with the anti-imperialist cause. Egypt was flooded with Soviet arms and advisors, even though the local Communists languished in jail. The country remained a bastion of Soviet influence in the Middle East, through the humiliation of the Six-Day War of 1967 and past the death of Nasser in 1970. His successor, Anwar Sadat, much less comfortable in the Soviet embrace, proceeded to purge pro-Russian officials and, in 1972, to expel all Soviet military advisors and weapons specialists. After Sadat's forces were humiliated in the Yom Kippur War against Israel in October 1973, the Soviets jumped at the opportunity to restore their influence: Kosygin flew to Cairo, replacement tanks and aircraft were rushed to the Egyptians, and Moscow issued ominous threats of possible intervention by Soviet "volunteers." But none of this aid deflected Sadat from a realist course after this last defeat at the hands of the Israelis: he would come to terms with the Jewish state and accept the mediation of the United States. In 1976 Sadat denounced his treaty with the Soviet Union, and the following year made his spectacular pilgrimage to Jerusalem. The Camp David Accords between Egypt and Israel, brokered by President Carter, represented Egypt's complete diplomatic turnabout from East to West, and one of the severest setbacks for Soviet diplomacy.

The Egyptian pattern—transitory alliances between the Soviets and restive third-world nationalists, ending in disillusionment and rupture—was repeated time and again in Africa. With the spread of independence in the late fifties and early sixties, Ghana, Guinea, and Algeria all turned to the Soviets for backing, as did radical Arab regimes that had seized power by coup d'état: Syria (1954, and again in 1966), Iraq (1958), and Libya (1969). The former Belgian Congo, valued for its uranium and other minerals, became independent in June 1960 and was subsequently torn by conflict between the Soviet-supported leftists, led by premier Patrice Lumumba, and the American- and Belgian-supported president Joseph Kasavubu. After the murder of Lumumba—now a martyr for the Soviets, who named their university for third-world students after him—the Western influence prevailed.

In response to the novel political opportunities offered by the third world, the Russians found that they had to modify standard Marxist theory. To accommodate friendly but backward regimes, they devised the concept of a "noncapitalist path of development" along which a country could move from feudalism directly toward modernization plus socialism. Nevertheless, most newly independent countries who were initially attracted sooner or later found the Soviet grip uncomfortable and the aid a bad bargain, and ended up expelling the Soviet presence in whole or in part. Here and there, notably in Guinea and Tanzania, the Russians had to compete with Chinese aid and influence from the mid-sixties on, though Peking was never able to make a serious dent in the politics of the third world as a whole.

Khrushchev's turn toward the Middle East led him to adopt a tactic that had universal appeal in the Moslem world and an old-fashioned echo in the Soviet Union itself. This was anti-Zionism, a propaganda line that tapped the springs of anti-Semitism at home and enhanced Soviet influence among Israel's enemies. Pro-Soviet nationalists elsewhere in the third world aped the Soviet line, and Israel became dangerously isolated in world forums except for the support of the United States. When the United Nations expanded by admitting the nations that won independence in the sixties, and thereby acquired a third-world majority, the Soviets, using the levers of anti-Zionism and anti-imperialism, were able to undermine the leadership of the United States and the European democracies and convert it into a Soviet sounding board on many issues. Similarly, the Soviets cultivated the organization of "nonaligned" countries (which included such transparently aligned governments as Havana and Hanoi) and induced it to lean more often than not against the West.

Generally speaking, the Soviet appeal to third-world nationalists of the Egyptian stripe was more an irritant and embarrassment to the West than an enduring strategic gain for the Soviet Union. Ultimately the Russians themselves recognized that alliances based only on passing interests and anti-imperialist emotion were unreliable and that they needed ties based more solidly on political, economic, and ideological grounds.

The model for this second kind of Soviet approach to the third world was provided more or less accidentally by the Cuban Revolution of 1959. In this instance the Russians found a local leader, Fidel Castro, who was not only amenable to diplomatic and military cooperation but also eager to adopt Communist political, economic, and ideological formulas as the framework for his own revolutionary regime. Thus, Cuba provided the pattern for capture of a third-world nationalist revolution and its integration into the Soviet system of power, more securely than either conventional Marxism or conventional alliances could assure. Castro's waverings toward Peking radicalism were restrained in the late 1960s by Soviet arms aid and sugar purchases, which assured Cuba's unique role as a remote but subservient satellite of Moscow, prepared to serve as a Soviet proxy in the third world.

Cuba remained an exceptional case until the mid-1970s, when a series of coups, revolutions, and belated independence movements made available to the Soviets a wide array of amenable regimes, mostly in Africa, where the new strategy could be pursued. They included former French African states (the Congolese Republic, Mali for a time, Dahomey/Benin), Afghanistan and Ethiopia after the republican revolutions of 1973 and 1974 respectively, the former Portuguese colonies in Africa when they gained independence in 1975, South Yemen (formerly the Aden protectorate, administered by Britain) after the coup of 1978, and, in the Western Hemisphere, Nicaragua and the island ministate of Grenada. For this category of states the Soviets devised a new theory and a new political model. The theory was "socialist orientation," meaning allegiance to the Soviet Union without the working-class base that normally legitimizes Communism; and the model was the "vanguard party," organized on Leninist lines to exercise a political monopoly. The many manifestations of this new revolutionary trend, unanticipated by American policymakers, reinforced concerns about the Russians' global influence and ambitions and turned the hopes of détente into the fears of the New Cold War.

The Soviets' success in wooing or capturing third-world regimes, even on a temporary basis, obviously cannot be explained by standard Marxist reasoning. Indeed, wherever a country has a substantial industrial base and working class, either the Communists have pulled away from Moscow (as in Italy) or the workers have shunned the Communists (as in Poland). Typically, the people most attracted to the Soviet cause in the third world are young nationalists, often in the military, who are Western-educated or at least touched by Western-style education, but rebel against the memory of Western domination and see in the Soviet Union an exemplar of anti-Western modernization. The enthusiasm of some of these Soviet clients verges on the embarrassing: the Russians worry about the cost of subsidizing these regimes and have to caution them against trying to socialize their countries too fast.

Soviet influence in the third world is the converse of the West's attraction in the East European satellites and among some of the Soviet minorities: any power that challenges the power that dominates them is their natural friend. Just as the Soviets have been faced with chronic unrest in their traditional zone of influence, so the Western powers have found themselves faced with a chain reaction of pro-Soviet, anti-imperialist movements in what used to be their privileged spheres. Cuba is the prototype of this rebellion in America's traditional zone of hegemony in the Western Hemisphere—rebellion that by the end of the seventies was beginning to spread dangerously in Central America. The United States with its Maginot Line attitude fixed on the defense of Western Europe, has been seriously, if not fatally, outflanked in the third world. But although the Soviet third-world campaign as it penetrates the Western Hemisphere has become one of the most divisive subjects for U.S. foreign-policy debate in the eighties, Americans have suggested few alternatives other than isolationist abandonment or military confrontation. If the Soviets' categorization of revolutionary movements in the third world has been shallow and hackneyed, the United States seems unable even to analyze the problem, let alone develop a strategy to cope with it.

▪ The Balance of Terror

The long era of stable East-West relations in the 1960s and 1970s rested in part on certain fundamental facts about military power in the late twentieth century. The advent of nuclear weapons had made general war between the superpowers, if not unthinkable, at least a terrible option of last resort. Agreements to minimize the possibility of a nuclear exchange became a matter of real mutual interest.

The Soviet leadership did not easily accept limits on the pursuit of national security through military strength. In keeping with Russian priorities since Muscovite times, Stalin had made military prowess the first objective of the state. To his successors, hardened by World War II, this goal could not be subordinated to any other norm. The function of socialism, ostensibly to advance the well-being of the masses, was diverted to the maintenance and enhancement of the world's greatest military machine.

The end of World War II in no way diminished the military orientation and style of the Soviet political structure. If anything, the trauma of the war and the new role of superpower put a greater premium than ever on the long-term priorities of the military and on achievement of parity with the United States. What followed from this was thoroughly compatible with the industrialist and technologist bent of the post-purge leadership: a mammoth share of the resources of a poor and devastated country was devoted to the development of military might and the modern economic base that it required.

It is difficult to establish the proportion of gross national product devoted to military purposes in the Soviet Union, since a great deal of the military effort has been buried in the budgets of civilian industrial ministries, and the ruble-dollar conversion is arbitrary. A rough estimate for recent years would be the equivalent of $150 billion out of a trillion-dollar GNP—in other words, an absolute level of defense spending of the same order of magnitude as that maintained by the United States, out of a total economic performance that is only around half of the American. However, the economists' estimates have become a subject of political controversy in the United States; hard-liners claim that the Soviet Union is outspending the United States, and adherents of détente argue that the American effort is more nearly equal to the Soviet. In any case, the relative share of the military establishment in the Soviet economy (12–15 percent) is far greater than the American commitment (around 5 percent).

After raising the degree of military effort in the late sixties and maintaining a steady rate of new industrial investment and economic growth, the Soviets were able to pull abreast of the United States in total military spending in the early 1970s, and they have continued to push ahead since then. However, with the slowdown in economic growth in the late seventies, they had to slacken the rate of increase in their defense budget, as the CIA finally acknowledged in 1983. Aggregate NATO defense spending remains at least equal to the total for the Warsaw Pact. Furthermore, it should be noted that the Soviet military effort is much nearer the USSR's wartime limit of total mobilization, which could be far exceeded by the United States in an effort comparable to that made in World War II.

The armed forces that the Soviet Union supports on the basis of its substantial economic commitment are, to say the least, very impressive. For years, ground forces have been maintained at a level of around three million men (against less than one million in the U.S. army), lavishly equipped with tanks and artillery. The Soviet tank force has long outnumbered the combined forces of the United States and its NATO allies by a factor of better than two to one. By 1980 the air force, with around half a million personnel and nearly 10,000 combat planes, equaled the American in every category except long-range bombers. Strategic missile forces, modestly governed by the U.S.–Soviet Strategic Arms Limitation Treaties, involve about 400,000 men. The navy (also about 400,000 strong), limited in its effectiveness by the geography of the Soviet Union, has traditionally been relegated to an auxiliary role concentrating on coastal defense and submarines. Recently it has developed a respectable high-seas capability, with aircraft carriers and guided-missile cruisers operating out of Murmansk, Odessa, and Vladivostok.

The Soviet armed forces are organized under a single Ministry of Defense staffed entirely by military officers. Ever since Zhukov's tenure (1956–57) the minister had been a career marshal, until Ustinov was appointed in 1976; but even he assumed military rank to maintain the protocol, and moreover his previous leadership of the armament industry (since 1941) was not unrelated to the new assignment. The military establishment, headed by a single chief of staff under the minister, is organized into ground forces, air force, air defense command, missile forces, navy, and logistical forces, each under the command of a marshal (or fleet admiral) who also holds the title of deputy minister of defense. Normally the officer next in status to the chief of staff is designated as the commander-in-chief of the Warsaw Pact forces.

The quality of the Soviet armed forces is a matter of controversy among Western observers. Command doctrine is highly centralist, in the Russian tradition, to the detriment of initiative in small unit operations. Soviet weaponry in the hands of Russia's Arab allies has usually proved to be inferior to U.S. and Israeli equipment. Pay and living conditions for rank-and-file personnel remain spartan, and there are frequent reports about the abuse of conscripts and corruption in the officer corps. Questions of morale that might arise from these considerations are basically addressed, as are other problems in Soviet society, through the system of political control.

Civilian control of the military has been maintained not through a civilian-led ministry, but through a mechanism that is unique to the Communist countries and that reflects their manner of political control in general. This is the system of political commissars (now officially "deputy commanders for political affairs"). These people are Communist Party officials with military rank and uniform, attached to military units at all levels down to the battalion. They combine the functions of chaplain, education and information, and counterintelligence in a Western army, with responsibility for troop morale, political indoctrination, and the loyalty of the professional officers. Allowing for the inevitable tension between professional and political officers, the latter have a separate chain of command, headed by the Main Political Administration under a general of the army (since 1962, Alexei Yepishev) who is also a full member of the Central Committee of the Party.

The Party also penetrates and coopts the armed forces through its normal system of membership and committees, while the KGB maintains its own network of informers in the armed forces just as everywhere else. Nearly all military officers are party members, and most noncoms are at least Komsomols. The top brass serve on the regional and central party committees according to their rank: Defense Minister Ustinov is a member of the Politburo; all marshals are full members of the Central Committee; military district commanders sit on their respective republic or provincial party committees; and so on down. Military officers made up 7 percent of the 545 members of the party leadership (Central Committee and Central Auditing Commission) elected in 1981, and were the third-largest category after the party apparatus and the central government. Thus, the relationship is reciprocal: the party controls the armed forces, but the armed forces are in turn institutionalized as an important voice and pressure group in the policymaking process.

Russia's orientation in military matters, like its foreign policy as a whole, has been powerfully conditioned since prerevolutionary times by the country's geopolitical situation and its economic and technological inferiority to the West. Soviet military thinking has remained essentially conservative, slow to respond to new technological and geopolitical realities, and only in the most superficial way influenced by Marxism. Its purposes have remained sufficiently traditional so that they could be expressed in terms of the thoroughly unrevolutionary thinking of Carl von Clausewitz, the great Prussian strategist whose theories were much admired by Lenin.

From the time of its earliest conflicts with the West, Russia has relied mainly on its army of unthinking but disciplined peasants, who would fall back and advance again across the country's vast spaces to best the invader regardless of casualties. Stalin, who fancied himself a great military theoretician, never got beyond this experience in his banal enumeration of the "five permanently operating factors" that determined the outcome of the war: the strength of the civilian rear areas, the morale of the troops, the number and quality of divisions, armament, and the organizational ability of the command. Not much room here for strategic innovation or tactical brilliance.

World War II only confirmed the old fear of foreign invasions and the belief in the efficacy of distance and massed forces to check aggressors. Soviet strategic doctrine from 1945 until the end of the sixties was geared to one overriding obsession: the possibility of a resurgence of forces in Western Europe, spearheaded by a revanchist Germany, that might repeat the treacherous invasion of 1941. From this fixation stemmed all the heavy-handed measures that brought on the Cold War—the Soviet grip on the East European security zone, the struggles and crises over Germany, and the maintenance of an army whose strength was unprecedented for any country in peacetime. As the history of the Cold War demonstrates, American responses simply convinced the Soviets that these policies were necessary, while recasting the United States in the place of Germany as the primary danger. In a similar way, Americans transferred the fall-of-France and Pearl Harbor traumas to their perception of the Soviet threat. Hence the expectation that World War III will begin as a surprise Soviet blitzkrieg against Western Europe.

Soviet thinking about nuclear weapons has always appeared out of date. Stalin did not believe that they portended a decisive change in the nature of war, even though the United States had already developed an atomic bomb and the Soviets were rushing to perfect their own. He showed no great fear of the American bomb and in no way yielded to it while he was setting up a conventional defense in depth.

The Americans, in contrast, quickly reorganized their strategy around atomic weapons, thinking of them less as a means to pressure or overcome the Russians than as a solution to the dilemma of great-power responsibility versus peaceful economic pursuits. By 1946 nuclear weapons had become, as they have remained to this day, the cheap American answer to the Soviets' superior ground forces: they would deter Communist aggression and avoid the cost of a wartime military establishment. This premise was shaken when the Soviets developed their own atomic bomb in 1949, but it nevertheless survived in the conviction, embodied in the 1950 decision to develop the hydrogen bomb, that the United States could and must maintain a technological lead over the Soviets in nuclear weaponry. Building on this premise, the Eisenhower administration enunciated the doctrine of "massive retaliation": Washington threatened first and unrestricted use of nuclear weapons against Soviet cities in order to deter a Soviet conventional assault on Europe, which was otherwise considered virtually inevitable and unstoppable. The degree of bluff in this stance was offset by the Soviets' lack of documented interest in such a westward assault.

Stalin's death opened a new era in Soviet military thinking. Under Malenkov it swung all the way to the view that nuclear war meant mutual annihilation. But this notion, and the theory of deterrence based on "mutually assured destruction," could never quite be assimilated within the Soviet ideological framework. From the late fifties on, while building an intercontinental deterrent equivalent to that of the United States, the Soviets consoled themselves with the notion that even if nuclear war were unleashed by the imperialists, it would not be decisive; in the end, socialism would prevail over capitalism. Nevertheless, there was at least implicit recognition that the two superpowers had a mutual interest in minimizing the likelihood of a nuclear exchange. During the early Khrushchev years, this brought Washington and Moscow to their closest point of accommodation in the nuclear arms race.

From the demise of the Baruch Plan in 1946 until the end of the Cold War in the mid-fifties, neither the Soviet Union nor the United States made any serious effort to negotiate the control of nuclear weapons. The ostensible stumbling block was always inspection and verification, which the United States insisted on to prevent Soviet cheating and which the Soviets resisted as an unacceptable intrusion

into their closed society. These psychological barriers still remain—
the American fear of being tricked, the Soviet fear of being exposed.
Even beyond these obstacles, neither side felt a compelling interest
in accepting controls. The Americans were reluctant to give up their
perceived nuclear advantage without conventional disarmament
first, and the Russians were reluctant to bargain from weakness and
tried to make up for it with antinuclear propaganda campaigns.

A potential breakthrough agreement in the more moderate climate of 1955 foundered on the inspection issue and on Washington's reluctance to accept a ban on the use of nuclear weapons (and
thus to surrender the nuclear deterrent), even though the Russians
offered to make cutbacks in their conventional forces. In 1956 and
1957 the Soviets vigorously campaigned for disarmament and particularly for a ban on nuclear testing (a popular position because of
the fallout controversy). But neither side was prepared to tailor its
proposals to make them acceptable to the other, preferring to press
for propagandistic advantages. Protracted negotiations from 1958 to
1960 over a nuclear test ban and the prevention of surprise attack
failed to overcome the underlying resistance on each side. No one
took seriously Khrushchev's 1959 UN proposal for "universal and
complete disarmament," and the whole disarmament effort came
temporarily to a halt when Khrushchev switched to his confrontationist policy in 1960.

What Khrushchev seems to have been most concerned about (as
Adam Ulam has persuasively argued in *The Rivals*) was the danger
of nuclear weapons in the hands of a revanchist Germany and an
unreliable China. It has been suggested that Khrushchev's real aim,
when he manufactured the Berlin crisis of 1958–1961 and proposed
the Rapacki Plan for a nuclear-free Central Europe (put forward on
Russia's behalf in 1957 by the Polish foreign minister), was to win
some assurance that the Bonn government would not get its finger
on the nuclear trigger. Unfortunately, Khrushchev could not
express these concerns in a sufficiently unambiguous way to allay
American fears of the Soviet threat to Europe. Ironically, the Western answer to the Rapacki Plan was NATO's decision in December
1957 to step up the deployment of American tactical nuclear weapons in Europe (already introduced as early as 1953) and to accept
intermediate-range missiles under collective NATO command.

It is interesting to speculate whether Khrushchev, who was not
averse to an internal thaw, might actually have agreed to allow rea-

sonable inspection if he had been offered the guarantees he wanted about Germany. But U.S. policy was by now so totally wedded to the new nuclear defense anchored in Germany that such concessions were not really negotiable. The underlying problem was that the United States, recognizing that its massive nuclear deterrent might itself be deterred and skeptical that Soviet conventional forces would be reduced to a tolerable level, was entertaining a shift in defense strategy that required keeping the technological initiative open. The new guiding spirit was Henry Kissinger, whose *Nuclear Weapons and Foreign Policy* promoted the theory of limited nuclear war and provided the rationale for an extensive American buildup of tactical nuclear weapons.

Khrushchev actually went an extraordinary distance in 1956–1959 to extend the olive branch of arms limitation to the West. He offered concessions in the very areas that Stalin had been most rigid about—namely, inspection and conventional force reductions. U.S. leaders at the time, as well as many subsequent commentators, have dismissed these Soviet proposals as propaganda gestures. The fact remains that during these years the Soviets took unusual initiatives in foreign policy and in domestic affairs, in distinct contrast to their practice both before and after. It is unlikely that any Soviet leader would take such steps as Khrushchev did (even including unilateral troop reductions and the 1958 test moratorium) for purely propaganda reasons. However, the Khrushchev initiatives, whatever their value, were not capitalized on by the United States and its allies; Soviet party and military leaders must have viewed them as a failure of monumental proportions. By increasing Khrushchev's vulnerability to the neo-Stalinist opposition in the party, the West's rebuff no doubt weakened him politically and contributed to his 1960 switch to a hard line in an effort to recoup.

Time and again in the fifties and sixties, the Russians were faced with American advances in weaponry: battlefield nuclear weapons, high-accuracy intercontinental missiles, missile-firing submarines, and the multiple-warhead missile, or MIRV ("multiple independently targeted reentry vehicle"). Their response was a relentless effort to catch up. As early as the U.S. election campaign in 1960, Soviet weaponry was sufficiently respectable to lend credence to John Kennedy's charges (actually cultivated by Khrushchev) that the Eisenhower administration had permitted the growth of a "missile gap." Soviet bomb testing during the Berlin crisis of 1961, plus the Cuban missile crisis the following year, provoked the great fall-out shelter panic in the United States and demonstrated that the American nuclear deterrent was itself finally deterred.

The limited Nuclear Test Ban Treaty of 1963 evidenced once again the superpowers' mutual underlying interest in controlling the arms race, as well as their capacity—not to be taken for granted—to recognize that mutual interest. The USSR and the United States were both concerned with curbing the spread of nuclear weapons to other powers (China had exploded its first atomic bomb in 1964). In the late sixties they proceeded slowly but surely with the Nuclear Nonproliferation Treaty (concluded in 1968) and the SALT Talks governing intercontinental ballistic missiles (ICBMs). The SALT negotiations began in 1969, after the United States had unilaterally accepted a ceiling of "sufficiency" on its long-range missile force and the Soviets had pulled abreast of the United States in the size of their arsenal. While negotiations moved toward the SALT I treaty in 1972, each side continued to press its advantage in its own characteristic way: the Americans, amid much controversy, pursued the technological lead in developing the antiballistic missile (ABM) and the MIRV; the Soviets forged ahead in the numbers and size of their missiles. Technology proved vulnerable to Soviet imitation, and was destabilizing besides: both the ABM and the MIRV made it possible for one side to launch a first strike that could so cripple the enemy's response capability that the aggressor's ABMs and civil defense could cope with the few missiles that might be fired back. Thus, nuclear war would become tolerable for the aggressor, and deterrence as a principle of superpower balance could break down.

This problem of second-strike deterrent capability was addressed throughout the arms control negotiations of the seventies. In 1972 SALT I confined ABMs to two experimental sites on each side and froze the installation of new ICBMs. In 1974 the Vladivostok Agreement placed a limit on the number of missiles that could have multiple warheads. And in 1979 the SALT II treaty, a long and complex document that was signed but never ratified, specified parity in the total of strategic nuclear-weapons launchers (intercontinental missiles, submarine-launched missiles, and bombers) and called for modest future reductions (which would actually affect the Soviet Union more than the United States). During these years, the Soviet government continued steadily to expand its conventional forces, especially naval power, and forged ahead with intermediate-range nuclear weapons (not covered in the treaties) targeted on Western Europe and China. This program, along with the Soviet push in the third world, was to prove the undoing of détente.

Nuclear weapons have intensified each shift in the climate of American-Soviet relations ever since the 1950s. They were the core of mutual interest during the years of détente, both in the late fifties and from the Test Ban Treaty of 1963 to the late seventies. They were a central issue during the years of tension from 1960 to 1962 and again in the American response to Soviet power that brought on the New Cold War in the late seventies.

American doubts about détente and the efficacy of arms control surfaced in 1976 in a heated controversy over the CIA's evaluation of Soviet capabilities; the in-house "Team A" was relatively sanguine, whereas the "Team B" of outsiders (headed by Richard Pipes of Harvard) viewed the Soviets with new alarm. The latter opinion was echoed by numerous writers on grand strategy who concluded that the buildup of Soviet forces—superior on the ground, catching up at sea, and advancing in the nuclear realm prior to the SALT agreements—constituted an unacceptable threat to American security. It was argued that improvements in missile accuracy and anti-submarine warfare on the one hand, and in civil defense on the other, created a "window of vulnerability"—a period of a few years when the Soviets would be able to execute a first-strike strategy with "acceptable" losses and thereby undercut the American nuclear deterrent. All these concerns were fueled by old fears: Washington once again assumed that the Soviets intended to export revolution by surprise attack, or (a more sophisticated version) that their ideologically bankrupt regime had to keep expanding externally in order to retain power internally.

Soviet military strategists responded to the changing balance of nuclear forces with far less apparent controversy than did the Americans. Relying on their own capability for deterrence, the Soviets threatened massive retaliation against any American nuclear initiative. But according to their conservative thinking, a nuclear exchange would not alone determine the outcome of a war, which would depend on conventional forces as well. This form of argument persuaded American strategists that the Soviets considered a nuclear war to be "winnable," which enhanced the fear of a Soviet first strike.

Under the Reagan administration, American strategic debate focused again on the deterrence of a Soviet conventional attack in Europe. In apparent disregard of the "window of vulnerability," U.S. strategy has continued to rest on the possible first use of tactical nuclear weapons and "theater" deterrents (that is, European-based missiles) to offset the Soviet ground threat to Europe (which hoary American theory still regards as paramount). This posture depends on the belief that nuclear war can be kept limited and therefore "winnable," even in the American sense of the word. Critics of this strategy find the first-use limited-war deterrence strategy extremely risky because, on the one hand, it could be considered a bluff in certain marginal situations, and, on the other, it would, if carried out, inevitably escalate (as the Soviets believe) into an unrestricted nuclear exchange. This concern gave rise to the no-first-use debate, initiated in *Foreign Affairs* (Spring 1982) by four prominent policymakers of the past—George Kennan; McGeorge Bundy and Robert McNamara from the Kennedy-Johnson era; and Gerard Smith, chief negotiator of the SALT I treaty—who took issue with the premises that had implicitly guided American strategy all through the years of détente and SALT. But the prevailing American judgment in the early eighties was that détente merely camouflaged Soviet preparations for a nuclear Pearl Harbor, and that America could restore its credible deterrent only by outbuilding the Soviets once again and reasserting the technological lead—this despite all the evidence that the Soviets invariably keep up both in quantity and quality. It was such reasoning, coupled with the *cause célèbre* of Afghanistan, that prompted the Carter administration to shelve the SALT II treaty and supplied the underpinnings for the foreign policy of the Reagan administration.

▪ The New Cold War

A rapid series of events in the late 1970s put an end to the growing Soviet-American amity of the previous decade and a half. The Soviets' progress toward military parity and their diplomatic accomplishments in the third world sharpened American anxieties, at the same time that U.S. political opinion was veering to the right. Moscow, too, became anxious as it lost its hold on satellites and sympathizers and as Washington-Peking exchanges led to a de facto alliance against the Kremlin. As in the beginning of the original

Cold War, each superpower found itself compelled to view the other as a threat that called for maximum attention to military power and strategic security.

Détente, at its peak in 1973, had been attacked in the United States as a policy of appeasement that allowed the Soviet Union to forge ahead politically and militarily. Skepticism about détente was strengthened by neoconservatism, a reaction to the welfare-state liberalism and counterculture agitation of the 1960s, and to the mea culpa isolationism engendered by the Vietnam War. With renewed indignation, critics attacked the USSR's civil rights record, treatment of dissidents, and restrictions on Jewish emigration—which ironically became an issue just when the Soviet authorities were allowing it to reach a significant level. Nixon's resignation in 1974 took the political drive out of détente, and the Helsinki agreement was concluded only on momentum. The ink was scarcely dry on the accords when President Ford, fighting for renomination against Ronald Reagan and the Republican right wing, repudiated the very word "détente."

We know little or nothing of the process by which the Soviet leadership arrived at the decision to go over to the geopolitical offensive around 1975. Indeed, there may have been no specific decision, but only a cumulative series of pressures and reactions reflecting both the external sense that the capitalist world along with China was passing them by, and the rising internal forces of military interest and nationalistic self-righteousness. In any case, Soviet actions from 1975 on gave credence to the critics of détente. A signal for Moscow's new moves was Washington's failure to come to the aid of South Vietnam early in 1975 when it was being overwhelmed by North Vietnamese forces, in direct violation of the Paris accords. Presumably seeing this disinterest as a green light, the Soviets began to intervene directly in third-world countries to implant Moscow-dominated "governments of socialist orientation."

The prototype for the new forward strategy was the former Portuguese colony of Angola, torn by competing nationalist movements after Portugal promised independence in 1975. The Soviets provided military aid to the most ideologically compatible of the rivals, the Popular Movement for the Liberation of Angola (MPLA), and prevailed upon Castro to send troops. Angola became virtually a Soviet satellite, and Portugal's great East African territory of Mozambique swung almost as close to the Soviet orbit. Thus, the last cases of decolonization in Africa provided the most successful foot-holds for the Soviets.

Their attention next shifted to the strategic Horn of Africa and the Arab regions opposite it, east of the Red Sea. Soviet aid to Somalia, beginning in 1974, bought bases and a military presence, until a new temptation presented itself: a revolution in Ethiopia. Commencing with the military overthrow of emperor Haile Selassie in 1974, the Ethiopian Revolution took a radical turn in 1977 and embraced Soviet aid as well as Marxist-Leninist ideology and Cuban troops. But here the Soviets overplayed their hand: the Somalis, locked in a border war with Ethiopia, promptly repudiated the Soviet connection, expelled the Russians from their bases, and turned to the United States for aid and comfort. Meanwhile, in South Yemen a classic coup was being prepared. When the nation's leadership showed signs in 1978 of looking to American or Chinese protection, the Yemen Socialist Party (actually Communist)—again with Cuban troops—staged a bloody uprising, executed president Salem Robaye Ali, and put the country firmly in the Soviet camp.

A similar venture, but with wider implications, took place almost simultaneously on Russia's Middle Eastern border. The traditional buffer state of Afghanistan had long been officially neutral. A coup in 1973 overthrew the monarchy and set up a republic, still officially non-Communist and neutral. In April 1978 a new coup, hailed by the Soviets as a true popular democratic revolution, put the pro-Communist Nur Mohammed Taraki in power and, as in South Yemen, moved the country definitely into the Soviet orbit. Neither the Soviets nor their local sympathizers were in full control, however. The Taraki government immediately came under attack from the right, in the form of guerrilla resistance by traditionalist tribes-men, and then from the left in a factional coup by extremists. Taraki was deposed and killed in September 1979 by the fanatic Hafizullah Amin, whose advent only prompted greater resistance among the anti-Communist rebels. The Soviets, confronted with a major security problem on a sensitive border (Afghanistan is adjacent to their own Moslem minority area), decided to restore order by direct intervention. The scene resembled Czechoslovakia in 1968: Soviet troops poured into Afghanistan, liquidated Amin and his entourage in favor of the rival Communist Babrak Karmal, and tried to pacify the country.

The invasion of Afghanistan demolished the already deteriorating structure of détente. The Carter administration, never consistent in its attitude toward the Soviets, had begun by proclaiming an end to "the inordinate fear of Communism" and at the same time throwing Moscow off balance with new arms-reduction proposals. It proclaimed its support of human rights everywhere against dictatorial repression. It played the "China card" by establishing de jure diplomatic relations with Peking, and confronted the Russians with a clear American-Chinese alignment. It concluded a treaty with the Soviets providing for cooperation in space research and extended the SALT I treaty pending the conclusion of SALT II; but simultaneously it announced plans to develop the neutron bomb for defense in Europe (countered by Soviet deployment of heavy missiles targeted on the population centers of Western Europe). Amid rising criticism about the effectiveness of arms control, SALT II was finally signed by Carter and Brezhnev when they met in Vienna in June 1979—the last meeting of heads of state during the Brezhnev era.

By this time America's new ally, China, had launched a punitive attack on Russia's ally, Vietnam, which had just intervened in Cambodia to overthrow China's allies. In the Middle East, fundamentalists in Iran had repudiated both Western and Soviet influence. The Carter administration was feeling the strain. A Soviet combat brigade was alleged to have been introduced into Cuba, in violation of the compromise of 1962, and then the American Embassy was seized in Tehran. In late 1979 momentous steps were already being taken—Carter had approved the development of the MX missile, with its first-strike capability, and NATO had agreed to locate American intermediate-range missiles (IRBMs) and cruise missiles in Europe if the Soviets would not consent to mutual reductions—when the news came of Soviet intervention in Afghanistan. Carter, announcing that he had come to understand more about the Communists in that one week than in all his previous experience, declared diplomatic war.

The Americans were outraged by the invasion of Afghanistan and frustrated at their inability to counter Soviet gains in the third world. Again, they thought, the Soviets were revealing their old intention of expanding by force, seeking global hegemony in the long run and the strangulation of the West's oil supply in the short run. But the Iranian Revolution and the Soviets' exploitation of Arab hostility to Israel had effectively denied the United States leverage in the region; the only country that might serve as a base for counteraction was a nervous Pakistan, which served the Afghan rebels as a sanctuary and supply conduit. For the most part, the American reaction to Afghanistan was one of enraged impotence. Carter placed an embargo on grain sales, which the Soviet easily made up for in the world market (until the Reagan administration rescinded the ban, to repair the damage to American agriculture), and ordered a boycott of the 1980 summer Olympic Games in Moscow, an otherwise tempting opportunity for foreign contact with Soviet society. Most serious in their future implications were Carter's decisions to extend the theory of "linkage" to the arms control process and to withdraw the SALT II treaty from consideration for ratification by the U.S. Senate (an action already rendered doubtful by widespread complaints of American nuclear inferiority).

With the inauguration of Reagan in January 1981, the United States acquired for the first time since the retirement of Dulles in 1958 a leadership suspicious of any agreement with the Russians. Once again the ideological theory of the Communist menace took hold in U.S. policymaking. President Reagan on various occasions described the Soviet Union as an "evil empire," and called its leaders "the focus of evil in the modern world." Referring to the nuclear freeze movement, he asserted, "I would agree to a freeze only if we could freeze the Soviets' global ambitions." But China, having become an implicit American ally, no longer figured in Americans' sense of the Communist threat, though the far right in Reagan's entourage remained uncomfortable about the Peking connection. It was as though the United States could live with one of the two Communist powers at a time, as long as it could make the other out to be a menace to civilization.

Going a step beyond Carter, the Reagan administration at first rejected the arms control process in general, and the SALT II treaty in particular, on the ground that they perpetuated American inferiority to the Soviets. Citing the "window of vulnerability," Reagan indicated his intention to force the Russians to a better arms bargain by upping the military budget and demonstrating America's ability to outbuild them. But this extreme position evoked the opposite reaction among the American public: there was renewed alarm about the horrors of nuclear war, and the nuclear freeze movement mobilized wide support to campaign for a halt to the arms race. In response, Reagan proposed late in 1982 not merely to arrest the arms race, as SALT had envisaged, but to attempt reductions through Strategic Arms Reduction Talks ("START") and a "build-down" (the destruction of two old missiles for every new one manufactured).

The Soviets were no more enthusiastic about these overtures than they were about the Carter proposal of 1977 for nuclear cutbacks. Their coolness gives some credence to the theory that the Soviet Union resists nuclear weapons reductions (as distinguished from a freeze on new weapons development) because it believes it wields much more international influence under the umbrella of mutual nuclear deterrence than it would in the competition of conventional forces alone. Given Soviet economic and manpower limitations, this surmise may have some truth to it, particularly with respect to China and Western Europe. It accords with Soviet boasts about the protection that the USSR offers to "national liberation movements" in the third world. In a global sense, the Soviet Union may have worked itself into a situation corresponding to the position of the United States in Western Europe: each depends on the nuclear balance to deter conventional intervention by the adversary. To the extent this is true, the prospects for substantial nuclear reductions in the near future (as against limits on further building) seem dim, and drastic American proposals for cutbacks cannot be expected to be taken seriously.

The arms issue became even more intractable when President Reagan proceeded to implement the NATO plan to install American land-based missiles at European sites from which they could strike Moscow quickly and accurately. The price demanded of the Soviets to avoid this threat was to dismantle all their SS-20 missiles aimed at Western Europe (the so-called zero option). Each government repeatedly rejected the other's terms for a settlement. A promising compromise allowing a reduced number of missiles on each side—the "Walk in the Woods" agreement worked out in Geneva in the summer of 1982 by American negotiator Paul Nitze and his Soviet counterpart Yuri Kvitsinsky—was disavowed both in Moscow and in Washington. Even Andropov's offer to reduce Soviet missiles aimed at Europe to the number possessed by the British and French (provided the United States gave up its own deployment plans) was rejected by the Western powers, concerned as they were to preserve the automatic American involvement in Europe's nuclear defense.

Europeans, for their part, were torn between ban-the-bomb senti-ments and the attraction of low-budget security offered by Ameri-can nuclear protection. In any case, they preferred to believe that détente was not dead. Economic ties between the Soviet Union and Western Europe—based mainly on the exchange of Soviet raw ma-terials and energy for Western industrial equipment—continued into the eighties as strong as ever, and Reagan's suspension of the embargo on American grain sales to the Soviet Union undercut U.S. objections to its allies' dependency on trade with the Soviets.

In the fall of 1983 Soviet-American relations reached a point of tension unmatched since the Cuban missile crisis of 1962. The tragic downing of a Korean airliner by a Soviet fighter plane in Septem-ber, and the exchange of invective this triggered between the U.S. and Soviet governments, were followed by a total impasse in nego-tiations on the Euromissiles. When the United States proceeded with deployment of IRBMs and cruise missiles in Europe, the So-viets broke off all strategic missile talks. The replacement of Andro-pov by Chernenko in February 1984 left the Soviets even less willing to pursue negotiations with the Reagan administration, an attitude that they underscored by their boycott of the 1984 summer Olympics in Los Angeles.

Meanwhile, the Soviets' flanking strategy in the third world reached perilously close to America's most traditional interests in Central America. The Sandinista revolutionary movement, which had taken power in Nicaragua in 1979, quickly showed signs of Communist ties, much as Cuba had after Castro's victory. Soviet-bloc military aid poured in, and some (the amount and duration are debatable) was diverted to support the similar insurgency in El Salvador. In great alarm, Washington extended military aid to the Salvadoran government and anti-Sandinista Nicaraguans, under circumstances reminiscent of the early U.S. commitment in Viet-nam. Direct U.S. intervention in the fall of 1983 overwhelmed the pro-Soviet revolutionaries on the island of Grenada, and demon-strated a readiness under some circumstances to defend the Ameri-can sphere as forcibly as the Soviets have guarded theirs. Nevertheless, despite these experiences, the United States made lit-tle effort to devise a workable political strategy to counter the po-tential Soviet appeal to third-world revolutionary movements.

The Soviet leaders of the 1980s have shown little or no disposition to temper the pursuit of military and political advantage that has caused such a rise in U.S. anxiety. They find a source of pride and perhaps of domestic popularity in their global role, and appear to believe that the march of history, led by pro-Communist vanguard parties, is in their direction. This is not to suggest that the pro-Soviet trend is irresistible; in fact, the Soviet position, which relies on concentric rings of domination—Russians over non-Russians in the Soviet Union, Soviets over satellites in the bloc, the Communist bloc over dependent third-worlders—is inherently shaky. The Soviets must ultimately rely on military power to win influence and advance their security.

The remarkable thing about the Soviet-American confrontation of the eighties, like the technologically less dangerous standoff of the original Cold War, is that it could persist for years without direct military conflict. None of the prophecies of doom uttered during the past third of a century have come true: the Soviets have not launched a general war of revolution, and the capitalists have not launched an anti-Soviet war of intervention. Such restraint hardly stems from international scruple, which plays a minimal role in bipolar relationships. It is a horror of the weapons of total war, plus the security that each nation enjoys within its sphere of influence, that persuades both sides to keep the peace between them.

Conclusion

Industrial ministries on Kalinin Prospect, Moscow

Confrontation or Accommodation?

Despite four decades of recurring confrontation, darkened by a sense of impending nuclear doom, neither the Soviet Union nor the United States ordinarily operates on the basis of a realistic understanding of the other. Articulate Soviet thinking—that is, official thinking—has made use of a combination of Marxist labels and old Russian assumptions to represent the U.S. government as a counter-revolutionary aggressor. Americans, grasping little of the peculiar sources of Soviet behavior, oscillate between fear of a moribund ideology and naive faith in expressions of peaceful intentions. Each side is primed to fit the other into its own preconceived view of the world rather than to appreciate how a different history has shaped the way its adversary thinks and acts.

Americans must face a basic fact: Russia is a mammoth power that will not disappear or cease to challenge the United States, regardless of the coloration of its government. The contest for world influence between the United States and Russia is grounded in history—indeed, it was foreseen by writers in Europe and America more than a century ago. Russia will continue to be guided by the pride, ambitions, and interests that have carried over from prerevolutionary times—and no mere alteration in regime or ideology will quickly eliminate them.

Russian ambitions and interests do not necessarily mean war with the United States, as American policymakers assumed during the Cold War era, when the ideological theory of Soviet expansion was in vogue. But the thinking of responsible Russians is warped by their tormented history and the political perpetuation of old obsessions. Although Russia has grown up in terms of its modernization and industrialization (as Khrushchev said, Russia is no longer wearing short pants), as a nation it still lacks the self-assurance of maturity. Russians who exercise governmental responsibility have no confidence in their ability to persuade others—either their own subjects or foreign powers—to do what they want or to respect their interests, and thus they resort to threats, duplicity, and force. There remains an element of infantilism in Russian political life, with its lack of trust, restraint, and give and take. Russians in government have no sense of how to win other people's good will because they have no belief that anyone's good will can be expressed through governmental institutions.

Russia's fixations stem from centuries of grim experience—the struggle for national identity and survival, the pursuit of security by expansion, and the tensions of the multinational society that resulted from the tsars' empire-building. Russia has been unable to shed its sense of being an outsider in the modern world, its inferiority complex, its obsessive distrust of foreigners, its mania for secrecy. As an autocracy, Russia has been able to put the highest priority on the mobilization of its natural and human resources for military purposes. As a participant in Europe's dynastic wars and alliances, Russia learned that security was an ephemeral goal, constantly threatened by new combinations of foes, and that any territory not under Russian military domination was a potential enemy. Russia has not broken with the diplomatic past: it has preserved to a unique extent the outlook and methods of an archaic European system of international relations. The Soviet experience has added much to old Russian tactics and assumptions in the international arena, but it has eliminated very little. Russia, for all of its revolutionary disguise, is really the last of the old-time militarist-imperialist states.

The Revolution is the great illusion in Russian history, both for its heirs within the country and its enemies without. To be sure, the Revolution installed a regime committed to the idea of socialism, but the eventual form of this socialism—the command economy—was a reincarnation of the old despotism. The "workers' state" remained an ideological myth, while the new hierarchy of militarized politics entrenched itself behind that façade. World revolution survived only as Soviet imperialism ironically allied with anti-imperialism. Its legacy is the opaque self-righteousness both of Russia's rulers and of anti-Communists abroad.

Postrevolutionary Russia is still with us as the regime of totalitarian coercion known appropriately as Stalinism, shorn perhaps of its arbitrary terror and its personalized egomania but no less despotic in its assertion of unlimited power. Nurtured on autocracy and backwardness as well as the inexorable backswing of revolution, Stalinism brought together the worst that prerevolutionary and revolutionary Russia had to offer.

Stalinism was powerfully reinforced by the life-and-death struggle of World War II. For Stalin and his apologists, victory over Germany was the validation of his entire system, which emerged from the ordeal even more militaristic and nationalistic than before. The war implanted a paranoiac fear of attack from the west—German revanchism is a constant propaganda theme—though it also left a residue of popular nostalgia for collaboration with the United States.

The Stalinist apparatus of control—the party, police, and military apparatus—has never had any interest in a genuine accommodation with the West; true détente and the free flow of ideas would under-cut the need for its own functions and open its legitimacy to question. Peaceful coexistence, as the Soviet leaders say, does not mean "ideological coexistence." Yet they are not the people to let mere Marxist theory make them risk everything in a Third World War. In its foreign policy, the Soviet government has never been constrained by ideology to do anything that was not in accord with its traditional power interests.

Although Marxism-Leninism is still the language in which the Soviet leaders justify their policies and legitimize their rule, it became outmoded long ago as a political program. As an explanation of the world, it does not work; as propaganda, it is exhausted both in the Soviet Union and in the industrialized world where it was supposed to find its following. The Soviet Union is a conservative post-revolutionary state relying heavily on the imperialist menace to justify totalitarian closure and to sustain its ambiguous appeal to third-world nationalists.

Within the Soviet Union today, there is only one real source of emotional support for the regime and its foreign policy. This is simply old-fashioned Great Russian nationalism, defensive in its primary instincts but proud of the global role that the country has won by virtue of its military power. "Thanks to international tension and ideological impoverishment," the French correspondent Michel Tatu has observed, "militant patriotism is about the only surviving reliable value." It has found expression in a Russian New Right, with roots among the masses and with branches in the hierarchy. The New Right cherishes the old Russian virtues over the decadence of the West; it is sometimes religious and often anti-Semitic; it wants the minorities to be assimilated and the satellites to submit; and it draws comfort from displays of national power and discipline.

Compatible with the Russian New Right is the ideology of national power as an end in itself—an ideology that has been implicit for decades in the economic and military priorities of the Soviet regime. Former anarchist Cornelius Castoriadis, in his book *Devant la guerre,* has gone so far as to suggest that the Soviet Union has become a "stratocracy," a state ruled by the military interest. Castoriadis' thesis settles the question of whether interest groups such as the military and the managers of heavy industry can influence the party leadership as special-interest lobbies do in the United States.

The answer is that they do not need to—military priorities are thoroughly infused into the ruling party hierarchy. Between the party and the military-industrial complex there is no divergence of interests but only a delegation of functions.

Are the Soviets therefore inherently expansionist and aggressive, entirely apart from or even in spite of their official ideology? This is how their Marxist adversaries in China and Yugoslavia have viewed them for years. Russia's history is a record of expansion wherever opportunity knocked, and Moscow still shows no inhibitions of principle on the extension of its influence into new areas. From the Soviet standpoint, it is right and natural for the superpower of the Eastern Hemisphere to aspire to as much strategic firepower and worldwide projection of force as the superpower of the Western Hemisphere enjoys. Two can play the role of world policeman, each guarding its sphere of responsibility from the other, which it brands as an outlaw.

The absolute in Soviet policy is not revolution but national security, construed, in the post–World War II bipolar world, in global terms. Centuries of threats, pressures, and temptations have reinforced in Russia's leaders a fundamentally suspicious and confrontationist attitude toward the outside world. Friendships are never dependable; alliances are always expedient; enmities, overt or covert, lurk everywhere. Like the Old Regime, the Soviets have been insatiable in the pursuit of security by dominating neighboring regions. They can be expected to be unyielding, regardless of cost or opportunities lost, in matters involving control of their satellite zone or free foreign access to their closed society—hence the past crises in Eastern Europe and the impasse on human rights and arms control inspection. The Soviet leaders certainly know from centuries of sad Russian experience that weakness and humiliation at the hands of foreign powers inevitably invite trouble for an unpopular and coercive regime. When the Soviets feel cornered by superior force or a superior combination of adversaries, they will turn to tactics of defiance and grasp at whatever nearby advantage presents itself. This belligerent reaction under pressure was shown in their response to the formation both of the Anglo-American coalition in the late forties and of the Sino-American coalition in the late seventies. From the Baruch Plan to the Euromissiles, it has always been easy to provoke the Soviets into the nasty rejection of high-sounding compromises with which the United States itself may have been uncomfortable.

Can the United States ever resolve its differences with Russia and find a path to peaceful cooperation? The goal is remote, if only because the existence of the two superpowers will continue to polarize world politics. More immediately, real friendship and understanding are ruled out because the Communist regime is driven by its national inferiority complex and its need for ideological justification to keep foreign contacts at a minimum. External cooperation is possible, as the record shows, when some common problem—Germany in the thirties and forties, nuclear weapons in the fifties and sixties, China in the sixties and seventies—brings Russia and the Western democracies together. But the grand settlement that so many Americans have longed for is highly unlikely, depending as it would on the demise of the present regime in the Soviet Union.

According to President Reagan, this is no great problem because Communism is destined for the ash heap of history. Unfortunately this notion bespeaks a misunderstanding of the Soviet Union on several planes. Communism in the genuine ideological sense—the achievement of the workers' state through revolution and dictatorship—is already on the ash heap of history, having yielded to a bureaucratic totalitarianism that merely uses the proletarian revolution as propagandistic legitimation. What is not on the ash heap of history, or likely to end up there short of a holocaust, is Russia as a great nation and a major power with aspirations to worldwide influence. No conceivable Russian government will willingly play second fiddle to the United States.

Are there grounds for hoping that Russia may somehow change internally, enough to transcend its needs for ideological pretense and military preponderance? Could the momentum of modernization and the education of the citizenry eventually remake Russian politics on Western lines? Would this in turn assure amity between the superpowers and free the world from the balance of terror? The theory of convergence would answer yes to all of these questions.

The notion of convergence has been debated and disputed on both sides since the beginning of détente in the 1960s. Many Western commentators remain deeply skeptical of the idea, and the Soviets have denounced it as a bourgeois propaganda ploy, even though they are striving to become as much like the West as possible in industrial prowess and consumer amenities. The validity of convergence obviously depends on which aspects of life one is comparing.

In many nonpolitical respects the Soviet and American societies have clearly become more alike. Russia is now highly industrial, urban, and technological. The United States, like all other industrial societies, has become more centralized, more hierarchical (in the private sector as well as the public), more manipulable through national communication and surveillance networks. Each country in its own way has gone through the managerial revolution, which vests power independently of private property in a class of public or quasi-public executives. Each has cultivated the norms of consumer affluence, though Russia has failed to fulfill public expectations. Each suffers increasingly from familiar postindustrial problems, ranging from environmental pollution to mental illness.

Convergence, as these points show, is most apparent in the material and personal aspects of life. But convergence in social structure cannot guarantee international accommodation without some basis for mutual understanding at the political level. Here a vast difference remains, reflecting the old gulf between Russia and the West in their traditions, assumptions, and distribution of power. So far, convergence in technology and industrial organization has not even dented the Soviets' political resistance to building mutual confidence and trust.

Can change in society overcome the ideological fixations and police regime of the Communist dictatorship, as many historical precedents, even Russia's, suggest? Other dictatorships, seemingly entrenched forever, have sometimes yielded to a liberalizing spirit after an old tyrant has died, or when the last phase of the revolutionary cycle calls for a return to the ideals with which it began. Khrushchev took a step toward such a renovation, though he failed to prevent the clock from being turned back again. Today the revolutionary cycle in Russia is long overdue for a new turn, away from Stalinist conservatism and toward a revival of the Revolution's early hopes for freedom and equality. The events of the Prague Spring of 1968, when the Communist Party of Czechoslovakia tried to democratize its own system from within, indicate the type of renewal for which Russia is ready. The Czechoslovaks would have succeeded had not the Russians intervened. If Russia undertakes reform, there is no one who will intervene to stop it.

The forces pressing for change in Russia could obviously have a substantial effect if the political situation gave them freer play. A large part of the Soviet population today has been neither nurtured nor scarred by Stalinism. The country's successful transformation into a modern, industrialized, educated, fairly sophisticated society collides with the system of totalitarian rule that effected that transformation. "The country cannot be governed in the old way," wrote dissident historian Roy Medvedev in the mid-seventies; "democratization is an objective necessity for our society." If Medvedev is correct, the dictatorship of the party bureaucracy contains the seeds of its own destruction.

The protracted postrevolutionary impasse between system and society in the Soviet Union is now manifested in multiple difficulties. Fear and anger have grown between the controllers and the controlled. The economy stagnates, consumers are frustrated, the populace is apathetic, the New Class tires of its expendable rulers. As Sakharov wrote in the late seventies, "a deeply cynical caste society has come into being." The country's potential affluence is sapped by a pointless arms race and by a quest for security through isolation and preponderant power, rather than international cooperation and a reasonable power balance.

Underlying the sclerotic and paranoid stance of the Soviet regime in matters both domestic and foreign is a colossal historical irony. The essence of the regime is not derived from "Communism" in any definable sense, or from the direct force of the Revolution. It lies, rather, in Russia's protracted failure to complete the revolutionary process by breaking the ice-jam of postrevolutionary conservatism obsessively legitimized by revolutionary ideology. Russia's problem is not that it is Communist. The problem is that it is not Communist, but cannot dispense with the pretense.

The barriers to change, however badly it is needed, are obvious. The Establishment of controllers tolerates no organized or expressed challenge to its supremacy. It is supported by the many Soviet citizens who fear political confusion and yearn for a *krepkii khoziain*— a "tough boss," like Stalin. This common attitude illustrates the congruence between old Russian political culture and Communist totalitarianism. "You don't know our people," said a party-line Soviet scientist recently when pressed about the lack of political freedom. Massive security precautions at sensitive moments like the death of a leader or even at May Day parades bespeak the anxiety that crowds cause the authorities, who know how their own revolution began. In the minority regions particularly, there is reason for such anxiety if political liberalization should signal the opportunity to resist control from Moscow. Russian nationalism cannot readily accept either the separatism of the non-Russian nationalities or the loss of control over Eastern Europe which any weakening of the Soviet presence would entail.

Nevertheless, there are reasons to expect that the political, intellectual, and economic stagnation that has characterized the Soviet Union in the sixties and seventies may soon be coming to an end. Reform must as a practical matter start from the top down, and the top itself is changing. Time alone is accomplishing a sweeping renovation of the Communist leadership and the replacement of the post-purge generation with younger people who, however much they may conform to the Stalinist heritage, were not molded by the same traumatic experiences of the purges and the war. Presumably they will be more flexible and more sophisticated, if not in some sense more liberal. Better educated, they will be more secure in their personal status and may feel less need for crude ideological justifications of their powers, privileges, and policies.

The new leaders will have at their disposal a prolific class of experts and technicians, who have been trained to serve in the maturing industrial economy and whose hopes both for economic betterment and a voice in the policymaking process are not to be denied. Soviet Russia may yet experience the revolution of rising expectations. If future leaders are to make any headway, they must better appreciate the complexity of their own system, give more heed to the experts, and allow some decentralization of the planning and policymaking process along the lines of the Hungarian model. Such steps may not be big enough or come soon enough to alleviate the growing tension between controllers and specialists, but it would be too much to expect any hasty tampering with the basic habits of the closed society, including the deception and prevarication on which the Soviet regime has regularly relied. This seems to rule out a Prague Spring in Moscow.

The overarching question, not only for U.S.–Soviet relations but for the future of the entire world, is whether the two superpowers can overcome the history that has set them at odds before some misstep triggers the explosive mixture of political primitivism and nuclear technology. Given the ossified political situation in the Soviet Union, initiatives to break the vicious spiral of confrontation are much more likely to come, if at all, from the United States, though this would mean rising above the ideological simplicities of anti-Communism that usually make such good politics at home. During the last four decades the United States has tended to overestimate the Soviet threat, while the Soviet Union has always overestimated the threat from the West. Unable to fathom the aggressive defensiveness of the Russians, Americans impatiently swing from naive optimism to offended idealism, and in their righteousness repeatedly back the USSR into a corner where its security demands allow no concession.

In two crucial areas the United States chose a course of action for its short-run security that ultimately, in the Soviet reaction it provoked, created grave and irreversible risks to the peace and security of the world. One was a specific region of contention, namely Germany, in the early years of the Cold War. The other area was the technological race in nuclear weaponry. In both cases the damage, long ago done, is difficult if not impossible to undo; the point is the lesson to be drawn in managing fear and bargaining for the best long-term outcome.

As a result of Soviet actions in Eastern Europe and elsewhere, seen through the lens of anti-Communist ideology, the U.S. government decided barely a year after the end of World War II that Germany, whole or truncated, had to be a Western stronghold against the Soviet Union. The united neutral Germany that the Soviets may have been prevailed upon to accept (on the model of Austria) was never really a subject for U.S. bargaining, and all the Soviet pressure tactics to dissuade the United States from its course only confirmed Washington's belief in a threat from the east. The resulting partition of Germany created a tense and enduring confrontation all along the iron-curtain line dividing Europe. It implied a U.S. commitment to the front-line defense of Europe down the middle of Germany and the need for tactical nuclear weapons that could stop a Soviet blitzkrieg. It removed a potential buffer and sacrificed the possibility that Czechoslovakia and perhaps Hungary could have escaped internal Communization as Finland had.

The East European satellites fell under complete Soviet domination not because the Yalta agreement approved this fate, as the myth still has it, but because the Soviets were on the scene and the West failed to hold out effective bargaining inducements—either sticks or carrots—for a region-wide compromise within the limits set by Soviet security demands. (Sweden successfully did this for Finland, offering its own neutrality to ransom Finnish democracy.) The West instead set up a loud and obviously justifiable clamor about the Soviets' oppressive behavior within their sphere, which only intensified Stalin's security mania and gave him no inducement to desist from the heavy-handed consolidation of his sphere. Ironically, the outcome was counterproductive for the USSR, which was left to depend for its security in Eastern Europe on methods of control that assured the hatred of the satellite peoples.

The partition of central Europe and the eyeball-to-eyeball alignment of NATO and Warsaw Pact armies contributed to the other, even more dangerous, area of lost opportunity: the nuclear weapons race. Convinced of the Soviet menace to Western Europe and despairing of conventional defense for strategic as well as economic reasons, the United States put its trust in the threat of nuclear retaliation and the maintenance of a technological lead in nuclear weapons development. Time after time, the United States spurned opportunities to negotiate a halt to the race, as far back as Truman's decision to develop the hydrogen bomb (recently called into question by McGeorge Bundy). Unwilling to acknowledge in the fifties and sixties that the nuclear deterrent was being deterred by the Soviet pursuit of parity, the United States stressed development of tactical nuclear weapons and achievement of technical feats such as the MIRV to redress the military imbalance. On grounds of alleged inability to verify Soviet compliance, proposed curbs on nuclear testing were repeatedly resisted, delayed (when they could have been agreed upon in the late fifties), and ultimately qualified to allow underground testing to go on. The 1963 treaty was nevertheless a landmark in the possibilities of negotiation, and another was the antiballistic missile treaty of 1972.

In the eighties, the momentum of the arms race is paralyzing efforts at U.S.–Soviet accommodation. The pursuit by both sides of security in Europe through the deployment of intermediate-range nuclear missiles drives each side toward launch-on-warning strategies. The old chimera of technological superiority presents itself again to American policymakers in even more destabilizing proposals to develop antimissile and antisatellite systems for use in outer space. Meanwhile, the Soviet Union, in its costly but successful efforts to match American quality and quantity in the nuclear realm, has discovered for itself a certain sense of impunity as it outflanks NATO by way of its third-world gambits, while it is protected from retaliation by the threat of mutually assured destruction. The nuclear monster finds military and political interests on both sides ready to satisfy its appetite.

The conditions for successful negotiations with the Soviets, if there is a real desire to pursue them, are fairly clear from the record of past decades. First, there must be reasonable detachment from the political temptation to wave the bloody shirt (a tactic that seems to have met with diminishing returns in the New Cold War, as compared with the 1950s). Second, there must be a realistic awareness—repugnant as it may be—that the USSR will not countenance any challenge to its security zone in Eastern Europe, let alone to the legitimacy of its authority at home and in the minority republics. It will not yield on what it considers military parity, and it is unlikely to accept such drastic cuts in arms, whether nuclear or conventional, that its superpower status will be endangered. It is still prey to a nonnegotiable fear of China. However, the Soviet Union is much less deeply committed in its third-world alliance ventures and in its relations with foreign Communists outside the East European bloc. Except for its involvement in Afghanistan, it has been notably cautious in the Middle Eastern trouble zone in recent years. It has usually been ready (aside from the on-site inspection problem) to negotiate restraints on new arms developments and to reach agreements on reducing the risk of accidental war. Negotiations over "mutual balanced force reductions" in Europe have been going on for years. Furthermore, the Soviets are eager for expanded commercial relations—to the extent of constructing a lavish International Trade Center in Moscow, including a Hotel International that rivals luxury accommodations in the West. Given all these circumstances, the problem for the United States is one of flexibility: to recognize when and where a firm stand or a tempting bargain will induce the Soviet Union to alter course, and then to be able to change tactics in order to encourage Moscow in the positive direction. The sequence of events in the early sixties that initiated the era of détente is a demonstration that if agreement is desired, it is possible.

However frustrating the outside world may find the rigidity and immobility of Soviet thinking, these traits do not preclude external influence on the decisions of the Soviet leadership. The Kremlin, in its devious but pragmatic way, responds readily to the pressures, inducements, and opportunities offered by other countries—far more readily than its rhetoric usually suggests. Soviet policymakers seem less fixated on particular tactics than their American counterparts, who, having won a political consensus on a certain form of action, find it difficult to revise a policy even when it has become counterproductive. Containment was an instance of the way in which an adversary power can induce the Soviets to change course, as well as an example of how hard it is for U.S. leaders to shift gears to take advantage of the momentum when their own policy succeeds.

The lesson to be learned from decades of dealing with the Russians is that change is possible and that American policy can contribute to it, but that the pace of change may be so slow as to create the illusion that nothing can be done. For the time being, some form of arms-length bargaining for global stability seems the best that can be expected, until the Soviet Union can cure itself of the need for pseudorevolutionary confrontation. This places on the United States the burden of maintaining its side of the military balance without succumbing to the simplicities of ideological righteousness. Otherwise, the world may lose real and perhaps final opportunities to reduce the threat of nuclear war and bring the superpowers closer to a peaceful reconstruction of their relationship.

Suggested Readings

Since the Revolution, Russia has evoked one of the most extensive bodies of polemical, critical, and apologetic literature in modern history. In the English language alone (to which this listing is restricted) there is an embarrassment of riches on almost every facet of Russia, past and present. What readers need above all as they wade through the flood of print is some guide to the most important studies and representative viewpoints on the main issues of interpreting the Russian experience.

1. General Reference

There are several convenient encyclopedias and data handbooks on the Soviet Union and its history, including Archie Brown et al., eds., *The Cambridge Encyclopedia of Russia and the Soviet Union* (Cambridge: Cambridge University Press, 1982); Barbara P. McCrea, Jack C. Plano, and George Klein, eds., *The Soviet and East European Political Dictionary* (Santa Barbara, Calif.: Clio, 1984); John Paxton, ed., *Companion to Russian History* (New York: Facts on File, 1983); Paul S. Shoup, ed., *The East European and Soviet Data Handbook* (Stanford, Calif.: Hoover Institution, 1981); and C. D. Kernig, ed., *Marxism, Communism and Western Society: A Comparative Encyclopedia,* 8 vols. (New York: Herder & Herder, 1972–1973). For the most recent data, see *The Soviet Union: Domestic, Economic and Foreign Policy* (New York: Holmes & Meier, 1975 and succeeding years); and John L. Scherer, ed., *USSR: Facts and Figures Annual* (Gulf Breeze, Fla.: Academic International Press, 1977 and succeeding years). *The Great Soviet Encyclopedia,* 3rd ed., 32 vols., has been translated in full (New York: Macmillan, 1973–1982). Biographical data can be found in Institute for the Study of USSR (Munich), *Prominent Personalities in the USSR* (Metuchen, N.J.: Scarecrow Press, 1968); and idem, *Who Was Who in the USSR* (Metuchen, N.J.: Scarecrow Press, 1972).

The most convenient bibliographic guide is Paul Horecky, ed., *Russia and the Soviet Union: A Bibliographical Guide to Western Language Publications* (Chicago: University of Chicago Press, 1965). This volume is supplemented for more recent publications by the two volumes of Stephan M. Horak, *Russia, the USSR, and Eastern Europe: A Bibliographic Guide to English Language Publications, 1964–1974* and *1975–1980* (Littleton, Colo.: Libraries Unlimited, 1978, 1982). See also David L. Jones, *Books in English on the Soviet Union, 1917–1973: A Bibliography* (New York: Garland, 1975); and Anthony Thompson, *Russia/USSR: A Selective Annotated Bibliography of Books in English* (Santa Barbara, Calif.: Clio, 1979). More specialized are Thomas T. Hammond, *Soviet Foreign Relations and World Communism: A Selected Annotated Bibliography* (Princeton: Princeton University Press, 1965); and Stephan M. Horak, *Guide to the Study of the Soviet Nationalities: Non-Russian Peoples of the USSR* (Littleton, Colo.: Libraries Unlimited, 1982). All these may be supplemented for more recent work by the annual volumes of *The American Bibliography of Slavic and East European Studies* (Bloomington: Indiana University Press); and by *The European Bibliography of Soviet, East European and Slavonic Studies* (Birmingham, England: University of Birmingham, 1979). Two surveys of the development of Russian studies, still not superseded, are Anatol G. Mazour, *Modern Russian Historiography,* rev. ed. (Westport, Conn.: Greenwood, 1975; orig. pub. 1958); and Clarence A. Manning, *History of Slavic Studies in the U.S.* (Milwaukee: Marquette University Press, 1957). For a Soviet critique of American Soviet studies, see B. I. Marushkin, *History and Politics: American Historiography on Soviet Society* (Moscow: Progress Publishers, 1975).

On the geographic background see A. F. Chew, *An Atlas of Russian History* (New Haven: Yale University Press, 1970); Theodore Shabad, *Geography of the USSR: A Regional Survey* (New York: Columbia University Press, 1951); V. V. Pokshishevsky, *Geography of the Soviet Union* (Moscow: Progress Publishers, 1974); Roy Mellor, *The Soviet Union and Its Geographic Problem* (London: Macmillan, 1982); and Demitri Shimkin, *Minerals: A Key to Soviet Power* (Cambridge, Mass.: Harvard University Press, 1953). The ethnic makeup of the Soviet Union is surveyed in Frederick Barghoorn, *Soviet Russian Nationalism,* rev. ed. (Westport, Conn.: Greenwood, 1976; orig. pub. 1956); and in Zev Katz, R. Rogers, and F. Harned, eds., *Handbook of Major Soviet Nationalities* (New York: Free Press, 1975). Languages are described in R. G. A. De Bray, *Guide to the Slavonic Languages,* rev. ed., 3 vols. (Columbus, Ohio: Slavica, 1980); and in Bernard Comrie, *The Languages of the Soviet Union* (New York: Cambridge University Press, 1981). Population data are analyzed in Frank Lorimer, *The Population of the Soviet Union: History and Prospect* (Geneva: League of Nations, 1946); Ansley J. Coale et al., *Human Fertility in Russia since the Nineteenth Century* (Princeton, N.J.: Princeton University Press, 1979); and Iosif Dyadkin, *Unnatural Deaths in the USSR, 1928–1954* (New Brunswick, N.J.: Transaction Books, 1983).

Among the most useful journals dealing with Russian affairs are *The Slavic Review* (quarterly, Stanford, Calif.:); *The Russian Review* (quarterly, Cambridge, Mass.); *Canadian Slavonic Papers* (semiannual, Toronto); *The Slavonic and East European Review* (semiannual, London); *Soviet Studies* (quarterly, Birmingham, England); *Survey* (quarterly, London); and *Problems of Communism* (bimonthly, U.S. Information Agency, Washington, D.C.). Soviet news and journal articles are translated, in abstract or in full, in *The Current Digest of the Soviet Press* (weekly, Columbus, Ohio). Extremely useful for keeping current on the details of Soviet life and politics are *Radio Liberty Research Reports* and *Research Bulletin* (prepared weekly or more often in Munich and distributed from New York). Soviet publications in English include *New Times* (weekly), *World Marxist Review* (monthly), and *Soviet Life* (monthly).

2. Historical Surveys and Interpretations

There are numerous good textbooks on the history of Russia and the Soviet Union, but an outstanding one is Nicholas V. Riasanovsky, *A History of Russia,* 4th ed. (New York: Oxford University Press, 1984). Robert Auty and Dimitri Obolensky, eds., *An Introduction to Russian History* (New York: Columbia University Press, 1976), offers chapters by specialists on all periods. See also J. N. Westwood, *Endurance and Endeavor: Russian History, 1812–1980* (Oxford: Oxford University Press, 1981); and Joel Carmichael, *An Illustrated History of Russia* (New York: Reynal, 1960). The Soviet view is available in A. P. Nenarokov, ed., *History of the USSR,* 3 vols. (Moscow: Progress Publishers, 1977).

A detailed survey of Russia to 1917 is Michael T. Florinsky, *Russia: A History and an Interpretation,* 2 vols. (New York: Macmillan, 1954). The exhaustive treatment planned by George Vernadsky and Michael Karpovich, *A History of Russia,* actually extended to five volumes by Vernadsky reaching to the seventeenth century (New Haven: Yale University Press, 1943–1969). Important prerevolutionary histories by Russians include: Sergei M. Soloviev, *History of Russia,* 35 vols. to date (Gulf Breeze, Fla.: Academic International Press, 1976; orig. Russian ed. 1864); Vasili O. Kliuchevsky, *A Course in Russian History,* 5 vols. (Chicago: Quadrangle, 1968; orig. Russian ed. 1904–1910); Paul M. Miliukov, Charles Seignobos, and L. Eisenmann, *History of Russia,* 3 vols. (New York: Funk & Wagnalls, 1968–1969; orig. French ed. 1932–1933); and for the Marxists, Mikhail N. Pokrovsky, *Brief History of Russia,* 2 vols. (Gulf Breeze, Fla.: Academic International Press, 1968; orig. Russian ed. 1920). Soviet views of prerevolutionary history are presented in Cyril E. Black, ed., *Rewriting Russian History: Soviet Interpretations* (New York: Praeger, 1956). An extensive collection of prerevolutionary primary sources is George Vernadsky et al., eds., *A Source Book for Russian History from Early Times to 1917,* 3 vols. (New Haven: Yale University Press, 1972).

Economic and social history are surveyed in Peter I. Lyashchenko, *History of the National Economy of Russia to the 1917 Revolution* (New York: Octagon, 1970; orig. Russian ed. 1939); James Mavor, *An Economic History of Russia,* 2 vols. (New York: Russell & Russell, 1965; orig. pub. 1914); and William L. Blackwell, ed., *Russia's Economic Development from Peter the Great to Stalin* (New York: New York University Press, 1975).

Special interpretations spanning imperial and Soviet times include Ernest J. Simmons, ed., *Continuity and Change in Russian and Soviet Thought* (New York: Russell & Russell, 1967; orig. pub. 1955); Cyril E. Black, ed., *The Transformation of Russian Society: Aspects of Social Change since 1861* (Cambridge, Mass.: Harvard University Press, 1960); James H. Billington, *The Icon and the Axe: An Interpretive History of Russian Culture* (New York: Random House, 1970); Adam B. Ulam, *Russia's Failed Revolutions: From the Decembrists to the Dissidents* (New York: Basic Books, 1981); Walter M. Pintner and Don K. Rowney, eds., *Russian*

Officialdom: The Bureaucratization of Russian Society from the Seventeenth to the Twentieth Century (Chapel Hill: University of North Carolina Press, 1980); and Ronald Hingley, *The Russian Secret Police: Muscovite, Imperial Russian, and Soviet Political Security Operations, 1565–1970* (New York: Simon and Schuster, 1970).

Convenient collections of primary sources and other readings are Basil Dmytryshyn, *Medieval Russia, Imperial Russia, and Soviet Russia,* 3 vols. (Hinsdale, Ill.: Dryden, 1973); and Alfred E. Senn, ed., *Readings in Russian Political and Diplomatic History,* 2 vols. (Homewood, Ill.: Dorsey, 1966).

3. Early Russia

Important works on the various phases and features of Russian history up to 1800 are noted here chronologically.

a. *Ancient and Medieval.* Omeljan Pritsak, *The Origin of Russia,* vol. 1 (Cambridge, Mass.: Harvard University Press, 1980); Samuel H. Cross, *Slavic Civilization through the Ages* (New York: Russell & Russell, 1968; orig. pub. 1948); Boris D. Grekov, *The Culture of Kievan Russia* (New York: Gordon, 1977; orig. Russian ed. 1944); John Fennell, *The Crisis of Medieval Russia, 1200–1304* (London: Holden, 1983); John Meyendorff, *Byzantium and the Rise of Russia* (New York: Cambridge University Press, 1981); and Jerome Blum: *Lord and Peasant in Russia from the Ninth to the Nineteenth Century* (Princeton: Princeton University Press, 1961).

b. *Muscovy.* A. E. Presniakov, *The Formation of the Great Russian State* (Chicago: University of Chicago Press, 1970; orig. Russian ed. 1918); John Fennell, *Ivan the Great of Moscow* (New York: St. Martin's, 1961); Baron Sigismund von Herberstein, *Notes upon Russia* (New York: Burt Franklin, 1965; orig. Latin ed. 1549); Robert I. Vipper, *Ivan Grozny* [a sympathetic Soviet biography of Ivan IV, The Terrible] (Moscow: Foreign Languages Publishing House, 1947; orig. Russian ed. 1922); Bjarne Nörretranders, *The Shaping of Czardom under Ivan Groznyj* (Copenhagen: Munksgaard, 1964); Alexander Yanov, *The Origins of Autocracy: Ivan the Terrible in Russian History* [an argument by an émigré historian that Ivan turned Russia away from the Western path] (Berkeley: University of California Press, 1981); Richard Hellie, *Enserfment and Military Change in Muscovy* (Chicago: University of Chicago Press, 1971); Sergei F. Platonov, *Time of Troubles: A Historical Study of the Internal Crisis and Social Struggle in Sixteenth and Seventeenth Century Muscovy* (Lawrence: University of Kansas Press, 1970; orig. Russian ed. 1924); Ruslan G. Skrynnikov, *Boris Godunov* (Gulf Breeze, Fla.: Academic International Press, 1983; orig. Russian ed. 1978); Paul Dukes, *The Making of Russian Absolutism, 1613–1801* (London: Holden, 1983); J. M. Hittle, *The Service City: State and Townsmen in Russia, 1600–1800* (Cambridge, Mass.: Harvard University Press, 1979).

c. *The Eighteenth Century.* Marc Raeff, *Imperial Russia, 1682–1825* (New York: Knopf, 1971); B. H. Sumner, *Peter the Great and the Emergence of Russia* (London: Macmillan, 1962; orig. pub. 1940); Robert K. Massie, *Peter the Great* (New York: Knopf, 1980); L. Jay Oliva, *Russia in the Era of Peter the Great* (Englewood Cliffs, N.J.: Prentice-Hall, 1969); Brenda Meehan-Waters, *Autocracy and Aristocracy: The Russian Service Elite of 1730* (New Brunswick, N.J.: Rutgers University Press, 1982); Isabel de Madariaga, *Russia in the Age of Catherine the Great* (New Haven: Yale University Press, 1981); Hans Rogger, *National Consciousness in Eighteenth-Century Russia* (Cambridge, Mass.: Harvard University Press, 1960); John Alexander, *Emperor of the Cossacks: Pugachev and the Frontier Jacquerie of 1773-1775* (Lawrence: University of Kansas Press, 1973); Paul Avrich, *Russian Rebels, 1600-1800* (New York: Norton, 1976).

4. The Nineteenth Century

Nineteenth-century Russia has been the subject of a great many American studies, as well as translations of Soviet and other works. Some important books on political themes are: W. Bruce Lincoln, *The Romanovs: Autocrats of All the Russias* (New York: Dial, 1981); Richard Pipes, *Russia under the Old Regime* (New York: Scribner's, 1974); Charles A. Ruud, *Fighting Words: Imperial Censorship and the Russian Press, 1804-1906* (Toronto: University of Toronto Press, 1982); Daniel T. Orlovsky, *The Limit of Reform: The Ministry of Internal Affairs in Imperial Russia, 1807-1881* (Cambridge, Mass.: Harvard University Press, 1980); Allen McConnell, *Tsar Alexander I: Paternalistic Reformer* (New York: Crowell, 1970); Marc Raeff, *Michael Speransky: Statesman of Imperial Russia* (Westport, Conn.: Hyperion, 1980: orig. pub. 1957); Eugene Tarlé, *Napoleon's Invasion of Russia* [by a Soviet historian representing the new nationalism] (New York: Octagon, 1970; orig. Russian ed. 1938); Phyllis P. Kohler, ed., *Custine's Eternal Russia: A New Edition of Journey for Our Time* [the journals of the Marquis de Custine] (Miami: University of Miami Press, 1976; orig. French ed. 1843); Edward Crankshaw, *The Shadow of the Winter Palace: Russia's Drift to Revolution, 1825-1917* (New York: Viking, 1976); Nicholas V. Riasanovsky, *Nicholas I and Official Nationality in Russia, 1825-1855* (Berkeley: University of California Press, 1959); Sidney Monas, *The Third Section: Police and Society under Nicholas I* (Cambridge, Mass.: Harvard University Press, 1961); S. Frederick Starr, *Decentralization and Self-Government in Russia, 1830-1870* (Princeton: Princeton University Press, 1972); Hugh Seton-Watson, *The Decline of Imperial Russia, 1855-1914* (New York: Praeger, 1952); Norman G. O. Pereira, *Tsar-Liberator: Alexander II of Russia* (Newtonville, Mass.: Oriental Research Parners, 1983); Peter A. Zaionchkovsky, *The Abolition of Serfdom in Russia* [by a major Soviet historian] (Gulf Breeze, Fla.: Academic International Press, 1978); Donald Mackenzie Wallace, *Russia on the Eve of War and Revolution* [a classic British traveler's account] (Princeton: Princeton University Press, 1984; orig. pub. 1877); Richard S. Wortman, *The Development of a Russian Legal Consciousness* (Chicago: University of Chicago Press, 1976); Heide Whelan, *Alexander III and the State Council: Bureaucracy and Counter-reform in Late Imperial Russia* (New Brunswick, N.J.: Rutgers University Press, 1982); Hans Rogger, *Russia in the Age of Modernization and Revolution* (New York: Longman, 1983).

Economic and social developments in the nineteenth and early twentieth centuries are addressed in Alexander Gershenkron, *Economic Backwardness in Historical Perspective: A Book of Essays* (Cambridge, Mass.: Harvard University Press, 1962); William L. Blackwell, *The Industrialization of Russia: An Historic*

Perspective (Arlington Heights, Ill.: Harlan Davidson, 1982); M. I. Tugan-Baranovsky, *The Russian Factory in the Nineteenth Century* (Homewood, Ill.: Dorsey, 1970; German ed. 1900); Theodore H. von Laue, *Sergei White and the Industrialization of Russia* (New York: Columbia University Press, 1963); John P. McKay, *Pioneers for Profit: Foreign Entrepreneurship and Russian Industrialization, 1885-1913* (Chicago: Chicago University Press, 1970); Daniel Field, *The End of Serfdom: Nobility and Bureaucracy in Russia, 1855-1861* (Cambridge, Mass.: Harvard University Press, 1976); Terrence Emmons, *The Russian Landed Gentry and the Peasant Emancipation of 1861* (Cambridge: Cambridge University Press, 1968); Roberta Manning, *The Crisis of the Old Order in Russia: Gentry and Government* (Princeton: Princeton University Press, 1982); Wayne S. Vucinich, ed., *The Peasant in Nineteenth Century Russia* (Stanford, Calif.: Stanford University Press, 1968); Geroid T. Robinson, *Rural Russia under the Old Regime* (New York: Longmans, Green, 1932); Donald W. Treadgold, *The Great Siberian Migration: Government and Peasant in Resettlement from Emancipation to the First World War* (Princeton: Princeton University Press, 1957); Cyril E. Black, "The Nature of Imperial Russian Society," *Slavic Review* 20 (December 1961): 656–600.

5. Prerevolutionary Thought and the Revolutionary Movement

The topic of Russian political and social thought and its relation to the Revolution has been studied exhaustively in the West. The most important overviews include Thomas G. Masaryk, *The Spirit of Russia*, 2 vols. [Masaryk was the first president of Czechoslovakia] (London: Allen & Unwin, 1919; orig. German ed. 1913); Nicholas Berdyaev, *The Russian Idea* [by an eminent émigré philosopher] (Boston: Beacon, 1962; orig. Russian ed. 1946); Ronald Hingley, *The Russian Mind* (New York: Scribner's, 1979); V. V. Zenkovsky, *A History of Russian Philosophy* 2 vols. [by an émigré philosopher] (New York: Columbia University Press, 1953); and Isaiah Berlin, *Russian Thinkers* (New York: Viking, 1978).

On more specific intellectual topics, the following are valuable: Marc Raeff, *Origins of the Russian Intelligentsia: The Eighteenth Century Nobility* (New York: Harcourt, Brace, Jovanovich, 1966); Philip Pomper, *The Russian Revolutionary Intelligentsia* (New York: Crowell, 1970); Richard Pipes, ed., *The Russian Intelligentsia* (New York: Columbia University Press, 1961); Richard Hare, *Pioneers of Russian Social Thought* (New York: Vintage, 1964); Franco Venturi, *Roots of Revolution: A History of the Populist and Socialist Movements in Nineteenth Century Russia* (New York: Knopf, 1960; orig. Italian ed. 1952); Alexander S. Vucinich, *Social Thought in Tsarist Russia: The Quest for a General Science of Society, 1861-1917* (Chicago: University of Chicago Press, 1976).

Representative works by or on particular thinkers and revolutionary groups include: Boris Menshutkin, *Russia's Lomonosov: Chemist, Courtier, Physicist, Poet* (Princeton: Princeton University Press, 1952; orig. Russian ed. 1937); D. M. Lang, *The First Russian Radical: Alexander Radishchev, 1749-1802* (Westport, Conn.: Greenwood, 1979; orig. pub. 1959); Alexander Radishchev, *Journey from St. Petersburg to Moscow* (Cambridge, Mass.: Harvard University Press, 1958); Anatol Mazour, *The First Russian Revolution, 1825: The Decembrist Movement* (Stanford, Calif.: Stanford University Press, 1937); Mikhail Zetlin, *The Decembrists* (New

York: International University Press, 1958; orig. Russian ed. 1933); Nicholas V. Riasanovsky, *Russia and the West in the Teachings of the Slavophiles* (Magnolia, Mass.: Peter Smith, n.d.; orig. pub. 1952); Martin Malia, *Alexander Herzen and the Birth of Russian Socialism* (Cambridge, Mass.: Harvard University Press, 1961); Alexander Herzen, *My Past and Thoughts*, 6 vols. (Berkeley: University of California Press, 1982; first complete Russian ed. 1921); Paul Avrich, *The Russian Anarchists* (Westport, Conn.: Greenwood, 1980; orig. pub. 1967); E. H. Carr, *Michael Bakunin* (New York: Octagon, 1975; orig. pub. 1937); Arthur P. Mendel, *Michael Bakunin: Roots of Apocalypse* (New York: Praeger, 1981); Isaiah Berlin, *The Hedgehog and the Fox: An Essay on Tolstoy's View of History* (New York: Simon and Schuster, 1953); George Fischer, *Russian Liberalism* (Cambridge, Mass.: Harvard University Press, 1958); Abbott Gleason, *Young Russia: The Genesis of Russian Radicalism in the 1860s* (New York: Viking, 1980); Nikolai Chernyshevsky, *What Is to Be Done?* [a revolutionary novel that had a great impact on Lenin] (New York: Vintage, 1961; orig. Russian ed. 1863); Philip Pomper, *Sergei Nechaev* (New Brunswick, N.J.: Rutgers University Press, 1979); idem, *Peter Lavrov and the Historical Letters* (Chicago: University of Chicago Press, 1972); David Footman, *Red Prelude* [on the People's Will terrorists] (Westport, Conn.: Hyperion, 1980; orig. pub. 1945); Robert F. Byrnes, *Pobedonostsev: His Life and Thought* (Bloomington: Indiana University Press, 1968); James Billington, *Mikhailovsky and Russian Populism* (Oxford: Clarendon Press, 1958); Peter A. Kropotkin, *Memoirs of a Revolutionist* (Magnolia, Mass.: Peter Smith, 1967; orig. pub. 1899); Albert L. Weeks, *The First Bolshevik: A Political Biography of Peter Tkachev* (New York: New York University Press, 1968); Jeremiah Schneiderman, *Sergei Zubatov and Revolutionary Marxism* (Ithaca: Cornell University Press, 1976); George Kennan, *Siberia and the Exile System* (New York: Russell & Russell, 1970; orig. pub. 1891).

For an introduction to Marxism see Edmund Wilson, *To the Finland Station* (London: Macmillan, 1972; orig. pub. 1940); Jerrold Seigel, *Marx's Fate: The Shape of a Life* (Princeton: Princeton University Press, 1978); David McLelland, *Marxism after Marx* (New York: Harper & Row, 1979); Robert C. Tucker, *The Marxian Revolutionary Idea* (New York: Norton, 1969); Lewis S. Feuer, ed., *Marx and Engels: Basic Writings on Politics and Philosophy* (New York: Anchor, 1959); Robert V. Daniels, *Marxism and Communism: Essential Readings* (New York: Random House, 1965); Alfred G. Meyer, *Marxism since the Manifesto* (Washington, D.C.: American Historical Association Service Center for Teachers of History, 1961). An encyclopedic survey is G. D. H. Cole, *History of Socialist Thought*, 5 vols. (London: Macmillan, 1953–1960). On the development of the Marxist movement in Russia see John L. H. Keep, *The Rise of Social Democracy in Russia* (New York: Oxford University Press, 1963); Allan Wildman, *The Making of a Workers' Revolution: Russian Social Democracy, 1891–1903* (Chicago: University of Chicago Press, 1967); Samuel H. Baron, *Plekhanov: The Father of Russian Marxism* (Stanford, Calif.: Stanford University Press, 1963); Georgi Plekhanov, *Fundamental Problems of Marxism* (New York: Beekman, 1962); Arthur P. Mendel, *Dilemmas of Progress in Tsarist Russia: Legal Marxism and Legal Populism* (Cambridge, Mass.: Harvard University Press, 1961); Richard Pipes, *Struve: Liberal on the Left, 1870–1905* (Cambridge, Mass.: Harvard University Press, 1970); idem, *Struve: Liberal on the Right, 1905–1944* (Cambridge, Mass.: Harvard University Press, 1980); Israel Getzler, *Martov: A Political Biography of a Russian Social-Democrat* (Cambridge, Mass.: Harvard University Press, 1967); Robert J. Brym, *The Jewish Intelligentsia and Russian Marxism* (New York: Schocken, 1978).

Important works on the rise of Bolshevism and the principal Bolshevik leaders include: Leopold Haimson, *The Russian Marxists and the Origins of Bolshevism* (Cambridge, Mass.: Harvard University Press, 1955); Theodore Dan, *The Origins of Bolshevism* [a translation of a work by a Menshevik émigré] (London: Secker & Warburg, 1964); Alain Besançon, *The Rise of the Gulag: Intellectual Origins of Leninism* (New York: Continuum Books, 1981; orig. French ed. 1977); Neil Harding, *Lenin's Political Thought: Theory and Practice in the Democratic and Socialist Revolutions* (London: Macmillan, 1983); Alfred G. Meyer, *Leninism* (Cambridge, Mass.: Harvard University Press, 1957); Bertram D. Wolfe, *Three Who Made a Revolution* [on Lenin, Trotsky, and Stalin to 1914] (New York: Dial, 1948); Donald W. Treadgold, *Lenin and His Rivals* (New York: Praeger, 1955); Adam B. Ulam, *The Bolsheviks* [a biography of Lenin] (New York: Macmillan, 1968); Louis Fischer, *The Life of Lenin* (New York: Harper & Row, 1964); Stefan Possony, *Lenin: The Compulsive Revolutionary* (Chicago: Regnery, 1964); V. I. Lenin, *Collected Works* (Moscow: Progress Publishers, 1975; most reliable Russian ed. 1928–1937); Isaac Deutscher, *The Prophet Armed: Trotsky, 1897–1921* (New York: Oxford University Press, 1954); idem, *The Prophet Unarmed: Trotsky, 1921–1929* (New York: Oxford University Press, 1959); idem, *The Prophet Outcast: Trotsky, 1929–1940* (New York: Oxford University Press, 1963); Baruch Knei-Paz, *The Social and Political Thought of Leon Trotsky* (New York: Oxford University Press, 1978); Leon Trotsky, *Our Revolution* (Westport, Conn.: Hyperion, 1974; orig. pub. 1918); Leon Trotsky, *My Life* (New York: Pathfinder, 1970; orig. pub. 1930); Isaac Deutscher, *Stalin: A Political Biography* (New York: Oxford University Press, 1948); Edward E. Smith, *The Young Stalin: The Early Years of an Elusive Revolutionary* (New York: Farrar, Straus and Giroux, 1967); Adam B. Ulam, *Stalin: The Man and His Era* (New York: Viking, 1973); Robert C. Tucker, *Stalin as a Revolutionary* (New York: Norton, 1973); Stephen F. Cohen, *Bukharin and the Bolshevik Revolution* (New York: Knopf, 1973).

6. Cultural Background

There are good books to introduce the reader to all the various aspects of Russian culture. A broad introduction to religion, literature, and the arts is Paul Miliukov, *Outlines of Russian Culture,* 3 vols. (Gulf Breeze, Fla.: Academic International Press, 1975; orig. Russian ed. 1896–1903). For the visual arts, see Robert Auty and Dimitri Obolensky, eds., *Introduction to Russian Art and Architecture* (New York: Cambridge University Press, 1980); and for music, James Bakst, *A History of Russian-Soviet Music* (Westport, Conn.: Greenwood, 1977). Scientific work is surveyed in Alexander S. Vucinich, *Science in Russian Culture,* 2 vols. (Stanford, Calif.: Stanford University Press, 1963, 1970); and the history of education is treated in James C. McClelland, *Autocrats and Academics: Education, Culture, and Society in Tsarist Russia* (Chicago: University of Chicago Press, 1979). I have made no attempt here to cover the vast amount of writing on Russian literature;

one of the many good surveys is Marc Slonim, *An Outline of Russian Literature* (New York: Oxford University Press, 1958).

On the Orthodox Church, see G. P. Fedotov, *The Russian Religious Mind,* 2 vols. (Belmont, Mass.: Nordland, 1976; orig. pub. 1946); Robert L. Nichols and T. G. Stavrou, eds., *Russian Orthodoxy under the Old Regime* (Minneapolis: University of Minnesota Press, 1978); and John S. Curtiss, *Church and State in Russia, 1900-1917* (New York: Octagon, 1965; orig. pub. 1940).

Representative works on national minorities include: Mikhail S. Hrushevsky, *History of the Ukraine* (New Haven: Yale University Press, 1941); Richard Pierce, *Russian Central Asia, 1867-1917* (Berkeley: University of California Press, 1960); Jonathan Frankel, *Prophecy and Politics: Socialism, Nationalism, and the Russian Jews, 1867-1917* (New York: Cambridge University Press, 1981); Eugene M. Kulischer, *Jewish Migration: Past Experiences and Post-War Prospects* (New York: American Jewish Committee, 1943); Nicholas Vakar, *Belorussia: The Making of a Nation* (Cambridge, Mass.: Harvard University Press, 1956); Edward C. Thaden, ed., *Russification in the Baltic Provinces and Finland, 1855-1914* (Princeton: Princeton University Press, 1981); David M. Lang, *The Georgians* (New York: Praeger, 1966); and idem, *Armenia: Cradle of Civilization* (London: Allen & Unwin, 1980).

7. Prerevolutionary Foreign Relations

Russia's foreign relations before and since the Revolution are treated in Ivo Lederer, ed., *Russian Foreign Policy: Essays in Historical Perspective* (New Haven: Yale University Press, 1962). Russian-American relations are surveyed in Thomas A. Bailey, *America Faces Russia: Russian-American Relations from Early Times to Our Day* (Magnolia, Mass.: Peter Smith, 1964; orig. pub. 1950); and William A. Williams, *American-Russian Relations, 1781-1947* (New York: Octagon, 1971; orig. pub. 1952).

More specialized books on Russian foreign relations before the Revolution include: Robert J. Kerner, *The Urge to the Sea* (New York: Russell & Russell, 1971; orig. pub. 1942); Sergei F. Platonov, *Moscow and the West* (Hattiesburg, Miss.: Academic International, 1972; orig. Russian ed. 1926); Barbara Jelavich, *A Century of Russian Foreign Policy, 1814-1914* (Philadelphia: Lippincott, 1964); Andrei Lobanov-Rostovsky, *Russia and Europe,* 2 vols. (Westport, Conn.: Greenwood, 1968; orig. pub. 1947 and 1951); John Langdon-Davies. *The Crimean War* (New York: Viking, 1968); Hans Kohn, *Pan-Slavism: Its History and Ideology* (Philadelphia: Porcupine, n.d.; orig. pub. 1953); William L. Langer, *The Franco-Russian Alliance, 1890-1894* (New York: Octagon, 1967; orig. pub. 1929); David V. Dallin, *The Rise of Russia in Asia* (New Haven: Yale University Press, 1949); D. C. B. Lieven, *Russia and the Origins of the First World War* (New York: St. Martin's, 1984).

Works dealing with Russian-American relations up to 1917 include: Nikolai N. Bolkhovitnikov, *The Beginnings of Russian-American Relations, 1775-1815* [translation of a work by the leading Soviet expert in this field] (Cambridge, Mass.: Harvard University Press, 1976); Nina N. Bashkina et al., eds., *The U.S. and Russia: The Beginning of Relations, 1765-1815* [a volume in the joint U.S.–Soviet documentary publishing project] (Washington, D.C.: U.S. Government

Printing Office, 1980); Max H. Laserson, *The American Impact on Russia: Diplomatic and Ideological, 1784-1917* (New York: Macmillan, 1950); Frank A. Golder, *Russian Expansion on the Pacific, 1641-1850* (New York: Paragon Reprints, 1971; orig. pub. 1914); Howard I. Kushner, *Conflict on the Northwest Coast: American-Russian Rivalry in the Pacific Northwest* (Westport, Conn.: Greenwood, 1975); S. B. Okun, *The Russian-American Company* (New York: Octagon, 1979; orig. Russian ed. 1939); Henry Winter Davis, *The War of Ormuzd and Ahriman in the 19th Century* (Baltimore: Waters, 1837); Hans Rogger, "Russia and the Civil War," in Harold Hyman, ed., *Heard Round the World: The Impact Abroad of the Civil War* (New York: Knopf, 1969); Frank A. Golder, "The Russian Fleet and the Civil War," *American Historical Review* 20 (July 1915): 801–814; Benson L. Grayson, *Russian-American Relations in World War I* (New York: Ungar, 1979); Ann E. Healy, "Tsarist Anti-Semitism and Russian-American Relations," *Slavic Review* 42 (Fall 1983): 408–425.

8. The Early Twentieth Century

The immediate prerevolutionary era in Russia has always been a subject of fascination for both writers and readers of history. Several works describe the Revolution of 1905, including Sidney Harcave, *First Blood: The Russian Revolution of 1905* (London: Bodley Head, 1964); Solomon M. Schwarz, *The Russian Revolution of 1905* (Chicago: University of Chicago Press, 1967); Paul Miliukov, *Russia and Its Crisis* (Chicago: University of Chicago Press, 1905); Howard D. Mehlinger and John M. Thompson, *Count Witte and the Tsarist Government in the 1905 Revolution* (Bloomington: Indiana University Press, 1972).

For politics between 1905 and 1917 see Harrison Salisbury, *Black Night, White Snow: Russia's Revolutions, 1905–1917* (New York: Doubleday, 1978); Robert K. Massie, *Nicholas and Alexandra* (New York: Atheneum, 1967); Mary Schaeffer Conroy, *P. A. Stolypin: Practical Politics in Late Tsarist Russia* (Boulder, Colo.: Westview, 1976); Alexander De Jonge, *The Life and Times of Grigorii Rasputin* (New York: Coward, 1982); William Gleason, *Alexander Guchkov and the End of the Russian Empire* (Philadelphia: American Philosophical Society, 1983); and Arno Mayer, *The Persistence of the Old Regime* (New York: Pantheon, 1981).

Society and thought on the eve of the Revolution are dealt with in W. Bruce Lincoln, *In War's Dark Shadow: The Russians before the Great War* (New York: Dial, 1983); Christopher Read, *Religion, Revolution and the Russian Intelligentsia, 1900-1912: The Vekhi Debate and Its Intellectual Background* (New York: Barnes and Noble, 1980); Boris Shragin and Albert Todd, eds., *Landmarks: A Collection of Essays on the Russian Intelligentsia* (New York: Karz Howard, 1977; orig. Russian ed. 1909); and Leopold Haimson, "The Problem of Social Stability in Urban Russia, 1905–1917," *Slavic Review* 23 (December 1964): 619–642, and 24 (March 1965): 1–24.

9. The Revolution

The classic work on the Revolution is William Henry Chamberlin, *The Russian Revolution, 1917-1921,* 2 vols. (New York: Macmillan, 1935). Edward Hallett

Carr, *The Bolshevik Revolution,* 3 vols. (New York: Macmillan, 1950–1953), is part of an exhaustive multivolume series entitled *History of Soviet Russia.* For a social history of the Revolution see Marc Ferro, *The Russian Revolution of February, 1917* (Englewood Cliffs, N.J.: Prentice-Hall, 1972; orig. French ed. 1967); and idem, *October, 1917: A Social History of the Russian Revolution* (London: Routledge & Kegan Paul, 1980; orig. French ed. 1976). John Thompson, *Revolutionary Russia, 1917* (New York: Scribner's, 1981), is a brief survey. P. N. Sobolev et al., eds., *History of the October Revolution* (Moscow: Progress Publishers, 1966), presents the Soviet view of 1917. Various interpretive essays are included in Richard Pipes, ed., *Revolutionary Russia* (Cambridge, Mass.: Harvard University Press, 1968); and Ralph Carter Elwood, *Reconsiderations on the Russian Revolution* (Columbus, Ohio: Slavica, 1976). For source materials see Robert P. Browder and Alexander F. Kerensky, eds., *The Russian Provisional Government, 1917: Documents,* 3 vols. (Stanford, Calif.: Stanford University Press, 1961); Robert V. Daniels, ed., *The Russian Revolution* (Englewood Cliffs, N.J.: Prentice-Hall, 1972); Z. A. B. Zeman, ed., *Germany and the Revolution in Russia, 1915–1918* (New York: Oxford University Press, 1958); James Bunyan and Harold H. Fisher, eds., *The Bolshevik Revolution, 1917–1918: Documents* (Stanford, Calif.: Stanford University Press, 1934); James Bunyan, ed., *Intervention, Civil War, and Communism in Russia, April–December, 1918: Documents* (New York: Octagon, 1973; orig. pub. 1936); and Martin McCauley, ed., *The Russian Revolution and the Soviet State, 1917–1921: Documents* (New York: Barnes and Noble, 1975).

Important comparative works bearing on the Russian Revolution include: Lyford P. Edwards, *The Natural History of Revolution* (Chicago: University of Chicago Press, 1970: orig. pub. 1927); Crane Brinton, *The Anatomy of Revolution,* rev. ed. (New York: Random House, 1965; orig. pub. 1952); Hannah Arendt, *On Revolution* (Harmondsworth: Penguin, 1977; orig. pub. 1963); idem, *The Origins of Totalitarianism* (New York: Harcourt, Brace, 1968; orig. pub. 1951); Dennis Brogan, *The Price of Revolution* (London: Hamilton, 1951); and Jonathan R. Adelman, *The Revolutionary Armies* (Westport, Conn.: Greenwood, 1980).

Successive episodes of the Revolution are treated in Bernard Pares, *The Fall of the Russian Monarchy: A Study of the Evidence* (New York: Knopf, 1939); Tsuyoshi Hasegawa, *The February Revolution: Petrograd, 1917* (Seattle: University of Washington Press, 1981): George Katkov, *Russia, 1917: The February Revolution* (Westport, Conn.: Greenwood, 1979; orig. pub. 1967); Paul Miliukov, *History of the Second Russian Revolution* (Gulf Breeze, Fla.: American International Press, 1978); William G. Rosenberg, *Liberals in the Russian Revolution: The Constitutional Democratic Party, 1917–1921* (Princeton: Princeton University Press, 1974); Oscar Anweiler, *The Soviets: The Russian Workers, Peasants and Soldiers Councils* (New York: Pantheon, 1974; orig. German ed. 1958); David Mandel, *The Petrograd Workers and the Fall of the Old Regime,* and idem, *The Petrograd Workers and the Soviet Seizure of Power* (New York: St. Martin's, 1984); Diane Koenker, *Moscow Workers and the 1917 Revolution* (Princeton: Princeton University Press, 1981); Allan Wildman, *The End of the Russian Imperial Army: The Old Army and the Soldiers' Revolt, March–April 1917* (Princeton: Princeton University Press, 1979); George Katkov, *The Kornilov Affair—Russia 1917: Kerensky and the Breakup of the Russian Army* (London: Longmans, 1980); John L. H.

Keep, *The Russian Revolution: A Study in Mass Mobilization* (New York: Norton, 1977); Graeme J. Gill, *Peasants and Government in the Russian Revolution* (New York: Barnes and Noble, 1979); Alexander Rabinowitch, *Prelude to Revolution: The Petrograd Bolsheviks and the July 1917 Uprising* (Bloomington: Indiana University Press, 1968); idem, *The Bolsheviks Come to Power: The Revolution of 1917 in Petrograd* (New York: Norton, 1976); Robert V. Daniels, *Red October: The Bolshevik Revolution of 1917* (Boston: Beacon, 1984; orig. pub. 1967); S. P. Melgunov, *The Bolshevik Seizure of Power* [translation of an émigré work] (Santa Barbara, Calif.: Clio, 1972; orig. Russian ed. 1953); Roy A. Medvedev, *The October Revolution* [a Soviet dissident work] (New York: Columbia University Press, 1979; orig. Russian ed. 1976); John Reed, *Ten Days That Shook the World* (Harmondsworth: Penguin, 1979; orig. pub. 1919); Robert A. Rosenstone, *Romantic Revolutionary: A Biography of John Reed* (New York: Knopf, 1975).

Memoir accounts of the Revolution include Paul Miliukov, *Political Memoirs, 1905-1917* (Ann Arbor: University of Michigan Press, 1967; orig. Russian ed. 1955); Alexander Kerensky, *Russia and History's Turning Point* (New York: Duell, Sloan and Pierce, 1965); Victor Chernov, *The Great Russian Revolution* [by the Socialist Revolutionary leader] (New York: Russell & Russell, 1966; orig. pub. 1936); N. N. Sukhanov, *The Russian Revolution of 1917* [an abridged translation of a famous Menshevik eyewitness record] (Princeton: Princeton University Press, 1984; orig. Russian ed. 1922–1923); Leon Trotsky, *The History of the Russian Revolution* (Ann Arbor: University of Michigan Press, 1957; orig. pub. 1932); Anton Denikin, *The White Army* [by the famous White general] (Gulf Breeze, Fla.: Academic International Press, 1973; orig. pub. 1930); Dmitri von Mohrenschildt, ed., *The Russian Revolution of 1917: Contemporary Accounts* (New York: Oxford University Press, 1971).

The Revolution in the minority areas is treated in John S. Reshetar, *The Ukrainian Revolution, 1917–1920* (Bala Cynwyd, Pa.: Ayer, 1972; orig. pub. 1952); Michael Palij, *The Anarchism of Nestor Makhno, 1918–1921* (Seattle: University of Washington Press, 1976); Clarence Jay Smith, *Finland and the Russian Revolution* (Athens, Ga.: University of Georgia Press, 1958); and Firuz Kazem-Zadeh, *The Struggle for Transcaucasia* (New York: Philosophical Library, 1951).

10. History of the Soviet Period

The most exhaustive history of the Soviet period is Edward Hallett Carr, *A History of Soviet Russia,* 9 vols. (New York: Macmillan, various years). This work includes *The Bolshevik Revolution,* 3 vols. (1951–1953); *The Interregnum* (1954); *Socialism in One Country,* 3 vols. (1958–1960); and, written with R. W. Davies, *Foundations of a Planned Economy,* 2 vols. (1969). The last is continued in R. W. Davies, *The Industrialization of Soviet Russia,* 2 vols. (Cambridge, Mass.: Harvard University Press, 1980).

Other surveys and interpretations include: Charles Bettelheim, *Class Struggles in the USSR,* 2 vols. (New York: Monthly Review Press, 1976, 1978; orig. French ed. 1974); E. H. Carr, *The Russian Revolution from Lenin to Stalin* (New York: Free Press, 1979); Robert V. Daniels, *The Nature of Communism* (New York: Random House, 1962); Basil Dmytryshyn, *USSR: A Concise History,* rev. ed.

[with documents, including Khrushchev's 1956 secret speech] (New York: Scribner's, 1981); Merle Fainsod, *How Russia Is Ruled,* rev. ed. (Cambridge, Mass.: Harvard University Press, 1963; orig. pub. 1953); Sheila Fitzpatrick, *The Russian Revolution, 1917–1932* (New York: Oxford University Press, 1982); Carl J. Friedrich and Zbigniew K. Brzezinski, *Totalitarian Dictatorship and Autocracy,* rev. ed. (Cambridge, Mass.: Harvard University Press, 1965; orig. pub. 1956); Walter Z. Laqueur, *The Fate of the Revolution: Interpretations of Soviet History* (New York: Macmillan, 1967); Martin McCauley, *The Soviet Union since 1917* (London: Holden, 1983); Leonard Schapiro, *The Communist Party of the Soviet Union,* rev. ed. (New York: Random House, 1971; orig. pub. 1960); Donald W. Treadgold, *Twentieth-Century Russia,* 5th ed. (Chicago: Rand McNally, 1981); Robert C. Tucker, *The Soviet Political Mind* (New York: Norton, 1971); Adam Ulam, *History of Soviet Russia* (New York: Praeger, 1976); Theodore H. von Laue, *Why Lenin? Why Stalin?* (New York: Harper & Row, 1971); Bertram D. Wolfe, *Revolution and Reality: Essays on the Origin and Fate of the Soviet System* (Chapel Hill: University of North Carolina Press, 1981). The most recent translation of an official Soviet text is Boris Ponomarev et al., eds., *History of the Communist Party of the Soviet Union* (Moscow: Foreign Languages Publishing House, 1960).

See also the biographies listed in Part 5 of these suggested readings.

There is a plethora of substantial works on particular periods and aspects of the Soviet experience.

a. *From the Revolution to the Stalin era.* Robert Service, *The Bolshevik Party in Revolution, 1917–1923: A Study in Organizational Change* (New York: Barnes & Noble, 1979); T. Harry Rigby, *Lenin's Government* (New York: Cambridge University Press, 1979); Leonard Schapiro, *The Origins of the Communist Autocracy* (Cambridge, Mass.: Harvard University Press, 1977; orig. pub. 1957); Oliver H. Radkey, *The Election of the Russian Constituent Assembly* (Cambridge, Mass.: Harvard University Press, 1958); David Footman, *Civil War in Russia* (Westport, Conn.: Greenwood, 1975; orig. pub. 1961); Peter Kenez, *Civil War in South Russia* (Berkeley: University of California Press, 1971); Richard Luckett, *The White Generals* (New York: Viking, 1971); Peter Kurth, *Anastasia: The Riddle of Anna Anderson* (Boston: Little, Brown, 1983); Bertrand Russell, *The Practice and Theory of Bolshevism* [an early impression by the famous philosopher] (London: Allen & Unwin, 1962; orig. pub. 1920); Paul Avrich, *Kronstadt 1921* (New York: Norton, 1974); John Maynard, *Russia in Flux* [focuses on the peasantry] (New York: Macmillan, 1948); Harold H. Fisher, *The Famine in Soviet Russia: 1919–1923* (Bala Cynwyd, Pa.: Ayer, n.d.; orig. pub. 1927); Richard Pipes, *The Formation of the Soviet Union: Communism and Nationalism, 1917–1923,* rev. ed. (New York: Atheneum, 1968; orig. pub. 1954); Moshe Lewin, *Lenin's Last Struggle* (New York: Monthly Review Press, 1978); Robert V. Daniels, *The Conscience of the Revolution: Communist Opposition in Soviet Russia* (Cambridge, Mass.: Harvard University Press, 1960); Robert V. Daniels, "Evolution of Leadership Selection in the Central Committee, 1917–1927," in Walter Pintner and Don K. Rowney, eds., *Russian Bureaucracy* (Chapel Hill: University of North Carolina Press, 1980); Leon Trotsky, *The New Course* (Ann Arbor: University of Michigan Press, 1965; orig. Russian ed. 1923); Nina Tumarkin, *Lenin Lives! The Lenin Cult in Soviet Russia* (Cambridge, Mass.: Harvard University Press, 1983); William G. Rosenberg, ed., *Bolshevik Visions: First Phase of the Cultural Revolution in Soviet Russia* (Ann Arbor: Ardis, 1983); Roger Pethybridge, *The Social Prelude to Stalinism* (New York: St. Martin's, 1974).

b. *The Stalin Era and Stalinism.* Svetlana Alliluyeva, *Twenty Letters to a Friend* [recollections by Stalin's daughter] (New York: Harper & Row, 1967); Anton Antonov-Ovseenko, *The Time of Stalin* [by the son of a revolutionary leader killed in the purges] (New York: Harper & Row, 1983; orig. Russian ed. 1980); John A. Armstrong, *The Politics of Totalitarianism* (New York: Random House, 1961); Zbigniew Brzezinski, *The Permanent Purge* (Cambridge, Mass.: Harvard University Press, 1956); Stephen F. Cohen and Robert C. Tucker, eds., *The Great Purge Trial* [includes transcript of the 1938 trial] (New York: Grosset & Dunlap, 1965); Robert Conquest, *The Great Terror* [on the purges of 1936–1938] (New York: Macmillan, 1968); idem, *Kolyma: The Arctic Death Camps* (New York: Oxford University Press, 1979); George S. Counts and Nucia Lodge, *The Country of the Blind: The Soviet System of Mind Control* [on the Zhdanov movement, 1946–1948] (Westport, Conn.: Greenwood, n.d.; orig. pub. 1949); Merle Fainsod, *Soviet Rule in Smolensk* [based on the captured party archive] (Cambridge, Mass.: Harvard University Press, 1958); George Fischer, *Soviet Opposition to Stalin: A Case Study in World War II* [on the Vlasov movement] (Westport, Conn.: Greenwood, 1970; orig. pub. 1952); Sheila Fitzpatrick, ed., *Cultural Revolution in Russia* (Bloomington: Indiana University Press, 1978); Sheila Fitzpatrick, "Stalin and the Making of the New Elite, 1928–1939," *Slavic Review* 38 (September 1979): 377–402; idem, *Education and Social Mobility in the Soviet Union, 1921–1934* (New York: Cambridge University Press, 1979); Werner G. Hahn, *Postwar Soviet Politics: The Fall of Zhdanov and the Defeat of Moderation, 1946–1953* (Ithaca: Cornell University Press, 1982); Arthur Koestler, *Darkness at Noon* [the famous novel on the purges] (New York: Macmillan, 1941); Moshe Lewin, *Russian Peasants and Soviet Power: A Study of Collectivization* (New York: Norton, 1975); Roy Medvedev, *Let History Judge: The Origins and Consequences of Stalinism* (New York: Knopf, 1971); Zhores Medvedev, *The Rise and Fall of T. D. Lysenko* (New York: Anchor, 1971); Roy A. Medvedev, *Nikolai Bukharin: The Last Years* (New York: Norton, 1980); idem, *On Stalin and Stalinism* (New York: Oxford University Press, 1979); idem, *All Stalin's Men* (New York: Doubleday, 1983); Boris Nicolaevsky, *Power and the Soviet Elite* (Ann Arbor: University of Michigan Press, 1975); Alec Nove, *Stalinism and After* (Winchester, Mass.: Allen & Unwin, 1980); Roger Pethybridge, "Stalinism as Social Conservatism?" *European Studies Review* 11 (October 1981): 461–485; Niels Erik Rosenfeldt, *Knowledge and Power: The Role of Stalin's Secret Chancellery in the Soviet System of Government* (Copenhagen: Rosenkilde and Bagger, 1978); Joseph Stalin, *Leninism: Selected Writings* (Westport, Conn.: Greenwood, 1975); idem, *Collected Works,* 13 vols. (Moscow: Foreign Languages Publishing House, 1952–1955); Nicholas Timasheff, *The Great Retreat* (Bala Cynwyd, Pa.: Ayer, 1972; orig. pub. 1946); Leon Trotsky, *The Revolution Betrayed,* rev. ed. (New York: Pathfinder, 1973; orig. pub. 1937; Robert C. Tucker, ed., *Stalinism* [interpretive essays] (New York: Norton, 1977); Arvo Tuominen, *The Bells of the Kremlin: An Experience in Communism* [by a Finnish ex-Communist] (Hanover,

N.H.: University Press of New England, 1983; orig. Finnish ed., 1957); Sidney and Beatrice Webb, *Soviet Communism: A New Civilization?* 2 vols. (London: Longmans, 1935); Alexander Werth, *Russia: The Post-War Years* (New York: Taplinger, 1972).

   c. *The Post-Stalin Era.* Georges Bortoli, *The Death of Stalin* (New York: Praeger, 1975); *The Anti-Stalin Campaign and International Communism* [documents, including Khrushchev's secret speech] (New York: Columbia University Press, 1956); Carl A. Linden, *Khrushchev and the Soviet Leadership, 1957-1964* (Baltimore: Johns Hopkins University Press, 1966); Edward Crankshaw, *Khrushchev: A Career* (New York: Penguin, 1971; orig. pub. 1966); Roy Medvedev, *Khrushchev* (New York: Anchor, 1983); Giuseppe Boffa, *Inside the Khrushchev Era* [by an Italian Communist correspondent] (New York: Marzani & Munsell, 1959); Roger Pethybridge, *A Key to Soviet Politics: The Crisis of the Anti-Party Group* (New York: Praeger, 1962); Robert Conquest, *Power and Policy in the USSR* (New York: Harper & Row, 1967); Sidney Ploss, *Conflict and Decision-Making in Soviet Russia: A Case Study of Agricultural Policy, 1953-1963* (Princeton: Princeton University Press, 1965); Thomas P. Whitney, ed. *Khrushchev Speaks: Selected Speeches, Articles and Press Conferences, 1959-1961* (Ann Arbor: University of Michigan Press, 1963); Strobe Talbott, ed., *Khrushchev Remembers* (Boston: Little, Brown, 1970); idem, *Khrushchev: The Last Testament* (Boston: Little, Brown, 1974); Leonard Shapiro, ed., *The USSR and the Future: An Analysis of the New Program of the CPSU* [contains the text of the 1961 Party Program] (New York: Praeger, 1963); Michel Tatu, *Power in the Kremlin: From Khrushchev to Kosygin* (New York: Viking, 1967; orig. French ed. 1966); George W. Breslauer, *Khrushchev and Brezhnev as Leaders: Building Authority in Soviet Politics* (London: Allen & Unwin, 1982); John W. Strong, ed., *The Soviet Union and Brezhnev and Kosygin* [topical articles] (New York: Van Nostrand, 1971); John Dornberg, *Brezhnev: The Masks of Power* (New York: Basic Books, 1974).

   d. *Economic History.* Alec Nove, *An Economic History of the USSR,* rev. ed. (Harmondsworth: Penguin, 1982; orig. pub. 1969); idem, *Political Economy and Soviet Socialism* (London: Allen & Unwin, 1980); Raymond Hutchings, *Soviet Economic Development* (New York: New York University Press, 1983; orig. pub. 1971); Alexander Erlich, *The Soviet Industrialization Debate, 1924-1928* (Cambridge, Mass.: Harvard University Press, 1960); Naum Jasny, *Soviet Industrialization, 1928-1952* (Chicago: University of Chicago Press, 1961); Donald R. Hodgman, *Soviet Industrial Production, 1928-1951* [statistical analysis] (Cambridge, Mass.: Harvard University Press, 1954); Moshe Lewin, *Political Undercurrents in Soviet Economic Debates* (Princeton: Princeton University Press, 1974); Holland Hunter, "The Overambitious First Five Year Plan," *Slavic Review* 32 (June 1973): 237–257; R. W. Davies and S. G. Wheatcroft, "Further Thoughts on the First Soviet Five Year Plan," *Slavic Review* 34 (December 1975): 790–803; Eugene Zaleski, *Stalinist Planning for Growth, 1933-1952* (Chapel Hill: University of North Carolina Press, 1980).

   e. *Other Topics.* T. Harry Rigby, *Communist Party Membership in the USSR* (Princeton: Princeton University Press, 1968); Myron Rush, *Political Succession in the USSR* (Ithaca: Cornell University Press, 1965); Simon Wolin and Robert M. Slusser, eds., *The Soviet Secret Police* (Westport, Conn.: Greenwood, 1975;

orig. pub. 1952); George Leggett, *The Cheka* (New York: Oxford University Press, 1981); Boris Lewytzky, *The Uses of Terror: The Soviet Secret Police, 1917-1970* (London: Sidgwick & Jackson, 1971); Alexander Solzhenitsyn, *The Gulag Archipelago, 1918-1956,* 3 vols. (New York: Harper & Row, 1973-1979); Dmitri Fedotoff-White, *The Growth of the Red Army* (Princeton: Princeton University Press, 1944); John S. Curtiss, *The Russian Church and the Soviet State, 1917-1950* (Boston: Little, Brown, 1953); Richard H. Marshall, Jr., et al., eds., *Aspects of Religion in the Soviet Union, 1917-1967* (Chicago: University of Chicago Press, 1971); Edward J. Brown, *Russian Literature since the Revolution,* 3rd ed. (Cambridge, Mass.: Harvard University Press, 1982); George M. Enteen, *The Soviet Scholar-Bureaucrat: M. N. Pokrovskii and the Society of Marxist Historians* (University Park: Pennsylvania State University Press, 1978); Konstantin Shteppa, *Russian Historians and the Soviet State* (New Brunswick: Rutgers University Press, 1962); David Joravsky, *The Lysenko Affair* (Cambridge, Mass.: Harvard University Press, 1970); idem, *Soviet Marxism and Natural Science, 1917-1932* (New York: Columbia University Press, 1961); Abraham Rothberg, *The Heirs of Stalin: Dissidence and the Soviet Regime, 1953-1970* (Ithaca: Cornell University Press, 1972); Peter Reddaway, ed., *Uncensored Russia—Protest and Dissent in the Soviet Union: The Unofficial Moscow Journal, a Chronicle of Current Events* (New York: American Heritage Press, 1972); Marshall S. Schatz, *Soviet Dissent in Historical Perspective* (New York: Cambridge University Press, 1981).

f. *The Nationalities.* Basil Dmytryshyn, *Moscow and the Ukraine, 1919-1952: A Study of Russian Bolshevik Nationality Policy* (New York: Bookman Associates, 1956); Robert S. Sullivant, *Soviet Politics and the Ukraine, 1917-1957* (New York: Columbia University Press, 1962); James E. Mace, *Communism and the Dilemmas of National Liberation: National Communism in Soviet Ukraine, 1918-1933* (Cambridge, Mass.: Harvard Ukrainian Research Institute, 1983); idem, "Famine and Nationalism in Soviet Ukraine," *Problems of Communism* 33 (May–June 1984): 37–50; Yaroslav Bilinsky, *The Second Soviet Republic: The Ukraine after World War II* (New Brunswick: Rutgers University Press, 1964); I. S. Lubachko, *Belorussia under Soviet Rule, 1917-1957* (Lexington: University of Kentucky Press, 1972); Romuald J. Misiunas and Rein Taagepera, *The Baltic States: Years of Dependency, 1940-1980* (Berkeley: University of California Press, 1983; David M. Lang, *A Modern History of Soviet Georgia* (Westport, Conn.: Greenwood, 1975; orig. pub. 1962); Mary A. K. Matossian, *The Impact of Soviet Policies in Armenia* (Westport, Conn.: Hyperion, 1981; orig. pub. 1962); Elizabeth Bacon, *Central Asians under Russian Rule: A Study in Cultural Change* (Ithaca: Cornell University Press, 1980; orig. pub. 1966); Alexandre Bennigsen and Marie Broxup, *The Islamic Threat to the Soviet State* (New York: St. Martin's, 1982); Solomon Schwarz, *The Jews in the Soviet Union* (Bala Cynwyd, Pa.: Ayer, 1972; orig. pub. 1951); Lionel Kochan, ed., *The Jews in Soviet Russia since 1917* (New York: Oxford University Press, 1978).

g. *Collections of Source Materials.* Robert V. Daniels, ed., *A Documentary History of Communism,* rev. ed., 2 vols. (Hanover, N.H.: University Press of New England, 1984; orig. pub. 1960); and Robert H. McNeal, ed., *Resolutions and Decisions of the Communist Party of the Soviet Union,* 5 vols. (Toronto: University of Toronto Press, 1974-1982).

11. History of Soviet Foreign Relations

The listings that follow are a bare sampling of the most important works on this inordinately controversial subject.

a. *General Works.* Robert D. Warth, *Soviet Russia in World Politics* (New York: Twayne, 1963); Adam B. Ulam, *Expansion and Coexistence: The History of Soviet Foreign Policy, 1917–1973*, rev. ed. (New York: Holt, Rinehart & Winston, 1974); John L. Gaddis, *Russia, The Soviet Union, and the United States: An Interpretive History* (New York: Wiley, 1978); George F. Kennan, *Russia and the West under Lenin and Stalin* (Boston: Little, Brown, 1960); Philip E. Mosely, *The Kremlin and World Politics: Studies in Soviet Policy and Action* (New York: Vintage, 1960); Philip E. Mosely, ed., *The Soviet Union, 1922–1962: A Foreign Affairs Reader* (New York: Praeger, 1963); Nikolai V. Sivachev and Nikolai N. Yakovlev, *Russia and the United States: U.S.-Soviet Relations from the Soviet Point of View* (Chicago: University of Chicago Press, 1979); Paul Hollander, *Political Pilgrims: Travels of Western Intellectuals to the Soviet Union, China and Cuba* (New York: Oxford University Press, 1981); A. A. Gromyko and B. N. Ponomarev, eds., *Soviet Foreign Policy, 1917–1980*, 2 vols. [official Soviet view] (Moscow: Progress Publishers, 1981); I. D. Ovsyany et al., *A Study of Soviet Foreign Policy* [official Soviet view] (Moscow: Progress Publishers, 1975).

b. *From the Revolution to World War II.* Rex A. Wade, *The Russian Search for Peace: February–October, 1917* (Stanford, Calif.: Stanford University Press, 1969); Robert D. Warth, *The Allies and the Russian Revolution* (New York: Russell & Russell, 1973); Michael Kettle, *Russia and the Allies, 1917–1920*, vol. 1: *The Allies and the Russian Collapse, March 1917–March 1918* (Minneapolis: University of Minnesota Press, 1981); Richard K. Debo, *Revolution and Survival: The Foreign Policy of Soviet Russia, 1917–1918* (Toronto: University of Toronto Press, 1979); John Thompson, *Russia, Bolshevism, and the Versailles Peace* (Princeton: Princeton University Press, 1966); Arno J. Mayer, *Politics and Diplomacy of Peacemaking: Containment and Counterrevolution at Versailles, 1918–1919* (New York: Knopf, 1968); John F. N. Bradley, *Allied Intervention in Russia* (Lanham, Md.: University Press of America, 1984); Richard H. Ullman, *Anglo-Soviet Relations, 1917–1921*, 3 vols. (Princeton: Princeton University Press, 1961–1968); Louis Fischer, *The Soviets in World Affairs: A History of the Relations between the Soviet Union and the Rest of the World, 1917–1929*, 2 vols. (Princeton: Princeton University Press, 1951; orig. pub. 1930); Teddy V. Uldricks, *Diplomacy and Ideology: The Origins of Soviet Foreign Relations, 1917–1930* (Beverly Hills, Calif.: Sage, 1979); Gerald Freund, *Unholy Alliance: Russian-German Relations from the Treaty of Brest-Litovsk to the Treaty of Berlin* (New York: Harcourt, Brace, 1957); Gustav Hilger and Alfred G. Meyer, *The Incompatible Allies: German-Soviet Relations, 1918–1941* [based on Hilger's recollections as a German diplomat] (New York: Hafner, 1971; orig. pub. 1953); Richard B. Day, *Leon Trotsky and the Politics of Economic Isolation* (New York: Cambridge University Press, 1973); Max Beloff, *The Foreign Policy of Soviet Russia, 1929–1941*, 2 vols. (London: Oxford University Press, 1947, 1949); F. W. Deakin and G. R. Storry, *The Case of Richard Sorge* (Boston: Merrimack, 1978; orig. pub. 1966).

c. *American-Soviet Relations, to World War II.* Benson L. Grayson, ed., *The*

American Image of Russia, 1917-1977 (New York: Ungar, 1979); William A. Williams, *The Tragedy of American Diplomacy* [revisionist view] (New York: Dell, 1972; orig. pub. 1959); Christopher Lasch, *The American Liberals and the Russian Revolution* (New York: Columbia University Press, 1962); Robert Lansing, *War Memoirs* [Lansing was U.S. secretary of state, 1915–1920] (Westport, Conn.: Greenwood, 1970; orig. pub. 1935); Peter G. Filene, *Americans and the Soviet Experiment, 1917-1933* (Cambridge, Mass.: Harvard University Press, 1967); Joan Hoff Wilson, *Ideology and Economics: United States Relations with the Soviet Union 1918-1933* (St. Louis: University of Missouri Press, 1974); George F. Kennan, *A History of American-Soviet Relations,* vol. 1: *Russia Leaves the War,* vol. 2: *The Decision to Intervene* (Princeton: Princeton University Press, 1956, 1958); idem, "The Sisson Documents," *Journal of Modern History* 28 (June 1956): 130–154; Richard Goldhurst, *The Midnight War: The American Intervention in Russia, 1918-1920* (New York: McGraw-Hill, 1978); Betty M. Unterberger, *America's Siberian Expedition, 1918-1920* (Westport, Conn.: Greenwood, 1969; orig. pub. 1956); William S. Graves, *America's Siberian Adventure, 1918-1920* (Bala Cynwyd, Pa.: Ayer, 1971; orig. pub. 1931); Benjamin M. Weissman, *Herbert Hoover and Famine Relief to Soviet Russia, 1921-1923* (Stanford, Calif.: Hoover Institution, 1974); Robert P. Browder, *The Origins of Soviet-American Diplomacy* (Princeton: Princeton University Press, 1953); Beatrice Farnsworth, *William C. Bullitt and the Soviet Union* (Bloomington: Indiana University Press, 1967); Joseph E. Davies, *Mission to Moscow* (Garden City, N.Y.: Garden City Publishing, 1943); George F. Kennan, *Memoirs, 1925-1950* (Boston: Little, Brown, 1967).

d. *Soviet Russia and the Communist Movement, to World War II.* Hugh Seton-Watson, *From Lenin to Khrushchev: The History of World Communism* (New York: Praeger, 1960); Franz Borkenau, *World Communism: A History of the Communist International* (Ann Arbor: University of Michigan Press, 1962); R. H. S. Crossman, ed., *The God That Failed* [accounts by ex-Communists] (New York: Arno, n.d., orig. pub. 1950); Robert C. North, *Moscow and Chinese Communists* (Stanford, Calif.: Stanford University Press, 1963); Conrad Brandt, *Stalin's Failure in China* (Cambridge, Mass.: Harvard University Press, 1958); William G. Rosenberg and Marilyn B. Young, *Transforming Russia and China: Revolutionary Struggle in the Twentieth Century* (New York: Oxford University Press, 1982); Irving Howe and Lewis Coser, *The American Communist Party: A Critical History, 1919-1957* (New York: Da Capo, 1974; orig. pub. 1957); Theodore Draper, *The Roots of American Communism* (New York: Octagon, 1977; orig. pub. 1957); Morris Ernst, *Report on the American Communist* (New York: Capricorn Books, 1962; orig. pub. 1952); William L. O'Neill, *A Better World: The Great Schism— Stalinism and the American Intellectuals* (New York: Simon and Schuster, 1982).

e. *War and Cold War.* Alan Clark, *Barbarossa* (New York: Morrow, 1965); John Erikson, *The Road to Stalingrad* (New York: Harper & Row, 1975); Alexander Dallin, *German Rule in Russia, 1941-1945* (New York: Octagon, 1980; orig. pub. 1957); Raul Hilberg, *The Destruction of the European Jews,* rev. ed. (New York: Harper & Row, 1979; orig. pub. 1961); William H. McNeill, *America, Britain, and Russia—Their Cooperation and Conflict, 1941-1946: Survey of International Affairs* (New York: Johnson Reprint, n.d.; orig. pub. 1953); George C. Herring, *Aid to Russia, 1941-46* (New York: Columbia University Press, 1973);

Vojtech Mastny, *Russia's Road to the Cold War: Diplomacy, Warfare and the Politics of Communism, 1941-1945* (New York: Columbia University Press, 1979); William O. McCagg, Jr., *Stalin Embattled, 1943-1948* (Detroit: Wayne State University Press, 1978); Christopher M. Woodhouse, *The Struggle for Greece, 1941-1949* (New York: Beekman, 1979); Herbert Feis, *From Trust to Terror: The Onset of the Cold War, 1945-1950* (New York: Norton, 1970); Gar Alperowitz, *Atomic Diplomacy: Hiroshima and Potsdam—The Use of the Atomic Bomb and the American Confrontation with Soviet Power* (New York: Simon and Schuster, 1965); Dana F. Fleming, *The Cold War and Its Origins, 1917-1960,* 2 vols. (New York: Doubleday, 1961); John L. Gaddis, *The United States and the Origins of the Cold War* (New York: Columbia University Press, 1972); idem, *Strategies of Containment: A Critical Appraisal of Postwar American National Security Policy* (New York: Oxford University Press, 1982); Thomas T. Hammond, ed., *Witnesses of the Origins of the Cold War* (Seattle: University of Washington Press, 1982); Joyce and Gabriel Kolko, *The Limits of Power: The World and United States Foreign Policy* [a revisionist view] (New York: Harper & Row, 1972); Walter LaFeber, *America, Russia, and the Cold War, 1945-1980,* 4th ed. (New York: Wiley, 1980); Vojtech Mastny, "The Cassandra in the Foreign Commissariat: Maxim Litvinov and the Cold War," *Foreign Affairs* 54 (January 1976): 366-376; Charles L. Mee, Jr., *The Marshall Plan: The Launching of Pax Americana* (New York: Simon and Schuster, 1984); William Taubman, *Stalin's American Policy: From Entente to Détente to Cold War* (New York: Norton, 1982); Richard J. Walton, *Henry Wallace, Harry Truman, and the Cold War* (New York: Viking, 1976); Walter Lippmann, *The Cold War* (New York: Harper, 1947); David Caute, *The Great Fear: The Anti-Communist Purge under Truman and Eisenhower* (New York: Simon and Schuster, 1979); Dean Acheson, *Present at the Creation: My Years in the State Department* (New York: Norton, 1969); Joseph M. Jones, *The Fifteen Weeks* [on the Truman Doctrine and the Marshall Plan] (New York: Harcourt, Brace & World, 1955); Thomas B. Larson, *Soviet-American Rivalry* (New York: Norton, 1981); Milovan Djilas, *Conversations with Stalin* [by the former Yugoslav leader] (New York: Harcourt, Brace & World, 1962); Marshall D. Shulman, *Stalin's Foreign Policy Reappraised* (Cambridge, Mass.: Harvard University Press, 1963); R. J. Maddox, *The New Left and the Origins of the Cold War* (Princeton: Princeton University Press, 1974); David Horowitz, *Containment and Revolution* (Boston: Beacon, 1967); Daniel Yergin, *Shattered Peace: The Origins of the Cold War and the National Security State* (Boston: Houghton Mifflin, 1978).

f. *The Fifties and Sixties.* Joseph S. Nogee and Robert H. Donaldson, *Soviet Foreign Policy since World War II* (New York: Pergamon, 1980); Adam B. Ulam, *The Rivals: America and Russia since World War II* (New York: Viking, 1983; orig. pub. 1971); David V. Dallin, *Soviet Foreign Policy after Stalin* (Westport, Conn.: Greenwood, 1975; orig. pub. 1961); William Zimmerman, *Soviet Perspectives on International Relations, 1956-1967* (Princeton: Princeton University Press, 1969); Zbigniew Brzezinski, *The Soviet Bloc: Unity and Conflict* (Cambridge, Mass.: Harvard University Press, 1967; orig. pub. 1961); Janos Radvany, *Hungary and the Superpowers: The 1956 Revolution and Realpolitik* (Stanford, Calif.: Hoover Institution, 1972); Donald S. Zagoria, *The Sino-Soviet Conflict, 1956-1961* (New York: Octagon, 1980; orig. pub. 1962); O. B. Borisov and B. T.

Koloskov, *Sino-Soviet Relations, 1945–1973: A Brief History* [official Soviet view] (Moscow: Progress Publishers, 1975); Curtis Cate, *The Ides of August: The Berlin Wall Crisis, 1961* (New York: Evans, 1979); Honoré Catudal, *Kennedy and the Berlin Wall Crisis* (Berlin: Berlin-Verlag, 1980); Henry M. Pachter, *Collision Course: The Cuban Missile Crisis and Coexistence* (New York: Praeger, 1963); Graham Allison, *Essence of Decision: Explaining the Cuban Missile Crisis* (Boston: Little, Brown, 1971); Glen T. Seaborg, *Kennedy, Khrushchev, and the Test Ban* (Berkeley: University of California Press, 1981); Donald S. Zagoria, *Vietnam Triangle: Moscow, Peking, Hanoi* (New York: Pegasus, 1967); Jiri Valenta, *Soviet Intervention in Czechoslovakia, 1968: Anatomy of a Decision* (Baltimore: Johns Hopkins University Press, 1981).

g. *Collections of Source Materials.* Alvin Z. Rubinstein, *The Foreign Policy of the Soviet Union*, 3rd ed. (New York: Random House, 1972); Robert V. Daniels, *A Documentary History of Communism*, vol. 2: *Communism and the World*, rev. ed. (Hanover, N.H.: University Press of New England, 1984); Jane Degras, ed., *Soviet Documents on Foreign Policy, 1917–1941*, 3 vols. (New York: Octagon, 1978; orig. pub. 1951–1953); U.S. Department of State, *Foreign Relations of the United States* [the volumes on Russia and the USSR] (Washington, D.C.: U.S. Government Printing Office, various years); Jane Degras, ed., *The Communist International, 1919–1943: Documents* (London: Oxford University Press, 1956); Xenia J. Eudin and Harold H. Fisher, eds., *Soviet Russia and the West, 1920–1927: A Documentary Survey* (Stanford, Calif.: Stanford University Press, 1957); Xenia Eudin and Robert M. Slusser, eds., *Soviet Foreign Policy, 1928–1934: Documents and Materials*, 2 vols. (University Park: Pennsylvania State University Press, 1967); Ministry of Foreign Affairs of the USSR, *Correspondence between the Chairman of the Council of Ministers of the USSR and the Presidents of the USA and the Prime Ministers of Great Britain during the Great Patriotic War of 1941–1945*, 2 vols. (Moscow: Foreign Languages Publishing House, 1957); Norman A. Graebner, *Cold War Diplomacy, 1945–1960* (Princeton: Van Nostrand, 1962); Thomas H. Etzold and John L. Gaddis, eds., *Containment: Documents on American Policy and Strategy, 1945–1950* (New York: Columbia University Press, 1978).

12. The Contemporary Soviet Union

The following listings are a fraction of the important work on recent Soviet affairs done in the West or available as translations of Soviet publications.

a. *General Descriptions.* Hedrick Smith, *The Russians* (New York: Times Books, 1983; orig. pub. 1976); Robert Kaiser, *Russia: The People and the Power* (New York: Atheneum, 1976); David Shipler, *Russia: Broken Idols, Solemn Dreams* (New York: Times Books, 1983); Kevin Klose, *Russia and the Russians: Inside the Closed Society* (New York: Norton, 1984); Michael Binyon, *Life in Russia* (New York: Pantheon, 1984); V. M. Sinitsyn et al., *The Soviet Way of Life* [official Soviet view] (Chicago: Imported Publications, 1974); Archie Brown and Michael Kaser, eds., *Soviet Policy for the 1980s* (London: Macmillan, 1982); Robert F. Byrnes, ed., *After Brezhnev: Sources of Soviet Conduct in the 1980s* (Bloomington: Indiana University Press, 1983).

b. *The Political System.* Jeremy R. Azrael, *Managerial Power and Soviet Policy* (Cambridge, Mass.: Harvard University Press, 1966); Harold Berman, *Justice in the USSR,* rev. ed. (New York: Vintage, 1963); Zbigniew Brzezinski, "The Nature of the Soviet System," with comments by Alfred G. Meyer ("USSR, Incorporated") and Robert C. Tucker ("The Question of Totalitarianism"), *Slavic Review* 20 (October 1961): 351–388; Hélène Carrère d'Encausse, *Confiscated Power: How Soviet Russia Really Works* (New York: Harper & Row, 1982; orig. French ed. 1980); Santiago Carrillo, *Eurocommunism and the State* [a critique of Soviet policies by the then leader of the Communist Party of Spain] (Westport, Conn.: Lawrence Hill, 1978; orig. Spanish ed. 1977); Paul Cocks, Robert V. Daniels, and Nancy Whittier Heer, eds., *The Dynamics of Soviet Politics* (Cambridge, Mass.: Harvard University Press, 1976); Stephen Cohen, Alexander Rabinowitch, and Robert Sharlet, eds., *The Soviet Union since Stalin* [topical articles] (Bloomington: Indiana University Press, 1980); Theodore H. Friedgut, *Political Participation in the USSR* (Princeton: Princeton University Press, 1979); Vladimir Gsovsky and K. Grybowski, *Government, Law and Courts in the Soviet Union and Eastern Europe* (London: Stevens, 1959); Darrell P. Hammer, *USSR: The Politics of Oligarchy* (Hinsdale, Ill.: Dryden, 1974); John N. Hazard, *Law and Social Change in the USSR* (Westport, Conn.: Hyperion, 1980; orig. pub. 1953); idem, *The Soviet System of Government,* 5th ed. (Chicago: University of Chicago Press, 1980); Ronald V. Hill and Peter Frank, *The Soviet Communist Party* (London: Allen & Unwin, 1981); Jerry F. Hough and Merle Fainsod, *How the Soviet Union is Governed* (Cambridge, Mass.: Harvard University Press, 1979); Jerry F. Hough, "Party 'Saturation' in the Soviet Union," in Paul Cocks et al., eds., *The Dynamics of Soviet Politics* (Cambridge, Mass.: Harvard University Press, 1976); T. Harry Rigby, Archie H. Brown, and Peter Reddaway, eds., *Authority, Power, and Policy in the USSR* (London: Macmillan, 1980); Leonard Schapiro, *Totalitarianism* (London: Macmillan, 1978; orig. pub. 1972); Robert W. Siegler, *The Standing Commissions of the Supreme Soviet: Effective Cooptation* (New York: Praeger, 1982); H. Gordon Skilling and Franklyn Griffiths, eds., *Interest Groups in Soviet Politics* [a collection of articles] (Princeton: Princeton University Press, 1970); Peter Vanneman, *The Supreme Soviet: Politics and the Legislative Process in the Soviet Political System* (Durham, N.C.: Duke University Press, 1977); Vladimir Voinovich, "The Trouble with Truth," *The New Republic,* November 28, 1983, pp. 26–30 [on the style of Soviet propaganda and the suppression of past documents]; Robert Wesson, *The Aging of Communism* (New York: Praeger, 1980); Stephen White, *Political Culture and Soviet Politics* (New York: St. Martin's, 1980); Julia Wishnevsky, "Estimates of the Prison Population of the USSR," *Radio Liberty Research,* August 31, 1982.

c. *Leadership Politics.* Dimitri K. Simes et al., *Soviet Succession: Leadership in Transition* (Beverly Hills, Calif.: Sage, 1978); Seweryn Bialer, *Stalin's Successors* (New York: Cambridge University Press, 1980); Donald R. Kelley, ed., *Soviet Politics in the Brezhnev Era* (New York: Praeger, 1980); Robert V. Daniels, "Office Holding and Elite Status: The Central Committee of the CPSU," in Paul Cocks et al., eds., *The Dynamics of Soviet Politics* (Cambridge, Mass.: Harvard University Press, 1976); Leonid Brezhnev, *Socialism, Democracy, and Human Rights* (New York: Pergamon, 1980); Seweryn Bialer and Thane Gustavson, eds., *Russia at the Crossroads: The Twenty-Sixth Congress of the Communist Party of the Soviet Union* (London: Allen & Unwin, 1982); Zhores Medvedev, *Andropov* (London: Blackwell, 1983); Jonathan Steele and Eric Abraham, *Andropov in Power: From Komsomol to Kremlin* (Oxford: Martin Robertson, 1983); Yuri V. Andropov, *Speeches and Writings* (Oxford: Pergamon, 1983); Konstantin U. Chernenko, *Selected Speeches and Writings* (New York: Pergamon, 1982).

d. *Economy.* Morris Bornstein, ed., *The Soviet Economy: Continuity and Change* (Boulder, Colo.: Westview, 1981); Zbigniew M. Fallenbuchl, *Economic Development in the Soviet Union and Eastern Europe,* 2 vols. (New York: Praeger, 1976); Marshall I. Goldman, *USSR in Crisis: The Failure of an Economic System* (New York: Norton, 1983); Paul K. Gregory and Robert C. Stuart, *Soviet Economic Structure and Performance* (New York: Harper & Row, 1981); Eric Hoffman and Robbin Laird, *The Politics of Economic Modernization in the Soviet Union* (Ithaca: Cornell University Press, 1982); Franklyn D. Holzman, *The Soviet Economy: Past, Present, and Future* (New York: Foreign Policy Association, 1982); Jean Karsavina, ed., *Guidelines for the Economic and Social Development of the USSR for 1981–85 and for the Period Ending in 1990* [official Soviet materials] (Moscow: Novosti, 1981); Alastair McAuley, *Economic Welfare in the Soviet Union: Poverty, Living Standards, and Inequality* (Madison: University of Wisconsin Press, 1979); James R. Millar, *The ABC's of Soviet Socialism* (New York: Cambridge University Press, 1982); Blair Ruble, *Soviet Trade Unions: Their Development in the 1970s* (Cambridge: Cambridge University Press, 1981); Leonard Schapiro and Joseph Godson, eds., *The Soviet Worker: Illusion and Realities* (New York: St. Martin's, 1981); Harry G. Shaffer, ed., *Soviet Agriculture* (New York: Praeger, 1977); Konstantin M. Simis, *USSR: The Corrupt Society—The Secret World of Soviet Capitalism* [by an émigré lawyer] (New York: Simon & Schuster, 1983); *The Soviet Economy Today* [Soviet articles] (Westport, Conn.: Greenwood, 1981); U.S. Congress, Joint Economic Committee, *Soviet Economic Prospects for the Seventies, The Soviet Economy in a New Perspective, The Soviet Economy in a Time of Change, The Soviet Economy in the 1980s—Problems and Prospects* (Washington, D.C.: U.S. Government Printing Office, 1973, 1976, 1979, 1982).

e. *Society.* Jerry G. Pankhurst and Michael P. Sachs, eds., *Contemporary Soviet Society: Sociological Perspectives* (New York: Praeger, 1980); Basile Kerblay, *Modern Soviet Society* (New York: Pantheon, 1983; orig. French ed. 1977); George Fischer, *Soviet Development and Theories of Modern Society* (New York: Atherton, 1968); Karl W. Ryavec, ed., *Soviet Society and the Communist Party* (Amherst: University of Massachusetts Press, 1978); Alex Inkeles, Raymond Bauer, and Clyde Kluckhohn, *How the Soviet System Works* [based on the Harvard Refugee Interview Project] (Cambridge, Mass.: Harvard University Press, 1956); Mervyn Matthews, *Class and Society in Soviet Russia* (New York: Walker, 1972); Walter D. Connor, *Socialism, Politics and Equality: Hierarchy and Change in Eastern Europe and the USSR* (New York: Columbia University Press, 1979); Donald C. Hodges, *The Bureaucratization of Socialism* (Amherst: University of Massachusetts Press, 1981); David Lane, *The End of Social Inequality? Class, Sta-*

tus, and Power under State Socialism (London: Allen & Unwin, 1982); Victor Zaslavsky, *The Neo-Stalinist State: Class, Ethnicity and Consensus in Soviet Society* (Armonk, N.Y.: M. E. Sharpe, 1982); Kent Geiger, *The Family in Soviet Russia* (Cambridge, Mass.: Harvard University Press, 1968); Gail Warshafsky Lapidus, *Women in Soviet Society: Equality, Development, and Social Change* (Berkeley: University of California Press, 1978); Jennie Brine et al., eds., *Home, School, and Leisure in the Soviet Union* (London: Allen & Unwin, 1981); John F. Besemeres, *Socialist Population Politics* (Armonk, N.Y.: M. E. Sharpe, 1980); Murray Feshbach, "Between the Lines of the 1979 Soviet Census," *Problems of Communism* 31 (January–February 1982): 27–37; Christopher Davis and Murray Feshbach, *Rising Infant Mortality in the USSR in the 1970's* (Washington, D.C.: U.S. Bureau of the Census, 1980).

f. *The Nationalities.* Hélène Carrère d'Encausse, *Decline of an Empire* (New York: Newsweek, 1979; orig. French ed. 1978); Ralph S. Clem, ed., *The Soviet West: Interplay between Nationality and Social Organization* (New York: Praeger, 1975); Peter J. Potichny, ed., *The Ukraine in the Seventies* (Oakville, Ont.: Mosaic, 1975); Michael Rywkin, *Moscow's Muslim Challenge: Soviet Central Asia* (Armonk, N.Y.: M. E. Sharpe, 1982); William Korey, *The Soviet Cage: Anti-Semitism in Russia* (New York: Viking, 1973); Paul Panish, *Exit Visa: The Emigration of the Soviet Jews* (New York: Coward, McCann and Geoghegan, 1981).

g. *Religion.* Dennis J. Dunn, ed., *Religion and Modernization in the Soviet Union* (Boulder, Colo.: Westview, 1978); William C. Fletcher, *Soviet Believers: the Religious Sector of the Population* (Lawrence: Regents' Press of Kansas, 1981); Christel Lane, *Christian Religion in the Soviet Union* (Albany: State University of New York Press, 1983).

h. *Education, Science, and Culture.* Mervyn Matthews, *Education in the Soviet Union: Policies and Institutions since Stalin* (London: Allen & Unwin, 1982); Paul Cocks, *Science Policy in the Soviet Union* (Washington, D.C.: National Science Foundation, 1980); Frederick Fleron, ed., *Technology and Communist Culture: the Social-Cultural Impact of Technology under Socialism* (New York: Praeger, 1977); Alexander S. Vucinich, *Empire of Knowledge: The Academy of Sciences of the USSR, 1917–1970* (Berkeley: University of California Press, 1984).

i. *Dissent.* Frederick C. Barghoorn, *Détente and the Democratic Movement in the USSR* (New York: Free Press, 1976); Stephen F. Cohen, ed., *An End to Silence: Uncensored Opinion in the Soviet Union* [articles from "samizdat"] (New York: Norton, 1982); Petro G. Grigorenko, *Memoirs* [by a Soviet general who became a dissident and later emigrated] (New York: Norton, 1983); Tatyana Mamonova, ed., *Women and Russia: Feminist Writings from the Soviet Union* (Boston: Beacon, 1984); Roy Medvedev, *On Socialist Democracy* (New York: Norton, 1977; orig. Russian ed. 1972); Andrei Sakharov, *On Progress, Coexistence, and Intellectual Freedom* (New York: Norton, 1968); Alexander Solzhenitsyn, *Letter to the Party Leaders* (New York: Harper & Row, 1974); Alexander Solzhenitsyn, ed., *From under the Rubble* [articles by dissidents] (Chicago: Regnery-Gateway, 1981; orig. pub. 1974); Alexander Yanov, *The Russian New Right* [an émigré critique] (Berkeley: University of California International Studies, 1978).

13. Contemporary Issues in Soviet Foreign Relations

Again, the listings that follow are a mere sampling of the most important recent literature on Soviet foreign policy and related topics.

a. *General Works.* G. A. Arbatov and Willem Olthaus, *The Soviet Viewpoint* [Arbatov is the chief Soviet expert on the United States] (New York: Dodd, Mead, 1983); Andrei A. Gromyko, *Peace Now, Peace for the Future* [by the Soviet foreign minister] (New York: Pergamon, 1984); Seweryn Bialer, ed., *The Domestic Context of Soviet Foreign Policy* (Boulder, Colo.: Westview, 1981); Leonid Brezhnev, *Peace, Détente, and Soviet-American Relations* (New York: Harcourt, Brace, Jovanovich, 1979); Brian Crozier, Drew Middleton, and Jeremy Murray-Brown, *This War Called Peace* (London: Sherwood, 1984); John B. Dunlop, *The Faces of Contemporary Russian Nationalism* (Princeton: Princeton University Press, 1984); Herbert J. Ellison, ed., *Soviet Policy toward Western Europe* (Seattle: University of Washington Press, 1984); Harry Gelman, *The Brezhnev Politburo and the Decline of Détente* (Ithaca: Cornell University Press, 1984); William E. Griffith, *The Superpowers and Regional Tensions: Russia, America, and Europe* (Lexington, Mass.: Lexington Books, 1981); Roger E. Kanet, ed., *Soviet Foreign Policy in the 1980's* (New York: Praeger, 1983); R. Judson Mitchell, *Ideology of a Superpower* (Stanford, Calif.: Hoover Institution, 1982); William Pfaff, "Reflections: A Second Cold War," *The New Yorker,* December 3, 1979, pp. 126–140; Jonathan Steele, *Soviet Power: The Kremlin's Foreign Policy from Brezhnev to Andropov* (New York: Simon and Schuster, 1983); Hugh Seton-Watson, *The Imperial Revolutionaries: Trends in World Communism in the 1960's and 1970's* (Stanford, Calif.: Hoover Institution, 1978).

b. *American-Soviet Relations.* Alexander George, ed., *Managing U.S.-Soviet Rivalry: Problems of Crisis Prevention* (Boulder, Colo.: Westview, 1983); Stanley Hoffman, *Dead Ends: American Foreign Policy in the New Cold War* (Cambridge, Mass.: Ballinger, 1983); John Lenczowski, *Soviet Perceptions of U.S. Foreign Policy: A Study of Ideology, Power and Consensus* (Ithaca: Cornell University Press, 1982); Joseph S. Nye, *The Making of America's Soviet Policy* (New Haven: Yale University Press, 1984); Richard Pipes, *U.S.-Soviet Relations in the Era of Détente* (Boulder, Colo.: Westview, 1981); Norman Podhoretz, *The Present Danger* (New York: Simon and Schuster, 1980); Anatol Rapoport, *The Big Two: Soviet-American Perceptions of Foreign Policy* (New York: Pegasus, 1971); Morton Schwartz, *Soviet Perceptions of the United States* (Berkeley: University of California Press, 1978); Alexander I. Solzhenitsyn, "Misconceptions about Russia Are a Threat to America," *Foreign Affairs* 58 (Spring 1980): 797–834; Strobe Talbot, *The Russians and Reagan* (New York: Vintage, 1984); Adam Ulam, *Dangerous Relations* (New York: Oxford University Press, 1983); U.S. International Communication Agency, "Soviet Perceptions of the United States: Result of a Surrogate Interview Project," mimeo, Washington, D.C., June 27, 1980; U.S. House of Representatives, Committee on Foreign Affairs, *Soviet Diplomacy and Negotiating Behavior: Emerging New Context for U.S. Diplomacy* (Washington, D.C.: U.S. Government Printing Office, 1979); U.S. Senate, Committee on Foreign Relations, *Perceptions: Relations between the United States and the Soviet Union* (Washington, D.C.: U.S.

Government Printing Office, 1978); Thomas W. Wolfe, *The SALT Experience* (Cambridge, Mass.: Ballinger, 1979).

    c. *Military, Strategic, and Arms Questions.* Christopher Bertram, *The Future of Arms Control* (London: Institute for Strategic Studies, 1978); McGeorge Bundy, "The Missed Chance to Stop the H-Bomb," *New York Review of Books,* May 13, 1982, pp. 13–22; McGeorge Bundy, George F. Kennan, Robert S. McNamara, and Gerard Smith, "Nuclear Weapons and the Atlantic Alliance," *Foreign Affairs* 60 (Spring 1982): 753–768; Andrew Cockborn, *The Threat: Inside the Soviet Military Machine* (New York: Random House, 1983); John M. Collins, *U.S.-Soviet Military Balance: Concepts and Capabilities 1960–1980* (New York: McGraw-Hill, 1980); Arthur M. Cox, *Russian Roulette: The Superpower Game* (New York: Times Books, 1982); Freeman Dyson, *Weapons and Hope* (New York: Harper & Row, 1984); S. G. Gorshkov, *The Sea Power of the State* [by the commander of the Soviet navy] (Annapolis: Naval Institute Press, 1979; orig. Russian ed. 1976); The Harvard Nuclear Study Group (Albert Carnesale et al.), *Living with Nuclear Weapons* (Cambridge, Mass.: Harvard University Press, 1983); David Holloway, *The Soviet Union and the Arms Race* (New Haven: Yale University Press, 1983); Franklyn D. Holzman, "Military Spending: Are We Falling Behind the Soviets?" *The Atlantic* 252 (July 1983): 10–18; International Institute of Strategic Studies, *The Military Balance* and *Strategic Survey* (London: published annually); C. J. Jacobsen, *Soviet Strategic Initiatives* (New York: Praeger, 1979); Robert H. Johnson, "Periods of Peril: The Window of Vulnerability and Other Myths," *Foreign Afffairs* 61 (Spring 1983): 950–970; Stephen S. Kaplan et al., *Diplomacy of Power: The Soviet Armed Forces as a Political Instrument* (Washington, D.C.: Brookings Institution, 1981); George F. Kennan, *The Nuclear Delusion: Soviet-American Relations in the Atomic Age* (New York: Pantheon, 1969); Henry Kissinger, *Nuclear Weapons and Foreign Policy* (New York: Harper & Row, 1969; orig. pub. 1957); Jonathan S. Lockwood, *The Soviet View of United States Strategic Doctrine: Implications for Decision-Making* (New Brunswick, N.J.: Transaction Books, 1983); Edward N. Luttwak, *Strategies and Politics: Collected Essays* (New Brunswick, N.J.: Transaction Books, 1980); Michael Mandelbaum, *The Nuclear Question: The United States and Nuclear Weapons, 1946–1976* (New York: Cambridge University Press, 1979); idem, *The Nuclear Revolution: International Policy before and after Hiroshima* (New York: Cambridge University Press, 1981); Robert S. McNamara, "The Military Role of Nuclear Weapons," *Foreign Affairs* 62 (Fall 1983): 59–80; Samuel B. Payne, Jr., *The Soviet Union and SALT* (Cambridge, Mass.: MIT Press, 1980); Andrew J. Pierre, ed., *Nuclear Weapons in Europe* (New York: Council on Foreign Relations, 1984); Richard Pipes, "Why the Soviet Union Thinks It Could Fight and Win a Nuclear War," *Commentary* 64 (July 1977): 21–34; Jonathan Schell, *The Fate of the Earth* (New York: Knopf, 1982); John W. Spanier and Joseph L. Nogee, *The Politics of Disarmament: A Study in Soviet-American Gamesmanship* (New York: Praeger, 1962); Viktor Suvorov, *Inside the Soviet Army* (New York: Macmillan, 1983); Graham D. Vernon, ed., *Soviet Perceptions of War and Peace* (Washington, D.C.: National Defense University Press, 1981); Edward L. Warner, *The Military in Contemporary Soviet Policy: An Institutional Analysis* (New York: Praeger, 1977); A. Y. Yefremov, *Nuclear Disarmament* [official Soviet view] (Chicago: Progress Press, 1980).

d. *Soviet Relations with Other Communist Countries and Parties.* Karen Dawisha and Philip Hanson, eds., *Soviet–East European Dilemmas: Coercion, Competition, and Consent* (New York: Holmes & Meier, 1981); Herbert Ellison, ed., *The Sino-Soviet Conflict: The Seventies and Beyond* (Seattle: University of Washington Press, 1982); Donald Shanor, *The Soviet Triangle: Russia's Relations with China and the West in the 1980's* (New York: St. Martin's, 1980); C. G. Jacobsen, *Sino-Soviet Relations since Mao: The Chairman's Legacy* (New York: Praeger, 1981); Rudolf L. Tökes, ed., *Eurocommunism and Détente* (New York: New York University Press, 1978); Vernon V. Aspaturian, Jiri Valenta, and David P. Burke, eds., *Eurocommunism between East and West* (Bloomington: Indiana University Press, 1980).

e. *Relations with the Third World.* Charles B. McLane, *Soviet–Third World Relations,* 3 vols. (New York: Columbia University Press, 1973–1974); A. Gafurov et al., *Lenin and the Revolution in the East* [official Soviet view] (Chicago: Imported Publications, 1978); Robert H. Donaldson, ed., *The Soviet Union in the Third World: Successes and Failures* (Boulder, Colo.: Westview, 1981); Elizabeth K. Valkenier, *The Soviet Union and the Third World: An Economic Bind* (New York: Praeger, 1983); Adeed and Karen Dawisha, eds., *The Soviet Union in the Middle East: Policies and Perspectives* (New York: Holmes & Meier, 1982); Stephen T. Hosmert and Thomas W. Wolfe, *Soviet Policy and Practice toward Third World Conflicts* (Lexington, Mass.: Lexington Books, 1983); Alexander R. Alexiev, *The New Soviet Strategy in the Third World* (Santa Monica, Calif.: RAND, 1983); U.S. House of Representatives, Committee on International Relations, *The Soviet Union and the Third World: A Watershed in Great Power Policy?* (Washington, D.C.: U.S. Government Printing Office, 1977); Charles Milene, *The Soviet Union and Africa: The History of the Involvement* (Lanham, Md.: University Press of America, 1980); Arthur J. Klinghoffer, *The Angolan War: A Study in Soviet Policy in the Third World* (Boulder, Colo.: Westview, 1980).

f. *Trade.* Franklyn D. Holzman, *International Trade under Communism: Politics and Economics* (New York: Basic Books, 1976); Lawrence T. Caldwell and William Diebold, *Soviet-American Relations in the 1980's: Superpower Politics and East-West Trade* (New York: McGraw-Hill, 1980); Joseph Finder, *Red Carpet* (New York: Holt, Rinehart and Winston, 1983).

Index

Items not otherwise identified refer to Russia or the Soviet Union.

27203